Prophecy and Society
in
Ancient Israel

ROBERT R. WILSON

Prophecy and Society in Ancient Israel

FORTRESS PRESS   Philadelphia

First paperback edition 1984

Library of Congress Cataloging in Publication Data

Wilson, Robert R   1942–
  Prophecy and society in ancient Israel.

  Bibliography: p.
  Includes indexes.
  1. Prophets. 2. Sociology, Biblical. 3. Bible.
O. T. Prophets — Criticism, interpretation, etc.
I. Title.
BS1198.W55   224 ′ .06   78–14677
ISBN 0-8006-1814-9

1114C84   Printed in the United States of America   1–1814

For
Sharyn

Contents

Preface

I first became interested in the social dimensions of Israelite prophecy as a result of having to teach courses in the interpretation of the prophetic literature. In spite of all of the scholarly work that has been done on the prophetic corpus, much of this material remains tantalizingly enigmatic. In the course of my exegetical work, I became increasingly convinced that some interpretive problems could be clarified, if not solved, if we possessed more detailed information on the social settings and characteristics of Israelite prophetic activity. I therefore began to survey the biblical evidence on this subject, and in the process of trying to understand what I had found, I was inevitably led to consult extra-biblical sources dealing with prophetic phenomena. This study of prophecy and society in ancient Israel presents some of the results of my research.

No single work can hope to explore all of the social dimensions of prophetic activity in Israel, and for this reason I have tried to achieve only two goals in this study. First, I have attempted to present a fairly comprehensive survey of ancient and modern comparative evidence relevant to the study of biblical prophecy. In the case of the modern evidence, I have provided a summary of recent anthropological studies on prophecy without trying to relate all of this material directly to the Israelite prophets. I hope that this format will make the material more accessible to biblical scholars who may wish to utilize the anthropological evidence but who do not share my views on its application to biblical prophecy. In the case of the ancient Near Eastern evidence, which is more familiar to biblical scholars, I have tried to use some of the anthropological material to interpret the ancient sources. Second, I have attempted to illustrate one way in which modern comparative material might be used to explore the problem of prophecy and society in Israel. Against the background of insights drawn from contemporary sources, I have employed form-critical and tradition-historical methods to reexamine the biblical accounts of prophetic activity and then have attempted a tentative historical synthesis of the biblical evidence. The results of this research cannot claim to be conclusive or even comprehensive, but I hope that they will at least stimulate further discussion and make some contribution to the ongoing debate on the nature of Israelite prophecy.

During my work on the problem of prophecy and society, I have received help from a number of individuals and groups. Students in my classes at Yale have made important contributions through their own research and through their willingness to challenge my suggestions. I have also benefited enormously from conversations with my former teacher and colleague S. Dean McBride, Jr. His brilliant reconstruction of the history of the Deuteronomic movement has heavily influenced my treatment of the Deuteronomic History, and my historical synthesis owes much to his views on the history of the Levites. His work, which will be published in his forthcoming Anchor Bible commentary on Deuteronomy, has made my own task much easier.

While I was preparing this study, a Yale University Morse Fellowship and a fellowship from the American Council of Learned Societies enabled me to devote a full year to scholarly research. I wish to thank both institutions for their support.

Finally, I owe an unrepayable debt to my wife, Sharyn. While listening to my tales of people possessed by spirits, she has had the misfortune to learn at first hand what it is like to live with someone possessed by a book. Her support and encouragement throughout the project have made its completion immeasurably easier.

Abbreviations

AA	*American Anthropologist*
ABL	R. F. Harper, *Assyrian and Babylonian Letters Belonging to the K. Collection of the British Museum* (14 vols.) Chicago: University of Chicago Press, 1892–1914
AcOr	*Acta Orientalia*
AfO	*Archiv für Orientforschung*
AHW	W. von Soden, *Akkadisches Handwörterbuch*, Wiesbaden: Otto Harrassowitz, 1965–
AJSL	*American Journal of Semitic Languages and Literatures*
ANET	J. B. Pritchard, ed., *Ancient Near Eastern Texts Relating to the Old Testament*, 3rd ed., Princeton: Princeton University Press, 1969
ARM(T)	Archives royales de Mari (texts in transliteration and translation)
ASR	*American Sociological Review*
ASTI	*Annual of the Swedish Theological Institute*
AusBR	*Australian Biblical Review*
BA	*Biblical Archaeologist*
BASOR	*Bulletin of the American Schools of Oriental Research*
BeO	*Bibbia e oriente*
Bib	*Biblica*
Bib Leb	*Bibel und Leben*
BJRL	*Bulletin of the John Rylands University Library of Manchester*
BO	*Bibliotheca orientalis*

BR	*Biblical Research*
BTB	*Biblical Theology Bulletin*
BZ	*Biblische Zeitschrift*
BZAW	Beihefte zur ZAW
CAD	*The Assyrian Dictionary of the Oriental Institute of the University of Chicago*, Chicago: Oriental Institute, 1956–
CBQ	*Catholic Biblical Quarterly*
CT	Cuneiform Texts from Babylonian Tablets . . . in the British Museum
CTA	A. Herdner, *Corpus des tablettes en cunéiformes alphabétiques*
CTM	*Concordia Theological Monthly*
DBSup	*Dictionnaire de la Bible, Supplément*
DN	Divine name
EvT	*Evangelische Theologie*
GN	Geographical name
HSS	Harvard Semitic Series
HTR	*Harvard Theological Review*
HUCA	*Hebrew Union College Annual*
IDB	G. A. Buttrick, ed., *Interpreter's Dictionary of the Bible*, 4 vols., New York: Abingdon Press, 1962
IDBSup	Supplementary volume to *IDB*
IEJ	*Israel Exploration Journal*
Int	*Interpretation*
JAAR	*Journal of the American Academy of Religion*
JANESCU	*Journal of the Ancient Near Eastern Society of Columbia University*
JAOS	*Journal of the American Oriental Society*
JBL	*Journal of Biblical Literature*
JCS	*Journal of Cuneiform Studies*
JNES	*Journal of Near Eastern Studies*
JRAI	*Journal of the Royal Anthropological Institute*
JSS	*Journal of Semitic Studies*
KAI	H. Donner and W. Röllig, *Kanaanäische und aramäische Inschriften*, 3 vols., Wiesbaden: Otto Harrassowitz, 1964ff.
KAR	E. Ebeling, *Keilschrifttexte aus Assur religiösen Inhalts*, Leipzig: J. C. Hinrichs, 1919, 1923
KD	*Kerygma und Dogma*
MT	Masoretic Text
NedTTs	*Nederlands theologisch tijdschrift*

Or	Orientalia
OrAnt	Oriens antiquus
PN	Personal name
PW	Pauly-Wissowa, Real-Encyclopädie der classischen Altertumswissenschaft
R	H. C. Rawlinson, The Cuneiform Inscriptions of Western Asia, London: R. E. Bowler; IV, with T. G. Pinches, 2d ed., 1891
RA	Revue d'assyriologie et d'archéologie orientale
RB	Revue biblique
RevExp	Review and Expositor
RHPR	Revue d'histoire et de philosophie religieuses
RSO	Rivista degli studi orientali
RSR	Recherches de science religieuse
SBLSP	Society of Biblical Literature Seminar Papers
Sem	Semitica
SJA	Southwestern Journal of Anthropology
TDNT	G. Kittel and G. Friedrich, eds., Theological Dictionary of the New Testament
TDOT	G. J. Botterweck and H. Ringgren, eds., Theological Dictionary of the Old Testament
TLZ	Theologische Literaturzeitung
TRu	Theologische Rundschau
UF	Ugarit-Forschungen
UVB	Vorläufiger Bericht über die von dem Deutschen Archäologischen Institut und der Deutschen Orient-Gesellschaft aus Mitteln der Deutschen Forschungsgemeinschaft unternommenen Ausgrabungen in Uruk-Warka, Berlin, 1930–
VT	Vetus Testamentum
VTSup	Vetus Testamentum, Supplements
WO	Die Welt des Orients
ZA	Zeitschrift für Assyriologie
ZAW	Zeitschrift für die alttestamentliche Wissenschaft
ZTK	Zeitschrift für Theologie und Kirche

Prophecy and Society
in Old Testament
Research

AN INTRODUCTION TO THE PROBLEM

Ancient Israelite prophecy was a complex phenomenon which has been studied extensively by biblical scholars. Since the beginning of the critical study of the Bible in the nineteenth century, they have produced a number of comprehensive treatments of prophecy and have written a great many books and articles on its various aspects. In recent years in particular, researchers have been able to elucidate many of the obscure features of Israelite prophecy and have contributed greatly to our understanding of the prophets themselves. Their theological views have been examined and placed within the context of Israelite religion. The prophetic literature has been thoroughly analyzed, and the literary history of the prophetic corpus has been traced. Scholars have succeeded in delineating the characteristic patterns of the prophets' words and in some cases have been able to relate the various forms of prophetic speech to their original social settings.[1]

1. For a brief survey of critical scholarship on prophecy, see R. E. Clements, *One Hundred Years of Old Testament Interpretation* (Philadelphia: Westminster Press, 1976) 51–75. An extensive bibliography of research since 1932 may be found in G. Fohrer, "Neuere Literatur zur alttestamentlichen Prophetie," *TRu* 19 (1951) 277–346; 20 (1952) 192–271, 295–361; idem, "Zehn Jahre Literatur zur alttestamentlichen Prophetie (1951–1960)," *TRu* 28 (1962) 1–75, 235–297, 301–374; idem, "Neue Literatur zur alttestamentlichen Prophetie (1961–1970)," *TRu* 40 (1975) 193–209, 337–377; 41 (1976) 1–12.

In the light of recent advances in prophetic research, it is all the more surprising that we still do not have a clear picture of the role that prophecy played in Israelite society. For purposes of study, the prophets have usually been isolated from their social matrix, and no comprehensive attempt has been made to examine the complex relationships that must have existed between the prophets and their society. We know little about the processes by which people became prophets, and the role that their society may have played in these processes remains to be studied. The nature of prophetic behavior is not precisely clear, and we do not know how society may have influenced that behavior. More important, we have only a vague understanding of the way in which prophecy actually functioned in Israelite society. We are uncertain about what the prophets did (or thought they were doing) for their society, and the society's reactions to their activities are often obscure. In short, most of the social dimensions of Israelite prophecy remain unclear, and for this reason the prophets themselves emerge from recent scholarly research as lifeless individuals.[2]

Yet, in spite of the fact that there is still no comprehensive study devoted exclusively to the problem of the relationship between prophecy and society in Israel, discussions of prophecy have frequently touched on various aspects of the problem. By collecting these scattered and sometimes oblique treatments, it is possible to reconstruct a schematic history of scholarship on the social dimensions of Israelite prophecy. This history reveals that the interaction between prophecy and society has been treated, at least peripherally, both by students of Israelite religious phenomena and by form critics concerned with the shape of biblical literature. These treatments, which are sometimes contradictory, have dealt in a limited way with three aspects of the overall problem: the social functions of prophecy, the nature of prophetic activity, and the social location of prophecy.

2. There have been a few scholarly attempts to deal with the social dimensions of prophecy, and these will be discussed below. In addition, see A. Jepsen, *Nabi: Soziologische Studien zur alttestamentlichen Literatur und Religionsgeschichte* (Munich: C. H. Beck, 1934); H. Junker, *Prophet und Seher in Israel* (Trier: Paulinus-Verlag, 1927); P. Kleinert, *Die Profeten Israels in sozialer Beziehung* (Leipzig: J. C. Hinrichs, 1905); A. Guillaume, *Prophecy and Divination among the Hebrews and Other Semites* (London: Hodder and Stoughton, 1938); and J. Lindblom, *Prophecy in Ancient Israel* (Philadelphia: Muhlenberg Press, 1962) 47–219.

PROPHECY AND SOCIETY IN THE STUDY
OF ISRAELITE RELIGION

From Ewald to Hölscher:
The Social Functions of Prophecy

Early critical scholars tended to see the prophets as inspired individuals who were responsible for creating the purest form of Israelite monotheism. This view of prophecy gave rise to works that concentrated on the intellectual and theological aspects of prophecy, with the result that little attention was given to the prophet as a human figure intimately related to a social setting. These early works on prophecy seldom comment on the precise nature of prophetic speech and behavior or on the social location of the prophet. Yet, at the same time, even the most theologically oriented studies do imply something about the social *functions* of prophetic activity. Heinrich Ewald, for example, saw the prophets as crucial figures in the history of Israelite religion. They were the first people in whom the divine spark of true knowledge was brought to consciousness by the spirit of God. For this reason they served as models of the spiritual heights which all people might someday reach. In this way the prophets functioned as individuals who had been divinely chosen to reform all aspects of human society.[3] Ewald thus saw the prophets as agents of social change, although he nowhere describes them explicitly in these terms.

A similar view of the social function of prophecy is implied in the early work of Bernhard Duhm. Like Ewald, Duhm saw the major significance of the prophets in their theology, which raised the level of Israelite religion to new moral and ethical heights. The prophets broke sharply with the ancient Israelite religious traditions, particularly those of the patriarchal period, and were powerful forces in shaping a religion free of superstitious cultic and magical practices.[4] Duhm thus believed that the prophets functioned as agents of social change, although their main contributions were moral, ethical, and theological. On the question of the nature of prophetic activity, Duhm had little to say. He was aware of the existence of ecstatic prophecy in the ancient Mediterranean world, but he drew such a

---

3. H. Ewald, *Die Propheten des Alten Bundes* (2d ed.; Göttingen: Vandenhoeck & Ruprecht, 1867), 1. 1–40.
4. B. Duhm, *Die Theologie der Propheten* (Bonn: Adolph Marcus, 1875) 1–34.

sharp distinction between "pagan" ecstatics and the Israelite prophets that he felt it unnecessary to use any type of comparative material in his study. He also recognized that the early writing prophets, particularly Amos and Isaiah, sometimes exhibited ec-static behavior. However, he believed that such behavior was pres-ent only early in the prophets' careers and that it was quickly replaced by normal, rational speech and behavior.[5] Although Duhm treated the prophets in particular historical contexts, he believed that those contexts played little role in shaping prophetic theology, which transcended particular historical settings. He therefore did not deal with the question of the social location of prophecy in any specific way.

Duhm's general approach to the question of prophecy and society was subsequently followed by a number of historians of Israelite religion. Wellhausen, who was otherwise the most influential of Duhm's contemporaries, made few contributions to the study of prophecy. He held that early prophecy in Israel had little impact on Israelite religion or society. Only with the work of the writing prophets were the older religious patterns destroyed and replaced by prophetic "ethical monotheism." In contrast to their predeces-sors, the writing prophets worked both inside and outside of the religious establishment in order to change it.[6]

Similar views were held by W. Robertson Smith, who recognized the existence of ecstatic prophecy within the Israelite religious es-tablishment but who argued that this phenomenon contrasted sharply with the rational behavior and ethical insights of the writing prophets.[7] However, Smith's approach moved beyond previous re-search at two important points. First, he made at least limited use of extra-biblical material to describe prophecy outside of Israel and to elucidate Israelite religious phenomena, although he ultimately denied that this material was relevant to the study of the writing

5. Ibid., 4, 19–24, 29–34, 86–91. Duhm later revised his views considerably in the light of subsequent research. See his *Israels Propheten* (Tübingen: J. C. B. Mohr, 1916 [2d ed., 1922]) 1–12, 61–88.

6. J. Wellhausen, *Prolegomena to the History of Ancient Israel* (London: Adam & Charles Black, 1885) 414–419, 467–477, 484–491; idem, *Israelitische und Jüdische Geschichte* (7th ed.; Berlin: Georg Reimer, 1914) 72–77, 91–92, 104–113, 122–132; idem., *Grundrisse zum Alten Testament* (ed. R. Smend; Munich: Chr. Kaiser, 1965) 87–97.

7. W. R. Smith, *The Old Testament in the Jewish Church* (London: Adam & Charles Black, 1895) 278–308; cf. his *The Prophets of Israel* (2d ed.; London: Adam & Charles Black, 1895).

prophets.[8] Second, he recognized the complex relationship which exists between religious phenomena and their social setting. He therefore paid a great deal of attention to the historical setting of the prophetic writings, and he noted the different social locations and functions of the various types of Israelite prophecy.[9]

The Legacy of Hölscher:
The Nature of Prophetic Activity

Although Smith's work on the question of prophecy and society treated some areas not previously considered, he still basically accepted the views of Duhm and Wellhausen. A major alternative view did not appear until the influential work of Gustav Hölscher, who shifted the focus of the inquiry from the social function of prophecy to the nature of prophetic activity.[10] Hölscher argued that all prophets, including those in Israel, shared the same ecstatic and visionary experiences. To prove his case, he systematically considered various psychological and behavioral characteristics of ecstatics and then demonstrated the existence of these characteristics among the Israelite prophets. Although Hölscher followed earlier scholars in maintaining that Israel's prophets received divine moral insights from their experiences, he stressed the cultural and historical links between Israelite ecstatic prophecy and ecstatic prophecy among Israel's neighbors. In spite of the thoroughness with which Hölscher treated the nature of Israelite prophecy, he made few comments on the social location of prophetic activity. He recognized that some early Israelite prophets were associated with the cult, but he denied that the writing prophets had cultic connections.[11]

Hölscher's work marks a turning point in the study of prophecy and society not only because of his conclusions but also because of

8. See, for example, the Arabic and Greek material cited by Smith in *The Old Testament in the Jewish Church*, 285–287, 292, 294, 297–298. For a discussion of Smith's general use of comparative material, see R. R. Wilson, *Genealogy and History in the Biblical World* (New Haven: Yale University Press, 1977) 13–14; and T. O. Beidelman, *W. Robertson Smith and the Sociological Study of Religion* (Chicago: University of Chicago Press, 1974) 27–28, 49–52.

9. Note, for example, Smith's reflections on the way in which a prophet's message is related to his psychological state and social setting ("Prophecy and Personality: A Fragment," *Lectures and Essays of William Robertson Smith* [ed. J. S. Black and G. Chrystal; London: Adam & Charles Black, 1912] 97–108). Cf. his treatment of Elijah (*Prophets of Israel*, 78–89).

10. G. Hölscher, *Die Profeten* (Leipzig: J. C. Hinrichs, 1914), esp. pp. 1–358.

11. Ibid., 143–147.

the method which he employed. He made extensive use of comparative material and thus established a pattern followed by a number of subsequent religio-historical treatments. Throughout *Die Profeten* his normal approach is to draw extensively on contemporary psychological studies of the characteristics of ecstasy and then to document the existence of those characteristics in antiquity.[12] In order to do this he uses a great quantity of ancient Near Eastern and classical material and relies particularly heavily on Arabic sources.

Hölscher's concern with the nature of prophetic activity has been shared by a number of subsequent religio-historical studies, all of which have focused on the ecstatic character of prophecy and have tried to come to grips with the basic problem posed by Hölscher's work: the relationship between the "irrational," ecstatic nature of prophecy and the coherent, theologically sophisticated, sometimes highly structured oracles of the Israelite writing prophets.[13] Treatments of this problem have followed three major lines of development, but to date no single solution has proven completely satisfactory.

First, some scholars have simply denied that the writing prophets and those nonwriting prophets whose words have been preserved were ecstatics. There are two major variations on this theme. Following the approach of scholars writing before the publication of Hölscher's work, some critics have admitted the existence of ecstasy early in the history of Israelite prophecy but have flatly denied the presence of ecstasy among the writing prophets.[14] In its extreme form, this approach is forced to overlook clear indications of ecstasy among the writing prophets, and most scholars following this line admit the occasional presence of "mild forms of ecstasy" in the writing prophets.[15] Taking a different tack, some scholars have ar-

---

12. The exact sources of Hölscher's psychological data are not always clear, but he seems to have been influenced greatly by the work of Wilhelm Wundt. See Clements, *One Hundred Years of Old Testament Interpretation,* 56–66.

13. For an overview of solutions to this problem, see H. H. Rowley, "The Nature of Old Testament Prophecy in the Light of Recent Study," *HTR* 38 (1945) 1–38 (= H. H. Rowley, *The Servant of the Lord* [2d ed.; Oxford: Blackwell, 1965] 95–134); and O. Eissfeldt, "The Prophetic Literature," *The Old Testament and Modern Study* (ed. H. H. Rowley; London: Oxford University Press, 1951) 134–145.

14. I. P. Seierstad, *Die Offenbarungserlebnisse der Propheten Amos, Jesaja und Jeremia* (Oslo: Jacob Dybwad, 1946); A. J. Heschel, *The Prophets* (New York: Harper & Row, 1962).

15. J. P. Hyatt, *Prophetic Religion* (New York: Abingdon-Cokesbury, 1947) 17; cf. J. Skinner, *Prophecy and Religion* (Cambridge: Cambridge University Press, 1922) 3–6; H. W. Robinson, "The Psychology and Metaphysic of 'Thus Saith Yahweh,'" *ZAW* 41 (1923) 5–8; A. Causse, "Quelques remarques sur la psychologie des prophètes," *RHPR* 2 (1922) 349–356.

gued that the "true prophets" in Israel were not ecstatics, while the "false prophets" described in the prophetic literature were ecstatics.[16] By assuming that all of the writing prophets were true prophets, this view is able to dissociate them from ecstasy. However, this approach underestimates the problems involved in differentiating true and false prophets in Israel, and it also overlooks the fact that there is no good biblical evidence to indicate that all of the so-called false prophets were ecstatics.

A second major line of development has taken an approach followed by Gunkel before the publication of Hölscher's work.[17] In contrast to Hölscher, who believed that the prophets delivered their oracles while in a state of ecstasy, Gunkel suggested that the prophets produced their oracles *after* their ecstatic experiences had ended. The oracles were thus the products of rational minds and were attempts to communicate what had transpired during the prophets' ecstasy. A number of scholars have accepted some form of Gunkel's position and have argued that the prophets composed their oracles either immediately after their ecstatic experiences or at a later date.[18] Although this view has the advantage of accounting for the more-or-less rational nature of the prophetic literature, it is based on very little evidence. In addition, there are clear indications that some prophets did deliver oracles while in a state of ecstasy. Jeremiah's oracle in 4:19 ("My anguish, my anguish! I writhe in pain!") seems closely connected to ecstasy, and the fact that Jeremiah's speech could be described as that of a madman (Jer 29:26) suggests that at least some of the prophet's utterances were given while in ecstasy. Ecstasy is also indicated by Jer 23:9, where

16. H. T. Obbink, "The Forms of Prophetism," *HUCA* 14 (1939) 25–28; S. Mowinckel, " 'The Spirit' and the 'Word' in the Pre-exilic Reforming Prophets," *JBL* 53 (1934) 199–227; Jepsen, *Nabi*, 208–217.

17. H. Gunkel, "Die geheimen Erfahrungen der Propheten Israels," *Suchen der Zeit* 1 (1903) 112–153; cf. his later treatment in "Einleitungen," H. Schmidt, *Die Schriften des Alten Testaments* 2 / 2: *Die grossen Propheten* (2d ed.; Göttingen: Vandenhoeck & Ruprecht, 1915) xxv-xxviii (="The Secret Experiences of the Prophets," *The Expositor*, 9th series, 1 [1924] 427–432).

18. T. H. Robinson, *Prophecy and the Prophets in Ancient Israel* (2d ed.; London: Duckworth, 1953) 50–51; idem, "The Ecstatic Element in Old Testament Prophecy," *The Expositor*, 8th series, no. 123, vol. 21 (1921) 217–238; J. Hempel, *Die althebräische Literatur* (Wildpark-Potsdam: Akademische Verlagsgesellschaft Athenaion, 1930) 62–63; S. Mowinckel, "Ecstatic Experience and Rational Elaboration in Old Testament Prophecy," *AcOr* 13 (1935) 264–291; G. Widengren, *Literary and Psychological Aspects of the Hebrew Prophets* (Uppsala: Lundequist, 1948) 98–120; Lindblom, *Prophecy in Ancient Israel*, 47–65, 105–108, 122–137, 177–182, 197–202, 216–219.

the prophet describes himself as shaking and like a drunken man because of the words of Yahweh.

The third approach to the problem of ecstasy has been taken by scholars who admit that even the writing prophets may have had mild and infrequent ecstatic experiences of some type. These scholars argue, however, that the *content* of the prophets' words must be distinguished from the ecstatic *means* by which those words were received.[19] This argument has the effect of shifting the focus of scholarly inquiry away from the problem of ecstasy, but by doing so it leaves unanswered the form-critical question of the relationship between ecstasy and the prophetic literature.

The Legacy of Mowinckel:
The Social Location of Prophecy

Just as Hölscher's work brought the question of the nature of prophecy to the attention of biblical scholars, so also Sigmund Mowinckel forced them to struggle with the problem of the social location of prophecy. Although Mowinckel's interests were primarily form-critical, he recognized the importance of dealing with the social setting in which stereotypical speech forms were used.[20] Therefore, in the course of his investigation of the Psalms, he suggested that the so-called prophetic psalms were originally prophetic oracles delivered in the context of the cult. His suggestion was made on the basis of the form of the language of the Psalms rather than on any actual description of prophetic activity in the cult, but he went on to argue that prophetic guilds functioned in the Jerusalem cult alongside the priests. To be sure, scholars had previously noted the existence of cult prophecy in Israel, but such activity was usually thought to have been confined to an early period in Israelite religious development.[21] In contrast, Mowinckel's work raised the possibility that cultic prophecy was to be found throughout the history of Israel and that even the writing prophets had cultic functions. On this last point Mowinckel was a bit vague, but he did argue that Joel

---

19. Rowley, "Old Testament Prophecy," 128–131; cf. Mowinckel, "Ecstatic Experience," 279–280.

20. As our next section will show, this has not always been the case among form critics. For a thorough discussion of Mowinckel's form-critical work, see J. H. Hayes, "The History of the Form-critical Study of Prophecy," SBLSP 1973, 1. 76–79.

21. See, for example, Hölscher, *Die Profeten*, 143–147.

and Habakkuk were cultic prophets, and he later extended his argument to include Isaiah and Micah as well.[22]

Mowinckel's work touched off a debate on the social location of Israelite prophecy which has persisted to the present day and shows no sign of abating.[23] So much has been written on the question of prophecy and the cult that it is impossible even to begin to sketch here a history of research after Mowinckel. However, it will be helpful to mention briefly three works which illustrate the types of approaches that have been taken.

The thesis that prophets in Israel were located in the cult was developed in a thorough way by Aubrey R. Johnson.[24] His work is significant not only because he concluded that Israelite prophets played an important role in the cult but also because he supported that conclusion with an analysis which recognized the complexities of prophetic phenomena. He collected evidence on the various types of prophetic figures and tried to distinguish their characteristic behavior and social functions. Although he took no stand on the relationship of the writing prophets to the cult, he did argue that they must be seen against the background of other types of prophecy.[25] Almost all of Johnson's arguments are supported by appeal to the biblical text alone, and he rarely uses extra-biblical data. In contrast to Mowinckel, who started from an analysis of speech patterns, Johnson makes little use of form criticism.

Alfred Haldar approached the question from a very different angle.[26] Haldar's work opens with a detailed analysis of various types of cultic functionaries in Mesopotamia and pays particular

22. Mowinckel's original suggestion was made in *Psalmenstudien III: Kultprophetie und prophetische Psalmen* (Oslo: Jacob Dybwad, 1923) 1–29. Cf. his later statement in *The Psalms in Israel's Worship* (Nashville: Abingdon Press, 1962) 2. 53–73; and note his article "Psalms and Wisdom," where he claims that "the majority of prophets formed an official class of cult functionaries . . . ." (*Wisdom in Israel and in the Ancient Near East* [H. H. Rowley *Festschrift*] [VTSup 3; ed. M. Noth and D. W. Thomas; Leiden: E. J. Brill, 1960] 206). Mowinckel argued that Isaiah and Micah were cult prophets in his *Jesaja-Disiplene* (Oslo: H. Aschehoug, 1926).

23. For a thorough discussion of the main lines of the debate, see H. H. Rowley, "Ritual and the Hebrew Prophets," *JSS* 1 (1956) 338–360 (=H. H. Rowley, *From Moses to Qumran* [New York: Association Press, 1963] 111–138); and L. Ramlot, "Prophétisme," *DBSup* 8 (1972) 1121–1166, where exhaustive, up-to-date bibliographies may be found.

24. A. R. Johnson, *The Cultic Prophet in Ancient Israel* (Cardiff: University of Wales, 1944; 2d ed., 1962).

25. Ibid., 29–30; cf. his remark in the preface of the 2d ed., p. v.

26. A. Haldar, *Associations of Cult Prophets among the Ancient Semites* (Uppsala: Almqvist & Wiksell, 1945).

attention to the *bārû* (the diviner, whom Haldar considers a "seer" or "oracle giver") and the *maḫḫû* (the ecstatic). Haldar then tries to make a direct connection between these Mesopotamian figures and Israelite priests and prophets. The function of the *bārû* was performed in Israel by the seers (*rōʾeh, ḥōzeh*) while the *maḫḫû* had a counterpart in the prophet (*nābîʾ*). Both the seers and the prophets were members of organized groups related to the cult, although the prophet's office was not hereditary.

A very different approach to the problem of prophecy and cult has been taken by the sociologist Peter L. Berger.[27] Berger's work is interesting not because of its conclusions, which will be familiar to biblical scholars, but because it is one of the few attempts to date to use a cross-disciplinary approach. Berger's basic concern is to test Weber's views of charisma against the contemporary scholarly consensus on the nature of Israelite prophecy. Berger focuses on the question of the social location of prophecy in Israel and specifically considers the relation of the prophets to the cult. After surveying recent research on the question, he concludes that biblical scholars today see little distinction between the writing prophets and the earlier *nābîʾ*s. In addition, he believes that most scholars would admit that the prophets were located in the cult. Berger then draws the important conclusion that charismatic figures such as prophets need not be only on the periphery of society but may function within established institutions as well. In practical terms this would mean that cultic prophets in Israel need not have been totally bound by institutional pressures but would have been free to promote innovative changes in their institutions. Whatever one may think of Berger's conclusions, it is unfortunate that he commits a common error in his use of evidence outside his own discipline: he assumes a consensus in another scholarly field where in fact no consensus exists.[28]

PROPHECY AND SOCIETY IN FORM-CRITICAL STUDY

Because there are several recent treatments of the history of form-critical research on the prophets, we need to make only a few

27. P. L. Berger, "Charisma and Religious Innovation: The Social Location of Israelite Prophecy," *ASR* 28 (1963) 940–950.

28. Berger's work was rightly criticized on this point by J. G. Williams, "The Social Location of Israelite Prophecy," *JAAR* 37 (1969) 153–165. However, the force

observations about form-critical perspectives on the relationship between prophecy and society.[29] Interest in the social dimensions of
prophetic activity first arose in form-critical circles in the work of
Gunkel. As early as 1906 Gunkel had developed the concept that all
literary genres had a setting in the life of the people who used them.
However, his discussions of this concept are somewhat vague. He
sometimes uses the phrase "setting in life" (Sitz im Leben) to refer
to the original social settings of the literary genres themselves, but
he also employs the phrase to refer to the social occasion on which
the genres were subsequently used.[30] The setting of the activity of
using a literary genre and the original setting of the actual language
and structure of the genre may sometimes be the same. For example, the language and structure of the lament originated on occasions of mourning, and the lament was subsequently used on similar
occasions. However, the original setting of the language of a genre
may not be the same as the setting in which the genre is actually
used. In the case of prophecy, the social matrix of prophetic language and the social location of prophetic activity may not be identical. A prophet who delivers oracles in the temple court may not
employ speech forms that originated in the temple.

Since the time of Gunkel form critics have had a great deal to say
about the literary genres of prophetic speech and about the original
social matrix of the language of those genres, but little attention has
been paid to the way in which the prophets actually used their
traditional speech patterns in Israelite society. Form critics have
generally overlooked the question of the social location of prophetic
activity. A clear case in point is the work of Claus Westermann,
whose *Basic Forms of Prophetic Speech* is the most recent com-

----

of Berger's conclusion is underestimated when Williams argues that prophets could
not have been located in the cult and still have criticized the cult.

29. For recent accounts of the history of form-critical research on the prophets, see
Hayes, "History," 60–99; R. R. Wilson, "Form-critical Investigation of the Prophetic
Literature: The Present Situation," SBLSP 1973, 1. 100–121; W. E. March,
"Prophecy," *Old Testament Form Criticism* (ed. J. H. Hayes; San Antonio: Trinity
University Press, 1974) 141–177; and G. M. Tucker, "Prophetic Speech," *Int* 32
(1978) 31–45.

30. H. Gunkel, "Fundamental Problems of Hebrew Literary History," *What Remains of the Old Testament* (London: George Allen & Unwin, 1928) 61–62. The
German original of this article was published under the title "Die Grundprobleme
der israelitischen Literaturgeschichte" in *Deutsche Literaturzeitung* 27 (1906), cols.
1797–1800, 1861–1866 and was reprinted in Gunkel's *Reden und Aufsätze* (Göttingen: Vandenhoeck & Ruprecht, 1913) 29–38.

prehensive study of prophetic literary genres. After a thorough survey of the history of research on prophetic speech forms and an examination of the relevant biblical material, Westermann concludes that prophetic speech was shaped by the notion that the prophet was God's messenger, who delivered divine messages to the people. The basic form of prophetic speech was the announcement of judgment against the individual, but this form later underwent a number of structural changes and was transformed into an announcement of judgment against the whole nation. In the course of Westermann's analysis he provides a thorough discussion of the various prophetic speech forms, but nowhere does he deal with the actual social settings in which the forms were used. His picture of the prophet as Yahweh's messenger suggests that prophets had the general function of serving as a bridge between the human and divine worlds, but the messenger image says nothing about the actual social location of prophetic activity. The title which Westermann gives to the basic prophetic literary genre *implies* that the prophets delivered their oracles in a judicial setting, but he does not actually press this argument.[31]

When form critics have considered the social location of prophetic activity, there has been a tendency to use the original setting of prophetic language to reconstruct the occasion on which the prophets used the language. An example of this tendency can be found in recent work on the *rîb,* the prophetic lawsuit. This genre was first analyzed by Gunkel, who suggested that it must have originally had a judicial setting.[32] This is an adequate explanation for the origin of the *language* and *literary structure* of the genre, but Gunkel's suggestion does not shed much light on the social setting in which the genre functioned. There is no biblical evidence that prophets normally delivered oracles in the course of judicial proceedings. Nevertheless, the judicial background of the language of the genre has led some scholars to *assume* that the prophets operated in legal contexts. Because God is also involved in the covenant lawsuit, some scholars have suggested that the prophets used this genre in a cultic trial in which the people were indicted for break-

---

31. C. Westermann, *Basic Forms of Prophetic Speech* (Philadelphia: Westminster Press, 1967). For a critique of Westermann's use of the messenger image and for a discussion of the adequacy of his form-critical analyses, see Wilson, "Form-critical Investigation of the Prophetic Literature," 100–109, 114–120.

32. H. Gunkel, *Einleitung in die Psalmen* (2d ed.; Göttingen: Vandenhoeck & Ruprecht, 1966) 364–365.

ing their covenant with Yahweh.[33] Still, it must be remembered that there are no biblical accounts of cultic trials for covenant breaking, and there is therefore no solid evidence that prophets actually participated in such trials. Their existence is based solely on a deduction from a literary genre.

THE IMPLICATIONS OF PRIOR RESEARCH

On the basis of the above history of the study of prophecy and society, it is possible to make two generalizations concerning the present state of the inquiry. First, it is clear that scholars have generally avoided dealing with *all* of the social dimensions of Israelite prophecy. The problem of the social role that the prophets played in Israel has rarely been treated at all in recent years. There are a number of discussions of the social location of prophecy, but they have been primarily concerned with the extent of prophetic involvement in the cult. Similarly, current treatments of the nature of prophetic activity have focused either on the behavior of the prophets (religio-historical studies of ecstasy) or on the structure of prophetic speech (form-critical studies of prophetic literature), but seldom are these two features of prophecy considered together. In addition, form critics concerned with the stereotypical structure of prophetic language have often simply ignored the questions of social location and function. Clearly, these fragmented approaches to the problem of prophecy and society must be superseded if any real progress is to be made. All of the social dimensions of Israelite prophecy must be considered before any accurate picture of the prophets can be formulated.

Second, the fact that no single approach has thus far been able to characterize accurately the distinctive social features of Israelite prophecy has gradually led scholars to recognize the complexity of the interaction between Israelite prophets and their societies. This tendency is best seen in Johnson's work on the different types of Israelite prophets and in Berger's work on the relationship between charisma and social institutions. Treatments of the problem of prophecy and society must take this complexity into account. It seems increasingly likely that not all of the Israelite prophets were

---

33. E. Würthwein, "Der Ursprung der prophetischen Gerichtsrede," *ZTK* 49 (1952) 7–8, 12–16. For a survey of recent work on the prophetic lawsuit, see R. North, "Angel-Prophet or Satan-Prophet?" *ZAW* 82 (1970) 31–67.

related to their societies in the same way. In addition, different relationships may have existed at various times in Israelite history, and this historical dimension must also be considered.

PROPHECY AND SOCIETY:
A CROSS-DISCIPLINARY APPROACH

The Use of Anthropological Evidence

Although it is easy to locate the weaknesses in prior research on the problem of prophecy and society, one of the chief reasons for these weaknesses must be readily acknowledged. In fact, there is very little biblical evidence on which to base a study of the social aspects of Israelite prophecy. Old Testament narratives describing prophetic activity can provide some clues about how the prophets may have been related to their society, and by carefully examining the literary history of the narratives it is sometimes even possible to reconstruct the changes that took place in these relationships. However, the major sources for the study of prophecy, the prophetic writings themselves, furnish little data that can throw light on the social matrix of the prophets. Only a few of the prophetic books contain accounts of prophetic activity, and even where such accounts exist it is often difficult to relate them to the oracles preserved elsewhere in the prophets' writings.

Because of this relative lack of biblical evidence, it will be helpful to approach the problem from another direction. In recent years contemporary anthropologists and sociologists have produced a number of competent field studies of a wide range of prophetic phenomena. Unlike the biblical material, these anthropological studies provide comprehensive accounts of the ways in which prophets are related to their societies. This comparative evidence indicates the complexity of the social dimensions of prophecy and can therefore suggest to the interpreter more precise and potentially useful questions that might be asked of the biblical text. In this way the anthropological data can provide a detailed background against which the biblical evidence can be better understood. By acquiring a more sophisticated understanding of the role of prophecy in modern societies, the interpreter should be better equipped to consider the social dimensions of prophecy in Israel.

Methodological Problems

The use of comparative material to elucidate Israelite religion raises certain methodological difficulties which must be faced at the beginning of any cross-disciplinary study. The value of comparative material is obvious, for it can supplement the meager biblical data on the nature and functions of prophecy. Yet, the methodological errors which we have already seen in the work of earlier scholars must be avoided. On the one hand, the interpreter must be fair to the biblical material by not imposing on it irrelevant and constricting external data. On the other hand, the interpreter must be fair to the comparative material by treating it properly in its own context. In order to avoid methodological errors, the following guidelines must be observed when comparative material is used.[34]

(1) Comparative material, particularly anthropological and sociological material, must be collected systematically by a trained scholar. Obviously the biblical scholar must rely on secondary literature for most comparative data, but an attempt should be made to be sure that the scholars whose work is used are reliable and that they have not themselves been overly selective or biased in their presentation of the data. In the case of anthropological material, this means that biblical scholars must rely on work done in the twentieth century.

(2) Comparative material must be properly interpreted in its own context before any attempt is made to apply it to the biblical text. Ancient Near Eastern cultural phenomena must therefore be seen in the whole context of the societies that produced them and must not simply be extracted from their own cultural matrix. Sociological and anthropological data on a particular phenomenon must be seen in the context of the whole society which produced the phenomenon. Only by doing this is it possible to understand the social function of the phenomenon. This means that the most useful comparative material will come from studies dealing with the totality of a single society or with the social function of a phenomenon within several societies. Theoretical or abstract studies that provide little hard data are likely to be less useful.

(3) When using sociological and anthropological material, the biblical scholar must survey a wide range of societies that contain the

34. For a more thorough discussion of these guidelines, see Wilson, *Genealogy and History*, 11–18.

phenomenon being studied. By doing this it is possible to avoid using atypical material for comparative purposes.

(4) The biblical interpreter must concentrate on the comparative data that has been collected and if possible must avoid the interpretive schemata into which sociologists, anthropologists, and Near Eastern scholars have placed the data. By doing this the biblical scholar can avoid biased presentations.

(5) When applying comparative material to the biblical text, the biblical scholar must be sure that the comparative material is truly comparable to the biblical material being studied. By limiting the comparative material in this way, the interpreter can eliminate data that might distort the interpretation.

(6) When applying comparative material to the biblical text, the interpreter must allow the biblical text itself to be the controlling factor in the exegetical process. The comparative material can thus be used only to form a hypothesis which must still be tested against the biblical text. The exegesis of the text itself will then support, disprove, or modify the hypothesis. If the exegesis of the text fails to provide enough evidence either to support or to deny the hypothesis, then the question must be allowed to remain open with respect to that particular text. The lack of exegetical evidence cannot cause either the acceptance or rejection of the hypothesis. Comparative data thus has a dual function. On the one hand, it can broaden the horizons of the biblical interpreter and suggest a wider range of hypotheses than the interpreter might be able to produce on the basis of the biblical text alone. On the other hand, comparative material may lend support to or cast doubt on hypotheses previously advanced.

The Complexity of the Biblical Traditions

Before anthropological material can be used to interpret the biblical evidence on prophecy and society, the complexity of Israel's own prophetic traditions must be taken into account. Even a cursory reading of the sources reveals that the biblical writers had divergent and sometimes conflicting views about prophecy. These views were presumably the product of a long period of development, and it is now difficult to determine how accurately they reflect historical reality. However, there is no reason to suspect that the various biblical conceptions of prophecy were simply created out of whole cloth.

Rather, they must be taken as an indication that the groups bearing the biblical traditions actually knew of different types of prophecy. If so, then each type must have had its own peculiar characteristics and must have existed for a definite historical period, while still developing in reaction to changing social, political, and religious conditions.

To suggest that the various biblical conceptions of *prophecy* are relatively accurate reflections of the types of prophecy that actually existed in Israel is not to suggest that all of the biblical pictures of individual *prophets* are historically accurate. The biblical writers sometimes allowed their personal attitudes about prophecy to influence their portrayal of particular prophets, with the result that these individuals are said to have spoken and acted in ways that conform to the authors' understanding of appropriate prophetic behavior but that are at variance with the individuals' actual behavior. Furthermore, relatively late conceptions of prophecy have occasionally been retrojected into an earlier time. Therefore, in some cases the biblical texts are a more reliable guide to the general nature of Israelite prophecy in the time the texts were written than they are to the actual characteristics of the prophets being described.

Although the groups that bore the Israelite traditions undoubtedly had a number of different conceptions of prophecy, only one of them can now be seen clearly in the biblical texts. The prominence of this one view of prophecy is due to the simple fact that almost all of the biblical narratives dealing with prophetic activity come from what is essentially a single theological and literary tradition. Scholars have long noted that the Deuteronomic History, the Elohistic layer of the Pentateuch, and the writings of Hosea and Jeremiah share certain traditions and theological perspectives. These sources also view prophecy in a similar way, and this distinctive view now pervades most of the prophetic narratives. Because all of these sources are usually thought to reflect a northern Israelite perspective, we will refer to them as representatives of the Ephraimite tradition.[35]

35. The continuity of the Ephraimite prophetic traditions has been clearly demonstrated by J. Muilenburg ("The "Office' of the Prophet in Ancient Israel," *The Bible in Modern Scholarship* [ed. J. P. Hyatt; Nashville: Abingdon Press, 1965] 74–97; idem, "The Intercession of the Covenant Mediator (Exodus 33:1a, 12–17)," *Words and Meanings: Essays Presented to David Winton Thomas* [ed. P. R. Ackroyd and B. Lindars; Cambridge: At the University Press, 1968] 159–181). For references to earlier discussions of these traditions and for a consideration of their origins, see E. W.

The groups who bore the Ephraimite tradition are difficult to identify with any certainty, but as a working hypothesis we will accept the theory that they originated in connection with some of the northern Israelite shrines during the period of the Judges. Some of the members of these groups may have been priests who officiated at the northern sanctuaries before David established a central shrine in Jerusalem. A few of the priests, represented by Abiathar, may have participated in David's Jerusalemite cult, while others remained outside of the royal establishment. Northern priestly influence in Jerusalem ended in the time of Solomon, and thereafter Ephraimite theological traditions were carried in different geographical areas by groups that retained an independent identity throughout the history of the monarchy. These groups expressed their views at various times in what we now know as the Elohistic layer of the Pentateuch and the Deuteronomic literature.[36]

Although the Ephraimite view of prophecy now dominates the biblical texts, there are also a few traces of other views. Some of these views are embedded in the Ephraimite literary corpus itself, but most of them are found in sources that can be linked with Jerusalemite or Judean authors. We will therefore assume that these views reflect Judahite traditions originating in the south but preserved after the rise of the monarchy at the royal court in Jerusalem. Unfortunately, because of the scarcity of information about Judean prophecy, it is unclear whether the sources reflect one coherent Judahite tradition or portions of several variant traditions.

Nicholson, *Deuteronomy and Tradition* (Philadelphia: Fortress Press, 1967) 58–106. Although the northern origin of the Elohistic and Deuteronomic traditions has occasionally been challenged, these challenges have not been serious enough to warrant modifying the scholarly consensus. For a recent discussion reaffirming the Ephraimite origin of these traditions, see A. W. Jenks, *The Elohist and North Israelite Traditions* (Missoula: Scholars Press, 1977) 2–18, 83–129.

36. This theory about the bearers of the Ephraimite traditions is based on F. M. Cross's reconstruction of Israel's early priesthood and to a lesser extent on his analysis of the Deuteronomic traditions (*Canaanite Myth and Hebrew Epic* [Cambridge: Harvard University Press, 1973] 195–215, 274–289). Although we cannot accept all of Cross's reconstruction, he has convincingly argued that when David set up a central sanctuary in Jerusalem, he also installed two priestly houses: Levitical priests from the old northern sanctuary at Shiloh (represented by Abiathar) and Aaronid priests from the southern Judahite shrine at Hebron (represented by Zadok). When Abiathar was exiled to Anathoth, control of the Jerusalem cult was left in the hands of the Aaronids, while the Levitical priests remained outside of the central cult. The suggestion that these Levitical priests were also the bearers of the old Ephraimite traditions, including the Deuteronomic traditions, I owe to S. Dean McBride, who will develop his suggestion in greater detail in his forthcoming commentary on Deuteronomy in the Anchor Bible.

The Scope of the Inquiry

In the study that follows we will first examine the anthropological evidence on various types of prophetic phenomena and will pay particular attention to the way in which modern prophets interact with their societies. Using the data drawn from this examination, we will then consider ancient Near Eastern evidence on prophecy. In this way we will be able to test the usefulness of the comparative data before attempting to apply it to the biblical material. Finally, in the light of our anthropological research, we will study the Old Testament evidence on prophecy and society. Our inquiry will focus on the Ephraimite prophetic traditions, for they provide the clearest evidence for the relationship between prophecy and society in Israel. However, we will also examine briefly the data on prophecy in Judah. The bulk of this data will come from prophetic narratives that have been preserved in the prophetic books themselves and in the work of the Chronicler. However, we will also use the little evidence that can be safely drawn from the oracles of Judean prophets.

The study of the biblical material can be approached in two ways. First, several crucial biblical texts can be examined in detail, and on the basis of this examination hypotheses can be formulated and then tested in later studies. Second, all of the biblical evidence on prophecy can be surveyed. The first approach has the advantage of being able to take into account the complexity of the biblical texts, but the concentration on only a few texts necessarily restricts the range of prophetic phenomena that can be considered. The second approach prevents a thorough examination of individual passages but has the advantage of permitting all of the evidence to be treated. Because previous studies of the problem of prophecy and society have failed to take into account all of the available material, we will follow the second approach, realizing that future detailed studies of specific passages may require the modification of our conclusions. Nevertheless, by at least surveying all of the biblical evidence we will be able to suggest the general outlines of a social history of Israelite prophecy.

2

Prophecy in Modern Societies

THE PROBLEM OF TERMINOLOGY

The writings of modern anthropologists contain much material that is potentially relevant to the study of biblical prophecy, but the usefulness of this material is sometimes obscured by the confusing and imprecise terms that anthropologists use in their discussions.[1] This imprecision is particularly visible in the titles that anthropologists have given to prophetic figures. Some writers simply reproduce the native terms for a society's religious specialists and then define these terms by describing the figures' activities. This approach has the advantage of faithfully reflecting the society's religious views, but the anthropologists discourage the use of their material for comparative purposes when they fail to relate the society's religious figures to similar figures in other societies. When anthropologists do attempt to describe religious specialists by using well-known English terms, the difficulties become even greater. Sometimes the English terms are not clearly defined or are not used consistently. Sometimes the anthropologists arbitrarily define their terms so that they accurately match the native categories but no longer carry the terms' common English meanings. Sometimes the

1. For a discussion of this problem by anthropologists, see I. M. Lewis, *Ecstatic Religion* (New York: Penguin Books, 1971) 12–14; and E. Bourguignon, "The Self, the Behavioral Environment, and the Theory of Spirit Possession," *Context and Meaning in Cultural Anthropology* (ed. M. E. Spiro; New York: Free Press, 1965) 40–42.

native figures are even made to fit the common meaning of the English terms. In order to avoid these terminological problems, we will begin our treatment of the anthropological material with a brief discussion of the English terms commonly applied to prophetic figures. Once we have outlined the scholarly consensus on the meaning of these terms, we will attempt to use them consistently in the remainder of our discussion.

The Prophet

Throughout the centuries the biblical prophets have served as the models with which other types of religious specialists have been compared. It is therefore somewhat surprising that anthropologists seldom use the word "prophet" in their writings.[2] There are two possible explanations for this state of affairs. First, when the title "prophet" is given to contemporary figures, a comparison with the biblical prophets is virtually inevitable. Anthropologists usually seek to avoid this sort of comparison because of the danger of distorting our understanding of the contemporary figures by forcing them into the classical biblical mold.

Second, the English word "prophet" is ambiguous, even when it is seen against its biblical background. The word "prophet" is ultimately derived from the Greek word *prophētēs,* an agent-noun which appears in Classical Greek texts as early as the fifth century B.C. *Prophētēs* is presumably formed from the verb *phēmi,* "to speak, to say," with the prefix *pro-,* "before," "forth," although the verb *prophēmi* is not attested until after the turn of the era. Because the prefix *pro-* is ambiguous, the meaning of *prophētēs* must be deduced from the contexts of its earliest appearances. In the early sources, the title *prophētēs* is usually given to a person connected with the oracles of Apollo and Zeus, and the word originally seems to have designated one who "speaks forth" or "proclaims" the message of the deity and interprets the divine word for people seeking oracles. The *prophētēs* thus seems to have occupied a mediatorial position between the people and the gods. Yet because divine messages sometimes deal with future events, the *prophētēs* later came

---

2. When anthropologists do use the designation "prophet," it is not always clear why this particular title has been applied. Note, for example, the use of the title in J. Middleton, *Lugbara Religion* (London: Oxford University Press, 1960) 258–264; E. E. Evans-Pritchard, *Nuer Religion* (Oxford: At the Clarendon Press, 1956) 303–310; K. Schlosser, *Propheten in Afrika* (Braunschweig: Albert Limbach, 1949); and B. G. M. Sundkler, *Bantu Prophets in South Africa* (2d ed.; London: Oxford University Press, 1961).

to be seen as one who "speaks of the future," who "speaks before" events actually take place.[3] The earliest descriptions of the activities of the *prophētēs* thus retain a certain ambiguity. The functions of the *prophētēs* seem to have overlapped those of the medium and the diviner. All of these specialists were concerned with proclaiming and interpreting divine messages and on occasion with speaking about the future. All three also provided means by which people could contact the gods.

The ambiguity surrounding the use of *prophētēs* in Classical Greek sources also extends to the use of the word in the Septuagint. When the Hebrew Bible was translated into Greek, the word *prophētēs* was consistently used to render the Hebrew word nābîʾ, the most common prophetic title used in the Hebrew text. Yet at the same time, *prophētēs* was sometimes used to translate the Hebrew titles rōʾeh and ḥōzeh ("seer" [1 Chr 26:28; 2 Chr 16:7, 10; 19:2; 29:25, 30; 35:15]), and once *prophētēs* was even used to render the Hebrew word malʾāk ("messenger" [2 Chr 36:15]). The Septuagint translators thus apparently did not distinguish the various types of Israelite prophetic figures but applied to all of them the title *prophētēs*, which the translators must have understood as a general term capable of characterizing diverse religious specialists.[4]

In the light of the difficulties associated with the Greek word *prophētēs* and its English derivative "prophet," it seems wise to follow most modern anthropologists and to avoid applying the word "prophet" to modern religious specialists. Therefore, in the remainder of our discussion, we will use the term "prophet" only to translate the Hebrew term nābîʾ. This use of the term "prophet" does not imply anything about the nature and function of the nābîʾ, whose role must be defined solely on the basis of the biblical texts.

The Shaman

The word "shaman" has been taken over from Tungus, the language spoken by the Siberian and Manchurian tribes among whom

3. For a thorough discussion of the Greek evidence, see E. Fascher, *Prophētēs* (Giessen: Alfred Töpelmann, 1927) 1–75. More recent treatments may be found in H. Krämer, "*Prophētēs*," *TDNT* 6 (1968) 783–796; E. R. Dodds, *The Greeks and the Irrational* (Berkeley: University of California Press, 1951) 64–101; M. C. van der Kolf, "Prophetes," *PW* 23 / 1 (1957) 797–814; and L. Ramlot, "Prophétisme," *DBSup* 8 (1972) 934–942.

4. The Septuagint's use of the term *prophētēs* is treated in detail in Fascher, *Prophētēs*, 102–108. Cf. Ramlot, "Prophétisme," 942–943. The relevant Hebrew terminology will be discussed at the appropriate points in our analysis of the biblical evidence.

figures bearing this title were first encountered by Westerners in the seventeenth century. Although the derivation of the word is unclear, its meaning is certain. "In all Tungus languages this term refers to persons of both sexes who have mastered spirits, who at their will can introduce these spirits into themselves and use their power over the spirits in their own interests, particularly helping other people, who suffer from the spirits; in such a capacity they may possess a complex of special methods for dealing with the spirits."[5] The distinguishing characteristic of the shaman is thus the ability to control spirits which might otherwise harm the living but which, if handled properly, can be harnessed and even made beneficent. In contrast to the specialists who are uncontrollably possessed by spirits, shamans must retain their command over the spirits at all times. Shamans accomplish this task either by incorporating the spirits into themselves in various ways or by sending their own spirits out of their bodies and into the spirit world.[6]

Since the first anthropological studies of shamanism, there has been a general tendency to use the word "shaman" to describe a wide variety of religious specialists, many of whom do not exhibit the classic characteristics of Tungus shamans. However, to avoid confusion, it seems best to understand the shaman in the traditional way as a "master of the spirits" and to avoid unnecessary generalization of the title.[7]

The Witch / The Sorcerer

The terms "witch" and "sorcerer" are not clearly distinguished in modern English, and both are generally taken to refer to a person who uses supernatural power or magic to achieve socially harmful goals.[8] However, many societies which are concerned with the

5. S. M. Shirokogoroff, *Psychomental Complex of the Tungus* (London: Kegan Paul, Trench, Trubner, 1935) 269.

6. For a general description of characteristic shamanic activity, see M. Eliade, *Shamanism* (Princeton: Princeton University Press, 1964) 4–8; and W. Bogoras, *The Chukchee* (Memoirs of the American Museum of Natural History 11 / Jesup North Pacific Expedition 7; Leiden: E. J. Brill, 1904–9) 413–468.

7. For a survey of some of the broader definitions of shamanism, see R. W. Firth, "Shaman," *A Dictionary of the Social Sciences* (ed. J. Gould and W. L. Kolb; New York: Free Press, 1964) 638–639; and M. Bouteiller, *Chamanisme et guérison magique* (Paris: Presses Universitaires de France, 1950) 6–7. The restricted definition we are using here follows R. Firth, "Problem and Assumption in an Anthropological Study of Religion," *JRAI* 89 (1959) 141.

8. For the patterns of usage connected with these two terms, see *The Oxford English Dictionary*, s.v. "sorcerer" and "witch."

malevolent use of supernatural power have specific titles to identify the various distinct categories of malefactors.[9] There is no simple way to translate these fine distinctions into English, but to simplify anthropological analysis some scholars have advocated distinguishing witchcraft and sorcery on grounds actually used by some tribal societies. If this procedure is followed, then witchcraft can be defined as the use of an innate power to cause harm to other people, and a witch can be defined as a person who exercises such a power. Thus, by definition witches can never be observed practicing witchcraft, for the process has no externally visible component. In contrast, sorcery can be defined as the magical manipulation of objects in order to bring about a harmful result, and a sorcerer can be defined as a person who manipulates magical objects for the purpose of bringing about harm. Unlike witchcraft, sorcery can be observed and identified more or less objectively.[10] This distinction between witchcraft and sorcery is a useful one and will be used in the remainder of our discussion. However, it must be remembered that the distinction is actually made only by a few groups and that its application to other societies is only for the sake of analytical precision.

The Medium

The term "medium" is found frequently in the anthropological literature, although the word is seldom explicitly defined. In general the term is used as a broad designation for anyone who acts as a channel of communication between the human and divine realms. People come to the medium to ask questions of the spirits, and the spirits, in turn, speak to the inquirers in a recognizable way through the medium. Because the word "medium" is usually defined func-

9. For examples, see R. F. Gray, "Some Structural Aspects of Mbugwe Witchcraft," *Witchcraft and Sorcery in East Africa* (ed. J. Middleton and E. H. Winter; London: Routledge & Kegan Paul, 1963) 143–144; B. Saler, "Nagual, Witch, and Sorcerer in a Quiché Village," *Ethnology* 3 (1964) 306–321; E. E. Evans-Pritchard, *Witchcraft, Oracles and Magic among the Azande* (Oxford: At the Clarendon Press, 1937) 8–12; and C. Kluckhohn, *Navaho Witchcraft* (Boston: Beacon Press, 1967) 22–24.

10. This distinction between witchcraft and sorcery has been cautiously advocated by J. Middleton and E. H. Winter ("Introduction," *Witchcraft and Sorcery in East Africa*, 2–8) and L. Mair (*Witchcraft* [New York: McGraw-Hill, 1969] 16–27), among others. For a criticism of this distinction, see V. Turner, *The Forest of Symbols* (Ithaca: Cornell University Press, 1967) 112–127.

tionally, the title can be given to various types of religious specialists and need not be applied to one particular type.[11]

The Diviner

Anthropologists usually use the term "diviner" to refer to a religious specialist who seeks from the spirits hidden information about the past, present, or future. In addition, the diviner's method of inquiry is usually said to involve the manipulation or interpretation of physical objects or natural phenomena, although this position is not maintained by all anthropologists.[12] However, when the divinatory process does not involve physical objects or natural phenomena, then it is difficult to distinguish the diviner from the medium, who has a similar function but whose methods are unspecified. Therefore, for the sake of analysis, we will follow the usual anthropological practice and see the identifying characteristic of the diviner in the particular physical or natural means used to obtain information. These means vary widely, but all are thought to have a certain objective character that puts them beyond the influence of the diviner.[13] The term "diviner," like the term "medium," has a functional definition, with the result that in many societies "diviner" is not an exclusive title but can be applied to various sorts of religious specialists.

The Priest

The commonly accepted anthropological definition of the title "priest" was originally formulated by Max Weber, who held that the priest was a specialist "in the continuous operation of a cultic enterprise, permanently associated with particular names, places, and times, and related to specific social groups."[14] Weber stressed con-

11. This definition of "medium" generally follows Firth, "Problem and Assumption," 141, although Firth restricts mediumship to cases of spirit possession, a move which other anthropologists would not make.

12. For a discussion of the problem of defining the word "diviner," see V. W. Turner, "Religious Specialists: Anthropological Study," *International Encyclopedia of the Social Sciences* 13 (New York: Macmillan Company and Free Press, 1968) 439. For more comprehensive definitions, see J. Beattie, "Divination in Bunyoro, Uganda," *Sociologus* 14 (1964) 44–48; and V. Turner, *Revelation and Divination in Ndembu Ritual* (Ithaca: Cornell University Press, 1975) 15–16.

13. In fact, many societies recognize that divinatory procedures are open to human manipulation, but the dogma of objectivity is still maintained. For a discussion of this phenomenon, see G. K. Park, "Divination and Its Social Contexts," *JRAI* 93 (1963) 195–209.

14. M. Weber, *The Sociology of Religion* (Boston: Beacon Press, 1964) 30. Cf. Turner, "Religious Specialists," 438; and W. A. Lessa and E. Z. Vogt, eds., *Reader in*

tinuous involvement in the maintenance of a cult as the hallmark of priesthood and considered the priest's authority to be derived from traditional participation in the cult.[15] Weber's definition is useful so long as its limitations are recognized. Like other functionally defined titles, the title "priest" can be applied to any specialist who participates in the regular maintenance of a cult. Thus, prophets, shamans, witches, mediums, and diviners can also be priests if they have regular cultic roles in their societies. In turn, priests can on occasion function as diviners, prophets, or mediums. Such overlapping of religious roles does not take place in all societies or even at all times in a single society, but the fact that priests sometimes have other religious functions prevents sharply distinguishing the priest from other religious specialists.

The Mystic

The term "mystic" is rarely used by anthropologists, and when it does appear it does not usually refer to a social role but to a particular type of relationship between an individual and the divine world. The mystical experience typically involves temporary union with divine reality and is intensely personal in nature. Mystics are frequently unwilling or unable to verbalize their experiences and often have no clearly defined religious role within their societies. Therefore, the mystic will generally fall outside of the scope of our inquiry.[16]

The Intermediary

The above discussion has helped to define more clearly some of the common religious titles and has provided a vocabulary for talking about the unique features of each specialist. However, it is still the case that some of these titles overlap and can be borne by the same individual. This overlapping of titles is due to the fact that several of these figures share certain characteristic social functions. To simplify our discussion of these common features, it will be helpful to adopt a neutral, general title that can embrace several reli-

----

Comparative Religion: An Anthropological Approach (Evanston: Row, Peterson, 1958) 410–411.

15. In contrast, Weber held that the prophet's authority was based on personal revelation and charisma (*Sociology of Religion,* 46–47).

16. For attempts to define mysticism, see W. James, *The Varieties of Religious Experience* (New York: New American Library, 1958) 292–294; and R. Otto, *Mysticism East and West* (New York: Macmillan, 1932).

gious specialties. This move will also allow us to incorporate a wider range of evidence than might otherwise be the case. Because the prophet, shaman, medium, and diviner are all characterized by the fact that in some way they serve as intermediaries between the human and divine worlds, we will use the term "intermediary" to refer collectively to all of them and will describe their activities in general terms as "intermediation." It should be noted that we have not designated the priest an intermediary, even though the two figures do sometimes share similar functions. This action has been taken because in most societies, including Israel, priests have many unique functions that must be the subject of separate investigation. To treat the priest along with the other specialists does not take sufficient account of his uniqueness.

THE SOCIAL PREREQUISITES
OF INTERMEDIATION

In order for intermediaries to exist within a society, certain general conditions and attitudes must be present. At first glance some of these social prerequisites seem obvious and scarcely worth mentioning, but their importance cannot be overestimated. They create the supportive social environment which permits intermediation to occur. Intermediaries will not automatically appear in all societies having the required characteristics, but when the proper social environment is lacking, intermediation cannot take place. When these crucial social features disappear after having once been present, existing intermediaries must also disappear or be relegated to subgroups where the necessary conditions are still present.

The first social prerequisite for the existence of intermediaries is a belief in the reality of a supernatural power or powers. This belief may be articulated in various ways, but no matter how it is expressed it must involve the recognition of powers that differ from the natural powers that are a part of everyday human experience. The world of the supernatural powers must in some way be distinct from the normal human world, so that there is a "gap" between the two. Without a belief in the existence of a separate realm populated by supernatural powers, no "gap" needs to be bridged, and there is no need for the services of an intermediary.[17]

17. J. Beattie and J. Middleton, "Introduction," *Spirit Mediumship and Society in Africa* (ed. J. Beattie and J. Middleton; New York: Africana Publishing Corporation, 1969) xviii–xix.

Second, if intermediaries are to exist in a society believing in supernatural powers, then the society must also believe that those powers can influence earthly affairs and can in turn be directly influenced by human agents. If the supernatural powers cannot become involved in normal human activity, then they cannot communicate directly with the world and so have no need for intermediaries. If the powers cannot be influenced by humans, then it is unnecessary for the society to have specialists for this purpose.

Even in societies where people believe in the possibility of communication between the human and supernatural worlds, all of the supernatural powers are not always thought to be equally accessible. There is a tendency for extremely powerful gods, such as creator gods, to become glorified to the point that they cease to have any real contact with the human world. They can be reached only through a hierarchy of subordinate ghosts, spirits, and gods, who serve as intermediaries for the otiose high gods. In such cases, only the lesser spirits are likely to have human intermediaries, for only these spirits have direct contact with human beings. The older high gods are isolated from the world and do not usually have cults or human intermediaries.

It is not unusual for changes to take place within the hierarchy of the spirit world. Lesser gods are elevated to the rank of high gods, and their places in the pantheon are taken by newcomers. When such changes take place, they will normally be reflected in the society's system of intermediaries. The intermediaries of the newly exalted high gods will tend to disappear, while the intermediaries of the newer spirits will become more prominent.[18]

---

18. There are numerous classical examples of this process. In Mesopotamia god lists and theogonies record several generations of otiose deities before listing the great gods of the cult. The history of these ancient gods is obscure, but presumably they were once active powers that were replaced by younger gods. By the second millennium the great gods of the cult were themselves thought to be inaccessible, and there developed the concept of the personal deity, who served as a divine intermediary through whom people could contact the great gods. For a discussion, see T. Jacobsen, *The Treasures of Darkness* (New Haven: Yale University Press, 1976) 159–164; H. Vorländer, *Mein Gott* (Kevelaer: Butzon & Bercker, 1975) 5–167; A. L. Oppenheim, *Ancient Mesopotamia* (Chicago: University of Chicago Press, 1964) 194–198; S. N. Kramer, *The Sumerians* (Chicago: University of Chicago Press, 1963) 118–123, 126–129; and F. M. Cross, "The 'Olden Gods' in Ancient Near Eastern Creation Myths," *Magnalia Dei: The Mighty Acts of God* (ed. F. M. Cross et al.; Garden City, N.Y.: Doubleday, 1976) 329–339. For a modern example of the close correlation existing between the divine hierarchy and the hierarchy of intermediaries, see G. K. Garbett, "Spirit Mediums as Mediators in Korekore Society," *Spirit Mediumship and Society in Africa*, 107–110; and G. Lienhardt, *Divinity and Experience: The Religion of the Dinka* (Oxford: At the Clarendon Press, 1961) 80–83.

A similar phenomenon can be seen in societies such as the Lugbara, where there is a highly developed ancestor cult. Among the
Lugbara the ghosts of dead lineage members are thought to retain
an interest in the social stability of their lineages. These ghosts
watch over the living and can cause trouble if lineage harmony is
threatened. To prevent such ghostly activity, living lineage members must resolve social tensions and make cultic offerings to placate the ghosts. However, not all ghosts have an equal stake in
human affairs. The most deeply involved ghosts are those that have
recently died. They are the primary focus of the cult and the ones
most likely to have intermediaries. As time passes, the ghosts become less involved with the living, and cultic activity diminishes.
Finally the ghosts reach the point that they are absorbed into the
anonymous mass of ancestral ghosts, and all intermediation ceases.[19]

Third, intermediaries can exist only where they are viewed positively and where their specific actions are encouraged or at least
tolerated. This statement introduces a point which we will explore
in greater detail later in our discussion. However, at the outset the
point needs to be stated in its sharpest form. Intermediaries cannot
exist without some sort of social support, although that support may
be minimal and come only from a small group within the society.
There can be no socially isolated intermediaries. Where intermediation is not socially acceptable, the society will discourage the appearance of intermediaries and will attempt to suppress any intermediaries who do appear.

This point can be illustrated with data drawn from a number of
societies, but one of the clearest illustrations comes from the Tonga,
who live in the southern part of Zambia. Two of the subdivisions of
the Tonga—the Plateau Tonga and the Valley Tonga—are geograph-
ically adjacent and have similar languages and cultures. Yet the two
groups differ in their views of spirit mediums. The relatively accessible Plateau Tonga have been greatly influenced by European
civilization, and as a result the possession cults which were once
common have come to be viewed as somewhat backward and un-
sophisticated. The cults themselves tried to combat this trend, and
possessed mediums warned the people to resist foreign cultural influences, but the people ignored this advice. Since the late 1940s the
cults have been disappearing rapidly, and spirit mediums are now

19. Middleton, *Lugbara Religion*, 25–28, 32–69.

rare because the society is not interested in supporting them. In contrast, the relatively isolated Valley Tonga have retained a complex system of spirit mediums. The Valley Tonga have also been influenced by Western civilization, but these influences have been incorporated into the possession cults. Thus, in addition to being possessed by the traditional animal spirits, some modern mediums are possessed by the "spirits" of airplanes, motorboats, and guitars. In this case the intermediaries have survived because they have enjoyed continuous social support.[20]

Finally, intermediaries will exist only in those societies where social conditions require the services of an intermediary. Therefore, intermediaries are often found in societies undergoing stress and rapid social change. Sudden economic reversals, wars, natural disasters, and cross-cultural contact can all lead to social instability. Under such conditions a society may seek to restore its equilibrium by renewing its contacts with the supernatural world. Intermediaries may have a role in this process, and if so, their numbers will increase as social conditions deteriorate. The converse is also true. As social conditions become more stable, the need for intermediaries lessens, and their numbers are likely to decrease.

Many societies provide illustrations of this link between social stability and the appearance of intermediaries. However, a striking case comes from the oral traditions of the Fipa, the inhabitants of Ufipa in southwest Tanzania. During the early nineteenth century, Ufipa underwent a great deal of social change as a result of increased political and economic activity. The country was on a crucial trade route between the coast and mineral-rich Katanga farther inland. Agricultural products and raw materials moved through Ufipa to shipping points along the coast, while manufactured goods from Europe, including firearms, were relayed from the coast to the interior. This trade brought prosperity to Ufipa, and to develop the economy even more, the chiefs of Ufipa demanded from the people increasingly heavy taxes of goods and labor. This move quite naturally fostered the growth of the bureaucracy responsible for supervising trade and collecting taxes. To support the growing political power of the chiefs, the army was enlarged, and this too required an increase in taxes. As a result of all of this activity, the population

20. E. Colson, *The Plateau Tonga of Northern Rhodesia* (Manchester: Manchester University Press, 1962) 92–96; idem, "Spirit Possession among the Tonga of Zambia," *Spirit Mediumship and Society in Africa*, 69–103.

increased, but social and economic power shifted from the people to the central government. By the latter part of the nineteenth century, there were large numbers of Fipa who were deprived of economic and political power. As dissatisfaction with the government increased, there was a corresponding increase in spirit possession. At this time the medium Kaswa appeared and brought messages that are still preserved in oral tradition. Kaswa predicted a further decline in traditional values and morality, together with war and an invasion from the East. The European invaders would finally destroy the power of the chiefs, but in the process Fipa society would be irrevocably changed. After delivering his message, Kaswa disappeared into the ground, at a place aptly called "Loss of Mind."[21]

Even in societies which are supportive of intermediation in general, intermediaries tend to be forgotten or disappear when they have no social function. Just as the supernatural powers themselves may safely be ignored as long as they do not disrupt everyday life, so also their intermediaries may be neglected as long as there is no need to communicate with the supernatural world.[22]

THE MECHANISMS OF INTERMEDIATION

Societies are able to recognize and validate intermediaries because of their distinctive behavior.[23] In every society intermediaries exhibit certain stereotypical characteristics which indicate supernatural involvement. Yet, not everyone who manifests these behavioral characteristics is automatically considered to be an intermediary. Although modern Western observers tend to think that "primitive" peoples routinely trace all aberrant and mentally deranged behavior to divine influence, in fact this is not the case. Most societies recognize multiple causes for the behavior typical of intermediaries, and not all examples of such behavior are seen as indications that genuine intermediation is occurring.

21. R. G. Willis, "Kaswa: Oral Tradition of a Fipa Prophet," *Africa* 40 (1970) 248–256. This example is noteworthy not only because the text of the medium's message has been preserved but also because of the remarkable parallels between conditions in Ufipa and conditions in Israel after the Solomonic period.

22. Lewis, *Ecstatic Religion*, 35–37. Note also the examples discussed by Y. K. Bamunoba and F. B. Welbourn, "Emandwa Initiation in Ankole," *The Uganda Journal* 29 (1965) 14–15; and P. Fry, *Spirits of Protest* (Cambridge: Cambridge University Press, 1976) 1–5.

23. We will discuss below the nature of this characteristic behavior and the process of social validation.

In many Western societies, the behavior associated with intermediation receives a naturalistic explanation. The person exhibiting such behavior is sometimes thought to be under the influence of hypnosis, mild psychological stress, sensory deprivation, alcohol, or drugs. More often, various types of physical and mental illness are invoked to account for the intermediary's peculiar behavior.[24] The same sorts of naturalistic explanations are sometimes found in societies that also recognize the supernatural origins of the intermediary's actions. Such societies are aware that illness can cause symptoms that resemble the traits of genuine intermediation and that people who are ill must be distinguished from people who are in some way involved with the spirit world. The former require treatment for their physical and psychological maladies and are often referred to Western doctors and psychiatrists. The latter are dealt with in a completely different way and are treated by using traditional methods.[25]

When societies recognize supernatural explanations for the characteristic behavior of intermediaries, details of the explanations vary widely and are usually couched in somewhat vague, spiritual terms. Still, it is possible to discern two general types of explanations.

Possession

Many societies attribute the characteristic behavior of intermediaries to some sort of spirit possession. At the outset, it is important to distinguish possession from trance, which in religious contexts is sometimes called "ecstasy." The two phenomena are often confused in scholarly discussions, and many writers use the word "possession" and the word "trance" interchangeably. However,

24. For a brief survey of naturalistic explanations, see E. Bourguignon and L. Pettay, "Spirit Possession, Trance and Cross-Cultural Research," *Symposium on New Approaches to the Study of Religion* (Proceedings of the 1964 Annual Spring Meeting of the American Ethnological Society, ed. J. Helm; Seattle: American Ethnological Society, 1964) 39–41; and A. M. Ludwig, "Altered States of Consciousness," *Trance and Possession States* (ed. R. Prince; Montreal: R. M. Bucke Memorial Society, 1968) 70–75. A detailed example of a typical psychological explanation may be found in J. Silverman, "Shamans and Acute Schizophrenia," *AA* n.s. 69 (1967) 21–31.

25. For examples of societies distinguishing the symptoms of illness from the symptoms of intermediation, see T. Modarressi, "The Zar Cult in South Iran," *Trance and Possession States*, 151; Bourgignon, "The Self, the Behavioral Environment, and the Theory of Spirit Possession," 41–42; M. J. Field, *Search for Security* (Evanston: Northwestern University Press, 1960) 66–71; and S. S. Walker, *Ceremonial Spirit Possession in Africa and Afro-America* (Leiden: E. J. Brill, 1972) 104–115.

strictly speaking, *trance* is a *psycho-physiological state marked by dissociation* and can have a number of different causes besides spirit possession. A person in a state of trance exhibits certain characteristic mental and physical traits, which frequently lead to the alteration of normal behavioral patterns. All of these traits are not present in every case of trance, but a comprehensive list of trance characteristics would include the following items:

(1) changes in thought processes, including alterations in concentration, attention, memory, and judgment

(2) distorted perception of time

(3) loss of conscious control over physical and mental processes

(4) uninhibited expression of rapidly changing emotions

(5) changes in body-image, sometimes involving feelings of isolation from reality or of an expanded consciousness

(6) distortions of perception, including hallucinations

(7) altered views of the meaning or significance of events, including experiences of "illumination" or profound insight

(8) inability or reluctance to communicate the trance experience, sometimes involving amnesia with respect to everything done and said in trance

(9) feelings of rejuvenation

(10) extreme sensitivity to suggestions, instructions, or commands[26]

It is important to note that the common characteristics of trance are general physiological and psychological conditions which may lead to a wide variety of specific behavioral manifestations. As we will soon see, trance behavior tends to follow definite patterns within a given society, but many factors influence the precise nature of these patterns. They cannot necessarily be predicted on the basis of the characteristics of the trance state itself.[27]

In contrast to trance, *possession* is a *cultural theory that explains how contact takes place between the supernatural and natural worlds.* The distinctive behavior of certain people is explained by saying that their bodies have been entered by a spirit or deity.[28] The precise description of this process varies, but usually it is said that

26. This list is a slight adaptation of the one found in Ludwig, "Altered States of Consciousness," 75–83.

27. We will consider the nature and causes of trance behavior when we discuss the behavioral characteristics of intermediaries.

28. On the distinction between trance and possession, see Bourguignon, "The Self, the Behavioral Environment, and the Theory of Spirit Possession," 40–43. The dis-

the spirit temporarily takes up residence in the host's body. The host is rarely possessed continuously but is only visited intermittently by the spirit. On these occasions the spirit and the possessed individual become one, but it is the spirit that dominates the relationship.[29] When the individual speaks and acts, it is actually the spirit speaking and acting through the individual's body. The host "clothes" or "embodies" the spirit and in the process takes on the spirit's distinctive identity. The host's own human identity is lost, and in some cases the spirit actually drives out and then replaces the individual's soul, with the result that the possessed person is no longer fully human.[30]

The unity of the possessing spirit and its host is often reflected in the language used to express possession. When the spirit and host are of different sexes, their union is frequently described in sexual and marital terms. Women are said to be the wives of male spirits, while men are seen as the husbands of female spirits. There are even cases in which wedding ceremonies are held to solemnize spirit marriages, and thereafter the supernatural spouses play a regular role in the family life of their human mates.[31] When possession occurs under these circumstances, the human partner exhibits the behavioral characteristics of the possessing spouse. Thus, for exam-

---

tinction that we are making between trance and possession is similar to the one that Firth makes between spirit possession and spirit mediumship ("Problem and Assumption," 141).

29. An exception to this rule is found in the case of the shaman, who must be able to control the spirits that he incarnates. Shamans who are possessed by spirits that cannot be controlled are usually regarded as ineffective and are removed from office. See Shirokogoroff, *Psychomental Complex*, 271, 352, 366.

30. Possession beliefs involving soul replacement are usually found among groups such as the Haitian voodoo cultists, the Saora of India, and the Tungus of Siberia, all of which believe that the normal human has more than one soul. See Lewis, *Ecstatic Religion*, 47, 57. For discussions of the general features of spirit possession, see Walker, *Ceremonial Spirit Possession*, 47–53; M. J. Field, "Spirit Possession in Ghana," *Spirit Mediumship and Society in Africa*, 3–5; L. de Heusch, "Cultes de possession et religions initiatiques de salut en Afrique," *Religions de Salut* (Annales de Centre d'Étude des Religions 2; Brussels: Université Libre de Bruxelles, Institut de Sociologie, 1962) 128–138; S. F. Nadel, "A Study of Shamanism in the Nuba Mountains," *JRAI* 76 (1946) 25; K. M. Stewart, "Spirit Possession in Native America," *SJA* 2 (1946) 323–325; and Bourguignon and Pettay, "Spirit Possession, Trance and Cross-Cultural Research," 39–46.

31. Spirit marriages have been observed in Haitian voodoo cults and among the trance mediums of Bali. In many societies shamans are regarded as "married" to spirits of the opposite sex. See A. Métraux, *Voodoo in Haiti* (London: Andre Deutsch, 1959) 212–219; J. Belo, *Trance in Bali* (New York: Columbia University Press, 1960) 21; V. Elwin, *The Religion of an Indian Tribe* (London: Oxford University Press, 1955) 130–135; and Lewis, *Ecstatic Religion*, 58–64.

ple, male shamans possessed by their spirit wives may follow typical female behavior patterns and may ultimately undergo a sexual transformation. Similarly, women who are possessed by male spirits may speak and act in ways that are usually typical of males.[32] The sexual and marital language used to describe possession is probably also related to the equine images which are often employed. The spirits are said to "mount" and "ride" their hosts, who are referred to as "horses."[33]

Societies evaluate possession and its accompanying behavior in different ways. On the basis of these evaluations, it is possible to distinguish three different types of possession, any or all of which may exist within a given society. Because of the subjective nature of the evaluation process, the distinctions between the different types of possession are not always absolute. What is viewed negatively by the whole society may be viewed positively by a minority group within it, and what the whole society values highly may be rejected by the minority. In addition, societies and groups sometimes change their evaluations of possession phenomena or of specific cases of possession. Still, once this subjective element is taken into account, the recognition of three types of possession is a useful analytical device.[34]

Possession Viewed Negatively

Societies tend to evaluate possession negatively when it is the work of evil or harmful spirits and when the behavior of the possessed individual is socially harmful. When evil spirits or demons are involved, societies do not usually believe that genuine intermediation takes place. The spirits are not thought to be interested in communicating with the world. Rather, they cause illness which must be cured by exorcism. The best examples of demonic possession are provided by the numerous cases recorded in Europe during the Middle Ages, but the phenomenon exists in modern societies as well.[35]

32. Examples are provided in Bogoras, *The Chukchee*, 448–454; Belo, *Trance in Bali*, 22–23; and Métraux, *Voodoo*, 213–219.

33. Lewis, *Ecstatic Religion*, 58.

34. The following schema of possession types is similar to the tripartite analysis suggested by Bourguignon and Pettay, "Spirit Possession, Trance and Cross-Cultural Research," 43–45.

35. Numerous examples are collected in T. K. Oesterreich, *Possession: Demoniacal and Other among Primitive Races in Antiquity, the Middle Ages, and Modern Times* (New York: Richard R. Smith, 1930).

Demonic possession is almost never voluntary. Although some societies believe that it can be invoked by a third person, the hallmark of demonic possession is that it appears unbidden at the sole volition of the spirits. Not only is the appearance of possession outside of the control of the victim, but frequently the behavior of the victim is also uncontrolled. In some cases demonic possession leads to behavior that is virtually identical to that of people possessed by more benevolent spirits, but in other cases the demons provoke their hosts to self-destructive actions or to antisocial crimes such as robbery, rape, assault, and murder. No society will tolerate such behavior, and all available means are used to render the possessed person harmless.

Even in societies where possession is tolerated, people must constantly be alert to the possibility that intermediaries have suddenly become possessed by malevolent rather than benevolent spirits. Intermediaries are thus viewed as potentially dangerous, for most societies believe that someone capable of being possessed by friendly spirits can also be possessed by harmful spirits. Shamans are a particular problem in this respect, since they habitually use their own protective spirits to control evil spirits. When a shaman becomes too weak to control his own spirits, then he may become the prey of the evil spirits and may do great damage to the society. Shamans and other intermediaries must therefore be watched closely so that the first signs of evil spirit possession can be detected. When such signs appear, the society tries to deal with the evil spirits by exorcising them, but if this approach fails, then the intermediaries must be driven out or killed. In this way societies subtly exercise control over their intermediaries, who are always open to the potentially fatal charge of demonic possession. We will see the social importance of this control mechanism when we examine the social functions of intermediation.[36]

Possession Viewed Negatively but Tolerated

Many societies recognize a type of possession which begins as an unwanted and uncontrollable illness but which develops into a more or less controlled form of possession that is tolerated by the majority of the society. While the deities involved in this type of

---

36. For a discussion of this control process with respect to shamans, see Shirokogoroff, *Psychomental Complex*, 371–377; and A. Balikci, "Shamanistic Behavior among the Netsilik Eskimos," *SJA* 19 (1963) 393.

possession are not demonic, neither are they usually the chief deities of the society. Rather they tend to be minor spirits, perhaps originally foreign to the society, or "old gods" whose cults have been subordinated to the official cults of newer, more powerful deities. Because of the nature of the possessing deities, and also because the people possessed tend to lack status and social power, anthropologists usually refer to this type of possession as *peripheral possession* and refer to the possessed individuals as *peripheral intermediaries.*[37]

Although the specific characteristics of peripheral possession vary somewhat from society to society, on the whole the development of the phenomenon follows the same pattern in most societies. The possession process typically begins with the host suddenly becoming ill and manifesting symptoms consistent either with physical illness or with possession. Attempts are usually made to treat the illness by normal means, but when this approach is ineffective, the patient is taken to a medium or to the priest of a peripheral possession cult. By various means the medium seeks to determine whether or not spirit possession is involved. Sometimes this is done by divination, but usually the medium or priest seeks to force the possessing spirit to reveal itself. If the medium is successful, the spirit confirms the diagnosis of spirit possession by clearly possessing the host and identifying itself. During this initial possession the host acts and speaks in ways characteristic of the possessing spirit. Through the host genuine intermediation takes place. The spirit makes known its demands and tells the medium how to remove the host's unwanted symptoms. After the initial possession has been completed, the necessary steps are taken to meet the spirit's requests and remove the patient's affliction. Frequently the spirit requires that the patient become an intermediary, a process which involves becoming a member of a peripheral possession cult or serving the society as the spirit's official representative. When this requirement has been met, the individual is possessed periodically by the spirit, but now possession is controlled and frequently even invoked. The possessed person has become a true intermediary, serving as a channel of communication between the human and

37. For a general description of peripheral possession, see Lewis, *Ecstatic Religion*, 66–126. V. W. Turner's term "liminal" seems roughly equivalent to the more common anthropological designation "peripheral" (*The Ritual Process* [Chicago: Aldine, 1969] 125–129).

divine worlds. Possession takes place in specific social and cultic contexts, and the new intermediary takes on a regular religious role.[38]

The society's attitude toward peripheral possession is somewhat ambiguous. At first, possession is evaluated negatively by the majority of the society. The symptoms of spirit activity are interpreted as indicative of illness, and the society takes the necessary steps to cure the patient. As part of this process, the society is willing to meet the demands of the possessing spirit, although the society may act reluctantly and will observe certain limits beyond which it will not go to placate the spirit. Once the possessed person becomes an established intermediary, the society will tolerate his behavior within certain limits and will usually try to be attentive to further supernatural messages. On the other hand, the person who is possessed has a somewhat different view of the experience than the society as a whole. Like the society, the possessed individual at first consciously evaluates his experience negatively and seeks to be cured. If the person is required to become an intermediary, he may actively resist the spirit's demands. However, once the person has become an intermediary, he usually evaluates his experience positively. Furthermore, if he is a member of a peripheral possession cult he will be supported in his evaluation by other cult members, all of whom are similarly possessed. He now may actively seek possession, while the society as a whole simply tolerates it and attempts to keep it within bounds.[39]

Possession Viewed Positively

When societies view possession positively, they see it as a genuine means of intermediation. Possession of this sort is com-

---

38. Anthropological literature provides numerous descriptions of peripheral possession. For a representative sample, see Beattie and Middleton, eds., *Spirit Mediumship and Society in Africa;* J. H. M. Beattie, "Initiation into the Cwezi Spirit Possession Cult in Bunyoro," *African Studies* 16 (1957) 150–161; Fry, *Spirits of Protest,* 68–106; J. Nicolas, *"Les juments des dieux": Rites de possession et condition féminine en pays Hausa* (Études Nigériennes 21; n.pl.: IFAN-CNRS, 1968); G. Harris, "Possession 'Hysteria' in a Kenya Tribe," *AA* n.s. 59 (1957) 1046–1066; H. B. Barclay, *Buurri al Lamaab* (Ithaca: Cornell University Press, 1964) 188–207; Bamunoba and Welbourn, "Emandwa Initiation," 13–25; L. B. Kaggwa and F. B. Welbourn, *"Lubaale* Initiation in Buganda," *The Uganda Journal* 28 (1964) 218–220; and J. Hamer and I. Hamer, "Spirit Possession and Its Socio-Psychological Implications among the Sidamo of Southwest Ethiopia," *Ethnology* 5 (1966) 395–401.

39. Bourguignon and Pettay, "Spirit Possession, Trance and Cross-Cultural Research," 43–45.

pletely controlled and appears only in appropriate social and cultic settings.

Positively viewed possession can occur under two circumstances. First, as we have already seen, it occurs among peripheral intermediaries and members of peripheral possession cults. In this case the positive evaluation is limited to minority groups within the society and is not likely to be shared by the society as a whole. Second, positively viewed possession sometimes occurs as part of a society's established religion. In this case, possession has important functions within the central cult and must occur at the appropriate points in the ritual. Societies carefully control possession within the central cult and have regular mechanisms for assuring an orderly supply of appropriately trained intermediaries. Because this type of possession is an established part of the central social structure, anthropologists usually refer to it as *central possession* and refer to the possessed individuals as *central intermediaries*.[40]

Societies and groups which view possession positively do not usually wait for the spirits to initiate possession but instead use a number of means to induce it. Alcohol, drugs, flashing lights, dancing, singing, fasting, smoke, and self-hypnosis are all used, but rhythmic stimulation is probably the most common method. Drums of various sorts play an important role in most possession cults, and the shaman's drum is the symbol of his authority. Scientific studies have correlated brain-wave patterns with typical African and Haitian possession rhythms, and there are indications that most normal people are susceptible to sonic stimulation. In places such as Haiti, where the use of drums to induce possession is a highly developed art, each spirit is invoked with its own characteristic rhythm. This suggests that the drummers are able to induce different types of possession behavior by subtly varying their rhythmic patterns, although to date it has not been possible to check this theory scientifically. However, regardless of the means used to induce possession, it is important to note that the people involved do not believe that the method used affects the validity of the possession experience. Possession induced by alcohol, drugs, or rhythmic stimulation is not considered a fraud or less valid than spontaneous possession. The people who use these means clearly recognize the connection be-

40. For a general description of central possession, see Lewis, *Ecstatic Religion*, 127–177.

tween the physiological stimulus and the response, but they maintain that genuine possession nevertheless occurs.[41]

Nonpossession

Nonpossession theories are the second major way that societies attempt to account for the distinctive behavior of intermediaries. These theories occur principally in connection with mysticism and shamanism, although even in these contexts they may be linked with some sort of possession theory. In contrast to possession theories, nonpossession theories typically involve the belief that an individual's soul or spirit can leave his body and travel to a supernatural world. When this occurs the individual ceases to be human and is vulnerable to invasion by foreign spirits or to accidents that might keep his soul from returning.

Soul migration or soul loss is frequently evaluated negatively. In some societies it is associated with witchcraft, for witches are thought to have the power to steal the souls of their victims. Various attempts are therefore made to protect the soul and prevent its being stolen. More often, soul loss is simply associated with illness. The patient's soul either leaves voluntarily or is driven out by a malevolent spirit. If the soul cannot be restored, it may eventually be destroyed, and the patient will die. In cases of witchcraft and illness, no intermediation actually takes place. Even when a sick person's soul is restored, it brings back no messages from the supernatural world.

In some instances soul loss is evaluated positively. This usually occurs in societies having shamans who function by sending their own spirits to the supernatural realm. The flight of the shaman's soul is always controlled and has several purposes. The shaman's spirit can be sent to battle evil spirits and prevent them from harming the society. By means of soul flight the shaman can obtain information from the supernatural realm. This process is usually associated with dreams or visions, and it results in genuine intermediation. Similarly, the shaman can heal illness by retrieving from the

41. Walker, *Ceremonial Spirit Possession,* 15–25; Stewart, "Spirit Possession in Native America," 325; Shirokogoroff, *Psychomental Complex,* 348; Field, "Spirit Possession in Ghana," 6–8; J. Middleton, "Spirit Possession among the Lugbara," *Spirit Mediumship and Society in Africa,* 225; A. D. Ross, "Epileptiform Attacks Provoked by Music," *The British Journal of Delinquency* 7 (1956–57) 60–63; M. J. Herskovits, "Drums and Drummers in Afrobrazilian Cult Life," *The New World Negro* (ed. F. S. Herskovits; Bloomington: Indiana University Press, 1966) 183–197.

spirit world souls that have been stolen or driven out.[42] As is also the case with spirit possession, soul flight is frequently induced. Intermediaries use the same techniques to bring about soul flight as they do to bring about possession.

While the societies containing shamans tend to evaluate their periods of soul migration positively because of the social benefits that the shamans provide, the shamans themselves view soul migration ambiguously. On the one hand, the ability to send their souls on controlled flights leads to a secure role in the social structure and to a certain amount of social status. On the other hand, soul loss is potentially dangerous for the shamans, and many of them undertake their duties reluctantly. The shaman whose soul is absent is more vulnerable than ordinary people to attack by malevolent spirits. It is always possible that something will happen to the shaman's body so that his soul cannot return. The soul itself may be overpowered by evil spirits and destroyed. There are even cases where the shaman's own spirits are so frustrated in their fruitless attempt to accomplish their mission that they return and attack their helpless master.[43]

Soul migration is unequivocally evaluated positively only by mystics, who seek to lose their own identity in the supernatural realm. However, mystics are usually not interested in serving as intermediaries, so little communication with the spirit world actually takes place.

THE MAKING OF AN INTERMEDIARY

People become intermediaries in a variety of ways and for a variety of reasons. Just as each intermediary has unique personal characteristics, so also each undergoes a unique set of formative

42. In many societies shamanism is explained by using a combination of nonpossession and possession theories. The shaman is thought to send out his own primary soul only on rare occasions. The more normal process is for him to induce possession by his helping spirits or to replace one of his subsidiary souls with his helping spirits. These spirits, which the shaman has the power to control, are then sent on errands to the supernatural realm, while the shaman's primary soul remains intact. The process thus resembles highly controlled possession more closely than it does nonpossession. See Shirokogoroff, *Psychomental Complex*, 317–322.

43. For a discussion of nonpossession theories, see ibid., 317–322; Eliade, *Shamanism*, 5; J. M. Murphy, "Psychotherapeutic Aspects of Shamanism on St. Lawrence Island, Alaska," *Magic, Faith, and Healing* (ed. A. Kiev; New York: Free Press, 1964) 61–63; Balikci, "Shamanistic Behavior," 384–392; K. Rasmussen, *Intellectual Culture of the Iglulik Eskimos* (Copenhagen: Gyldendalske Boghandel,

experiences. Yet, when the process by which people become intermediaries is examined cross-culturally, certain general patterns do
emerge. These patterns help to provide a clearer understanding of
the individuals involved in intermediation, but it must always be
remembered that no single intermediary is likely to fit the patterns
perfectly.

It is popularly believed that individuals become intermediaries
by virtue of possessing certain religious, psychological, or social
characteristics. People who have these characteristics are thought to
develop naturally, even inevitably, into intermediaries. Popular descriptions of the development process vary, depending on the incli-
nations of the narrator, but they all share one common feature. They
all portray the process as a personal one taking place in relative
isolation. The sensitive person has a mystical experience that leads
him to become an intermediary. The "charismatic" individual becomes a prophet by receiving a "call" which validates him in the
eyes of his society. The psychotic or neurotic goes into trance,
claims to be possessed by spirits, and is accredited as an intermediary. The social misfit decides to become an intermediary to
enhance his social status.

The difficulty with this popular individualistic approach is that it
cannot adequately explain why people with the required personal
characteristics do not automatically develop into intermediaries or
why intermediaries do not always have the expected characteristics.
Mystics, charismatics, neurotics, and social misfits do not inevitably
become intermediaries, and in turn intermediaries are not all mystics, charismatics, neurotics, or social misfits.[44] Clearly, other factors
must be involved, and anthropological studies have shown that societies themselves play an important role in the process by which
some of their members become intermediaries. People do not normally become intermediaries in isolation from the rest of the society, but the society is intimately involved in the process. It is therefore necessary to examine not only the personal characteristics
which predispose a person to become an intermediary but also the
social factors which shape and control his development. Personal

---

Nordisk Forlag, 1929) 123–129; de Heusch, "Cultes de possession," 129–137; and
E. Bourguignon, "World Distribution and Patterns of Possession States," *Trance and
Possession States*, 4–9.

44. On this point, see Bouteiller, *Chamanisme*, 40–42.

and social factors are interrelated in complex ways, and only by considering both can the development of intermediaries be adequately understood.

Mental and Social Predisposition

From the outset it must be recognized that most discussions of the mental and social characteristics of intermediaries are the work of outside observers, who are not usually a part of the culture they are describing. Societies rarely use psychological and sociological terms to describe how intermediaries are formed, and as a result observers interested in such issues are forced to make deductions from the intermediaries' behavior and the observable aspects of the formative process. The major difficulty with this approach is that the observer is likely to use his own cultural norms to interpret what he sees. For example, to many Western psychiatrists any talk of spirit possession is abnormal and an indication that the possessed individual is out of touch with reality. Belief in spirits is not part of the normal Western world view, so people who think that they are possessed by spirits are thought by psychiatrists to be deluded and suffering from hallucinations. In addition, the characteristic behavior of intermediaries has a parallel in the West in the behavior of acute schizophrenics. Therefore, it is common for Western psychiatrists to conclude that all intermediaries are full-fledged psychotics or at least suffer from some sort of psychological abnormality.[45]

Yet this conclusion is the result of judging the intermediary by Western views of normality and abnormality. When the intermediary is seen within his own cultural context, then a very different conclusion must be drawn. In a society that believes in spirit possession, there is nothing abnormal about a person claiming to be possessed by spirits. Furthermore, where possession takes place regularly, people have fairly clear ideas about how possessed individuals normally act. As long as the intermediary's behavior conforms to what is normal and expected, then he will be considered well-adjusted mentally and socially. Only when his behavior violates the social norms will he be adjudged abnormal or insane. The determination of what is normal and abnormal must thus be made with reference to the norms of the society in which the behavior

45. Silverman, "Shamans and Acute Schizophrenia," 21–31; S. A. Freed and R. S. Freed, "Spirit Possession as Illness in a North Indian Village," *Ethnology* 3 (1964) 152.

occurs. Only in this way can the observer be fair to the phenomena being studied.[46]

When intermediaries are seen in the context of their own societies, the vast majority appear to be psychologically normal. Even when judged by Western standards, most intermediaries do not appear to be mentally unbalanced. Although some of them may be unusually susceptible to trance, they are able to control themselves relatively well and to function normally as members of their societies. In Bali, for example, many people who are not professional mediums are capable of being possessed in the proper religious contexts, but people considered insane by the Balinese *do not* go into trance. Among the Akan of Ghana, normal people are frequently possessed at dances, and those who are strongly possessed sometimes develop into professional intermediaries. Nuba shamans lead normal lives when they are not performing and can in no way be considered abnormal. If the Nuba detect signs of insanity in a shaman, he is removed from office. A similar situation exists among the Zezuru of Zimbabwe, where many normal people become spirit mediums and where accusations of insanity are sometimes used to depose a medium.[47]

The psychological normality of intermediaries is particularly apparent among those who become functionaries in central possession cults. These intermediaries are typically well-adjusted members of their societies and have above-average intelligence. As participants in the cult they are frequently required to carry out complex rituals while in trance and must oversee the cult's financial and religious operations. If divination is part of the cult, then the proper techniques must be learned and applied while in trance. Many of these techniques require a shrewd perception of human nature as well as an intimate knowledge of the society, so they can be mastered only by those who are in complete control of their mental faculties.

46. Belo, *Trance in Bali,* 7–10. It must also be remembered that there is evidence that trance states have physiological as well as psychological causes. If this is the case, then such states must be considered normal, for they can be induced in the average individual by using the appropriate techniques. For a discussion of the problem of the normality of possession states, see Walker, *Ceremonial Spirit Possession,* 10–40, 104–113.

47. Belo, *Trance in Bali,* 5–10; Field, *Search for Security,* 61; Nadel, "Study of Shamanism," 35–36; Fry, *Spirits of Protest,* 38; cf. J. Beattie, "Spirit Mediumship in Bunyoro," *Spirit Mediumship and Society in Africa,* 161; R. E. S. Tanner, "The Theory and Practice of Sukuma Spirit Mediumship," *Spirit Mediumship and Society in Africa,* 275; Beattie and Middleton, "Introduction," xxiv; and Walker, *Ceremonial Spirit Possession,* 10, 36.

Among many groups, such as the Tungus, would-be shamans are judged on their ability to master the ritual and to control their trance behavior. Candidates who lack the intelligence to acquire the necessary knowledge or who do not have the necessary mental and physiological discipline are disqualified.[48]

Even though the majority of intermediaries seem to be sane, there are some examples of marked mental instability. Shamans seem particularly prone to mental disorders. Because shamans are constantly in touch with the potentially dangerous spirit world, they are watched closely for signs of insanity. Some shamans eventually become isolated from their societies and go through periods of madness, but it is interesting to note that they do not practice their art while in this condition. Shamanizing is done only in lucid moments, and when these moments become too rare, the shamans are removed from office and not infrequently driven out or killed.[49] Thus, even though there are indications that some intermediaries are insane, there is no evidence to support the view that insanity is a prerequisite for becoming an intermediary.

While it is difficult to isolate particular *psychological* characteristics that predispose someone to become an intermediary, people who develop into intermediaries do tend to share common *social* characteristics. For the most part, these people play peripheral roles within their societies prior to becoming intermediaries and sometimes belong to an oppressed or minority group. Although they may have social status, they have little actual social, political, or religious power.

Intermediaries with peripheral social backgrounds can be found in many cultures, but the best examples come from Asian and African societies dominated by Islam or by some other type of patriarchally oriented religion. In these societies political and religious power is usually concentrated in the hands of the older males, while younger males and women play little role in government or in the official cult. Yet most of the intermediaries come precisely from these powerless groups. Many of the intermediaries are women,

48. Shirokogoroff, *Psychomental Complex*, 352, 363, 384; Bouteiller, *Chamanisme*, 39; Colson, "Spirit Possession," 90–93; Nadel, "Study of Shamanism," 35–36; Fry, *Spirits of Protest*, 38–42.

49. L. Krader, "Buryat Religion and Society," *SJA* 10 (1954) 330; Bouteiller, *Chamanisme*, 40–41; Bogoras, *The Chukchee*, 415–417; Murphy, "Psychotherapeutic Aspects of Shamanism," 55, 74–78; Nadel, "Study of Shamanism," 36; S. G. Lee, "Spirit Possession among the Zulu," *Spirit Mediumship and Society in Africa*, 142–150.

who frequently experience peripheral possession and become members of peripheral possession cults which are the counterparts of the male-dominated central cults. The males that participate in peripheral cults are usually social outcasts or individuals that for some reason have been excluded from the society's centers of power.[50]

Typical examples can be found in Bali, where the various types of male and female intermediaries usually come from peripheral backgrounds. Women generally lack political power in Balinese society, and they frequently become possessed during cultic dances. Sometimes possession leads the women along the traditional route to becoming an intermediary and a member of a peripheral possession cult, although this is not always the case. Outcast men also occasionally experience possession, and they usually become intermediaries participating regularly in the cult. Young children are sometimes possessed at dances, although possession usually ends as the children mature and does not lead them to become intermediaries. Important roles in cultic dances are taken by males who are possessed as they play the part of a particular deity. Many of these males belong to noble families that have lost their political power but have retained some of their social status. By becoming intermediaries of the gods, the men temporarily reclaim some of their former glory and gain cultic power in the context of the dance. A different type of ritual role is played by the *kris* dancers. These men are mostly young and come from very low castes having virtually no social or religious power. While being possessed they execute violent dances, slashing themselves with knives.[51]

Although a socially peripheral individual may become an intermediary at any time, the process is most likely to take place when the individual is under stress or is experiencing uncertainty about his proper social role. In some societies both men and women typically experience their initial possession with the onset of puberty, when they first encounter rigid social rules governing the relationship between the sexes. Marriage frequently marks the beginning of

---

50. For examples, see Beattie, "Spirit Mediumship in Bunyoro," 169–170; Walker, *Ceremonial Spirit Possession,* 6–7, 106; Lee, "Spirit Possession among the Zulu," 132; Beattie and Middleton, "Introduction," xxv–xxvi; Lewis, *Ecstatic Religion,* 72–74; Fry, *Spirits of Protest,* 37–42; Colson, "Spirit Possession," 78–93; and H. B. Barclay, "Muslim 'Prophets' in the Modern Sudan," *The Muslim World* 54 (1964) 250–255.

51. Belo, *Trance in Bali,* 2–6, 17–74, 150–153.

possession for women, particularly when the bride is young and strictly controlled by her husband and his family. Some men also experience possession at the age when they would normally marry, and their becoming an intermediary sometimes inhibits or prevents a normal married life. Aside from these personal crisis periods, people may become intermediaries whenever unbearable family tensions arise. Disputes over authority, property, or inheritance may lead to the possession of one or more of the participants. Finally, people may become intermediaries when their society's attitude toward them changes or becomes unpredictable. The social insecurity caused by such changes sometimes gives rise to initial possession.[52]

Although peripheral individuals usually become involved with peripheral possession and become intermediaries in peripheral possession cults, intermediaries connected with a society's central cult may also come from a peripheral background. The clearest examples of this phenomenon are shamans, whose cultic activities are essential to the well-being of their societies and who are therefore the chief figures in central possession cults. Yet many shamans are originally social outcasts who experience their initial possession long before they are allowed to function as their society's intermediaries. By learning to control their trances and master their spirits, the shamans are able to enter the central cult and thus upgrade their peripheral status, at least while they are carrying out their cultic duties.[53]

Mystical Experience and Supernatural Choice

While scholars may examine a person's psychological and social background in order to explain why he became an intermediary, intermediaries themselves and the societies that support them provide a very different sort of explanation. In most societies people are thought to become intermediaries as a direct result of supernatural action. Spirits or deities choose their own intermediaries, either by granting them a mystical experience of some sort or by possessing

52. R. Horton, "Types of Spirit Possession in Kalabari Religion," *Spirit Mediumship and Society in Africa*, 34–38; Lewis, *Ecstatic Religion*, 73–76; Walker, *Ceremonial Spirit Possession*, 81–90; Fry, *Spirits of Protest*, 68–106; P. J. Wilson, "Status Ambiguity and Spirit Possession," *Man* n.s. 2 (1967) 366–378; L. L. Langness, "Hysterical Psychosis in the New Guinea Highlands: A Bena Bena Example," *Psychiatry* 28 (1965) 276.
53. Murphy, "Psychotherapeutic Aspects of Shamanism," 74–76.

them directly. In the former case the person's spirit leaves his body during a trance or during a dream and travels to the supernatural realm, where the spirits inform him of his future vocation. In the latter case a spirit or deity possesses the chosen individual and compels him to become an intermediary.

On occasion an individual will seek to become an intermediary and attempt to induce a mystical experience or attract the attention of the spirits. Such tactics are not always successful, however, and in the end the spirits remain in control of the process. Without evidence of divine choice and the observable signs that it produces, a person will not be accredited as an intermediary in most societies.[54]

In contrast to the few who actively seek to become intermediaries, most candidates shun the position and resist the demands of the spirits. This initial reluctance is not due to feelings of theological or moral inadequacy but stems from practical considerations. In societies where the intermediary's position is inherited, the legal heir may try to avoid his responsibilities because of the rigorous training and social restrictions that are frequently involved. In most societies initial possession is a terrifying experience that drains an individual physically and emotionally. Not only is the experience itself unpleasant, but the person who answers the spirits' call and becomes an intermediary may face inhibiting social and religious rules. The intermediary's family life cannot be normal, and daily activities must be altered. Some intermediaries are required to play exhausting cultic roles and provide other services demanded by the society. Although some intermediaries receive social prestige and monetary compensation for their efforts, others are barely tolerated by their societies and are under the constant threat of ostracism.[55]

Although most societies understand why a person would seek to resist becoming an intermediary, they usually consider this course of action foolish and even dangerous. The symptoms of supernatural choice are usually similar to those of insanity, and it is commonly believed that a person who rejects the spirits' call will be driven mad. The spirits are not to be denied. They will have their chosen

---

54. Colson, "Spirit Possession," 73.
55. Fry, *Spirits of Protest*, 30; Belo, *Trance in Bali*, 30; Bogoras, *The Chukchee*, 418–419; and W. Bascom, *Ifa Divination* (Bloomington: Indiana University Press, 1969) 88–100.

intermediary, or they will destroy him in their anger. Therefore, many societies put subtle pressure on potential intermediaries to force them to agree to the demands of the spirits. This pressure, in addition to the persistent urging of the spirits themselves, usually convinces possessed individuals to accept the intermediary's role.[56]

The supernatural choice of an intermediary usually takes place in one of two ways. The first, and most common, way begins when the person involved experiences symptoms which are recognized by the society as signs of illness or as indicators of spirit possession. These symptoms vary, but they may include fits, sensitivity to trance, fainting, uncontrollable behavior, loss of appetite, allergies, and general malaise. At first, the person experiencing such symptoms is usually assumed to be ill, and steps are taken to cure him by using normal medical procedures. If this approach does not work, then spirit activity is assumed to be involved, and the patient is taken to a diviner, medium, or shaman. The practitioner performs various rituals designed to make the possessing spirit identify itself, and if the rituals are successful, the spirit possesses either the practitioner or the patient, gives its name, and announces its demands. Frequently the demands include a requirement that the patient become the spirit's intermediary. If this is the case, then the patient is initiated into the spirit's cult and after suitable instruction becomes an intermediary. This sequence of events is particularly common where peripheral possession is involved.[57] However, a similar process takes place in societies having central possession cults. In this case people manifesting the characteristic symptoms of spirit possession are taken to established mediums or shamans for diagnosis. If the people are destined to become intermediaries, this is revealed at a seance, and they begin an apprenticeship with an established intermediary.[58]

56. Bogoras, *The Chukchee*, 418–419; Walker, *Ceremonial Spirit Possession*, 38–40; Lewis, *Ecstatic Religion*, 66–68; Bascom, *Ifa Divination*, 88.

57. For a description of peripheral possession, see above, pp. 37–39. A detailed description of the making of a peripheral intermediary may be found in Fry, *Spirits of Protest*, 68–106. Cf. the cases cited in E. H. Ashton, *Medicine, Magic, and Sorcery among the Southern Sotho* (Cape Town: University of Cape Town, 1943) 3–5; Colson, "Spirit Possession," 73–74; Field, *Search for Security*, 61–73; Horton, "Types of Spirit Possession," 34–35; and P. Verger, "Trance and Convention in Nago-Yoruba Spirit Mediumship," *Spirit Mediumship and Society in Africa*, 51.

58. Examples may be found in Balikci, "Shamanistic Behavior," 382–383; Lewis, *Ecstatic Religion*, 70–72; D. MacR. Taylor, *The Black Carib of British Honduras* (New York: Wenner-Gren Foundation for Anthropological Research, 1951) 110–111; and A. Balikci, *The Netsilik Eskimo* (Garden City, N.Y.: Natural History Press, 1970)

The second way in which spirits choose their intermediaries is to act initially through an established medium, diviner, or shaman. In this case no preliminary symptoms appear. Rather, the spirit simply announces its choice through an intermediary, and the person selected is then inducted into the spirit's cult and trained in his new occupation. This process is particularly common in central possession cults, where there are orderly procedures for recruiting and training intermediaries, but it sometimes appears in other contexts as well.[59]

The Role of the Society

Throughout our discussion of the creation of intermediaries, we have referred to the role that society plays in the process. We now need to examine this role more systematically. Intermediaries do not operate in a vacuum. They are integral parts of their societies and cannot exist without social guidance and support. This support need not come from the whole society, but it must be present in some form, or the intermediaries will disappear. For example, intermediaries in a peripheral possession cult are usually only tolerated by the society as a whole, but they are strongly supported by other cult members. This small support group is sufficient to allow the intermediaries to continue their activities, and without it the intermediaries might be suppressed by the larger society. In addition to providing the necessary support groups for intermediaries, societies also regulate the various processes by which people become intermediaries. These aspects of social control must also be examined if the relationship between the society and the intermediary is to be understood.

Group Validation and Belief

In addition to supplying the general social matrix that allows intermediaries to exist, societies also validate incipient intermediaries, provide guidance to aid their development, and ulti-

---

225. A more formalized procedure for creating intermediaries is described in A. Southall, "Spirit Possession and Mediumship among the Alur," *Spirit Mediumship and Society in Africa*, 246–249.

59. For examples, see Bamunoba and Welbourn, "Emandwa Initiation," 16–19; Beattie, "Initiation into the Cwezi Spirit Possession Cult," 151; Beattie and Middleton, "Introduction," xxv; Belo, *Trance in Bali*, 4; and Horton, "Types of Spirit Possession," 24.

mately support their vocation by believing in their powers.[60] The role of the society in the validation process varies somewhat, depending on whether the intermediary is to function on the periphery of the society or in the central social structure.

In cases of peripheral possession, the society is involved at the very beginning of the intermediary's developmental process. Because the initial symptoms of peripheral possession can be indicative both of illness and of spirit possession, the society must ultimately decide the actual cause. This is a crucial decision, for it either encourages the individual involved to develop as an intermediary or it permanently prevents him from doing so. The society's decision is made in various ways. Sometimes the society simply provides the means by which the decision can be made more or less objectively. The person is taken to a doctor for cure, and if that approach fails, an established intermediary is asked to investigate the possibility of supernatural involvement. The society then accepts the decisions of its specialists, although portions of the society may do so reluctantly. When such differences of opinion occur, the stage is set for future social tension between groups that accept the new intermediary and those that tolerate or reject him. Intergroup conflict over the validity of intermediaries is particularly common in cases of peripheral possession, which by definition involves people and groups on the periphery of society rather than the society as a whole.

Sometimes the society takes a more active role in evaluating the credentials of an incipient intermediary. Without relying on the opinions of specialists, groups will immediately support a particular intermediary but just as firmly reject another. The reasons lying behind these evaluations are not usually clear, perhaps because both rational and irrational factors are involved. However, a major role is played by the would-be intermediary's social status, personal characteristics, behavior, and point of view. A person who is a well-integrated, respected member of a group is more likely to be accredited as an intermediary than someone who arouses the group's antagonism. A person who delivers a divine message that is in line with group expectations—even though the message is unpopular—is more likely to be accredited than a person who delivers outra-

60. For a discussion of the general social characteristics that are necessary in order for intermediaries to exist, see above, pp. 28–32. Note also the comments of Walker, *Ceremonial Spirit Possession*, 59–78.

geous and disruptive messages. Thus, for example, in some Muslim societies *possession* by minor spirits is tolerated, and they are served by peripheral cults and intermediaries outside of the Islamic religious structure. The demands of these spirits usually involve only personal gifts to their intermediaries and do not have important theological or social implications. However, Islamic theology will not admit that *prophets* might exist after Muhammad. Therefore, anyone claiming to have *prophetic* revelations from Allah will be considered heretical and insane, even if the content of the new revelations does not contradict established doctrine.[61]

When incipient intermediaries are to function within a society's central social structure, the whole society is likely to play a role in the validation process. In some cases, the whole society or the group which requires an intermediary simply elects or appoints one of its members to the position, even though the designated individual has no apparent qualifications. Particularly in societies where each family or group is expected to have an intermediary, individuals are forced to accept the task and are then trained in the proper techniques.[62]

Usually, however, societies use more subtle methods to validate central intermediaries. Official ceremonies are created in order to encourage potential intermediaries to be possessed. The atmosphere at these ceremonies can be quite conducive to possession, so that even people who do not believe in the spirits or in possession are sometimes possessed and chosen as divine representatives.[63] As soon as the spirits have selected an individual who is acceptable to the society on social and personal grounds, the society immediately views the candidate as a full-fledged intermediary and believes in his supernatural powers. The effect of this group belief is usually to convince the individual to accept the intermediary's role. The candidate is frequently trained at the request of the society and is encouraged in his attempts to bring about the expected intermediation. Because the group believes in the intermediary, he tends to be

61. Barclay, *Buurri al Lamaab*, 136, 188–207. For a description of the status of modern "prophets" in Islam, see Barclay, "Muslim 'Prophets,' " 250–255. The role of the society in accrediting peripheral intermediaries is discussed and illustrated in Walker, *Ceremonial Spirit Possession*, 59–78; and Field, *Search for Security*, 66–72.

62. See the cases cited in Bamunoba and Welbourn, "Emandwa Initiation," 16; and Colson, "Spirit Possession," 70.

63. Note, for example, the ceremony described in Kaggwa and Welbourn, "*Lubaale* Initiation in Buganda," 218–219. In this case candidates were repeatedly exposed to the ceremony until possession occurred.

successful. His success attracts further group support and establishes him more firmly as an intermediary.

The power of group belief can be seen in a remarkable autobiographical account dictated by Qaselid, a Kwakiutl shaman. Qaselid began his career with the assumption that all shamans are frauds. In order to test the accuracy of his assumption, he began frequenting shamanic performances in order to observe the shamans' healing techniques. He witnessed some impressive performances but still suspected that trickery might lie behind them. His suspicions were confirmed when a group of shamans invited him to join them. He did so and asked that they teach him their secret techniques. The shamans agreed to his request and taught him how to simulate trance and how to behave so that people would recognize him as a shaman. He was also taught a dramatic curing ritual, involving the "sucking out" of sickness in the form of a bit of bloody eagle down, which was produced from the shaman's mouth at the proper moment. This experience confirmed Qaselid's belief that all shamans are frauds, but he decided to pretend to be a shaman in order to explore the matter further. In his capacity of apprentice shaman, he visited a nearby village and was met by the chief, who informed Qaselid that the chief's sick son had recently had a dream predicting Qaselid's arrival. The chief urged Qaselid to see the boy, suggesting that even if Qaselid was not really a shaman he could cure the patient because he believed in Qaselid's powers. Qaselid visited the chief's son, performed for the first time the healing ritual, and the boy was immediately cured. Qaselid recognized that the cure was not due to his own powers but to the belief of the patient. Nevertheless, word of the apprentice's cure began to spread among the Kwakiutl tribes. He was invited to examine other patients, and in each case he gave an impressive performance and brought about a miraculous cure. He was then called in as a consultant on difficult cases that had defied the powers of local shamans. He recognized the fraud involved in these shamans' techniques and became convinced that his own method was superior. The people agreed. He continued to enjoy a high rate of success, and his fame spread. More and more of the people believed in his powers. Group after group rejected their old shamans and sought the services of Qaselid. As more and more people believed in his abilities, Qaselid's fame and power grew. Rival shamans tried to discover his secrets, but he refused to reveal them. He would no longer admit to other shamans that he used trickery, for he had become convinced of the power of his techniques. Other shamans were shamed by Qaselid's success. Many ceased to practice, and some even committed suicide. The Kwakiutl now saw Qaselid as a great shaman, and he himself became convinced that he had genuine supernatural powers. He continued to believe that other shamans were frauds, and he delighted in exposing them, but he accepted the people's evaluation of his own skills. The mounting pressure of group belief finally convinced him that he *was* a genuine shaman.[64]

The importance of group support in the creation of intermediaries can be seen even when the formation process itself is "objective" and formal. Clear examples are provided by S. M. Shirokogoroff in his detailed descriptions of two shamanic elections. In the first case, the old shaman had died without training a successor, so the clan was forced to hold a trial to elect a new shaman. The only likely candidate was a man who was a relatively successful politician. However, many in the group thought that he was too old and that he would be unable to sustain a strenuous performance for any length of time. He therefore received little cooperation from the group in preparing for his performance, and even his own son would not encourage him. At the trial he was unable to induce possession even by using alcohol. His failure to go into trance was undoubtedly due to the clan's lack of support, for normally he was able to drink himself into a stupor and would do so whenever he had the opportunity. After several unsuccessful trials, he ceased to be a candidate, but then his son decided to seek the position. The father immediately vetoed this move, and as a result the clan elected no shaman at all.

In the second case, the election process was more complex, for several candidates were involved. At the beginning, the group's sympathies were clearly with a woman who seemed to be an ideal candidate. She could achieve trance easily and had some group support. However, at the trial she had difficulty inducing possession. After a long time she was able to introduce into herself a group of spirits, but when asked by the people to name all of the spirits in the group, she was unable to do so. Prior to the trial she had tried repeatedly to memorize the complex spirit hierarchies of the Tun-

64. Qaselid's account may be found in F. Boas, *The Religion of the Kwakiutl Indians* (New York: Columbia University Press, 1930), 1. 1–40 (Kwakiutl text), 2. 1–41 (English translation).

gus, but she was unable to learn them. Because of her inability to master the body of knowledge traditionally required of shamans, the group reacted unfavorably to her performance, and she began to lose her initial support. A second candidate was then asked to perform. He was able to recite the names of the spirits, and his trance performance was successful. Members of the group slowly began to shift their support from the first candidate to the second, but on the second day of the trial the second candidate also made a mistake in naming the spirits. The group debated the importance of this error, but because group support was now fairly strong, it was decided that the mistake was unimportant. After several days of additional trial performances, the second candidate was accepted as the group's shaman.[65]

Just as societies support intermediaries and provide the conditions necessary for them to function, so societies can also withdraw their support. This sometimes happens because the intermediaries involved can no longer function adequately. They may become unable to make contact with the spirit world, or their performances may cease to be convincing. Usually, however, societies withdraw their support because of the content of the message which the intermediary brings from the spirits. When supernaturally derived information about the future is incorrect on too many occasions, people begin to lose faith in the intermediary. Similarly, when the intermediary brings a message which deviates too far from traditional values or violates group morality, he is in danger of losing his social support. When a society rejects an intermediary, it usually interprets this action as the rejection of an incompetent or fraudulent individual. The society does not discard the theory of intermediation but continues to believe that valid intermediation can take place when a genuine intermediary is involved. The society simply ceases to believe in the powers of the individual and does not lose its faith in the system.[66]

Society and the Charismatic Individual

Since the time of Max Weber, it has been standard scholarly procedure to describe prophets, shamans, and other intermediaries as

65. Shirokogoroff, *Psychomental Complex*, 347–349, 353–358.

66. For examples of the process of rejecting intermediaries, see Fry, *Spirits of Protest*, 33, 42; Garbett, "Spirit Mediums as Mediators," 118; and Horton, "Types of Spirit Possession," 27–28. For a discussion of the way in which groups react to the incorrect utterances of intermediaries, see L. Festinger et al., *When Prophecy Fails* (New York: Harper & Row, 1964) 193–233.

charismatic individuals. In spite of this common practice, we have thus far avoided using the concept of charisma in our discussion, and we will continue this policy in what follows. Our reluctance to use the concept of charisma does not necessarily stem from doubts about its potential usefulness but rather is due to the recognition that proper use of the concept would require more discussion of psychological and sociological theory than is possible in this brief treatment. In recent years questions have been raised about the nature and applicability of the concept, and they must be fully explored before the concept can be safely applied.[67] Nevertheless, at this point something needs to be said about the relationship between the popular view of intermediaries as charismatic individuals and the above data on the role of the society in shaping intermediaries.

Weber's clearest definition of "charisma" appears in the context of a discussion of various types of authority:

> The term "charisma" will be applied to a certain quality of an individual personality by virtue of which he is set apart from ordinary men and treated as endowed with supernatural, superhuman, or at least specifically exceptional powers or qualities. These are such as are not accessible to the ordinary person, but are regarded as of divine origin or as exemplary, and on the basis of them the individual concerned is treated as a leader.[68]

For Weber, charismatic authority is distinct from traditional authority. The latter involves the rules which have been handed down from past generations, while the former has no system of abstract rules but involves new demands which frequently break with tradition. The paradigmatic charismatic figure is thus the prophet, who brings a new divine word to challenge the traditional structures of society. Charismatics exist outside of the normal social structures, although charisma can be "routinized" when groups and organizations are formed to perpetuate and transmit it.[69]

---

67. For a brief discussion of some of the issues involved, see W. H. Friedland, "For a Sociological Concept of Charisma," *Social Forces* 43 (1964) 18–21; Fry, *Spirits of Protest*, 45–47; S. N. Eisenstadt, "Introduction," in M. Weber, *On Charisma and Institution Building* (ed. S. N. Eisenstadt; Chicago: University of Chicago Press, 1968) ix–lvi; P. Worsley, *The Trumpet Shall Sound* (2d ed.; New York: Schocken Books, 1968) 266–272; and D. Emmet, "Prophets and Their Societies," *JRAI* 86 (1956) 13–23.

68. M. Weber, *The Theory of Social and Economic Organization* (New York: Free Press, 1964) 358–359.

69. Ibid., 359–373; cf. Weber, *Sociology of Religion*, 46–59.

Although Weber was aware that charismatics must be supported by groups or disciples, he did not stress this point.[70] As a result, his work sometimes gives the impression that charismatics are lonely individuals completely outside of their societies. This reading of Weber has in turn given rise to the popular image of the prophet as a divinely inspired individual who reforms society with his radical message and who refuses to be a part of the corrupt social order that he condemns. Clearly, this picture cannot be supported by the anthropological data that we have examined thus far. The evidence indicates that few intermediaries actually fit Weber's pattern. Many are not leaders, although they do derive their authority from their ability to communicate with the divine realm. Furthermore, they are usually well integrated into their support groups, either on the periphery of society or at its center. Most important, intermediaries owe their position ultimately to the validation of their support groups. As we have already seen, numerous factors enter into the validation process, and more practical considerations are involved than Weber's theory would admit. In short, the anthropological evidence suggests that if charisma is a "gift of the gods," it is also a gift of the society.

To be sure, there are some intermediaries that do come close to Weber's ideal type. However, they appear only in times of extreme social crisis, when the normal mechanisms of society have broken down and are unable to cope with the people's fears and anxieties about the future. At such times people experience much more social anxiety than that which usually leads to the creation of intermediaries. In these crisis situations, individuals who can articulate group discontent, provide a plan to alleviate it, and convince the group of the viability of the plan will be supported as charismatic leaders. But even in this case the leaders depend on the group for support and will remain in their position only so long as they are successful in expressing and directing group fears and goals.[71]

70. See, for example, Weber, *Social and Economic Organization*, 359–360; and Fry, *Spirits of Protest*, 45–47.

71. For further discussion of the roles that society plays in supporting charismatic individuals, see Friedland, "For a Sociological Concept of Charisma," 18–26; D. F. Aberle, "Religio-Magical Phenomena and Power, Prediction, and Control," *SJA* 22 (1966) 221–230; T. K. Oommen, "Charisma, Social Structure and Social Change," *Comparative Studies in Society and History* 10 (1967) 85–99; G. Devereux, "Charismatic Leadership and Crisis," *Psychoanalysis and the Social Sciences* 4 (1955) 145–157; and A. R. Willner and D. Willner, "The Rise and Role of Charismatic Leaders," *The Annals of the American Academy of Political and Social Science* 358 (March 1965) 77–88.

Peer Validation

In some societies potential intermediaries must first be validated by other intermediaries before being accepted by a support group or by the whole society. Where such systems exist, a small group of professional intermediaries controls entrance into their profession, and their decisions on potential candidates are usually accepted by larger units of the society. In the case of peripheral intermediaries, peer validation usually takes place at the point where the patient's symptoms must be diagnosed. An established medium or diviner in effect decides whether or not the patient will have a career as an intermediary. These professionals wield a great deal of power, but they are usually sympathetic to the patient because they tend to share the patient's social background. They too were once patients who were "cured" by becoming established intermediaries. Therefore, most people with the proper symptoms are accepted as peripheral intermediaries without difficulty. Once the new intermediaries have been validated by their peers, there is usually a period of initiation during which the newcomers are taught the required rituals and behavior. The initiation, which can last for months or even years, is also under the control of professionals, who teach their characteristic behavior to the novices. In this way, the professionals insure the homogeneity of their group and guarantee similar behavioral characteristics on the part of all group members.[72]

In the case of central intermediaries, the peer validation process is usually more rigorous than it is in the case of peripheral intermediaries. Central intermediaries usually have some degree of wealth, social power, and prestige, and they are cautious about sharing their privileges with outsiders. The validation process is frequently a lengthy one, and careful attention is paid to the background and qualifications of the candidate. His family history may be explored, and he is tested on the authenticity of his trance behavior and his knowledge of the spirit world. Candidates who are favored by the professional group have little difficulty with this exam-

---

72. For examples of peer validation of peripheral intermediaries, see Ashton, *Medicine, Magic, and Sorcery*, 3, 28–32; Beattie, "Spirit Mediumship in Bunyoro," 165–166; Bamunoba and Welbourn, "Emandwa Initiation," 22–25; Beattie, "Initiation into the Cwezi Spirit Possession Cult," 150–161; Belo, *Trance in Bali*, 1–3, 49–51; Kaggwa and Welbourn, "*Lubaale* Initiation in Buganda," 218–220; Lee, "Spirit Possession among the Zulu," 134–138; Verger, "Trance and Convention," 57–66; H. Cory, "The Buswezi," *AA* n.s. 57 (1955) 923–952; and J. Beattie, "Group Aspects of the Nyoro Spirit Mediumship Cult," *The Rhodes-Livingstone Journal* 30 (1961) 20–23.

ination, for they are usually coached in advance on the proper behavior. However, it is sometimes difficult for candidates not favored by the group to gain entrance. In this respect, the procedure resembles a guild system, with entrance into the guild strictly controlled by its present members. Once a candidate is accepted, he is subjected to a long initiation period, during which he is taught how to perform his duties. Even if the new intermediary eventually leaves the group and practices on his own, he will always exhibit the behavior ingrained in him during his initiation.[73]

Apprenticeship

True apprenticeship is not common among intermediaries, but it does exist. Particularly where groups of central intermediaries are organized in a guild system, new members must be trained in the characteristic behavior, practices, and techniques of the guild. Apprenticeship is likely to be required particularly in cases where technical skill is involved. For example, in many societies diviners must learn the manipulative techniques of their art, and where guilds of diviners exist, this training may take place during an apprenticeship. A clear example is found among the Yoruba, where Ifa diviners learn their highly refined skills by apprenticing themselves to active practitioners. Ifa divination involves the manipulation of various devices, such as nuts, chains, cups, or powder, and the recitation of poetic verses that are associated with various configurations of the devices. There are numerous verses for each configuration, and the diviner simply recites these verses until the customer recognizes one that bears on his problem. Successful divination thus depends on the diviner's being able to recite a sufficiently large number of verses. Apprentice diviners learn the verses from established diviners after undergoing an extensive initiation. Within the guild, diviners are ranked in grades according to skill, with each grade having its own insignia. Children may become apprentices at age five or six and require years of training before being allowed to practice independently.[74]

---

73. For examples of peer validation of central intermediaries, see Garbett, "Spirit Mediums as Mediators," 115–116; S. D. Messing, "Group Therapy and Social Status in the Zar Cult of Ethiopia," *AA* n.s. 60 (1958) 1120–1121; and G. K. Garbett, "Religious Aspects of Political Succession among the Valley Korekore (N. Shona)," *The History of the Central African Peoples* (Lusaka, Northern Rhodesia: Rhodes-Livingstone Institute, 1963) 7–8.

74. Bascom, *Ifa Divination*, 68–75, 81–100.

In some societies shamans also acquire their skills through apprenticeship. Individuals who have manifested the characteristic signs of spirit involvement become the pupils of established shamans in order to learn proper performance techniques and the names of the spirits. During the learning period the apprentices "practice" controlling the spirits and performing normal shamanic functions, but the novices are not regarded as full-fledged shamans. When the teacher thinks that the student is prepared, a public trial is arranged, and the society determines whether or not the apprentice has in fact become a shaman. Upon successful completion of the trial, the student may be given a helping spirit by the teacher as a sign that the apprenticeship has been completed. The new shaman then moves to another community to practice. Only rarely does the new shaman remain in the society where he was trained unless he succeeds his teacher. Most societies will tolerate only one shaman at any given time, for to have more than one raises the possibility of confusing and contradictory shamanic advice.[75]

Although apprenticeship is required primarily of diviners and shamans, it may occasionally be required of other types of intermediaries as well. Mediums of various sorts require training after their initial possession in order to be able to serve the spirits properly. Usually this training takes place informally, but on occasion a formal apprenticeship is involved. In addition, a type of apprenticeship sometimes takes place before initial possession. Would-be mediums associate with established mediums in order to learn the specific types of behavior that are likely to be interpreted as signs of genuine possession. However, in most societies this learning takes place informally, with no formal association being involved.[76]

Succession and Inheritance

The supposedly spontaneous nature of peripheral possession usually precludes peripheral intermediaries from inheriting their

75. For descriptions of shamanic apprenticeships, see Balikci, "Shamanistic Behavior," 382–383; Bogoras, *The Chukchee,* 420–425; Balikci, *The Netsilik Eskimo,* 225; Nadel, "Study of Shamanism," 28; Shirokogoroff, *Psychomental Complex,* 351–358, 375; and C. G. Seligmann and B. Z. Seligmann, *The Veddas* (Cambridge: At the University Press, 1911) 128–129. Cf. the briefer accounts in Eliade, *Shamanism,* 13–19; Rasmussen, *Intellectual Culture of the Iglulik Eskimos,* 109–115; Taylor, *Black Carib,* 110; and S. Wavell, A. Butt, and N. Epton, *Trances* (London: George Allen & Unwin, 1966) 38–42.

76. For examples of other types of apprenticeships, see Bamunoba and Welbourn, "Emandwa Initiation," 17–19; Field, *Search for Security,* 66–72; Garbett, "Spirit Mediums as Mediators," 115–117; Tanner, "Theory and Practice," 275–276; and Walker, *Ceremonial Spirit Possession,* 52–53.

offices or passing them on to their descendants. Occasionally *spirits* remain in a single family for generations, but the spirits freely choose a new intermediary within the family when the old intermediary dies, and the society plays no role in the process.[77] In contrast, central intermediaries sometimes inherit their offices and are able to transfer them to future generations. In this case, the society or the guild regulates the inheritance procedure and thus indirectly determines who may and who may not take the intermediary's role. For example, the society may limit the position to members of one sex or decree that it may not be held by people in adjacent generations within the same family line. By tradition the position may go to members of a single family or to a small group of families, and the society may even specify the relative age of the officeholder within a single generation. The rules governing inheritance vary in their strictness, but they are usually applied in such a way as to insure the orderly transmission of the intermediary's office.[78]

THE BEHAVIORAL CHARACTERISTICS
OF INTERMEDIARIES

Stereotypical Behavior

Although the behavioral characteristics of intermediaries vary from society to society, within a given society these characteristics tend to follow predictable patterns. Several different types of behavior patterns may exist in the same society, depending on the type of intermediary and support group involved, but each individual will exhibit the same behavior that typifies other intermediaries in his group. Thus, for example, all intermediaries in a peripheral possession cult will act and speak in roughly the same way while they are being possessed, but their behavior may differ from that of intermediaries in the society's other peripheral cults and from that of intermediaries in the central cult. Yet within each group, behavior will conform to the standard pattern.[79]

77. For examples, see Bouteiller, *Chamanisme*, 57–59; and Nadel, "Study of Shamanism," 27.
78. For cases where the intermediary's position is inherited, see Barclay, *Buurri al Lamaab*, 197–198; Bouteiller, *Chamanisme*, 58–59; Eliade, *Shamanism*, 13–19; Garbett, "Spirit Mediums as Mediators," 116; Krader, "Buryat Religion," 331; M. Leiris, *La possession et ses aspects théâtraux chez les Éthiopiens de Gondar* (Paris: Librairie Plon, 1958) 13: and Shirokogoroff, *Psychomental Complex*, 344.
79. Field, *Search for Security*, 56; Horton, "Types of Spirit Possession," 23; Ross,

As we have already seen, societies will not tolerate certain types of behavior. Most groups will not permit excessively violent, antisocial, or uncontrolled actions, and if such behavior appears, it will be viewed as the result of illness, witchcraft, or possession by evil spirits. Attempts will be made to cure the malady, but if the symptoms are not alleviated, the patient may be driven out or killed. For this reason, the behavior of intermediaries is always marked by conscious or subconscious self-control. Not all intermediaries go into trance when they are in contact with the spirit world, but even when trance occurs the intermediary's speech and actions remain under his control. During the trance the individual may seem to be in the power of the spirits, and afterward he may have no memory of what transpired, but his trance behavior will still conform to the expected controlled stereotypes. He may act and speak rationally or perform complex rituals, but even when he does not do so he will follow the typical patterns.[80]

In spite of what has just been said about the ability of intermediaries to control their behavior, there appear to be times when this control is lost. For example, in the typical peripheral possession syndrome, the individual initially exhibits symptoms that seem to be outside of his control. Only after possession has been diagnosed and the individual has been initiated into a peripheral possession cult does his behavior appear reasonable and controlled. Similarly, when shamans first introduce spirits into themselves at the beginning of a performance, the spirits sometimes appear to have the upper hand. The shaman seems to act incoherently, struggling with the spirits. Only after a dramatic battle is the shaman again able to gain control and master the spirits so that the "rational" portion of the performance can begin. However, the appearance of uncontrolled behavior in these instances is deceptive. It must be remembered that peripheral possession *stereotypically* begins with apparently uncontrollable behavior. Thus the "uncontrollable" behavior is itself part of a larger pattern. Furthermore, although the individual's initial behavior appears uncontrolled, it is nevertheless charac-

----

"Epileptiform Attacks," 62; Bamunoba and Welbourn, "Emandwa Initiation," 13; R. B. Lee, "The Sociology of !Kung Bushman Trance Performances," *Trance and Possession States*, 42.

80. On the intermediary's control of trance and nontrance behavior, see Bourguignon, "World Distribution," 13; Field, *Search for Security*, 57; and Taylor, *Black Carib*, 123.

teristic of spirit activity. The behavior conforms to the society's expectations about how possessed individuals act. Similar "uncontrolled" symptoms are exhibited initially by *all* possessed individuals in the society, and in this way the society is able to recognize that possession rather than illness is involved. In the same way, the shaman's "struggle" with the spirits is a stereotypical part of his performance in some societies. A shaman is supposed to be able to master his spirits, and his ability to do so is demonstrated concretely at the beginning of each performance. If this standard element were to be omitted from the performance, people might suspect that the shaman was a fraud who had not really embodied the spirits. The people expect the shaman to have to struggle with the spirits, and his apparently uncontrolled behavior is a way of meeting that expectation.[81]

In some societies the stereotypical behavior of intermediaries can be highly complex. In Bali, for example, several different types of intermediaries exist, and each follows a complicated behavioral pattern. Mediums connected with temples are possessed in ritual contexts, and each represents a specific god. The medium's behavior is characteristic of the god possessing him, and the identity of the god can easily be recognized on the basis of the behavior. The same thing is true in the case of nonprofessionals who become possessed at dances. Even though these individuals have never been possessed before, they exhibit the characteristic behavior of the possessing spirits clearly enough that they can be identified. The trance behavior of Balinese children takes the form of highly stylized classical dances that the children have never been taught. Still other intermediaries perform at trance ceremonies and take part in ritual dance dramas while wearing the masks of the gods Barong and Rangda. These dramas have a traditional plot, although there is still room for individual creativity. Finally, the traditional behavior of possessed *kris* dancers involves slashing themselves with knives.[82]

In many societies possession behavior involves exhibiting the characteristics thought to be those of the possessing spirit or deity. According to the theory of possession, the individual loses his per-

81. For further discussion of apparently uncontrolled behavior, see Garbett, "Spirit Mediums as Mediators," 115; Verger, "Trance and Convention," 51; Walker, *Ceremonial Spirit Possession*, 37; Bogoras, *The Chukchee*, 437–439; and G. Obeyesekere, "The Idiom of Demonic Possession: A Case Study," *Social Science & Medicine* 4 (1970) 97–100.
82. For detailed descriptions of Balinese trance behavior, see Belo, *Trance in Bali*, 4, 52–66, 96–102, 200.

sonal identity and becomes the embodiment of the possessing spirit, which totally controls him. The two become one, so that the speech and actions of the individual are actually the speech and actions of the spirit. Thus women possessed by male spirits may speak and act in ways that are appropriate to males, and the reverse is also true. Individuals of one caste will change their mode of acting and speaking when they are possessed by spirits of a different caste, and members of the society will treat the possessed individuals as if they actually occupied the caste of the spirits. If the possessing spirits have more specific characteristics, these too will be reflected in the behavior of their intermediaries. Among the Yoruba, people possessed by the blacksmith god speak and act in an appropriately crude way, while the mediums of the thunder god perform a jolly dance. The mediums of the warrior god are coarse, those of the creator god serene, those of the god of smallpox agitated, and those of divine messengers abusive.[83] The tendency to duplicate the possessing spirit's behavior persists even when the spirit is that of an animal or inanimate object. Nyoro hunters are sometimes possessed by the spirits of large animals they have killed, and the hunters' possession behavior resembles that of the possessing animal.[84] Among the Tonga, people are sometimes possessed by the spirits of trains, bicycles, airplanes, boats, chains, pumps, guitars, and accordions. In each case the possessed individual performs a dance which contains behavior characteristic of the possessing object.[85]

Just as intermediaries act in a stereotypical way, so they also use stereotypical speech patterns. In some cases the intermediaries speak in an unknown tongue that is not intelligible to bystanders. The unintelligible words are regarded as the secret language of the spirits, known only to their intermediaries, who translate after the spirits have spoken.[86] In other cases, however, the language of the

83. For a more detailed discussion, see Verger, "Trance and Convention," 50–51; Belo, *Trance in Bali*, 22–23; Colson, "Spirit Possession," 82–85; Leiris, *La possession*, 17; Walker, *Ceremonial Spirit Possession*, 37; and A. J. N. Tremearne, *The Ban of the Bori* (London: Heath, Cranton & Ouseley, [1914]) 281–391.

84. J. H. M. Beattie, "A Note on the Connexion between Spirit Mediumship and Hunting in Bunyoro, with Special Reference to Possession by Animal Ghosts," *Man* 63 (1963) 188–189; cf. Colson, "Spirit Possession," 71, 82–90.

85. Colson, "Spirit Possession," 84–90.

86. For examples of secret "spirit languages," see Bogoras, *The Chukchee*, 416, 425, 437–439; Balikci, "Shamanistic Behavior," 384; Horton, "Types of Spirit Possession," 29; Leiris, *La possession*, 26; Lienhardt, *Divinity and Experience*, 72; Lee, "Spirit Possession among the Zulu," 131; and J. H. M. Beattie, "The Ghost Cult in Bunyoro," *Ethnology* 3 (1964) 136.

intermediaries is intelligible to normal individuals, although it may be slightly different from the language currently in general use. For example, mediums in the Ethiopian *zar* possession cult speak a form of Amharic—which, of course, is intelligible to the rest of the society—but the dialect of the spirits differs from normal speech in that the former makes use of only a few loanwords and uses a large number of paraphrastic expressions, metaphors, and comparisons. In this respect, the language seems almost formulaic, since it consistently uses the same unusual circumlocutions for common words and phrases. The morphology of the language is clearly Amharic, but occasionally unusual changes are made in the spelling of words, and some words are abnormally lengthened.[87]

The stereotypical language of intermediaries sometimes even extends to their accounts of their revelatory dreams. Nuba shamans, for example, are usually drawn into their profession when they have strange dreams involving snakes, leopards, and red and white horses. These same images are common in shamanistic dreams and regularly appear in the shamans' accounts of their initial experiences with the spirits.[88]

Society and the Behavior of the Intermediary

Just as societies play an integral role in the creation of intermediaries, so also social forces are involved in shaping the intermediaries' stereotypical behavior. As we have already seen in our discussion of peer validation and apprenticeship, societies sometimes influence behavior directly by requiring would-be intermediaries to undergo formal training. By this means they are taught the necessary speech and behavior patterns, and uniformity in professional behavior is assured.

More often, however, societies play an indirect role in determining the behavior of their intermediaries. Indirect influence takes place in an obvious way when societies provide role models for potential intermediaries. If a society contains established intermediaries, then their characteristic behavior is visible and can serve as a pattern for people who experience possession for the first time.

---

87. For one of the few studies of a "spirit language" that has been made by a knowledgeable linguist, see W. Leslau, "An Ethiopian Argot of People Possessed by a Spirit," *Africa* 19 (1949) 204–212. Cf. J. H. M. Beattie, "Consulting a Diviner in Bunyoro: A Text," *Ethnology* 5 (1966) 209–211.
88. Nadel, "Study of Shmanism," 28–29.

Newly possessed individuals are likely to want to express their experience in some form, and it is natural for them to adopt the behavior of others in their society who have had the same experience. By observing established intermediaries, the neophytes are able to learn behavioral patterns which can be slightly modified and developed to fit individual needs. This learning process does not usually take place consciously, but it is one that goes on subconsciously over a period of years. In most societies people are first exposed to possession behavior as children and may even play at being possessed. Balinese children learn their traditional trance dances in this way, and in many societies adults exhibit stereotypical possession behavior that they have learned through childhood observation.[89]

In addition to providing obvious role models, societies also influence the behavior of intermediaries in more subtle ways. Societies usually have preconceived notions about how intermediaries should act and speak. The origin of these notions is usually difficult to trace, for they are traditional, but whatever their source they are enforced through a system of rewards and punishments. Societies encourage the behavioral conformity of intermediaries by granting them economic and social rewards and by recognizing them as genuine intermediaries. At the very least, societies will tolerate the presence of intermediaries who do not depart too far from the expected norms. On the other hand, by withholding rewards and recognition, societies discourage intermediaries who do not conform to the expected behavior. If the behavior of an intermediary diverges too far from the society's expectations, then he is regarded as a threat to the stability of the society and may be forcibly repressed or even expelled. Would-be intermediaries are therefore under subtle pressure to conform to their society's behavioral expectations, for only by doing so can they receive the desired rewards and recognition.

The pressure that societies exert on their intermediaries sometimes places them in a difficult position. On the one hand, the intermediary believes that he is in contact with the spirits and that

89. For a discussion of the importance of role models in shaping the behavior of intermediaries, see Walker, *Ceremonial Spirit Possession*, 39, 47, 59–69, 74–77; Bourguignon, "World Distribution," 11–12; Beattie, "Spirit Mediumship in Bunyoro," 166; Fry, *Spirits of Protest*, 34–35; Bourguignon, "The Self, the Behavioral Environment, and the Theory of Spirit Possession," 48; Belo, *Trance in Bali*, 60–62; L. Marshall, "The Medicine Dance of the !Kung Bushmen," *Africa* 39 (1969) 372; and A. Métraux, "La comédie rituelle dans la possession," *Diogène* 11 (1955) 34–38.

this contact requires a certain behavioral response. The spirits have particular reasons for contacting the intermediary, and he feels compelled to do and say what the spirits request. On the other hand, the intermediary's words and deeds must take a form that corresponds to the society's expectations. If the expected behavior is not present, then the intermediary will not be recognized as authentic. His divine message will not be taken seriously, and his behavior will not be tolerated. The intermediary who wants to be accredited must therefore strike a balance between the pressures of his society and the pressures exerted by the spirits. He must act and speak in a way that is both acceptable to the society and true to his own supernatural experience. If he is unable to strike this balance, then he will either be rejected by his society, or he will compromise his own integrity as an intermediary.

The problems facing intermediaries become even more complex when more than one group is involved. This is particularly true in the case of peripheral intermediaries, who must deal both with their small support groups and with the society as a whole. Here three factors must be taken into consideration: the behavior which is dictated by the spirits, the behavioral expectations of the support group, and the behavioral expectations of the whole society. Because the peripheral intermediary cannot exist without a support group, the behavioral expectations of this group play the crucial role in shaping his words and actions. However, because the support group is already on the periphery of society, conformity to the group's behavioral expectations almost inevitably brings the intermediary into conflict with the society as a whole. In general, members of peripheral groups are more tolerant of behavioral excesses and unorthodox words than are members of the society's central social structure, who typically expect relatively normal and controlled behavior and orthodox speech from their intermediaries. The intermediary who wants to remain within his society must seek to minimize his conflicts with the society without jeopardizing his position in his support group. While remaining true to the demands of the spirits, he must conform to the expectations of his support group without stretching the tolerance of the society too far. If he is unable to do this, he runs the risk of being rejected by his support group or being suppressed by the larger society.[90]

90. For a more thorough discussion of the issues involved, see Lewis, *Ecstatic Religion*, 34–35, 76–78, 176; Horton, "Types of Spirit Possession," 24–28; W. Mischel

THE SOCIAL FUNCTIONS OF INTERMEDIATION

In addition to the obvious religious function of serving as links between the human and supernatural worlds, intermediaries also have important social functions. Some of these functions are common to both peripheral and central intermediaries but other functions are not. For this reason, it is necessary to consider these two types of intermediaries separately. However, at the outset, it must be recognized that the distinction between the two types is not absolute. Some intermediaries can be seen either as peripheral or as central, depending on the point of reference used to make the classification. Thus, for example, an intermediary who functions within a peripheral possession cult is peripheral to the society as a whole, for he is a minority voice in the society and plays no role within the central cult. Yet, when seen from the perspective of the peripheral cult, the intermediary must be considered a central intermediary, for he plays an important part in maintaining that cult. Members of the larger society would certainly consider intermediaries in peripheral cults to be peripheral intermediaries, but members of a peripheral cult might, under certain conditions, see themselves and their intermediaries as central and the rest of the society as peripheral. To complicate the picture even further, central intermediaries may have once been members of peripheral social groups, with the result that these individuals must be considered peripheral with respect to personal background but central with respect to their present function. When dealing with the categorization of intermediaries, it is therefore important to know the person or group responsible for assigning the categories and the point of reference that was used in the process.

The Functions of Peripheral Intermediation

Peripheral intermediation has several interrelated social functions. First, by becoming intermediaries people on the periphery of society are sometimes able to improve their personal situations.

----

and F. Mischel, "Psychological Aspects of Spirit Possession," *AA* n.s. 60 (1958) 254–260; Walker, *Ceremonial Spirit Possession*, 91; Beattie, "Spirit Mediumship in Bunyoro," 166; Messing, "Group Therapy and Social Status," 1120; Shirokogoroff, *Psychomental Complex*, 363; Belo, *Trance in Bali*, 3, 68–74; and L. P. Mair, "Independent Religious Movements in Three Continents," *Comparative Studies in Society and History* 1 (1958–1959) 124.

While a society might not normally grant the requests of such powerless individuals, when they speak as intermediaries they speak
with the voices of the spirits, who have more authority and whose
demands carry more weight. In most cases societies recognize the
authority of the spirits and are willing to agree to the demands that
are made through the intermediaries.[91]

Thus, seen from a personal perspective, peripheral intermediation is a tool that powerless individuals can use to modify their
status and obtain additional benefits from the society. Sometimes
these benefits are quite tangible. For example, in societies where
women have little political or religious power and are completely
dominated by males, some women become possessed by spirits that
demand more money or better food, clothing, and living conditions
for their intermediaries. These requests are usually granted, so long
as they are not too outrageous, and the result is an improvement in
the intermediary's material status. Other social outcasts may use the
same approach, and, if they are interested only in improving their
life-style, they may cease to be intermediaries when they have
amassed sufficient wealth and power.[92]

More often, however, individuals derive less tangible benefits by
becoming peripheral intermediaries. Higher status usually accom-
panies the intermediary's position, and by occupying this position
individuals can increase the amount of respect that they receive from
the society. If the intermediary becomes a member of a peripheral
possession cult, he finds himself in a supportive environment where
he enjoys a great deal of power. His importance and authority

91. For examples of this process in operation, see Bamunoba and Welbourn,
"Emandwa Initiation," 13, 16; Lewis, *Ecstatic Religion*, 66–116; Beattie, "Group
Aspects," 11–38; F. B. Welbourn, "Spirit Initiation in Ankole and a Christian Spirit
Movement in Western Kenya," *Spirit Mediumship and Society in Africa*, 290–303;
Beattie, "Spirit Mediumship in Bunyoro," 159–170; Barclay, *Buurri al Lamaab*,
196–205; Leiris, *La possession*, 13–38; Messing, "Group Therapy and Social Status,"
1120–1126; Ashton, *Medicine, Magic, and Sorcery*, 3–4, 28–32; Colson, "Spirit Possession," 71, 78–90; S. Fuchs, *Rebellious Prophets: A Study of Messianic Movements
in Indian Religions* (Bombay: Asia Publishing House, 1965) 1–17; M. Gelfand,
Shona Ritual (Cape Town: Juta, 1959) 10–13, 121–123; B. Stefaniszyn, *Social and
Ritual Life of the Ambo of Northern Rhodesia* (London: Oxford University Press,
1964) 138–147; E. H. Winter, *Beyond the Mountains of the Moon* (Urbana: University of Illinois Press, 1959) 22–25; and Nicolas, *"Les juments des dieux."*

92. There are numerous examples of this function of peripheral intermediation. A
representative sample may be found in Lewis, *Ecstatic Religion*, 66–116; Hamer and
Hamer, "Spirit Possession," 400–401; Obeyesekere, "The Idiom of Demonic Possession," 98–101; Harris, "Possession 'Hysteria,'" 1046–1054; and I. M. Lewis, "Spirit
Possession in Northern Somaliland," *Spirit Mediumship and Society in Africa*,
189–190, 198–213.

within the cult help to compensate for his powerlessness in the society as a whole.[93]

A second important function of peripheral intermediation is to help bring about social change. In this case the interests of the spirits and their intermediaries turn away from personal aggrandizement and focus on the society as a whole. Through their intermediaries the spirits demand changes in the social order. Because the intermediaries speak not only as representatives of the spirits but also as representatives of support groups, the demand for social change takes a form that is acceptable to the peripheral group which the intermediary represents. Group members who are also intermediaries communicate with the spirits, clothe the supernatural message in stereotypical language that meets group expectations, and then deliver the message, which is supported by the authority of the spirits and the group. In practical terms this means that the demands of the spirits and the demands of the support group are the same. Therefore, both the interests of the spirits and the interests of the group are advanced when the intermediary delivers his message. From the perspective of the support group, the intermediary becomes the means by which group goals, desires, and programs are communicated to the larger society. Because of the supernatural authority that lies behind the intermediary's message, the society is usually willing to make some of the desired reforms, and thus the intermediary's support group at least partially achieves its goals.

The social reforms demanded by peripheral intermediaries usually fall into one of two categories. Sometimes the intermediaries seek to arrest social change by reaffirming traditional values. The intermediaries, along with their spirits and support groups, are a conservative voice in a society undergoing rapid social change. In these cases the possessing spirits are frequently old deities that were once part of the society's central cult but that have been displaced by newer gods. The old deities seek a rejection of recent innovations and demand to return to a place of preeminence in the cult. A return to older social and moral practices may also be in-

93. On this aspect of an intermediary's membership in peripheral cults, see Firth, "Problem and Assumption," 144–145; Horton, "Types of Spirit Possession," 28–47; Walker, *Ceremonial Spirit Possession*, 7–9, 85–91; Fry, *Spirits of Protest*, 36–38; H. Kuper, *An African Aristocracy* (London: Oxford University Press, 1947) 165–169; J. G. Kennedy, "Nubian Zar Ceremonies as Psychotherapy," *Human Organization* 26 (1967) 189–190; Lee, "Spirit Possession among the Zulu," 140–155; Messing, "Group Therapy and Social Status," 1120–1121; Tanner, "Theory and Practice," 284–286; and Southall, "Spirit Possession," 232–245.

volved in this process. If the intermediary's support group once had an important position in the old social order, a demand for the restoration of this position may be included.[94]

More often, however, peripheral intermediaries seek innovative changes in the society. Through the intermediaries the spirits and the support group advocate new patterns of action and behavior. New deities may also be urged on a society in this way, and peripheral spirits may seek to upgrade their status. The group itself may demand a larger role in the society's affairs. A plan for the restructuring of society will be advanced, and the group will seek to institute a new social order built around previously powerless individuals.[95]

A final function of peripheral intermediation is to help maintain social stability. By becoming peripheral intermediaries, repressed and powerless individuals can communicate their frustrations to the larger society. Because these communications are attributed to the spirits, the society tolerates the behavior of the intermediaries and makes an effort to alleviate their frustrations. This process works on two levels. On the personal level, individuals are provided with a socially acceptable means of venting their frustrations. Because the intermediary attributes his behavior to the action of the spirits, he avoids taking responsibility for his actions and is able to do and say things that would not be permitted under normal conditions. By tolerating this sort of psychological escape valve, the society prevents the intermediary from working out his frustrations in a way that might endanger the social order.[96] On the level of the support group, peripheral intermediation provides the mechanisms through which the group can relieve its discontent by realizing part of its program. The group voices its demands through its intermediaries,

94. For examples of peripheral intermediaries reaffirming traditional social values, see Colson, "Spirit Possession," 78–90; Beattie and Middleton, "Introduction," xxviii; R. G. Willis, "Kaswa: Oral Tradition of a Fipa Prophet," 248–256; Horton, "Types of Spirit Possession," 25–28; and Lienhardt, *Divinity and Experience,* 73–83.

95. For further discussion, see Horton, "Types of Spirit Possession," 31, 45–47; Beattie and Middleton, "Introduction," xxviii; Firth, "Problem and Assumption," 145; and M. Douglas, "Social Preconditions of Enthusiasm and Heterodoxy," *Forms of Symbolic Action: Proceedings of the 1969 Annual Spring Meeting of the American Ethnological Society* (ed. R. F. Spencer; Seattle: American Ethnological Society, 1969) 70–73.

96. For detailed examples, see Belo, *Trance in Bali,* 124–135; D. Parkin, "Politics of Ritual Syncretism: Islam among the Non-Muslim Giriama of Kenya," *Africa* 40 (1970) 224–225; and A. Doutreloux, "Prophétisme et culture," *African Systems of Thought* (ed. M. Fortes and G. Dieterlen; London: Oxford University Press, 1965) 224–239.

and the society takes those demands seriously because they come from the spirits. Social stability is achieved when a balance is struck between the demands of the group and the desire of the society to preserve its structure intact. Neither the group nor the society ever achieves precisely what it wants. The group will effect some of its desired changes but not all of them. The society will make some alterations in its structure but will make as few as possible. Peripheral intermediation thus provides a dynamic way of alleviating tensions between minority and majority groups. The process is a continuous one, for peripheral groups continue to press their demands, and the central society continues to meet those demands grudgingly. Yet, so long as both sides want to maintain the unity of the society, the process of give-and-take results in relative social stability and orderly social change.[97]

Peripheral Intermediation and Witchcraft Accusations

We have noted at several points in our discussion that peripheral intermediaries can exist only as long as they have the support of a group and are at least tolerated by the society as a whole. To insure this support and toleration, intermediaries express themselves in a way that is acceptable both to the group and to the society. An analogous situation exists with respect to peripheral groups that use intermediaries to advocate reforms in the larger society. The peripheral group must make reasonable demands, or else it runs the risk of alienating the society by its unacceptable behavior. We must now consider what happens when the demands of peripheral intermediaries and groups become too outrageous. A powerless minority sometimes feels that the society is not responsive enough to the group's demands and that the supernatural message of the intermediaries is not being taken seriously. These feelings usually lead to an increase in the group's frustrations and to an escalation of its demands. This escalation in turn antagonizes the society. Social tensions between the group and the society increase, and as these tensions grow the society comes to regard the group as a threat to social stability. When the point of toleration is passed, the society

97. For further discussion, see Beattie, "Spirit Mediumship in Bunyoro," 167–170; Walker, *Ceremonial Spirit Possession*, 97–99; Southall, "Spirit Possession," 232–245; Colson, "Spirit Possession," 89–90; Field, "Spirit Possession in Ghana," 10–12; and Obeyesekere, "The Idiom of Demonic Possession," 104.

will take steps to reduce social tensions and to restore the social order.

Societies have various ways of dealing with situations of rivalry and social friction, but the one which is most important for our discussion is the witchcraft accusation. Accusations of witchcraft are employed in cases where there are social tensions that cannot be handled by normal rational or legal means. Individuals or groups in conflict with each other may resort to witchcraft accusations in order to repress the party regarded as the source of the conflict. Such accusations are not to be made lightly, for in most societies witches are regarded as "inverts," beings that in every respect are the opposite of normal human beings. Witches are stereotypically pictured as night creatures, who fly or walk upside down. They break all social taboos and indulge in such heinous acts as incest, infanticide, and cannibalism.[98] The witch is a cancer in the social organism and must be excised in order to preserve the society. Most societies therefore require the death penalty for witchcraft, for only in this way can the witch's power finally be curbed. The judgment against the witch is frequently rendered by the spirits themselves, after the accused has been subjected to an ordeal designed to execute the guilty and spare the innocent.[99]

In the context of intermediation, societies use the threat of witchcraft accusations to control peripheral intermediaries and groups. When the society accuses a peripheral intermediary of witchcraft, the initial judgment which the society made on the intermediary is in effect reversed. Rather than attributing the intermediary's behavior to benign spirit contact, the society accuses him of involvement with demonic powers. The witchcraft accusation is a radical way of dealing with a troublesome intermediary, for it solves the problem by physically removing the offender, either by killing or banishing him. In the case of peripheral groups, accusations of witchcraft lead inevitably to a rupture in the social structure. By killing or banishing the group's intermediary, the society rejects the group itself,

98. For a discussion of the stereotypical characteristics of witches and the social functions of witchcraft accusations, see H. Debrunner, *Witchcraft in Ghana* (2d ed.; Accra: Presbyterian Book Depot, 1961) 20–47; Field, *Search for Security*, 38; J. LaFontaine, "Witchcraft in Bugisu," *Witchcraft and Sorcery in East Africa*, 197, 202–214, 217; and M. G. Marwick, *Sorcery in Its Social Setting* (Manchester: Manchester University Press, 1965) 95.

99. In Africa various types of poison ordeals were traditionally employed for this purpose. For descriptions, see M. Douglas, *The Lele of Kasai* (London: Oxford University Press, 1963) 241–244; and Evans-Pritchard, *Witchcraft*, 258–386.

forces it out of the society, and in the process stills the group's demands for social reform. Both peripheral intermediaries and their support groups usually seek to avoid provoking the society into making witchcraft accusations, for once this step is taken all hope of realizing the group's goals is lost. The *threat* of witchcraft accusations is therefore an effective deterrent against the excesses of peripheral individuals and groups.[100]

The witchcraft accusation, however, is a two-edged sword. It can be used by societies that want to repress difficult minority groups, but it can also be used in various ways by minority groups and individuals. Sometimes peripheral groups will indirectly use this weapon by deliberately increasing social tension so as to *force* the society to use witchcraft accusations. In this way the groups are able to shatter the social structure and place the blame for the destruction on the larger society. Peripheral intermediaries usually simply use the authority of their position to present their message to the society, but they may also hurl witchcraft accusations at vulnerable individuals in the central social structure. Political leaders, priests, and other intermediaries are likely targets for such accusations, for these figures are prominent exponents of the society's views. By using this technique, the peripheral intermediary not only claims supernatural support for his own views but demolishes his adversary's views by attributing them to demonic origins.[101]

Because witchcraft accusations always result in the fragmentation of a society, they appear only when social tensions have reached the point that social fission is inevitable. The appearance of witchcraft accusations in a society can therefore be used as an index of the society's stability. When a society is able to integrate its peripheral groups successfully, accusations of witchcraft are rare. But as social

---

100. For a discussion of the ways in which societies use witchcraft accusations to control obstreperous intermediaries, see Lewis, *Ecstatic Religion*, 33, 117–126. For other examples of societies using witchcraft accusations to repress minorities, see M. Douglas, "Techniques of Sorcery Control in Central Africa," *Witchcraft and Sorcery in East Africa*, 126; T. O. Beidelman, "Witchcraft in Ukaguru," *Witchcraft and Sorcery in East Africa*, 87; J. Buxton, "Mandari Witchcraft," *Witchcraft and Sorcery in East Africa*, 107; and M. Gluckman, *Politics, Law and Ritual in Tribal Society* (Chicago: Aldine, 1965) 216–226.

101. For examples of peripheral individuals using witchcraft accusations against superiors, see Mair, *Witchcraft*, 204–221; Buxton, "Mandari Witchcraft," 108; Douglas, *The Lele*, 223; idem, "Techniques of Sorcery Control," 125; J. Middleton, "Witchcraft and Sorcery in Lugbara," *Witchcraft and Sorcery in East Africa*, 268; Middleton and Winter, "Introduction," 13–14; and D. Tait, "Konkomba Sorcery," *JRAI* 84 (1954) 73–74.

instability and tension between groups and individuals increase, the number of accusations also increases. Societies where witchcraft accusations are common are likely to be highly unstable and in danger of fragmenting as dissidents break away to form independent groups.[102]

Intermediaries, Simple Support Groups, and Millenarian Movements

Up to this point in our discussion of the functions of peripheral intermediation, we have focused our attention on the roles that intermediaries play in their support groups and in the larger society. In dealing with these peripheral support groups we have spoken in general terms, for our interest has been in the intermediaries themselves. However, at this point in the discussion it is necessary to examine these peripheral support groups more closely, for in fact they are of different types and have different characteristics. For the sake of analysis, we will designate one common type of group a "simple support group." This sort of group is best exemplified by the typical peripheral possession cult, which we have already described, although simple support groups need not have such a formal structure. The other common type of peripheral support group that we will consider is the millenarian group. Anthropological material on millenarian groups and movements is probably more relevant to the study of Israelite apocalyptic than to the study of Israelite prophecy.[103] Nevertheless, because some scholars have used data on millenarian movements to interpret biblical prophecy, it is important to examine the relationship between simple support groups and millenarian groups.[104]

Anthropologists are still debating the precise nature of millenarian movements, and there are even arguments about the name that should be given to these movements.[105] Clearly, they are complex

102. Douglas, "Techniques of Sorcery Control," 124; M. G. Marwick, "The Social Context of Cewa Witch Beliefs," *Africa* 22 (1952) 232; J. C. Mitchell, *The Yao Village* (Manchester: Manchester University Press, 1956) 125–165.

103. For an attempt to apply some of this material to Israelite apocalyptic, see R. R. Wilson, "This World—And the World to Come," *Encounter* 38 (1977) 117–124.

104. For an example of the use of millenarian material to interpret Israelite prophecy, see T. W. Overholt, "The Ghost Dance of 1890 and the Nature of the Prophetic Process," *Ethnohistory* 21 (1974) 37–63; and his "Jeremiah and the Nature of the Prophetic Process," *Scripture in History and Theology: Essays in Honor of J. Coert Rylaarsdam* (Pittsburg: Pickwick Press, 1977) 129–150.

105. Millenarian movements are sometimes referred to as prophetic movements, messianic movements, revitalization movements, deprivation cults, cargo cults, and

social phenomena, and it is unlikely that any single interpretive schema can be made to fit all of them. However, at the risk of oversimplification, we may list several features that usually characterize millenarian movements and groups.

First, millenarian movements are made up of people who are on the periphery of society. They lack political and social power and have little social status. Furthermore, they *recognize* that they are on the periphery. They feel repressed and deprived of something which they might reasonably expect to possess. The feelings of deprivation that these people experience may come from a number of different sources. At a basic level, these peripheral individuals may lack food, clothing, useful work, or adequate housing. At a more abstract level, they may be politically powerless and socially ostracized. They may feel that they no longer have a voice in the way in which the society or the government is run. They may even believe that they can no longer control their own lives and destinies. On the other hand, they may simply have the vague feeling that the quality of their lives is poorer than it was in a real or imagined past.

The sort of deprivation involved in millenarian groups is rarely absolute but is usually measured in relation to something else. People may measure their present condition against the condition of others in the same culture or in neighboring cultures, or they may measure their present condition against their own past condition. This process can be carried to a rather high level of abstraction. People who feel deprived because the quality of social life has deteriorated frequently measure present conditions against past

----

crisis cults. For a discussion of the various designations that have been suggested, see W. La Barre, "Material for a History of Studies of Crisis Cults: A Bibliographic Essay," *Current Anthropology* 12 (1971) 3–44. General treatments of millenarian movements may be found in H. G. Barnett, *Indian Shakers: A Messianic Cult of the Pacific Northwest* (Carbondale: Southern Illinois University Press, 1957); I. C. Jarvie, *The Revolution in Anthropology* (Chicago: Henry Regnery Co., 1969); K. Burridge, *New Heaven, New Earth* (New York: Schocken Books, 1969); B. R. Wilson, *Magic and the Millennium* (New York: Harper & Row, 1973); W. La Barre, *The Ghost Dance* (New York: Dell, 1972); J. Mooney, *The Ghost-Dance Religion and the Sioux Outbreak of 1890* (ed. A. F. C. Wallace; Chicago: University of Chicago Press, 1965); P. Lawrence, *Road Belong Cargo: A Study of the Cargo Movement in the Southern Madang District, New Guinea* (Manchester: Manchester University Press, 1964); P. Worsley, *The Trumpet Shall Sound;* S. L. Thrupp, ed., *Millennial Dreams in Action* (The Hague: Mouton, 1962); N. Cohn, *The Pursuit of the Millennium* (rev. ed.; New York: Oxford University Press, 1970); V. Lanternari, *The Religions of the Oppressed* (New York: Knopf, 1963); and J. Lofland, *Doomsday Cult* (Englewood Cliffs, N.J.: Prentice-Hall, 1966).

conditions which may never have existed. There is a tendency for the past to be idealized, and as a result every generation feels that things were better "in the old days." The fact that "the old days" were not really any better does not keep feelings of deprivation from existing.

Although it is normal for there to be some feelings of deprivation in every society, certain conditions tend to intensify those feelings and create larger numbers of dissatisfied and deprived individuals. Such conditions are present particularly in times of rapid social change. Wars, famines, climatic changes, national economic reversals, and the shock of sudden cross-cultural contact can all lead to unusually widespread and severe feelings of deprivation. Not only do such periods of social upheaval produce political and social inequities that lead to genuine cases of deprivation, but crises such as wars and clashes with other cultures provide opportunities for people to compare their own situation with that of outsiders. These comparisons may lead to feelings of relative deprivation and fuel social unrest. Times of social crisis frequently give rise to millenarian groups, for in such times feelings of deprivation are increased beyond tolerable levels.

Although members of millenarian groups are peripheral individuals, it is important to note that they normally remain physically within the larger society. They may sense a gap of some sort between themselves and the rest of the society, but this gap is usually more psychological than spatial. Participants in millenarian groups do not always separate themselves from the society as a whole, nor do they always cut their ties to other groups in which they participate. They may remain within the larger society and still feel that they are a minority within it.[106]

The second characteristic of millenarian movements is that their members form themselves into groups having relatively cohesive

106. For a discussion of the role that relative deprivation and social crisis play in millenarian movements, see D. F. Aberle, "A Note on Relative Deprivation Theory as Applied to Millenarian and Other Cult Movements," Millennial Dreams in Action (S. L. Thrupp, ed.; New York: Schocken Books, 1970) 209–214; Burridge, New Heaven, New Earth, 9–10; B. Barber, "Acculturation and Messianic Movements," ASR 6 (1941) 664–668; Lanternari, Religions of the Oppressed, 243–249; Fuchs, Rebellious Prophets, xii, 2–3, 16–17; D. F. Aberle, "The Prophet Dance and Reactions to White Contact," SJA 15 (1959) 79–81; and A. J. F. Köbben, "Prophetic Movements as an Expression of Social Protest," International Archives of Ethnography 49 (1960) 117–164. For a critique of relative deprivation theory, see L. Spier, W. Suttles, and M. J. Herskovits, "Comments on Aberle's Thesis of Deprivation," SJA 15 (1959) 84–88.

structures. Group members share common beliefs, perspectives, and goals and sometimes pay allegiance to a single leader. Members perceive themselves as a corporate body, which is capable of directing its actions in a unified way. This perspective is shared by people outside the group, who see it as an entity capable of focused political and social action. The group has a visible system of governance that coordinates group efforts and provides mechanisms for the group's maintenance.[107]

The third characteristic of millenarian groups is that they contain some sort of catalytic agent to articulate the feelings of group members and to formulate a plan to relieve their discontent. In some groups this role is played by an intermediary, who brings from the spirits the encouragement necessary to sustain the group. The spirits, speaking through the intermediary, may also supply a plan designed to improve the group's powerless situation. In this case the intermediary is a crucial figure in the group, for he is the means by which the group gains access to the spirits, who are directing the group's journey toward salvation. The intermediary relays practical suggestions from the spirits and helps to set up short-term goals toward which the group can work. The achievement of these short-term goals is important, for it gives the group a feeling of success and accomplishment, without which group members would despair of ever reaching their ultimate goals. The intermediary may also represent the group in contacts with the larger society and help to articulate group plans and demands.

However, the catalytic agent need not be an intermediary but may be a "charismatic" leader, who holds the group together by making its members recognize their common bonds and goals. Once the leader has begun the process of group formation and has sketched a program for the group to follow, his actual physical presence within the group is no longer necessary for its successful growth. History is full of examples of charismatic leaders who were martyred or who simply disappeared early in the process of group formation. In many cases these leaders became more effective catalysts after their departure than they were before. Still, it would be a mistake to think that the catalytic agent in a millenarian group

---

107. On the importance of group structure and maintenance mechanisms, see A. F. C. Wallace, "Revitalization Movements," *AA* 58 (1956) 273–274; and Y. Talmon, "Pursuit of the Millennium: The Relation between Religious and Social Change," *Archives européennes de sociologie* 3 (1962) 134–135.

must necessarily be a single intermediary or leader. In some cases there may be a succession of intermediaries and leaders, or the leadership role may be taken by a group.[108]

The fourth feature of millenarian groups is that they have some sort of program for meeting the difficulties experienced by group members. Such programs are usually both forward- and backward-looking. The primary concern of millenarian groups is with the future, for they look forward to the solution of their present difficulties. If group problems cannot be solved in the future in this world, then they will be solved in "the world to come." They will be solved in a world which lies beyond this world of time and space. However, if a millenarian program is to be successful, it must deal with the immediate future as well as with the distant future and must provide group members with immediate realistic goals. If this is not done, the group may lose faith in its comprehensive program and eventually dissolve. A striking feature of millenarian programs is that they frequently look to the past for a picture of the future. Either they seek to *preserve* remnants of the past in the face of present threats, or they seek to *revive* the conditions believed to have existed before the present time of deprivation.[109]

The final characteristic of millenarian groups is that they provide their members with some practical means of realizing group programs. These means may be either active or passive. If a millenarian group uses active means, it will outline specific, usually rational, steps which group members can take to move the group toward its goals. If the group adopts a passive stance, it will take no direct action at all but will simply wait for the achievement of its goals by supernatural means.[110]

This brief sketch of some of the characteristics of millenarian groups is sufficient to illustrate the similarities and differences between such groups and simple support groups. Both groups are

108. For a discussion of the various kinds of catalytic agents involved in the formation and maintenance of millenarian groups, see Wallace, "Revitalization Movements," 270–273; Worsley, *The Trumpet Shall Sound,* ix–xxxix; Fuchs, *Rebellious Prophets,* 5–6; and J. Fabian, "Führer und Führung in den prophetisch-messianischen Bewegungen der (ehemaligen) Kolonialvölker," *Anthropos* 58 (1963) 773–809.

109. R. Linton, "Nativistic Movements," *AA* 45 (1943) 230–240; Talmon, "Pursuit of the Millennium," 130–133; Fuchs, *Rebellious Prophets,* ix–x, 11–15.

110. Wallace, "Revitalization Movements," 273–278; B. Wilson, "Millennialism in Comparative Perspective," *Comparative Studies in Society and History* 6 (1963) 93–114; J. F. Zygmunt, "When Prophecies Fail: A Theoretical Perspective on the Comparative Evidence," *American Behavioral Scientist* 16 (1972) 245–268.

similar in their overall composition and social location. They are both composed of peripheral individuals who lack political and social power. The groups themselves function at the margins of the society and are always a minority within it. Periods of stress and rapid social change encourage the development of both types of groups. Both types support the activities of intermediaries and allow them to function, and in turn both may use intermediaries to articulate group attitudes.

However, there are also marked differences between simple support groups and millenarian groups. First, millenarian groups are organized more rigidly than are simple support groups. Although intermediaries must have a support group of some sort, it need not be formally organized. Members of the group may have in common only their support of a particular intermediary and may share no particular attitudes or goals. The composition of the group tends to fluctuate, and members may not even perceive themselves as a group at all. Even when a formally organized peripheral cult group is involved, members of the group may share only their experience with the spirits and may have no long-range plans or goals. In contrast, millenarian groups are more cohesive and better organized. Members think of themselves as a group. They share common feelings and goals and may recognize the authority of a single leader. There are mechanisms to insure group survival and to prevent the group from disintegrating. There is a well-articulated statement of group aspirations, and the group has a plan for reaching its goals. Second, the role of the intermediary is slightly different in the two types of groups. When the intermediary's simple support group is not formally organized, he may do nothing for it at all. The group supports the intermediary but the intermediary has no definite role in the group. He fulfills the expectations of his support group in his behavior, but he is not expected to be a spokesman for the group. Even if the intermediary joins a peripheral cult composed of people who have had similar experiences with the spirits, he simply becomes a member of the group. In this context he may help to articulate group views, but this role could also be played by others in the group. In contrast, intermediaries may be the focal point of millenarian groups and act as the catalysts that are necessary to make such groups cohere and develop. The intermediary is a leader within the group and is expected to formulate and express group hopes and plans. Finally, because simple support groups do not have a strongly developed structure, they are unable to exist outside of the larger society. They do not have the organization that is necessary to permit them to exist independently. In contrast, millenarian groups are sometimes capable of withdrawing from the larger society and surviving as independent units. On occasion political separation is involved, although usually the group simply becomes a new religious entity. In either case the group is capable of supporting itself.

In summary, then, we may say that all millenarian groups are capable of supporting intermediaries, but not all simple support groups are millenarian. The millenarian group is more specialized, more cohesive, and better organized than the simple support group. Still, distinctions between the two types of groups are not always easily drawn, and it is necessary to see them as part of a continuum. If we were to place both types of groups and their intermediaries on a continuum moving from loose group organization to highly developed organization, the following picture would emerge.[111] At one end of the spectrum would be intermediaries who have no social support and whose behavior is regarded by the society as an indication of illness. In this case no support group exists at all, and the intermediary cannot survive. Further along the spectrum would be intermediaries who are supported by their societies or by simple support groups but who play no formalized role in these groups. Members of the simple support group lack a sense of group identity and have in common only their support of the intermediary. Still further along the continuum would be those intermediaries who are members of formally organized peripheral groups which also function as simple support groups. These may be cult groups composed of individuals who have had "calls" from the spirits, or the groups may be organized along other lines. As these groups develop more structure, they shade into fully developed millenarian groups. These groups are well organized, and their intermediaries play a crucial role in communicating group programs. Finally, at the end of the continuum would be the central cult groups that are integral to the functioning of a society. These groups are highly structured and involve well-developed rituals, beliefs, and programs. The intermediaries that are supported by such groups have official duties connected with the promulgation of group ideas and are under great pressure to conform to group expectations. This pressure does not

111. The following schema is a development of the one suggested by I. M. Lewis, "Spirit Possession and Deprivation Cults," *Man* n.s. 1 (1966) 322–329.

rob the intermediaries of all of their freedom to act as messengers of the spirits, but it does impose restrictions that are not shared by peripheral intermediaries.

Intermediaries and groups may originate at any point along this continuum. For example, an individual may receive from the spirits a message that articulates the feelings and hopes of his neighbors, and the result may be the formation of a millenarian group led by the individual. Similarly, an intermediary might bring supernatural messages that result only in the formation of a simple support group lacking a rigid structure. On the other hand, groups and individuals may move from point to point on the continuum. A simple support group may become more highly organized and become a full-fledged millenarian group capable of directed action and independent existence. A millenarian group might also be formed when a dissident segment of a central cult breaks away and is able to sustain itself as a peripheral group. It would even be possible for a group to travel the whole length of the continuum, developing from a simple support group into a millenarian group and finally into a central cult group. Such a development is not common, but it does occasionally occur.

The Functions of Central Intermediation

Central intermediaries occupy an established position within the social structure. They are sometimes part of a society's central cult, or they may simply be part of its political bureaucracy. In either case, they are the official links between their societies and the spirit world. Societies depend on their central intermediaries to provide access to the spirits whenever necessary and to relay important messages from the supernatural realm. When the spirits indicate their displeasure by sending sickness, social discord, or natural disaster, central intermediaries are expected to diagnose the problem and devise a remedy that will placate the spirits. In some societies central intermediaries are even responsible for preventing spirit-caused problems from occurring in the first place. Shamans, for example, are expected to protect their societies from malevolent spirits that might cause disease or natural catastrophes.[112]

Central intermediaries may also play important political roles. In

112. Netsilik shamans are supposed to insure a ready supply of game, control thunder and snowstorms, stop the cracking of ice, and ward off illness (Balikci, "Shamanistic Behavior," 386–387).

times of war a society may depend on its intermediaries to supply supernatural guidance for the army. When a ruler dies or is deposed, intermediaries may play a crucial role in regulating the succession by communicating the leadership preferences of the spirits. If the intermediaries are attached to a royal court or to a royal cult, they may serve as political advisers to the ruler and will certainly supply spiritual support for royal decisions and policies.[113]

Central intermediaries, then, are primarily responsible for maintaining their societies and for promoting community welfare. The intermediaries therefore have not only the specific duties that we have already mentioned but also the general task of insuring social stability. This task is accomplished first of all by providing supernatural legitimation for the existing social order and by supplying divine sanctions for traditional religious, political, and social views. Because the social and political establishment constitutes the support group for central intermediaries, they are under strong pressure to conform to traditional behavioral expectations and to avoid doing and saying things that might lead to social instability. This means that central intermediaries are usually more conservative than their peripheral colleagues. Central intermediaries safeguard social stability by avoiding unnecessary innovation. They are cautious about accepting new ideas and usually resist outside influences. Still, central intermediaries are by no means totally opposed to social change. They are simply interested in regulating the speed at which changes take place. Central intermediaries foster gradual and orderly change in order to retain social tradition and to preserve social stability. They are therefore fully capable of criticizing their societies but are likely to do so under the guise of retaining or restoring traditional beliefs and attitudes. New practices and ideas are anchored firmly in the past. In this way innovations are integrated into the tradition and their disruptive potential is minimized.[114]

The second way in which central intermediaries preserve social stability is by easing social tension. They represent the supernatural world when speaking to the people, but they also represent the

---

113. For examples, see Bouteiller, *Chamanisme*, 31; Garbett, "Spirit Mediums as Mediators," 106; Southall, "Spirit Possession," 246–252; and especially Garbett, "Religious Aspects of Political Succession," 1–2, 5–17.

114. Lewis, *Ecstatic Religion*, 127–177; Beattie and Middleton, "Introduction," xxvii–xxix; Garbett, "Spirit Mediums as Mediators," 119–120; Horton, "Types of Spirit Possession," 22–24; Nadel, "A Study of Shamanism," 30–31; Colson, *Plateau Tonga*, 92–93; and Colson, "Spirit Possession," 70–71, 73–78.

people when communicating with the spirits. This identification with the people allows the intermediaries to serve as representatives of public opinion. By virtue of the nature of their office, they are in a position to assess their society's moods and to observe developing attitudes and opinions. Diviners and mediums are particularly well-situated in this respect, for they are the specialists to whom people come for help in decision making. As long as the society is divided on a particular issue, the intermediaries will rarely express a definite opinion, for to do so would lead to social discord. However, when they sense that a consensus has developed, they will reinforce it by lending it supernatural support. In this way divisive issues are resolved, and group solidarity is restored.[115]

In a similar way, shamans, diviners, and mediums may provide the opportunity for people to air their disagreements and resolve them. This frequently happens in societies such as the Lugbara, where there is a well-developed ancestor cult. The ancestors are thought to retain an interest in their descendants and to become disturbed when social discord develops among them. When social conflicts develop, the ancestors may be invoked by one of the participants and asked to intervene. The ancestors respond by sending an illness to one of the involved parties, who must then be taken to an intermediary for diagnosis. As part of the diagnostic process, the patient confesses the nature of the social conflict, and the ancestor, through the intermediary, proposes a conciliatory remedy. In this way interpersonal disagreements are brought to light and publicly arbitrated. A version of this process also occurs in some shamanic performances, where the shaman seeks the cause of a disaster or illness by inviting confessions of wrongdoing from those present. People respond by confessing their sins against the society, and by the end of the session social problems have been aired and solved.[116]

Peripheral and Central Intermediaries

Both peripheral and central intermediaries can exist in the same society at the same time. Furthermore, the lines between the two

115. For examples of this ratification process, see Garbett, "Spirit Mediums as Mediators," 119–125; Park, "Divination and Its Social Contexts," 197–200; Bascom, *Ifa Divination,* 70; Field, *Search for Security,* 76; and Firth, "Problem and Assumption," 142–143.

116. Middleton, *Lugbara Religion,* 79–148; Beattie, "The Ghost Cult in Bunyoro," 146–147; W. La Barre, "Confessions as Cathartic Therapy in American Indian Tribes," *Magic, Faith, and Healing,* 36–49; Balikci, "Shamanistic Behavior," 387–389, 394.

are not always firmly drawn. Given individuals may move from one category to the other if their support group changes, and as this movement takes place, the characteristics and functions of the intermediaries will also change. As we have already noted, both types of intermediaries are part of a continuum, and individuals may move along that continuum in either direction. Thus, if a central intermediary violates the norms that his society has established, he may be forced out of his position and onto the periphery, where he may find a new support group and be able to function as a peripheral intermediary. As his status and social functions change, he will give up the formal, traditional behavior typical of central intermediaries and take on the freer, more spontaneous behavior of peripheral intermediaries. Conversely, a peripheral intermediary may be able to enlarge his support group to the point that it becomes a majority in the society. The intermediary then becomes a central intermediary. When this shift takes place, he takes on the appropriate functions and adopts the appropriate behavior patterns. His behavior becomes more rigidly controlled, and he takes a new interest in maintaining the society that supports him.[117]

CONCLUSIONS

The anthropological material we have surveyed suggests that the relationship between Israelite prophets and their societies may be much more complex than previous studies have realized. For this reason, biblical scholars can no longer confine their investigations only to the three aspects of the problem that have usually been treated, but the social dimensions of a whole range of prophetic activity must be considered. On the basis of the comparative evidence, we may expect Israelite society to have been involved in every phase of prophetic activity, from the prophet's "call" to the delivery of his message. To derive maximum benefit from this evidence, we must not oversimplify or schematize it but must apply it in all of its complexity to the biblical material. Still, at this point it will be helpful to indicate the major implications of the anthropological data for the three areas that scholars have traditionally considered when commenting on prophecy and society in Israel.

117. Colson, "Spirit Possession," 75; Walker, *Ceremonial Spirit Possession*, 91.

The Nature of Prophetic Activity

The anthropological material suggests that any study of prophetic behavior in Israel must take into account the role of social groups in creating prophets and in shaping their behavior. Although intermediaries may receive their messages directly from the spirits, those messages are expressed in words and deeds that conform to group expectations about how intermediaries should talk and act. As a result, all of the intermediaries within a particular group tend to act and talk in the same way. An attempt must therefore be made to determine whether or not Israelite prophets also exhibited stereotypical behavior. This attempt must move beyond the traditional discussion of the role of "ecstasy" in prophetic behavior, for ecstasy is itself only one stereotypical behavior pattern. Other forms of prophetic speech and action must also be considered. If stereotypical behavioral patterns are discovered, then their origins must be traced and they must be related to prophetic support groups or to the society as a whole. Divergent behavioral patterns will imply different social situations and support groups, and this social complexity must be taken into account in analyzing biblical prophecy.

The Social Location of Prophecy

The anthropological material suggests that there are two dimensions to the question of the social location of prophecy. First, intermediaries in every society are related to some sort of support group that allows them to continue to function. Seen from a social perspective, these groups and their intermediaries are located either on the periphery of society or within the central social structure. Second, intermediaries actually carry out their activities in various physical locations within the society. Sometimes the intermediary carries out his activities only within the support group, but other locations may also be involved. Studies of Israelite prophecy must deal with both of these aspects of social location. The support groups of the biblical prophets must be investigated, and an attempt must be made to discover where these groups lay in the social spectrum. In addition, the physical locations in which the prophets operated must also be explored. This exploration must consider locations other than the cult, and the full range of possible social and political settings must be considered.

The Social Functions of Prophecy

The anthropological material indicates that the functions of intermediaries vary depending on the type of intermediation involved. In general, peripheral intermediaries are usually involved in advancing the views of the spirits and of the intermediaries' own support groups. The aim is to improve the status of peripheral groups and individuals and to bring about changes in the social order. In contrast, central intermediaries are concerned with maintaining the established social order and with regulating the pace of social change. The investigation of the social functions of the Israelite prophets must also take this distinction into consideration. The different functions of peripheral and central prophets must be recognized, and the relation of each type of prophet to the whole society must be explored. The tensions that existed between prophet and society must be analyzed, and an attempt must be made to discover how those tensions were finally resolved. Only by considering all of these issues can insight be gained into the complex functions of prophecy in Israel.

3

Prophecy in the Ancient Near East

Ancient Near Eastern evidence was first brought to bear on biblical prophecy by scholars searching for foreign influences in Israel's prophetic traditions. At various times Egypt, Canaan, Syria, and Mesopotamia have all been suggested as possible sources for particular features of prophetic thought and behavior. Some scholars have even argued that certain types of Israelite prophecy were originally borrowed from another culture.[1] However, contemporary scholarship has been cautious about accepting the idea of direct borrowing, and this caution seems appropriate in the light of the anthropological material that we have just surveyed. Given the

---

1. Arguments for strong Egyptian influences on Israelite prophecy were presented by E. Meyer, *Die Israeliten und ihre Nachbarstämme* (Halle: Max Niemeyer, 1906) 451–455; and H. Gressmann, *Der Messias* (Göttingen: Vandenhoeck & Ruprecht, 1929) 417–445. For a critique of these arguments, see S. Herrmann, "Prophetie in Israel und Ägypten: Recht und Grenze eines Vergleichs," *Congress Volume, Bonn, 1962* (VTSup 9; Leiden: E. J. Brill, 1963) 47–65. The Canaanite or Syrian origin of ecstatic prophecy in Israel has been advocated by a number of scholars, including the following: E. Kautzsch, *An Outline of the History of the Literature of the Old Testament* (London: Williams and Norgate, 1898) 46–47; R. Smend, *Lehrbuch der alttestamentlichen Religionsgeschichte* (Freiburg i.B.: J. C. B. Mohr, 1899) 80; R. Kraetzschmar, *Prophet und Seher im alten Israel* (Tübingen: J. C. B. Mohr, 1901) 10–19; G. Hölscher, *Die Profeten* (Leipzig: J. C. Hinrichs, 1914) 140–143; A. Jepsen, *Nabi: Soziologische Studien zur alttestamentlichen Literatur und Religionsgeschichte* (Munich: C. H. Beck, 1934), 144–152; T. H. Robinson, *Prophecy and the Prophets in Ancient Israel* (2d ed.; London: Duckworth, 1953) 33–35. For a critique, see J. Lindblom, "Zur Frage des kanaanäischen Ursprungs des altisraelitischen Prophetismus," *Von Ugarit nach Qumran* (BZAW 77; ed. J. Hempel and L. Rost; Berlin: Töpelmann, 1961) 89–104.

proper social conditions and cultural attitudes, intermediaries can appear in any society. The existence of intermediation can be explained on the basis of internal social and religious conditions. Borrowing need not be involved, although outside influences may be present and in particular may help to shape the form that intermediation takes in a given society.

Even though contemporary scholars have generally rejected the idea that Israelite prophecy was borrowed from one of the surrounding cultures, the use of ancient Near Eastern material to elucidate Israelite prophecy has continued. In recent years scholarly attention has focused on Mesopotamia, where the Mari letters contain references to various types of "prophetic" figures. Thorough comparisons have been made between these figures and the biblical prophets, and the similarities and differences have been carefully analyzed.

However, to date most studies of ancient Near Eastern prophecy have concentrated on the behavior and the messages of prophetic figures while ignoring the larger question of their social roles. Yet, because some of the texts contain descriptions of the settings in which the "prophets" worked, this material is a potentially valuable source for analyzing the social dimensions of intermediation in the cultures that surrounded Israel. We will therefore examine the available Near Eastern evidence, paying particular attention to the way in which the intermediaries were related to their societies. To aid in this investigation we will use the anthropological material that we have just surveyed, although the limitations of the Near Eastern data must be recognized. At many points the ancient texts will yield a picture far less complete than the one we have drawn from modern sources.

PROPHECY IN MESOPOTAMIA

The Role of Divination in Mesopotamia

The Use of Omens in Theory and Practice

The importance of divination in Mesopotamia is indicated by the relatively large number of tablets that deal with omens and related matters. By the Old Babylonian period (ca. 1894–1595 B.C.) scribes had already begun to collect and systematize certain types of omens, and this process continued throughout Babylonian and Assyrian history. In this way a highly technical body of scholarly data was created, and this material can shed some light on the role of omens in Mesopotamian society.[2]

Although Mesopotamian scribes never formally stated the theory lying behind the use of omens, it is possible to deduce at least two important components of this theory. First, the Mesopotamians saw all aspects of reality as an interlocking totality. Historical occurrences and elements of human experience were not thought to be isolated phenomena but were seen as part of a much larger matrix. While modern Western observers see no significance in the juxtaposition of historical occurrences having no causal link, the Mesopotamians saw such occurrences, no matter how insignificant, against the background of the whole of reality. Thus, for example, if a fox wandered into the square of a town and the next day the town was destroyed by an enemy army, the modern observer would see no connection between the two events. However, for the Mesopotamian they would have been related by virtue of being part of the same larger historical moment. One event would not have been considered the *cause* of the other, but both would have been seen as part of an interlocking whole. Because of the interlocking character of reality, it could be assumed that if an event recurred, all other events that were originally part of the same historical matrix would also recur. To return to our example, if a fox wandered into a second town, then it could be predicted that that town too would be destroyed the next day. Every event thus has predictive potential if the past context of the event is known. In order to take advantage of this potential, Mesopotamian scribes very early began to catalogue all sorts of unusual occurrences together with the events that accompanied them. These catalogues presumably served as manuals that could be used by future diviners.[3]

A second component of Mesopotamian divination theory is re-

2. For general surveys of divination in Mesopotamia, see A. L. Oppenheim, *Ancient Mesopotamia* (Chicago: University of Chicago Press, 1964) 206–227; J. Nougayrol, "La divination babylonienne," *La divination* (ed. A. Caquot and M. Leibovici; Paris: Presses Universitaires de France, 1968) 1. 25–81; C. J. Gadd, *Ideas of Divine Rule in the Ancient Near East* (London: Oxford University Press, 1948) 50–59; and J. Nougayrol, "Trente ans de recherches sur la divination babylonienne (1935–1965)," *La divination en Mésopotamie ancienne* (Paris: Presses Universitaires de France, 1966) 5–19. Note also the older work of G. Contenau, *La divination chez les Assyriens et les Babyloniens* (Paris: Payot, 1940).

3. For a discussion of Mesopotamian views of historical reality, see J. J. Finkelstein, "Mesopotamian Historiography," *Cuneiform Studies and the History of Civilization* (Proceedings of the American Philosophical Society 107; Philadelphia: American Philosophical Society, 1963) 461–472.

lated to the first. Because reality includes both natural and supernatural elements, the gods themselves are intimately involved in
everyday happenings. Every historical event or natural occurrence
thus becomes a means by which the will of the gods can be communicated. It is only necessary to interpret events properly in order
for the desires of the gods to be uncovered.[4]

Because the Mesopotamians considered all events as potentially
ominous, it is not surprising that many different divinatory techniques were employed.[5] One major class of omens involved the
systematic recording of casual phenomena and the events that accompanied them. These records then became resources to be used
in interpreting future occurrences of the same phenomena. Several
early collections of omens from casual phenomena were eventually
gathered together in the great "canonical" omen series *šumma ālu*,
named after its first line, "if a city is situated on a hill. . . ." This
series contained more than a hundred tablets and included omens
based on events involving cities, houses, insects, snakes, cattle,
donkeys, dogs, fire, wild animals, and human relations.[6] Another
major series, *šumma izbu* ("if a newborn animal . . ."), recorded
omens based on the birth of malformed animals and humans.[7]
Ominous dreams were also catalogued, although this method of
divination does not seem to have been particularly popular.[8]

A second major class of omens depended on the use of special
techniques. Dice were manipulated to yield yes-or-no answers to
questions put to a deity. Diviners observed smoke rising from a

4. A. L. Oppenheim, "Perspectives on Mesopotamian Divination," *La divination
en Mésopotamie ancienne,* 35–36.

5. The general classifications used in the following discussion are based on those of
H. W. F. Saggs, *The Greatness That Was Babylon* (New York: Mentor, 1962) 307.

6. Unfortunately there is no up-to-date edition of this series. See the older work of
F. Nötscher, "Haus- und Stadtomina der Serie *šumma ālu ina mêlê šakin,*" *Or* o.s. 31
(1928); idem, "Die Omen-Serie *šumma ālu ina mêlê šakin,*" *Or* o.s. 39–42, 51–54
(1929–1930).

7. E. Leichty, *The Omen Series Šumma Izbu* (Locust Valley, N.Y.: J. J. Augustin,
1970).

8. A. L. Oppenheim, *The Interpretation of Dreams in the Ancient Near East*
(Transactions of the American Philosophical Society, vol. 46, part 3; Philadelphia:
American Philosophical Society, 1956). There is evidence that omens were sometimes derived from the flight of birds, although this method was apparently not used
after the Old Babylonian period. See E. Reiner, "Fortune-Telling in Mesopotamia,"
JNES 19 (1960) 24–25. The behavior of sacrificial animals was also considered ominous, and omens were taken from such unusual sources as shooting stars and
earthquakes (B. Meissner, "Omina zur Erkenntnis der Eingeweide des Opfertieres,"
AfO 9 [1933] 118–122; E. R. Lacheman, "An Omen Text from Nuzi," *RA* 34 [1937]
1–8).

censer and interpreted the changing patterns. Oil drops were placed on water, and the resulting configurations were studied. Attempts were made to induce ominous dreams, and specialists even attempted to derive omens from the behavior of an ox that had been sprinkled with water. However, the Mesopotamian divinatory specialists, the *bārûs*, apparently did not view these methods favorably, for they were rarely used after the Old Babylonian period.[9]

Among the specialists the preferred methods of divination were extispicy (the examination of the entrails of sacrificial animals) and hepatoscopy (the reading of animal livers). The latter is probably the older of the two techniques, and by the Old Babylonian period scribes had already collected numerous omens dealing with various configurations of the liver (and occasionally with conditions of the gall bladder and lungs). It is clear that these early omens were already part of a scholarly tradition. They are organized according to the feature of the liver with which they deal. They all follow a standard pattern and employ a great deal of technical terminology now only dimly understood. The omens almost always begin with a protasis describing the physical characteristic being considered and then give an apodosis detailing the events that will occur when this particular configuration appears. The apodosis frequently involves the king or the royal city and is usually stated in somewhat vague, stereotypical language that seems to be related to the clichés found later in treaties and chronographic texts.[10] Occasionally the apodosis contains a reference to historical events, but this is rare.[11] The connection between the protasis and the apodosis is not always obvious

9. For discussions of these rare forms of divination, see Reiner, "Fortune-Telling," 24–25; G. Pettinato, *Die Ölwahrsagung bei den Babyloniern* (2 vols.; Rome: Instituto di Studi del Vicino Oriente, 1966); idem, "Zur Überlieferungsgeschichte der aB-Ölomentexte," *La divination en Mésopotamie ancienne,* 95–107; idem, "Libanomanzia presso i Babilonesi," *RSO* 41 (1966) 303–327; and E. Leichty, "Literary Notes," *Essays on the Ancient Near East in Memory of Jacob Joel Finkelstein* (ed. M. de J. Ellis; Hamden, Conn.: Archon Books, 1977) 143–145.

10. For a discussion of these stereotypical descriptions of future prosperity and devastation, see Oppenheim, *Ancient Mesopotamia,* 211; Finkelstein, "Mesopotamian Historiography," 468–471; and A. K. Grayson, "Divination and the Babylonian Chronicles," *La divination en Mésopotamie ancienne,* 69–76.

11. For a discussion of the significance of these "historical" omens see Finkelstein, "Mesopotamian Historiography," 462–472; E. Reiner, "New Light on Some Historical Omens," *Anatolian Studies Presented to Hans Gustav Güterbock on the Occasion of His 65th Birthday* (ed. K. Bittel, P. H. J. Houwink ten Cate, and E. Reiner; Istanbul: L'Institut Historique et Archéologique Néerlandais de Stamboul, 1974) 257–261; and A. Goetze, "Historical Allusions in Old Babylonian Omen Texts," *JCS* 1 (1947) 253–265.

to the modern reader, particularly because the scribes sometimes attached several variant apodoses to the same protasis. The normality or abnormality of the liver may have helped to determine whether the apodosis was positive or negative, or the actual observation of events may have been the basis for linking protasis and apodosis. The following extracts from Old Babylonian tablets dealing with the right lobe and "palace gate" of the liver will serve to illustrate the form and content of these early omens:

> If the right lobe is normal (and) a second one reaches the foot of the left side of the "palace gate," the gods will return to the land and the land will dwell in a peaceful dwelling; the hand of an enemy king will not draw near.

> If the right lobe is in the area of the left, the king will capture a land not his own.

> If there are two "palace gates" and a filament connects their central area, the prince will receive income; (variant: the vizier will receive income).

> If there are two "palace gates" and three kidneys and at the right of the gall bladder there are two breaches, and they go all the way through, it is an omen of Apišalim whom Naram-Sin took prisoner when breaching (the wall of his city).[12]

After the Old Babylonian period these omen collections were elaborated in greater detail, so that by the middle of the first millennium extensive divinatory "handbooks" were available for the use of the *bārû*s. Also from this period come numerous extispicy reports describing in detail the exta of sacrificial animals and correlating the findings with questions that were asked before the sacrifice. These sorts of reports were rare in the Old Babylonian and Kassite periods but became increasingly common as diviners made more extensive use of extispicy.[13]

The third—and most famous—class of Mesopotamian omens was

---

12. A. Goetze, *Old Babylonian Omen Texts* (New Haven: Yale University Press, 1947) 13:5–8; 13:22–23; 24:5; 24:9. Note the ambiguity of the apodosis in the third omen. In one version the omen is favorable to the king: he will receive income. In the variant the omen is unfavorable to the king, for the income goes to his vizier.

13. For a collection of early extispicy reports, see A. Goetze, "Reports on Acts of Extispicy from Old Babylonian and Kassite Times," *JCS* 11 (1957) 89–105. A convenient collection of the elaborate Sargonic reports is available in E. G. Klauber, *Politisch-religiöse Texte aus der Sargonidenzeit* (Leipzig: E. Pfeiffer, 1913). For a comparison of the two types of reports, see I. Starr, "Extispicy Reports from the Old Babylonian and Sargonid Periods," *Essays on the Ancient Near East in Memory of Jacob Joel Finkelstein*, 201–208.

astrological. Omens based on celestial phenomena are attested as early as the Old Babylonian period, and by the beginning of the first millennium thousands of these omens had been assembled in the "canonical" series *enūma Anu Enlil* ("when Anu and Enlil . . ."). This series deals with the phases of the moon, the sun, the fixed stars, eclipses, and the movement of the planets, particularly Venus. Attention is also given to meteorological phenomena such as thunder, rain, hail, and cloud formations.[14] At a much later date astrological observations were coupled with birth reports to form horoscopes that predicted the future of newborn children.[15]

Until the middle of the first millennium, there is little information about the way in which omens were actually used in Mesopotamian society. Omens based on casual phenomena were presumably sought by the person who had observed them or were sought on behalf of the king. Rituals may have been connected with obtaining these types of omens, although there is little evidence on this point. However, when unfavorable omens appeared, a ritual could be performed to ward off the portended evil. Such rituals, which were given the title *namburbi,* consisted of actions, prayers, and incantations to be performed to counter specific omens. *Namburbi*s originally were used only in connection with casual omens of the type found in the series *šumma ālu* and *šumma izbu,* but gradually these rituals were also used with astrological omens such as those found in *enūma Anu Enlil.*[16]

In the case of omens based on the use of special techniques, the nature of the divinatory procedure is clearer. Texts from the time of Esarhaddon and Assurbanipal (680–627 B.C.) have preserved material dealing with extispicy, and some of this material can be used to reconstruct the way in which this particular type of divination functioned.[17] The extispicy texts fall into two general categories.

---

14. E. Reiner, *Babylonian Planetary Omens* (Malibu, Calif.: Undena, 1975); Oppenheim, *Ancient Mesopotamia,* 224–225; O. Neugebauer, *The Exact Sciences in Antiquity* (2d ed.; New York: Dover, 1969) 101; R. C. Thompson, *The Reports of the Magicians and Astrologers of Nineveh and Babylon* (2 vols.; London: Luzac, 1900).

15. A. J. Sachs, "Babylonian Horoscopes," *JCS* 6 (1952) 49–75.

16. For an introduction to the *namburbi* rituals, see R. I. Caplice, *The Akkadian Namburbi Texts: An Introduction* (Malibu, Calif.: Undena, 1974).

17. The basic publications of these texts are Klauber, *Politisch-religiöse Texte;* and J. A. Knudtzon, *Assyrische Gebete an den Sonnengott für Staat und königliches Haus aus der Zeit Asarhaddons und Asurbanipals* (2 vols.; Leipzig: Eduard Pfeiffer, 1893). For a general discussion, see J. Aro, "Remarks on the Practice of Extispicy in the Time of Esarhaddon and Assurbanipal," *La divination en Mésopotamie ancienne,* 109–117.

The first category consists of questions that were posed to the gods through the diviner. Texts in this group begin with the statement "Shamash, great lord whom I ask, answer me with a reliable positive answer." A specific question is then asked, and this is followed by statements requesting the deity to "disregard" conditions that might adversely affect the ritual. The question is then repeated, followed by a stereotypical prayer asking that a favorable omen be placed in the midst of the sacrificial sheep. This much of the tablet was completed before the sacrifice and was placed before the statue of the god. After the exta had been examined, the results were usually entered in the blank spaces left on the tablet. The results were recorded in the form of omen protases drawn from canonical omen series.

The second category of texts consists of extispicy reports. These tablets begin with a systematic catalogue of the condition of the exta of the sacrificial animal. The descriptions are in the form of omen protases, and when these protases have negative apodoses, they too are recorded. Both the protases and apodoses seem to be taken from the "canonical" omen catalogues. In some cases the survey of the exta is followed by a statement giving the total number of negative and positive omens. This information, in turn, was used to help determine the overall import of the entrails, as the following example makes clear: "There are five unfavorable omens; there are no favorable ones; it is unfavorable."[18] The next section of the report contains the question which was originally asked of the deity. These questions are frequently quite elaborate and filled with clichés similar to those found in chronographic texts of the same period.[19] The general response to the question is then given and sometimes elaborated. In some cases it is clear that the tone of the general response is based on the earlier totals of positive and negative omens, but the process by which the *bārûs* arrived at their specific conclusions is not always clear.[20] The reports conclude with the date the extispicy was performed, the location, and the names of the specialists that presided.

Both of these categories of extispicy texts indicate that omens were sought by the king whenever an important political or reli-

18. Klauber, *Politisch-religiöse Texte*, 105:obv. 18–20; cf. 106:16, where only the total of bad omens is mentioned.

19. See, for example, ibid., 105:rev. 1–14.

20. For a discussion of this problem, see I. Starr, "In Search of Principles of Prognostication in Extispicy," *HUCA* 45 (1974) 17–23.

gious matter required action. Specific questions were asked of the deity, a sheep was slaughtered, and the entrails were interpreted to provide an answer to the original question. As part of this process the *bārûs* drew on traditional collections of omens. In the case of negative results, the process was sometimes repeated to confirm or deny the original interpretation. Sometimes several diviners were set to work at once, and the majority opinion was accepted. There are even indications that astrology was sometimes linked with extispicy in order to "reinterpret" evil omens.[21]

Divination and Its Social Contexts

Many forms of Mesopotamian divination were highly complex, and for this reason diviners required extensive training before being allowed to practice their skill. At an early date diviners were organized into guilds, and in fact the *bārû* was sometimes given the title *mār bārî,* "member of the guild of diviners."[22] The guilds traced their ancestry back to the antediluvian king Enmeduranki, to whom the gods Shamash and Adad had taught the secret arts of divination by oil, by hepatoscopy, and by astrology. Entrance into the guild was strictly controlled. Initiates had to come from a priestly line and were required to be without physical blemish.[23] Those having the proper qualifications underwent an apprenticeship before being considered full members of the guild.

Although diviners may have originally been available for consultation by anyone in Mesopotamian society, most of them soon became an integral part of the central social structure. They were supported by the royal establishment, which required their services in order to make political, religious, and social decisions. The *bārûs* thus had social maintenance functions and were necessary for the very existence of the state. Political appointments could be made

21. A. L. Oppenheim, "A Babylonian Diviner's Manual," *JNES* 33 (1974) 197–220; R. Borger, *Die Inschriften Asarhaddons Königs von Assyrien* (Graz: Ernst Weidner, 1956) 82, ll. 20–21; W. H. P. Römer, "Religion of Ancient Mesopotamia," *Historia Religionum* (ed. C. J. Bleeker and G. Widengren; Leiden: E. J. Brill, 1969) 1. 172–178; Aro, "Remarks on the Practice of Extispicy," 109–116.

22. The title *mār bārî* was in use at least as early as the Old Babylonian period and was apparently interchangeable with the title *bārû.* See the evidence cited in *CAD* B 121–125.

23. The text describing the history and requirements of the diviners' guild reflects several different traditions that have been somewhat loosely joined. See W. G. Lambert, "Enmeduranki and Related Matters," *JCS* 21 (1967) 127, 132–133, 135, 137. *Bārûs* may have also cut their hair in a distinctive way, although this is not completely clear.

only after consulting the diviners, and religious rituals were also regulated by omens. The *bārû* played a crucial role in time of war, determining the sort of military activity that should be undertaken and the propitious times for attack. In some instances the diviner even led the army into battle.[24] Because of the political importance of divination, the king not only kept diviners in the royal court but sent them throughout the empire to work with royal officials.[25]

As we have already seen, the *bārû*s, as central intermediaries, were rigidly bound by tradition. Their activities were prescribed by rituals, and their mode of speech—or at least their mode of writing—was determined by "canonical" collections of omens. Still, the diviners were responsible for making decisions that inevitably led to social change. Such change was controlled, however, for the *bārû*s always acted in keeping with traditional methods and ideologies.

Prophecy in the Mari Letters

Since the discovery of references to oracular speakers in some of the Mari letters, numerous comparisons have been made between these figures and the biblical prophets.[26] Many of these comparisons

24. The fact that diviners not only accompanied the army but sometimes led it is clearly indicated by the Mari letter ARM(T) 2. 22:23–26, where the *bārû* Ilšu-nāṣir is said to have led a contingent of troops from Mari. For a discussion and a collection of additional examples, see A. Finet, "La place du devin dans la société de Mari," *La divination en Mésopotamie ancienne,* 87–93; J. M. Sasson, *The Military Establishments at Mari* (Rome: Pontifical Biblical Institute, 1969) 37; and *CAD* B 123–124, b, 1'.

25. For a discussion of the organization of the diviners' guilds and of the social functions of the *bārû*s, see J. Renger, "Untersuchungen zum Priestertum der altbabylonischen Zeit," *ZA* 59 (1969) 213–217.

26. The following Mari letters are generally thought to contain references to oracular speakers: A. 15 (G. Dossin, "Une révélation du dieu Dagan à Terqa," *RA* 42 [1948] 125–134); A. 455 (partially translated in G. Dossin, "Sur le prophétisme à Mari," *La divination en Mésopotamie ancienne,* 79–80); A. 1121 (G. Dossin's transliteration and translation included in A. Lods, "Une tablette inédite de Mari, intéressante pour l'histoire ancienne du prophétisme sémitique," *Studies in Old Testament Prophecy* [ed. H. H. Rowley; Edinburgh: T. & T. Clark, 1950] 103–107); A. 2731 (partially translated in Dossin, "Sur le prophétisme à Mari," 78); A. 4260 (partially translated in Dossin, "Sur le prophétisme à Mari," 85–86); A. 222 (unpublished; see, J.-G. Heintz, "Aux origines d'une expression biblique: *ūmūšū qerbū,* in A.R.M., X / 6, 8'?," *VT* 21 [1971] 529, n. 1); ARM(T) 2. 90; 3. 40, 78; 6. 45; ARM 10. 4, 6–10, 50–51, 53, 80–81, 94, 100, 117; ARMT 13. 23, 112–114. A full edition of all of the prophetic texts is being prepared by J.-G. Heintz for the ARMT series. For English translations of the texts, see W. L. Moran, *ANET,* 623–625, 629–632 (cf. his improved translation of the ARM 10 texts in "New Evidence from Mari on the History of Prophecy," *Bib* 50 [1969] 15–56); and H. B. Huffmon, "Prophecy in the Mari Letters," *The Biblical Archaeologist Reader,* vol. 3 (ed. E. F. Campbell, Jr. and D. N.

have been concerned primarily with determining whether or not prophecy of the Israelite variety actually existed in Mari and whether or not there were historical or cultural links between the Mari "prophets" and the later Israelite prophets. As part of this ongoing discussion, the speech patterns and messages of the Mari speakers have been analyzed extensively, but there have been only a few systematic attempts to study these figures in their social contexts. Where the social dimensions of Mari prophecy have been explored, scholars have usually concentrated on issues similar to those that have dominated the discussion of prophecy in Israel. Scholars have studied the nature and extent of prophetic ecstasy in Mari. The cultic role of the oracular speakers has been examined, and attempts have been made to determine whether the speakers gave their oracles spontaneously or only in response to a cultic inquiry. The extent to which the speakers saw themselves as divine messengers has also been debated.[27] Yet, because some of the Mari letters have preserved accounts of the social settings in which the oracular speakers delivered their messages, these sources can shed more light on the sociological dimensions of Mari prophecy than previous studies have recognized. We will therefore examine the various types of oracular speakers at Mari, paying particular attention to their behavior, their relationships to the larger society, and their social functions.

Freedman; Garden City, N.Y.: Doubleday, 1970) 199–224 (an improved reprint of an article that originally appeared in *BA* 31 [1968] 101–124). Many of the ARM 10 texts have also been edited in W. H. P. Römer, *Frauenbriefe über Religion, Politik und Privatleben in Mari* (Kevelaer: Butzon & Bercker, 1971). For bibliographical surveys, see F. Ellermeier, *Prophetie in Mari und Israel* (Herzberg: Erwin Jungfer, 1968) 21–23; and E. Noort, *Untersuchungen zum Gottesbescheid in Mari* (Kevelaer: Butzon & Bercker, 1977) 5–8. To these should be added J.-G. Heintz, "Prophetie in Mari und Israel," *Bib* 52 (1971) 543–555; H. B. Huffmon, "The Origins of Prophecy," *Magnalia Dei: The Mighty Acts of God* (ed. F. M. Cross, et al.; Garden City, N.Y.: Doubleday, 1976) 171–186; idem, "Prophecy in the Ancient Near East," *IDBSup*, 697–700; idem "Prophetic Oracles in the Ancient Near East," SBLSP 1974, 1. 101–104; J. J. Roberts, "Antecedents to Biblical Prophecy from the Mari Archives," *The Restoration Quarterly* 10 (1967) 121–133; H.-C. Schmitt, "Prophetie und Tradition," *ZTK* 74 (1977) 255–272; and S. D. Walters, "Prophecy in Mari and Israel," *JBL* 89 (1970) 78–81.

27. For a survey of research on these issues, see Noort, *Untersuchungen*, 9–34. An exception to the general tendency to neglect the sociological aspects of Mari prophecy is H. B. Huffmon's unpublished paper, "Prophetic Oracles in the Ancient Near East: Reflections on Their Use in Form-Critical Study of the Hebrew Bible," delivered October 26, 1974, at the Annual Meeting of the Society of Biblical Literature. In this paper Huffmon suggested using the neutral designation "oracular speaker" to refer to the prophetic figures at Mari, and we have followed his suggestion in our discussion.

Oracular Speakers at Mari: Characteristic Behavior and Social Contexts

The oracular speakers at Mari may be divided into two general groups. The first group is composed of individuals having special titles. The presence of these titles suggests that the persons designated by them occupied a relatively well-established position within the social structure. In contrast, the second group is composed of individuals who are given no particular title and who presumably played less clearly defined social roles.

THE *ĀPILU / ĀPILTU*

The title *āpilu* (fem. *āpiltu*) is attested only at Mari (ARM 10. 9, 53, 81; ARMT 13. 23; A. 1121; A. 2731; A. 4260) and is presumably a participial form of the verb *apālu*, "to answer."[28] The designation "answerer" might suggest that the *āpilu* gave oracles in response to questions put to a deity, but the letters give no indication that the *āpilu*s actually operated in this way. They seem to have exhibited no unusual behavior but confined themselves to delivering rational messages. However, some of these messages seem to use standard literary clichés, so it may be that the speech of the *āpilu*s was marked by characteristic formulaic patterns.[29]

The social location of the *āpilu*s' activities varied. The use of the plural form of the title (A. 1121: rev. 24) suggests that *āpliu*s may have sometimes acted as a group, although they certainly acted as individuals as well. Their relation to the cult is unclear. Some *āpilu*s represented a particular god, although it is not certain that all of

28. However, the form *aplû* found in ARMT 13. 23 suggests that there may be problems with this derivation. *Āpilu* also appears at Nuzi (HSS 13. 152:16; 14. 149:6) as the title of a person receiving supplies from the king, but the relationship between the Nuzi title and the one at Mari is unclear. A Neo-Babylonian lexical text equates *pil-pi-lu-u / a-pi-lu-u* with *assinnu, kurgarrû, ararû, šudararû,* and *kuluʾu,* all of which are titles of various temple personnel. However, the connection between *apillû* and *āpilu* is uncertain. See the discussion of A. Malamat, "Prophetic Revelations in New Documents from Mari and the Bible," VTSup 15 (1966) 212; Huffmon, "Prophecy in the Mari Letters," 203–204; CAD K 529, s.v. *kuluʾu,* A / 2 170; and Moran, ANET, 625, n. 29.

29. Unfortunately, the available evidence is not extensive enough to permit further exploration of this point. For a discussion, see M. Anbar (Bernstein), "Aspect moral dans un discours 'prophetique' de Mari," UF 7 (1975) 517–518; and J.-G. Heintz, "Langage prophétique et 'style de cour' selon *Archives Royales de Mari* X et l'Ancien Testament," *Sem* 22 (1972) 5–12. Moran ("New Evidence," 24–26) suggests that the use of the verb *tebû,* "to stand up," to describe the actions of the *āpilu* prior to speaking indicates that he remained crouched on the floor until he was possessed by a deity. This is a plausible suggestion, but the texts remain vague about the specific behavior of the *āpilu*.

them did. On some occasions the *āpilu* delivered oracles in the
temple (A. 1121; ARM 10. 53; ARMT 13. 23), but this was not always the case. In one instance an *āpiltu* delivered her message at
the palace gate (ARM 10. 9), and one letter (A. 4260) was sent directly to the king by an *āpilu*. Furthermore, in the only detailed
example of an *āpilu* delivering messages in a temple, his presence
seems to be intrusive. In A. 1121 the writer implies that the *āpilu*s
habitually appeared while omens were being taken and pressed the
demands of Adad for some hereditary property. There is no indication that the *āpilu*s' message was related to the omens, and the
writer seems to feel that the *āpilu*s were disrupting the normal ritual
process. A subsequent letter (A. 2731) apparently refers to the same
events, and the writer implores the king to grant the *āpilu*s' request
so that they will cease their activities.[30] Thus, even if some of the
*āpilu*s represented a particular deity, there is no evidence on the
role that they may have played in the deity's cult.

The relationship of the *āpilu*s to the central social structure of
Mari can be inferred from the content of their messages and from
the reactions of the letter writers to them. The fact that *āpilu*s were
at least tolerated by the central government is indicated by ARM(T)
9. 22:14, which lists an *āpilu* as the recipient of a garment from the
palace. Yet, several lines of evidence suggest that the *āpilu*s were
peripheral to Mari's central social structure and were not always
viewed positively by the royal establishment. First, in several instances *āpilu*s represent local deities in areas outside of Mari. The
*āpilu*s mentioned in A. 1121 and A. 2731 speak in the name of Adad
of Aleppo, while A. 4260 was written by an *āpilu* of Shamash of
Sippar. Both Aleppo and Sippar were at this time not being governed by Zimri-Lim, the ruler of Mari to whom the letters were
addressed. ARMT 13. 23 mentions an *āpilu* of Dagan of Tuttul.
Although these *āpilu*s may have played an important cultic role
locally, they were certainly peripheral to the central cults of Mari.[31]
Second, where the *āpilu*s' messages can be determined, they do not
seem to deal with matters pertaining to the cult or central government of Mari but are concerned with obtaining royal favors for the

30. Unfortunately, the crucial phrases in A. 1121 describing the *āpilu*s' appearance are difficult to interpret. For a discussion of the various possibilities, see Moran,
ANET, 625, nn. 25, 30, "New Evidence," 21; Huffmon, "Prophecy in the Mari Letters," 204–205; and B. F. Batto, *Studies on Women at Mari* (Baltimore: Johns Hopkins University Press, 1974) 120.
31. On this point see Moran, "New Evidence," 16–18.

deities and cults represented by the *āpilus*. A. 1121 and A. 2731 involve the *āpilus'* demand that the king give them some hereditary property, while A. 4260 requests a throne for Shamash of Sippar, some sort of "consecrated property" (*asakku*) for Adad of Aleppo, and a bronze sword for Nergal of Nishalim. Such requests are typical of peripheral intermediaries who are seeking to improve their own position or change the social structure. Third, the king apparently did not take the messages of the *āpilus* seriously. The writer of A. 2731 reminds the king that five previous letters have been written concerning the request of the *āpilus* and chides the king for taking no action. Fourth, there were apparently no official channels for reporting the words of the *āpilus* to the royal court. The writer of A. 1121 states that he had previously reported the words of the *āpilus* in Mari and that he would continue to do so in the future, but he clearly implies that he does this only because of his concern for the king. The *āpilu* responsible for A. 4260 found it necessary to write to the king, while the *āpilus'* messages in ARM 10. 81, 53, 9 were relayed by women in the royal court. Such haphazard reporting of the activities of the *āpilus* does not suggest that they played an important role in the religious life of Mari. Finally, the *āpiltu* in ARM 10. 81 sends a lock of her hair and the fringe of her garment to the capital so that her message can be tested by divination. This procedure is attested several times in the prophetic letters from Mari and was apparently required whenever the oracular speaker delivered a message publicly. The use of omens to test the veracity of the *āpilus'* words suggests that the religious establishment at Mari did not consider the *āpilus* a reliable means of divine-human communication. In addition, by requiring *āpilus* who spoke publicly to send the hair and fringe, the government exercised some control over their activities. Presumably there were penalties for *āpilus* whose words were not supported by the omens, so the knowledge that public utterances would be tested served to deter the *āpilus* from speaking rashly. This use of the hair and the fringe resembles the use of witchcraft accusations to control obstreperous intermediaries.[32] All of these lines of evidence suggest that the *āpilu* played a peripheral role within the social structure of Mari.

---

32. For a discussion of the significance of the hair and the fringe, see ibid., 19–20; Malamat, "Prophetic Revelations," 225–227; Huffmon, "Prophecy in the Mari Letters," 220–221; J. F. Craghan, "Mari and Its Prophets," *BTB* 5 (1975) 42–44, "The *ARM X* 'Prophetic Texts': Their Media, Style, and Structure," *JANESCU* 6 (1974)

THE *MUḪḪÛ / MUḪḪÛTU*

The title *muḫḫû* (fem. *muḫḫûtu*) is given to several people at Mari (ARM[T] 3. 40, 78; 6. 45; ARM 10. 50; A. 455) and in the form *maḫḫû* is attested elsewhere as well.[33] *Muḫḫû* is derived from the verb *maḫû*, "to go into trance," and is a *purrus* form, a nominal pattern indicating physical deformities or defects.[34] The *muḫḫû* is therefore a trancer or ecstatic. The precise nature of the characteristic trance behavior of the *muḫḫû* is unclear, but there are indications that it was violent and at times almost uncontrolled. In a literary text from Ras Shamra the writer complains, "My brothers bathe in their own blood like ecstatics" (*ki-ma maḫ-ḫe-e* [*Ugaritica* 5. 162:11']). In the creation epic *enūma eliš*, Tiamat "became like an ecstatic" (*maḫ-ḫu-tiš i-te-mi*) and "lost her mind" when challenged to single combat by Marduk (*enūma eliš* iv 88). The same phrase is used much later by Esarhaddon and Assurbanipal to describe the reaction of their enemies when faced with the might of the Assyrian army. The opponents "turn into ecstatics" and become totally incapable of fighting. Esarhaddon gives a similar characterization of his brothers, who "unlawfully" opposed his succession. They "went into trance" (*im-ma-ḫu-ma*) and "did things that were evil before god and man."[35] These passages suggest that in some circles the trance behavior of the *muḫḫû* was considered irrational, incapacitating, and potentially destructive, so much so that by the Neo-Assyrian period the activities of the *muḫḫû* were seen as a form of insanity.

Still, it may not automatically be assumed that the trance behavior of the *muḫḫû*s at Mari was as violent as it was elsewhere. The anthropological evidence indicates that trance behavior can vary from group to group and that features which are characteristic of

---

53–55; and A. Finet, "Les symboles du cheveu, du bord, du vêtement et de l'ongle en Mésopotamie," *Eschatologie et cosmologie* (Annales du centre d'étude des religions 3; Brussels: Editions de l'Institut de Sociologie de l'Université Libre de Bruxelles, 1969) 101–130.

33. The forms *maḫḫû* and *muḫḫû* are undoubtedly related, although the precise relationship is not clear. For a discussion of the problem, see H. Wohl, "The Problem of the *maḫḫû*," *JANESCU* 3 (1970–71) 112–118. ARM(T) 2. 90 may also involve a *muḫḫû*, but the text is broken at the point where the title would have been given.

34. Malamat, "Prophetic Revelations," 210–211. Cf. Hebrew *měšuggā ʿ*, "mad, insane."

35. Borger, *Die Inschriften Asarhaddons*, 44, col. 1, ll. 72–73; 42, col. 1, ll. 41–42; M. Streck, *Assurbanipal und die letzten assyrischen Könige* (Leipzig: J. C. Hinrichs, 1916) 2. 8, col. 1, l. 84; 158, l. 19.

trance in one group may not be present in another group. At the moment there is not enough evidence from Mari to permit a more specific reconstruction of the *muḥḥûs'* characteristic behavior. However, it is important to note that their oracles seem to have been intelligible and to have required no translation before being delivered. In ARM(T) 3. 40, 78, *muḥḥûs* are pictured delivering oracles in normal situations. The texts imply that the divine messages were received some time before they were actually delivered, so the texts shed no light on the relationship between the *muḥḥûs'* trance behavior and their speech. However, ARM 10. 50:21–26 and A. 455 describe *muḥḥûs* acting in a temple, and they may have spoken while in trance. If so, there is no indication that the trance state affected their ability to act rationally and speak coherently.

The social settings of the *muḥḥûs'* activities are clear. Although *muḥḥûs* sometimes delivered oracles in noncultic situations (ARM[T] 3. 40, 78), these figures also played regular cultic roles. In two cases the texts show *muḥḥûs* speaking in a cultic setting (ARM 10. 50:21–26; A. 455), and their messages sometimes dealt with specifically cultic matters (ARM[T] 3. 40; A. 455). Furthermore, a ritual text from Mari describes the participation of the *muḥḥû* in the cult of Ishtar. Unfortunately, the text is broken at crucial points, but the relevant lines seem to read, "if, at the beginning of the month, the *muḥḥû* comes and is not able to go into trance. . . ." The text becomes unclear at this point, but there are two references to a cage. At the end of the text are instructions for providing food and drink and setting up vessels for the needs of the *muḥḥûs*.[36] This passage may suggest that one of the ritual duties of the *muḥḥû* was to go into trance at appropriate times and that trance was induced if it could not be achieved spontaneously. Outside of Mari the *maḥḥû* also played regular cultic roles, although the precise nature of his participation is unclear, and some of the references may not actually refer to the ecstatic.[37]

36. G. Dossin, "Un rituel du culte d'Ištar provenant de Mari," *RA* 35 (1938) 6, col. 2, ll. 21–27; col. 4, ll. 34–36. The translation used here follows *CAD* M / 1 90a. For alternative translations, see Huffmon, "Prophecy in the Mari Letters," 211; and J. M. Sasson, "The Worship of the Golden Calf," *Orient and Occident* (ed. H. A. Hoffner, Jr.; Kevelaer: Butzon & Bercker, 1973) 152, n. 9.

37. See the references in *CAD* M / 1 90; and the discussion of Wohl, "The Problem of the *maḥḥû*," 112–118. Huffmon ("Prophecy in the Mari Letters," 213) uses ARM 10. 50:21–26 to argue that the *muḥḥû* supplied oracles in response to cultic inquiries. However, the relevant lines are too ambiguous to support this argument. See the alternative interpretation of Moran, "New Evidence," 38–40.

The relationship of the *muḫḫû* to the central social structure of Mari is more complex than was the case with the *āpilu*. On the one hand, the *muḫḫû* played a regular role in the cult of Ishtar, although it is impossible to determine the centrality of that role. As a cultic participant the *muḫḫû* was entitled to supplies, some of which undoubtedly came from the royal court. However, many of the same pieces of evidence that indicate the peripherality of the *āpilu* also suggest the peripherality of the *muḫḫû*. The *muḫḫû*s represent gods that are not part of Mari's central cult. Dagan of Tuttul and Dagan of Terqa are both represented by *muḫḫû*s (A. 455; ARM[T] 3. 40), and a *muḫḫūtum* of Annunitum is also mentioned (ARM 10. 50:21–26). This *muḫḫūtum* was located in Mari itself, but at the time the letter was written the goddess she represented was apparently not in favor with the king.[38] Although ARM 10. 50:21–26 indicates that *muḫḫû*s in Mari were somewhat concerned for the safety of the king and the stability of the government, the *muḫḫû*s outside of the capital were concerned with the well-being of their cults and deities. A. 455 describes a royal sacrifice to Dagan of Tuttul which was interrupted by a *muḫḫû* presenting the god's somewhat ungrateful demand for "pure water to drink." The *muḫḫû* of Dagan of Terqa, the ancestral home of Zimri-Lim's dynasty, sent the king an exhortation to perform a mortuary ritual (*kispu*) for the shade of the dynastic founder, Yahdun-Lim (ARM[T] 3. 40).[39] The haphazard way in which these requests were relayed to the king is again apparent. As was also the case with the *āpilu*, the *muḫḫû*'s utterances were sometimes tested by divination, and the *muḫḫû*'s hair and fringe were sent to the king (A. 455; ARM[T] 6. 45).[40] All of this evidence suggests that the *muḫḫû* played a peripheral role in the central cult of Mari.

However, there are indications that some groups took the *muḫḫû* more seriously. Esarhaddon's inscriptions on several occasions refer to favorable oracles which the king received from *maḫḫû*s, and in one of his treaties he required his vassal to swear not to withhold information that might come from a *maḫḫû*.[41] Esarhaddon's son,

38. See ARM 10. 8:9–11 and the discussion of Moran, "New Evidence," 18–19.
39. ARM(T) 3. 78 deals with a *muḫḫû*'s exhortation not to build a gate, but the circumstances are unclear.
40. ARM(T) 6. 45 simply reports that the writer is sending the hair and fringe of a *muḫḫû* whose message is contained in another tablet. The incident involved may be the same one reflected in ARM 10. 50:21–26. See Moran, "New Evidence," 20.
41. Borger, *Die Inschriften Asarhaddons*, 2, col. 2, ll. 12–13; 45, col. 2, ll. 6–7; D. J. Wiseman, "The Vassal-Treaties of Esarhaddon," *Iraq* 20 (1958) 37, ll. 108–122.

Assurbanipal, also mentions favorable omens from *maḫḫûs*, along with revelations through dreams.[42] It therefore appears that the *maḫḫû* was regarded favorably in the Assyrian royal court during this period, although the *maḫḫû* certainly did not replace the *bārû* as the primary divine-human intermediary.

THE *ASSINNU*

The *assinnu* appears in three of the Mari letters (ARM 10. 6, 7, 80) and is known from later sources as a member of the cultic personnel of Ishtar. If the relatively late descriptions of the *assinnu* are a reliable guide to the behavior of the *assinnus* at Mari, then it is clear that they acted in certain stereotypical ways and may have possessed characteristic physical features. However, the precise nature of the *assinnu*'s behavior is a matter of debate because of a vague reference in the Era Epic. The text refers to "the *kurgarrûs* and *assinnus* whose masculinity (*zikrūtu*) Ishtar changed into femininity (*sinnišūtu*) in order to teach the people religious fear."[43] This has been variously interpreted to mean that the *assinnu* was a eunuch, homosexual, transvestite, male cult-prostitute, or pederast.[44] However, none of these interpretations can unambiguously be supported by reference to other texts mentioning the *assinnu,* and for this reason some scholars hold that the *assinnu* was simply an actor who took a female role in cultic dramas.[45] An alternative solution to the problem of the *assinnu*'s behavior is suggested by ARM 10. 7:5–7, 23–27, which indicates that the *assinnu* Šelebum went into trance (*im-ma-ḫu*) in the temple of Annunitum before delivering an oracle for the king. Annunitum is a manifestation of the warrior aspect of Ishtar, so this text may indicate that trance was a characteristic part of the *assinnu*'s behavior when he participated in the goddess's cult.[46] If this was the case and if the trance was due to possession by the goddess, then the anthropological literature provides an expla-

42. Streck, *Assurbanipal,* 120, col. 5, ll. 93–96; T. Bauer, *Das Inschriftenwerk Assurbanipals* (Leipzig: J. C. Hinrichs, 1933) 2. 61, l. 8; Oppenheim, *The Interpretation of Dreams,* 201–202, 249–250.

43. L. Cagni, *L'epopea di Erra* (Rome: Istituto di Studi del Vicino Oriente, 1969) 110, col. 4, ll. 55–56.

44. See Moran, "New Evidence," 30; the discussion of *CAD* A / 2 341–342; and the review of H. W. F. Saggs, *JSS* 18 (1973) 272. In support of such interpretations note the lexical equation of the *assinnu* and the *kuluʾu,* who in one text is said not to be masculine (*zikaru*) (*AfO* 10 [1935–1936] 3:21). Note also the omen which begins, "if a man has intercourse with an *assinnu* . . . ." (CT 39. 41:23).

45. Moran, "New Evidence," 30; *CAD* A / 2 341–342.

46. On the relationship between Annunitum and Ishtar, see K. B. Gödecken, "Bemerkungen zur Göttin Annunītum," *UF* 5 (1973) 141–163.

nation for the *assinnu*'s behavior. When individuals are possessed by a deity of the opposite sex, they act and speak in ways appropriate to the possessing deity. When the goddess Ishtar possessed the male *assinnu*s, their behavior and speech would have been feminine rather than masculine, although this condition would have lasted only as long as the trance state itself. This switching back and forth between male and female behavior can explain the characterization of the *assinnu*s in the Era Epic, but unfortunately this theory of possession behavior cannot further specify the activities of the *assinnu*s when they played female roles in trance.

The cultic setting of the *assinnu*'s activities is well established, and within the cult he played certain prescribed roles. During the *akītu* festival *assinnu*s accompanied the goddess and gave cultic responses. On other occasions they sang special songs and performed dances. In one ritual they put on masks of a goddess, perhaps indicating that they wore special costumes while playing the feminine role. However, none of the references outside of Mari specifically indicate that trance was a regular part of the *assinnu*'s behavior, and nowhere else is the *assinnu* portrayed delivering oracles.[47]

The relationship of the *assinnu* to the central social structure of Mari is again ambiguous. As we have already seen, the *assinnu* played a regular role in the cult of Annunitum (Ishtar) in Mari, and both of the *assinnu* oracles that have been published indicate a concern for the stability of the central government and the protection of the king (ARM 10. 6, 7). However, at the time these oracles were delivered Annunitum was peripheral to the interests of Zimri-Lim, and the divine messages can be interpreted as attempts to win the king's attention and favor. Furthermore, in both instances the *assinnu*'s words were verified by using divination, either by sending the king the hair and the fringe or by making an independent inquiry.[48] Thus, like the *āpilu* and the *muḫḫû*, the *assinnu* seems to have had a peripheral relation to Mari's central cult.

---

47. For descriptions of the *assinnu*'s role in cultic rituals, see S. A. Pallis, *The Babylonian Akîtu Festival* (Copenhagen: Andr. Fred. Høst, 1926) 145–146; *KAR* 42:29; S. Lackenbacher, "Un nouveau fragment de la 'fête d'Ištar,'" *RA* 71 (1977) 46, l. 25'–26'; and W. G. Lambert, "The Problem of the Love Lyrics," *Unity and Diversity* (ed. H. Goedicke and J. J. M. Roberts; Baltimore: Johns Hopkins University Press, 1975) 104–105, 128, BM 41005, l. 17.

48. The crucial lines in ARM 10. 6 are difficult to interpret, but there is no doubt that the *assinnu*'s oracle was tested in some way. See Moran, "New Evidence," 36–38; and Huffmon, "Prophecy in the Mari Letters," 209–210.

THE *QABBĀTUM*

ARM 10. 80 may contain a reference to a *qabbātum*, a "speaker," although this word has also been interpreted as a personal name. If the word is actually a title, it is not attested elsewhere, and even its reading and derivation are uncertain.[49] In ARM 10. 80 this figure speaks in the name of Dagan of Terqa and warns the king against the deceptive acts of the ruler of Ešnunna. Nothing can be said about the characteristic behavior of the *qabbātum*, and it must be assumed that this figure played a peripheral role in the central cult.

ORACULAR SPEAKERS WITHOUT TITLE

Thirteen of the oracular speakers at Mari have no particular title related to their revelatory activities, although in some cases this may be due to the poor preservation of the texts. These figures seem to have exhibited no stereotypical behavior in connection with the *delivery* of their oracles, although the letters indicate that almost all of the lay speakers *received* their oracles in stereotypical ways. The emphasis which the letters place on the means of divine-human communication suggests that nonprofessionals felt compelled to demonstrate the authority of their utterances so that they would be taken seriously by the society.

Although two of the letters simply record that an individual received a message from a deity (ARMT 13. 114, ARM 10. 100), the remainder describe processes of revelation that are attested elsewhere and that are sometimes connected with professional oracle-givers. In ARM 10. 8 the speaker is said to have gone into trance (*im-ma-ḫi*) in the temple of Annunitum, and the reference in ARM 10. 10 to a woman who "saw" (*i-mu-ur*) an ominous vision in the temple of Itur-Mer may also indicate trance. ARM 10. 4 describes a "man and a woman" who were asked questions by a member of the royal family and who replied with *egirrû*-utterances. Such utterances are attested elsewhere, but nothing is known about their form or about how they were obtained.[50] However, the majority of the

---

49. The title has also been read as *qamatum*. For a discussion of the problems involved, see Moran, "New Evidence," 53; Huffmon, "Prophecy in the Mari Letters," 214; W. von Soden, "Einige Bemerkungen zu den von Fr. Ellermeier in 'Prophetie in Mari und Israel' (Herzberg 1968) erstmalig bearbeiteten Briefen aus ARM 10," *UF* 1 (1969) 198; and Craghan, "The *ARM X* 'Prophetic' Texts," 47–48.

50. For a discussion see Moran, "New Evidence," 48–49; and *CAD* E 44–45. Note also the Late Babylonian omen protasis which reads, "if a man continually has *egirrû*-utterances spoken behind him, [he will . . .] an *assinnu*" (CT 39. 41:23;

nonprofessional oracle-givers received their messages in dreams (A. 15; ARMT 13. 112, 113; ARM 10. 50, 51, 94, 117). Even where the actual message came in a theophany in the temple, the recipients described the theophany as occurring in a dream (A. 15; ARM 10. 50).[51] This suggests that nonprofessional speakers stereotypically derived their messages from dreams and that dreams were an acceptable means of revelation in some circles at Mari.

Some of the nonprofessional oracular speakers seem to have lacked social status within the community and may have played subsidiary social roles. Eight of the thirteen speakers were women, who presumably had less social and religious influence than men in the patriarchal society of Mari. Several of the women were servants (ARM 10. 8, 110, 117[?]), as was one of the men (ARMT 13. 112). The latter case is particularly interesting, for it has close parallels with anthropological descriptions of the onset of peripheral possession. The man involved had a recurring dream containing a divine prohibition against building a house or a temple. The dreamer's behavior is not specified, but it was apparently capable of being interpreted either as an indication of illness or as a sign of possession. To determine whether the individual was actually possessed or simply ill, the letter writer submitted the divine message to divination. However, in spite of these indications that the nonprofessional oracle-givers were located on the fringes of society at Mari, not all of the figures seem to fit the peripheral mold. One of the men was a šangu-priest (ARM 10. 51), and several of the men and women were "free citizens" (ARMT 13. 113, 114; A. 15). In two instances women within the royal establishment may have been involved in giving oracles (ARM 10. 50, 94[?]).

In spite of the uncertainty about the social status of some of the nonprofessional oracular speakers, the content of their messages and the way in which the government reacted to them indicate that these figures played a peripheral role in the religious establishment at Mari. Several of the divine messages concern personal requests which the speaker wished to present to the government (ARM 10. 94, 100, 117[?]). Two speakers delivered oracles from deities seeking better treatment from the king (ARM 10. 8; A. 15), while another

----

restoration from *CAD* A / 2 341). *Egirrû*-utterances were also received by *maḫḫûs* (Streck, *Assurbanipal*, 2. 120, col. 5, ll. 95–96).

51. For a discussion of the peculiar dream report in A. 15, see Oppenheim, *The Interpretation of Dreams*, 195–196.

offered advice on the proper conduct of a battle (ARM 10.51). Even in the cases where oracles were given in support of the central government, there is no indication that they were encouraged by the religious establishment (ARM 10. 4, 8, 10, 50). As was also the case with the titled oracular speakers, the oracles of the nonprofessionals were sometimes tested by divination (ARM 10. 8, 50, 94; ARMT 13. 112). Thus the diviners within the religious establishment made the final decision concerning which speakers and messages would be authenticated and which would not.

Oracular Speakers at Mari: Social Functions

Oracular speakers at Mari seem to have been peripheral intermediaries within the social structure. Their utterances were intended to bring about changes in the social and religious establishments, particularly by improving the lot of the gods and cults which the intermediaries represented. Most of their messages were innovative and designed to bring about changes in existing conditions. However, some of the speakers from Mari itself were concerned with preserving the social order and maintaining the status quo. Still, it must be assumed that even this quietism was intended to alter existing political policies.

In spite of the fact that the oracular speakers were peripheral intermediaries, they did receive support from some groups within the society. These groups encouraged the activities of the speakers or at least tolerated their existence. Some of the speakers found support in various peripheral cults, while others seem to have been of interest to segments of the royal family.[52] Through the intermediaries the support groups were able to articulate their views in an authoritative way. However, the demands of these groups were held in check by the diviners within the central religious establishment, who determined the truth or falsity of the intermediaries and their messages.[53]

52. Šibtu, the chief wife of Zimri-Lim, seems to have been particularly interested in the utterances of the oracular speakers, and she sometimes included reports of their messages in her letters to the king (ARM 10. 4, 6, 7, 8, 9, 10). Šibatum, who may have been a daughter of the king, seems to have been the recipient of the ominous dream mentioned in ARM 10. 94, while Inibšina, the wife of the governor of Mari and perhaps a member of Zimri-Lim's family, also reported oracular messages (ARM 10. 80–81). For a discussion of the role of these women in the royal court, see Batto, *Women at Mari*, 8–21, 42–48, 59–60.

53. In addition to the oracles contained in the Mari archives, an oracle from the Old Babylonian period has been found in the royal palace at Uruk (UVB 18 [1962]

Prophecy in the Neo-Assyrian Period

After the Old Babylonian period, there are no reports of prophetic figures until Neo-Assyrian times and the reigns of Esarhaddon and Assurbanipal (680–627 B.C.). During the intervening period the use of divination continued, but little is known about the development or even the existence of oracular speakers and the type of inter-mediation that they represented. However, the Neo-Assyrian sources indicate that sometime during this interim an important change took place in Mesopotamian society's evaluation of at least certain types of oracular speakers. To date, the earliest records of these figures come from Mari, which was on the periphery of the Mesopotamian heartland and which was heavily influenced by West Semitic or Amorite culture. It has even been suggested that this form of intermediation was actually a feature of West Semitic reli-gion and was able to exist in Mesopotamia only on the fringes of society. In contrast, the Neo-Assyrian sources show oracular speak-ers operating in the Assyrian royal court and indicate that this type of intermediation had become part of the core cultural tradition of Mesopotamia. It is unclear whether this shift took place gradually or whether it was due to Western influences in Assyria during the reigns of Esarhaddon and Assurbanipal.[54] In either case, it is evident that Neo-Assyrian prophecy had a social matrix that was somewhat different from that of the sort of prophecy attested at Mari.

Oracular Speakers in the Neo-Assyrian Period

In addition to the *maḫḫû*, whose existence in the Assyrian royal court we have already noted,[55] several other titled oracular speakers appear in Neo-Assyrian sources. The most widely attested figure is the *raggimu* (fem. *raggintu*) ("caller," "shouter"). Although this title may indicate that *raggimu*s delivered oracles in a distinctive way, the texts throw no light on the *raggimu*s' characteristic behav-

---

61–62, and plates 20d–f, 28c; English translation in *ANET*, 604). The tablet contains a message of Ishtar to an unnamed intermediary, who apparently delivered it to the king. Unfortunately, the content of the oracle is obscure, but it may have dealt with the establishment of Sin-kašid's dynasty and may have contained an exhortation to restore the goddess's temple. If so, then the tablet may be another example of pe-ripheral intermediation.

54. On the latter possibility, see H. Tadmor, "Assyria and the West: The Ninth Century and Its Aftermath," *Unity and Diversity* (ed. H. Goedicke and J. J. M. Roberts; Baltimore: Johns Hopkins University Press, 1975) 36–48.

55. See above, pp. 105–106.

ior. Their social roles are equally obscure, although there are indications that *raggimus* sometimes operated in cultic contexts. A letter to Esarhaddon reports a *raggintu*'s demand that a throne be removed from a temple, although the text is too broken to permit a reconstruction of the background of this message.[56] Clearer evidence comes from a letter to Esarhaddon detailing the death and burial of the substitute-king (*šar pūhi*). According to the letter writer, before these events took place a *raggintu* had delivered a divine message to the substitute confirming his appointment. She also delivered another oracle to him in the "assembly of the country" (UKKIN *ša* KUR), although the meaning of this oracle is uncertain. The letter thus suggests that the *raggimu/raggintu* had a role in the ritual for the substitute-king, although the precise nature and official status of that role are unclear.[57]

Some of the messages of the *raggimus/raggintus* have been preserved in the Neo-Assyrian oracle collections. The oracles come from the goddesses Ninlil and Ishtar and seem to be words of reassurance to Assurbanipal. However, nothing can be said of the original function of the messages or the context in which they were delivered.[58]

A second title given to Neo-Assyrian oracular speakers is *šabrû*. This designation is presumably derived from the Š-stem of the verb *barû*, "to show, to reveal," which is often used specifically in con-

---

56. ABL 149, reedited and translated in S. Parpola, *Letters from Assyrian Scholars to the Kings Esarhaddon and Assurbanipal* (Kevelaer: Butzon & Bercker, 1970) 1. 270–271. B. Landsberger (*Brief des Bischofs von Esagila an König Asarhaddon* [Amsterdam: Noord-hollandsche Uitgevers Maatschappij, 1965] 47–50) connects the *raggintu*'s demand with the ritual for the installation of the substitute-king (*šar pūhi*). However, parts of Landsberger's interpretation are problematic in the light of Parpola's new edition of the text.

57. ABL 437, reedited and translated in Parpola, *Letters*, 1. 228–230. See also the translation in *ANET*, 625–626; and the study of Landsberger, *Brief*, 38–57. Additional references to the *raggimu / raggintu* are found in ABL 1216:9 and 1285:31, but the contexts of these references are too fragmentary to permit any conclusions to be drawn from them. The title is also attested in a Middle Assyrian letter, which orders the imprisonment of a palace ploughman who has "seen" a *raggintu* (H. W. F. Saggs, "The Tell al Rimah Tablets, 1965," *Iraq* 30 [1968] 161–162). This reference suggests that the *raggintu* had a special cultic status.

58. A *raggintu* is credited with the oracles in K 883 (S. A. Strong, "On Some Oracles to Esarhaddon and Ašurbanipal," *Beiträge zur Assyriologie* 2 [1894] 633, 645, l. 1 = J. A. Craig, *Assyrian and Babylonian Religious Texts* [Leipzig: J. C. Hinrichs, 1895] 1. 26–27, l. 1; cf. *ANET*, 450–451); and a *raggimu* is mentioned at the end of the oracle collection K 2401 (Craig, *Assyrian and Babylonian Religious Texts*, 1. 25, col. 4, l. 32!). However, the context of the latter occurrence is almost completely unintelligible.

nection with dreams or visions.[59] The derivation of the title suggests that the *šabrû*'s messages usually came through dreams, and this suggestion is supported by the only text that preserves a picture of this specialist at work. Assurbanipal's annalistic account of his seventh campaign relates that when he was informed of the impending attack of the Elamites, he prayed to Ishtar of Arbela, asking her to help him in the coming battle. Assurbanipal reports that Ishtar answered and reassured him. Then, the annal continues, in the same night that the king appeared before the goddess, a *šabrû* went to sleep and had a revelatory dream. It is unclear whether this dream was the original source of the words of assurance that Assurbanipal received or whether the dream simply confirmed the goddess's private message to the king. In any case, the *šabrû* reported that the goddess had appeared, dressed in battle array, and spoken words of encouragement to the king. The vision ended with Ishtar rushing away to defeat Assurbanipal's enemies.[60]

Although this text suggests that the *šabrû* may have been a professional dreamer or visionary, nothing more is known of the social contexts of his activities. If he was indeed a professional visionary, he may well have operated in cultic contexts and may have induced visions, but there is no evidence on either of these points. However, it is noteworthy that Assurbanipal apparently did not question the truth of the *šabrû*'s vision and did not test it by divination. Rather, on the basis of the oracle's assurances he mounted an aggressive attack against the Elamites. If the account of the *šabrû*'s vision is not simply a fabrication designed to justify Assurbanipal's conduct of the Elamite war, then the content and social context of the oracle might indicate that the *šabrû* played an established role within the central social structure and helped to maintain the society by providing divine guidance for the king. However, before such a conclusion can be safely drawn, it will be necessary to have additional evidence, preferably from sources outside of the royal annals.

An oracular speaker with the title [lú]KAL also appears in Assur-

59. See the references collected in *CAD* B 118, 5b. Lexical texts equate *šabrû* and *raggimu*, although it is difficult to know how to interpret this equation. See *AHW*, 1120, s.v. *šabrû(m)*.

60. Streck, *Assurbanipal*, 108–119; partially translated in *ANET*, 606. See also the translation and discussion of Oppenheim, *The Interpretation of Dreams*, 249, 188, 190, 200, 207.

banipal's annals. The reading of this logogram is uncertain, although the annalistic description of the ^{lú}KAL is so similar to that of
the *šabrû* that the two figures may have been related or even identical.[61] The ^{lú}KAL appears in Assurbanipal's account of Šamaš-šum-
ukin's rebellion. At the height of the revolt, a ^{lú}KAL went to sleep
and had a vision of the statue of the moon god Sin. The base of the
statue was inscribed with a message promising that the god would
destroy all who plotted evil against the king. In the vision the scribal
god Nabu repeatedly read this inscription aloud to reassure the
king, who believed the divine message and mounted a campaign
against Šamaš-šum-ukin.[62] The striking feature of this vision report
is that the words which Sin uses to describe the fate of Assurbanipal's opponents appear again in the annalistic account of the destruction of Babylon and the slaughter of the rebels who supported
Šamaš-šum-ukin.[63] There are two possible explanations for this state
of affairs. First, both the vision report and the annalistic account may
reflect stereotypical descriptions of military disaster. If this is the
case, then it may indicate that the ^{lú}KAL used stereotypical language in expressing his message. Second, the vision report may have
been shaped to reflect the events that actually occurred during the
siege and destruction of Babylon. If this was the case, then it would
suggest that Assurbanipal used the fabricated vision report to justify
his harsh treatment of his brother Šamaš-šum-ukin and the Babylonians. In turn, the use of such a tactic would imply that divine
oracles were an acceptable way of supporting royal decisions and
that the people who delivered such oracles had social maintenance
functions within the government.

The only other titled oracular speaker to appear in Neo-Assyrian
sources is the *šēlūtu*, the (female) votary. The *šēlūtu* was a woman
dedicated to the service of a particular deity. She therefore had
regular cultic functions, although her status within the cult and the
precise nature of her functions are unclear. In one of the oracle
collections, a "*šēlūtu* of the king" (*še-lu-tu ša* LUGAL) is said to
have delivered a long oracle from Ishtar of Arbela to Esarhaddon

61. Note the comment of Streck, *Assurbanipal*, 32, n. *f*. However, more evidence
must be collected before the ^{lú}KAL and the *šabrû* can be identified with each other.
62. Ibid., 28–33; see the translation and interpretation of Oppenheim, *The Interpretation of Dreams*, 249–250, 201–202.
63. Streck, *Assurbanipal*, 32–33, ll. 122–126; 36–39, ll. 41–76.

assuring the king of the goddess's constant support.[64] On the basis of this single example it is impossible to determine whether or not oracle-giving was one of the *šēlūtu's* regular functions.

In addition to the oracular speakers having titles, Neo-Assyrian sources also record oracles delivered by individuals who are given no titles and who were presumably not professional intermediaries. Assurbanipal himself claims to have received communications from deities in response to his prayers, although sometimes it is not clear whether he actually received the divine messages himself or whether they were relayed through an intermediary.[65] In the oracle collections a number of messages are attributed to speakers having no specific title, although the status and social roles of these people are unknown.[66]

The Neo-Assyrian Oracle Collections

Neo-Assyrian sources have preserved several collections of oracles which were originally delivered to Esarhaddon and Assurbanipal. Some of these texts are not available in transliteration or translation, and even the existing cuneiform copies are occasionally inaccurate or misleading. In addition to being poorly published, the oracles themselves are often fragmentary and enigmatic. Still, these oracle collections can shed some light on the relationship between prophecy and society in the Neo-Assyrian period, so we will discuss them briefly. However, our remarks must be considered tentative

---

64. K 4310, col. 5, l. 11 (IVR 61; translated in *ANET*, 605). The phrase *"šēlūtu* of the king" presumably indicates that the king donated the girl to the deity. Cf. the Nimrud contract ND. 2309 dealing with the purchase of a girl for dedication as a *šēlūtu* (B. Parker, "The Nimrud Tablets, 1952—Business Documents," *Iraq* 16 [1954] 39); and note the discussion of Huffmon, "Prophetic Oracles in the Ancient Near East: Reflections on Their Use in Form-Critical Study of the Hebrew Bible," 3.

65. See, for example, the prayer and oracular response in K 1285 (Streck, *Assurbanipal*, 342–351). At least part of this response is said to have come from a *zaqiqu* (obv. l. 23), a "spirit" or "ghost" thought to emanate from a diety.

66. See, for example, K 4310, col. 1, ll. 29–30; col. 2, ll. 9–10, 13–15, 40; col. 5, ll. 64–65; col. 6, ll. 71–72. In addition to the oracular speakers that we have discussed, Late Babylonian texts also mention a *zabbu / zabbatu,* who was a type of ecstatic. The characteristic behavior of this figure may have involved self-mutilation, and there are indications that the *zabbu* may have had functions similar to those of the *maḫḫû*. However, little more can be said about this figure until more evidence is available. See the references and discussion of *CAD* Z 7, s.v. *zabbu*.

and subject to revision after the publication of new editions of the texts.[67]

The Neo-Assyrian oracle collections as a whole exhibit no overall organizational patterns and appear to consist of originally independent messages that have been strung together in a random sequence. Various deities are represented, but the majority of the preserved oracles come from goddesses, particularly Ninlil (K 883) and Ishtar of Arbela (K 2401, K 4310, K 12033+82-5-22, 527, K 6259). Most of the speakers are women, but a few men are also represented (K 4310, col. 1, ll. 29–30; col. 6, l. 30). With only a few exceptions (K 881, l.1 [*raggintu*]; K 4310, col. 5, l. 10[*šēlūtu*]; K 2401, col. 4, l.32 [*raggintu*]), the speakers do not seem to have had titles.

Where complete oracles have been preserved, there is some evidence that the divine messages themselves may have followed a standard pattern. Many oracles begin with the introductory formula, "word of DN" (K 2401, col. 2, l.33; col. 3, l.15; K 883, l.2; K 6259, l.1), and this phrase is followed by the name and/or the title of the addressee. The oracles frequently conclude with a formula designating the speaker: "from the mouth of PN of (the city of) GN" (K 4310, col. 1, l. 29; col. 2, ll. 9, 40; col. 5, ll. 10, 24–25; col. 6, l. 31; K 12033+82-5-22, 527, col. 1, ll. 14[?], 35[?]; col. 2, l. 28; col. 3, l. 18).

67. K. Deller and S. Parpola have promised a new edition of the Neo-Assyrian oracle collections, and H. B. Huffmon will treat the texts in a comprehensive study to be published in the near future. Huffmon has examined all of the available tablets, and much of the following discussion is based on his research. See in particular Huffmon, "The Origins of Prophecy," 175–176; idem, "Prophecy in the Ancient Near East," 699–700; idem, "Prophetic Oracles in the Ancient Near East," 102–103 (with full bibliography); and idem, "Prophetic Oracles in the Ancient Near East: Reflections on Their Use in Form-Critical Study of the Hebrew Bible," 3–13. I have also been able to examine new photographs of some of the tablets, including the unpublished fragment K 12033. Oracle collections are found in the following texts: K 883 (Strong, "Oracles to Esarhaddon and Ašurbanipal," 633–635, 645; copied also in Craig, *Assyrian and Babylonian Religious Texts*, 1. 26–27; translated in *ANET*, 450–451); K 6259 (S. H. Langdon, *Tammuz and Ishtar* [Oxford: At the Clarendon Press, 1914], plate 4); K 2401 (partially edited and copied in Strong, "Oracles to Esarhaddon and Ašurbanipal," 627–633, 637–643; inaccurately copied in Craig, *Assyrian and Babylonian Religious Texts*, 1. 22–25); K 4310 (IVR 61; translated in *ANET*, 605; transliteration in E. J. Banks, "Eight Oracular Responses to Esarhaddon," *AJSL* 14 [1897–98] 267–277; note also the partial translation, transliteration, and comments in M. Weippert, " 'Heiliger Krieg' in Israel und Assyrien," *ZAW* 84 [1972] 473–474); K 12033 + 82-5-22, 527 (82-5-22, 527 is inaccurately copied and translated in Langdon, *Tammuz and Ishtar*, pp. 137–140, and plates 2–3; and is partially edited in A. Parrot and J. Nougayrol, "Asarhaddon et Naqiʾa sur un bronze du Louvre," *Syria* 33 [1956] 158–159; K 12033 is unpublished); K 2647 + Rm II, 99 (CT 35. 14, 15, 13; edited by Bauer, *Assurbanipal*, 2. 79–81); K 6064 (CT 35. 26–27; edited by Bauer, *Assurbanipal*, 2. 82); and Rm II, 236 (CT 35. 30; edited by Bauer, *Assurbanipal*, 82).

Within the messages themselves, there are also hints of stereotypical speech. This is particularly true of the oracles collected in K 4310, most of which come from Ishtar of Arbela. The exhortation "do not be afraid" (*lā tapallaḥ*) occurs frequently (col. 1, ll. 6, 31; col. 2, ll. 16, 33; col. 3, l. 38; col. 5, l. 21). The deities insert the identifying and authenticating formula "I am DN" throughout their messages (col. 1, ll. 13, 19, 21–22; col. 2, ll. 17, 30, 38; col. 3, l. 15), and there are frequent exhortations to praise the deity (col. 2, ll. 33, 39). Stereotypical language may also appear in K 2647+Rm II, 99, where oracles dealing with Šamaš-šum-ukin's revolt against Assurbanipal bear a marked resemblance to the annalistic descriptions of this event. However, it is unclear whether the stereotypical form and language of the oracles actually indicate that the oracular speakers used standard speech patterns or whether the distinctive vocabulary is the result of the scribal activities of the compilers.

Little can be said about the settings in which the oracles were originally delivered. However, there is some evidence that they were given in response to a prayer or inquiry. In an obscure portion of K 883, Ninlil refers in highly symbolic terms to the actions that she will take when the enemy gathers against Assurbanipal. This reference is followed by an explanation of the symbols and is introduced in the following way: "should you (Assurbanipal) ask, 'what does "like a furtively walking person (*ḥallalatti*), like a proudly walking person (*enguratti*)" mean?,' (I explain) like a furtively walking person he will enter Egypt, like a proudly walking person he will come out (of Egypt)."[68] This passage could be interpreted to mean that Assurbanipal had received an enigmatic oracle from the goddess or had received an unclear omen and then had asked Ninlil for further clarification, which was forthcoming in the oracle just quoted. A clearer example is found in K 2401, where the deity (Ashur?) describes Esarhaddon's response when he was surrounded by enemies: "You (Esarhaddon) opened your mouth. I heard your distress." An oracle of assurance is then given to the king (K 2401, col. 2, ll. 10–14). It is probable that the entire oracle was the result of Esarhaddon's prayer, a probability which is strengthened by the conclusion of the oracle, which reads: "This is the favorable oracle (*šulmu*) before the (divine?) statue. This tablet of Ashur's *adû-*

---

68. K 883, ll. 17–19; this translation is adapted from *CAD* Ḫ 43, s.v. *ḥallalatti*. The meaning of *enguratti* is unknown.

agreement will come before the king on a *ḫaʾūtu* . . . and they will read (the tablet) before the king."[69]

The role that these oracle collections might have played in the religious establishment of the Neo-Assyrian empire is unclear. The evidence of K 2401 that oracles were delivered in cultic contexts within the royal court suggests that this type of activity was an accepted part of court life. This suggestion is supported by the content of the oracles, which promise support for the king and his policies. The fact that the oracles were collected and preserved suggests that they were judged worthy of preservation by the court scribes, although given scribal "list-making tendencies" it is difficult to make too much of this point. The attitude of the king toward this type of intermediation is unknown, although obviously he at least tolerated it within his court. A more positive attitude on the part of the king is suggested by K 2647+Rm II, 99, where the deity's role in the suppression of Šamaš-šum-ukin's rebellion is described in the past tense in terms similar to those used by Assurbanipal in his annals. We have already noted this phenomenon in a dream report coming from the time of Assurbanipal, and it is possible that K 2647+Rm II, 99 and the dream report both had the same function. The collection of "prophetic" oracles may have been used to justify the king's actions by attributing them to a deity. If so, then the text is either a piece of political propaganda or an indication that oracular speakers had regular social maintenance functions within Assurbanipal's court.

In contrast to the indications that oracular speakers played a role in the central social structure of Assyria, there are also signs that this type of activity was still socially peripheral. The speakers were primarily women and seem to have had no special status within the court. Most of the oracles come from Ishtar of Arbela, who was the consort of Ashur but who was apparently not ranked at the top of the pantheon.[70] The content of some of Ishtar's messages also suggests that she was not enjoying the king's favor and was seeking through the oracles to improve her status. In K 4310 in particular she exhorts the king to trust in her rather than in other humans (col. 2, l. 29) and

---

69. K 2401, col. 2, ll. 26–32. For an alternate translation, see *CAD* Ḫ 162, s.v. *ḫaʾūtu*. The meaning of *ḫaʾūtu* is unknown.

70. Note the position of Ishtar of Arbela in the god lists preserved in Esarhaddon's inscriptions (Borger, *Die Inschriften Asarhaddons*, 40, 43), and compare the lists in the ritual texts from the cult of Ashur (G. van Driel, *The Cult of Aššur* [Assen: Van Gorcum, 1969] 99, 101).

complains that the king's mother has been criticizing the goddess's care of Esarhaddon (col. 5, ll. 12–20). All of this leads to the conclusion that although the oracular speakers were located in the royal court and may have had certain social maintenance functions, they still were not completely in the mainstream of Assyrian society.

The Social Functions of the Neo-Assyrian Oracular Speakers

Just as the Neo-Assyrian texts indicate that by this period oracular speakers had moved from the periphery of the Assyrian empire to its center, so the texts also suggest that Neo-Assyrian speakers had functions that were closer to being central than they were to being peripheral. Although there are some indications that the speakers acted on the periphery of society and tried to reform religious and political practices, there is also evidence to indicate that these figures had social maintenance functions and supported the religious and political policies of the kings. Presumably the speakers who had cultic roles received some support from the religious establishment, and the royal court may have supported some of the speakers, at least as long as they did not disagree radically with the king's views. If the king himself used oracular messages as political propaganda, then it would indicate that this type of intermediation was an accepted feature of royal religious practice. However, there is still no evidence that the oracular speakers were numerous enough or powerful enough to replace the diviners as the primary intermediaries of the official cult. In general, then, the evidence indicates that Esarhaddon and Assurbanipal tolerated oracular speakers within the royal court, where they functioned as central intermediaries. However, they seem to have performed these functions only so long as the king found them useful. At other times the speakers seem to have been relegated to the fringes of society, where they had peripheral functions similar to those of their predecessors at Mari.

Akkadian "Prophecy" and "Apocalyptic"

For a number of years cuneiformists have applied the designation "prophecies" to a little-understood genre of Akkadian texts consisting of "predictions" of future events. Enough fragments of these texts have now been pieced together to provide some indication of their original function, so we will consider them briefly as part of our discussion of Mesopotamian prophecy. However, a comprehensive treatment of this material must await the discovery of more textual evidence.[71]

In contrast to the Assyrian oracle collections, the Mesopotamian prophecies do not consist of prophetic messages delivered on different occasions and then collected in a single tablet. Rather, the prophecies were apparently created as unified literary texts and show no signs of having been delivered orally. With minor variations, all of the known texts follow roughly the same organizational pattern. The prophecies seem to have begun with the identification of the speaker, although this point is unclear due to the poor condition of the beginning of the texts. In the two texts whose first lines have been preserved, the speaker is either a god (Marduk) or a deified king (Shulgi), but it is not certain that this is typical of all of the texts. Following the introduction, the speaker gives an overview of coming political events. This historical survey is expressed by the repeated use of a formula such as "a prince (*rubû* [NUN]) / king

71. The following Akkadian prophecy texts are extensive enough to be identified as examples of the genre: Text A (edited in A. K. Grayson and W. G. Lambert, "Akkadian Prophecies," *JCS* 18 [1964] 7, 12–16, 29; translated in *ANET* 606–607); the Marduk and Shulgi prophetic speeches (edited in R. Borger, "Gott Marduk und Gott-König Šulgi als Propheten: Zwei prophetische Texte," *BO* 28 [1971] 3–24; partially translated in W. Beyerlin, ed., *Near Eastern Religious Texts Relating to the Old Testament* [Philadelphia: Westminster Press, 1978] 119–122; the prophecies earlier published as Text C and Text D [Grayson and Lambert, "Akkadian Prophecies," 7–8, 19–22, 26–28, 30] belong to the Marduk and Shulgi speeches); the Uruk Prophecy (edited and translated in UVB 26–27 [1972] 87 and plate 25; H. Hunger, *Spätbabylonische Texte aus Uruk*, Teil 1 [Berlin: Gebr. Mann, 1976] 21–23; and H. Hunger and S. A. Kaufman, "A New Akkadian Prophecy Text," *JAOS* 95 [1975] 371–375); and the Dynastic Prophecy (A. K. Grayson, *Babylonian Historical-Literary Texts* [Toronto: University of Toronto Press, 1975] 24–37). In addition, several fragmentary prophecies have been identified. See the discussion of Grayson and Lambert, "Akkadian Prophecies," 8–9; and Grayson, *Historical-Literary Texts*, 22–23. Text B and LBAT 1543 were previously identified as prophecies (Grayson and Lambert, "Akkadian Prophecies," 7, 16–19, 24–25, 29; R. D. Biggs, "More Babylonian 'Prophecies,'" *Iraq* 29 [1967] 117–132). However, both of these texts have affinities with astrological omens and probably belong to one of the genres of omen literature rather than to the genre of the prophecies. On this point, see Grayson, *Historical-Literary Texts*, 15. Because the Akkadian prophecies more closely resemble biblical apocalyptic literature than they do biblical prophetic literature, some scholars have designated these texts "Akkadian apocalypses" (W. W. Hallo, "Akkadian Apocalypses," *IEJ* 16 [1966] 231–242). However, although the texts do indeed seem to be related to apocalyptic literature, they do not have the form of a classical apocalypse. Therefore, it seems best for the time being to retain the traditional designation "prophecies." For a brief form-critical study of the texts, see the original editions cited above and J.-G. Heintz, "Note sur les origines de l'apocalyptique judaïque à la lumière des 'prophéties akkadiennes,' " F. Raphaël et al., *L'apocalyptique* (Paris: Paul Geuthner, 1977) 71–87.

(*šarru* [LUGAL]) will arise." The rulers are never explicitly named, but sometimes their countries are identified and the exact length of their reigns indicated. Each reign is then evaluated positively or negatively. Usually the evaluation is given in general terms using stereotypical phrases drawn from omen apodoses, but sometimes there are specific references to military expeditions, building activities, or internal political affairs. The following example is typical of the standard pattern:

> A prince will arise and rule for thirteen years. There will be an Elamite attack on Akkad and the booty of Akkad will be carried off. The shrines of the great gods will be destroyed. Akkad will suffer a defeat. There will be confusion, disturbance, and disorder in the land. The nobility will lose prestige. Another man who is unknown will arise, seize the throne as king, and put his grandees to the sword. He will fill the wadis of Tuplijaš, the open country and hills, with half the extensive army of Akkad. The people will suffer need (and) hardship.[72]

The two texts whose endings have been preserved (the Marduk and Shulgi prophecies) conclude the historical survey with an elaboration of the reign of the ruler who was the real focus of the writer's interest.

It is clear that the Akkadian prophecies are "predictions after the event" (*vaticinia ex eventu*) and that at least some of them were produced in order to support their creators' views of current political events. By grounding contemporary events and the evaluation of those events in prophecies from ancient gods or kings, the writers were able to claim supernatural support for their own views. The propagandistic function of the prophecies can be seen most clearly in the Marduk prophetic speech. This text was undoubtedly produced during the reign of Nebuchadnezzar I (ca. 1124–1103 B.C.), who succeeded in bringing back the statue of Marduk from captivity in Elam. With this act began the renaissance of Babylonian power and the exaltation of Marduk to a position of preeminence in the pantheon.[73] These events are prophesied in the Marduk prophetic speech, where the god predicts the coming of an unnamed king who

72. Text A, side 1, col. 2, ll. 9–18; translation from Grayson and Lambert, "Akkadian Prophecies," 14.

73. For the evidence bearing on these events, see W. G. Lambert, "The Reign of Nebuchadnezzar I: A Turning Point in the History of Ancient Mesopotamian Religion," *The Seed of Wisdom: Essays in Honour of T. J. Meek* (ed. W. S. McCullough; Toronto: University of Toronto Press, 1964) 3–13.

will return the divine statue to Babylon and rebuild the god's temple. A long and successful reign is forecast for this king, and his rule is characterized as one of prosperity and fertility. This text was presumably used by the priests of Marduk to support the exaltation of their god and perhaps also by Nebuchadnezzar himself to lend authority to his political and religious policies. The text was probably created by scribes connected with the royal court and can therefore be analyzed as a literary form of central intermediation having social maintenance functions.

The function of the closely related Shulgi prophetic speech is not so easily determined because of the poor condition of the text, but the cities of Nippur and Babylon are frequently mentioned. It is therefore possible that the text was used to give divine support to the religious and political claims of one or both of these cities. If the text dealt with the exaltation of Babylon, then its general social setting might have been similar to that of the Marduk prophetic speech.[74]

The Uruk Prophecy may have also had functions analogous to those of the Shulgi prophetic speech, although it is difficult to determine precisely the historical events referred to in the Uruk text. However, the focus of the text is the fate of Uruk under a series of rulers, who either repress the city or allow it to flourish. The text ends by predicting the advent of a king in Uruk who will exercise worldwide dominion and establish an eternal dynasty. It is possible that the Uruk Prophecy was created by the unnamed king to support his royal claims.[75] On the other hand, the text's persistent focus on the city of Uruk itself suggests that the prophecies may have been used to undergird the city's claims to higher status or more benevolent royal treatment. If so, then the text had peripheral functions and was probably created by priests of Uruk as part of a campaign to secure better treatment for the city in exchange for supporting the new monarch.[76]

A peripheral function may have also been served by the Dynastic

---

74. For other suggestions, see Grayson, *Historical-Literary Texts*, 16.

75. Hunger and Kaufman ("A New Akkadian Prophecy Text," 373–375) argue that this unnamed king is Amel-Marduk (561–560), whose brief reign was plagued by instability. The text might therefore have been created by Amel-Marduk in order to bolster his own claim to power.

76. Note the similar suggestion of Hunger and Kaufman, ibid., 374–375. For a different interpretation, see P. Höffken, "Heilszeitherrschererwartung im babylonischen Raum," *WO* 9 (1977) 57–71.

Prophecy, which forecasts a series of good and evil kings. The text also predicts the fall of several dynasties, and after each change of dynasty the new dynastic founder is evaluated either positively or negatively. Good and evil dynastic founders seem to alternate regularly throughout the tablet, so that a good founding ruler is always followed by an evil one. The dynasties are never identified explicitly, but the ones at the end of the series are nevertheless readily identifiable. The text in its present broken form ends with the fall of the Persian Empire and the appearance of the first Macedonian king, an event which is evaluated positively. However, the original text apparently contained references to one more dynasty, which, if the pattern holds, would have been evaluated negatively. The event described on this missing end of the tablet may have been the capture of Babylon by Seleucus I (312 B.C.). If so, then the whole text may have been a piece of anti-Seleucid propaganda and may have expressed the oppressed Babylonians' views of their new rulers.[77] A similar peripheral function may have been served by Text A, although the poor state of the text does not permit speculation on this point.[78]

The Akkadian prophecies thus seem to have functioned peripherally and centrally, encouraging both the alteration of religious and social conditions and the preservation and support of the central social structure. The texts therefore had functions analogous to those of oral prophetic messages and demonstrate a basic similarity between written and oral prophecy.

The Nature and Social Functions of Prophecy in Mesopotamia

The limited evidence on prophecy in Mesopotamia suggests that the basic forms of intermediation attested there generally fit the patterns documented in contemporary anthropological studies of intermediation. In Mesopotamia, as in modern cultures, society played an important role in validating and training certain types of intermediaries, such as the diviners, and in discouraging other types, such as the oracular speakers. Both the diviners and oracular speakers seem to have exhibited stereotypical behavior, perhaps

77. Grayson, *Historical-Literary Texts*, 17–19.
78. For an attempt to reconstruct the historical events lying behind the predictions of Text A, see Hallo, "Akkadian Apocalypses," 235–239.

including characteristic speech patterns, and in both cases society seems to have played a role in regulating and even determining the intermediaries' behavior. Finally, intermediaries in Mesopotamia had social functions similar to those of their modern counterparts. The central intermediaries were clearly the diviners, who throughout Mesopotamian history operated within the central social structure to preserve it and to insure social stability and orderly change. In contrast, most of the oracular speakers were peripheral figures, operating on the fringes of society to bring about changes in social and religious conditions. These individuals were tolerated by the larger society but were also subject to subtle social pressures designed to curb their activities. The oracular speakers did have their own support groups, however, and sometimes played a role in peripheral cults. The peripheral status of oracular speakers changed somewhat in the Neo-Assyrian period, when some of these figures had functions that were more central than peripheral. However, even then the appearance of the speakers within the royal court may have been due at least in part to political expediency rather than to a genuine change in their status. In the end they never replaced the diviners as the central intermediaries of Mesopotamian society.

PROPHECY IN EGYPT

Egyptologists have traditionally applied the label "prophecies" to a relatively rare genre of Egyptian texts which contain predictions of future events. Although biblical scholars have sometimes used these texts to interpret Israelite prophecy and apocalyptic, they in fact reveal little about the nature of prophecy in Egypt. Most of the figures to which the "prophecies" are attributed are not intermediaries and do not claim to derive their messages from the supernatural world. Rather, the prophecies are usually thought to come from the wisdom and perceptiveness of the speaker. However, because these texts somewhat resemble the Akkadian prophecies and may be relevant to the study of apocalyptic, we will discuss briefly the Egyptian evidence.[79]

79. For a survey of the role that the Egyptian prophecies have played in the study of Israelite prophecy, see L. Ramlot, "Prophétisme," DBSup 8(1972) 812–823. The most thorough study of the whole subject is G. Lanczkowski, Altägyptischer Prophetismus (Wiesbaden: Otto Harrassowitz, 1960), although this work must be read along with the more balanced treatment of Ramlot, "Prophétisme," 818–868. See also the treatments of C. C. McCown, "Hebrew and Egyptian Apocalyptic Liter-

Almost all of the Egyptian prophecies have roughly the same form, although they do not all seem to have had the same social function. All of the texts picture the speaker standing in the presence of the king and delivering messages dealing with the future and sometimes with the present as well. This literary structure is particularly clear in the three longest texts. "King Cheops and the Magicians" (Papyrus Westcar), a text probably to be dated to the Twelfth Dynasty, shows the king being entertained by a succession of his sons, each of whom tells him a miraculous tale. The series of stories reaches its climax in the recital of a son who tells the king of a contemporary old man named Dedi, who possesses secret and particularly miraculous powers. The king visits Dedi, who demonstrates his powers and then predicts the birth of three kings who will found a new dynasty and bring to an end Cheops' royal line. A brief appendix to the tale describes the gods fulfilling the sage's prophecy.[80] The original social function of the text is unclear, and it may have been created simply as literature.

A similar structure is exhibited by "The Admonitions of an Egyptian Sage," in which a wise man named Ipuwer berates the king for permitting lawlessness and chaos in the land. After a long catalogue of social evils, Ipuwer describes the ideal society and exhorts the king to improve conditions. The social function of the text is not precisely clear, but it may have been used to instruct kings in the characteristics of good and bad government. Alternatively, the text may have been composed to praise and support a good king, whose prosperous reign was contrasted with the chaotic state of society under his predecessors.[81]

In "The Prophecies of Neferti" both the structure and the function of the text are clear. The work begins with the Fourth Dynasty king Snefru requesting his courtiers to supply him with entertain-

----

ature," *HTR* 18 (1925) 357–411; and F. Nötscher, "Prophetie im Umkreis des alten Israel," *BZ* n.s. 10 (1966) 163–170. Important bibliographical material on many of the texts has been collected in J. Leclant, "Éléments pour une étude de la divination dans l'Égypt pharonique," *La divination*, 1. 1–9. It should be noted that the title *ḥm-nṯr*, conventionally translated "prophet," actually designates a type of priest who in no way resembles the Israelite prophets.

80. For a translation and brief discussion, together with the original publication data, see W. K. Simpson, *The Literature of Ancient Egypt* (2d ed.; New Haven: Yale University Press, 1973) 15–30; and A. Erman, *The Ancient Egyptians* (ed. W. K. Simpson; New York: Harper & Row, 1966) xxiv, lxviii–lxix, 36–49.

81. Simpson, *Literature*, 210–229; Erman, *Ancient Egyptians*, xxix–xxx, 92–108; *ANET*, 441–444; J. van Seters, *The Hyksos* (New Haven: Yale University Press, 1966) 114–115.

ment. They respond by summoning the lector-priest Neferti, who describes to the king in horrifying detail the chaos that will descend on Egypt in the future. Order will finally be restored by a righteous king, who will once again bring justice and peace to the land. The text was undoubtedly composed in the time of the usurper king Ammenemes I (Twelfth Dynasty), who used it to support his government. The text was thus used as political propaganda within the social structure and in this respect had functions similar to those of some of the Akkadian prophecies.[82]

The remaining Egyptian prophecies are somewhat fragmentary, so it is sometimes difficult to know how to interpret them. "The Prophecy of the Lamb" is contained in a Demotic papyrus dated ca. 7 A.D., during the reign of Augustus. The papyrus relates that during the brief reign of the Egyptian king Bocchoris (ca. 718–712 B.C.) a "lamb" delivered to the king a long, detailed account of the events that would occur in Egypt during the next nine hundred years. For most of this time the kingdom was to be racked by social upheaval and injustice, although the lamb predicted that at the end of nine hundred years there would be a sudden change in Egypt's fortunes. Justice and political stability would again appear, and the former evil era would come to an end. The structural similarities between "The Prophecy of the Lamb" and "The Prophecies of Neferti" suggest that both texts may have had the same function, but the fragmentary condition of the former text prevents further speculation on this point.[83]

---

82. This text has been extensively studied and is available in several modern editions and translations. See Simpson, *Literature*, 7–8, 234–240; Erman, *Ancient Egyptians*, xxx, 110–115; *ANET*, 444–446; W. Helck, *Die Prophezeiung des Nfr.tj* (Wiesbaden: Otto Harrassowitz, 1970); and H. Goedicke, *The Protocol of Neferyt* (Baltimore: Johns Hopkins University Press, 1977). The propagandistic function of the text is thoroughly treated in G. Posener, *Littérature et politique dans l'Égypte de la XIIe dynastie* (Paris: Librairie ancienne Honoré Champion, 1956) 21–60, 145–157.

83. "The Prophecy of the Lamb" was originally edited in J. Krall, "Vom König Bokchoris," *Festgaben zu ehren Max Büdinger's* (Innsbruck: Wagner, 1898) 3–11; and has been reedited in J. M. A. Janssen, "Over Farao Bocchoris," *Varia Historica aangeboden aan Professor Doctor A. W. Byvanck* (Assen: Van Gorcum, 1954) 17–29. The precise nature of the "lamb" is uncertain. It has been suggested that "lamb" is a personal name, a title, or a reference to the ram god Amun or Ḥnum. On the other hand, other texts mentioning the lamb describe it as having had two heads, four horns, eight legs, and two tails. This description suggests that the lamb was envisioned as a genuine, though miraculous, animal. See the discussion of L. Kákosy, "Prophecies of Ram Gods," *Acta Orientalia* (Hung.) 19 (1966) 344–345; and R. Dunand, "L'oracle du potier et la formation de l'apocalyptique en Égypte," F. Raphaël et al., *L'apocalyptique* (Paris: Librairie Orientaliste Paul Geuthner, 1977) 50–51.

The function of the "Oracle of the Potter" is somewhat clearer. This work is known from a Greek papyrus written in the second or third century A.D., but the contents of the oracle undoubtedly reflect an older original. The text describes a speech that a potter made before an Egyptian king named Amenophis (Amenophis III?). The potter describes first the future evils that will appear when Egypt is governed by foreign rulers and then the return to normalcy that will accompany the restoration of Egyptian self-rule. The foreign rulers mentioned in the text are presumably the Persians and the Greeks, and the whole text is probably to be interpreted as the work of an oppressed group in Ptolemaic Egypt that was attempting to resist the pressures of Hellenism. If this interpretation is correct, then the text is a form of written prophecy that had peripheral functions within Egyptian society. By means of the prophecy, the oppressed authors sought to reform the current political situation and tried to return political power to their own hands. The text may have continued to function in this way in later times when the Romans would have replaced the Ptolemies as the oppressors.[84]

The work traditionally called "The Demotic Chronicle" may also have been created as political propaganda. This text was written in the Ptolemaic period and contains a number of obscure oracles, each of which is interpreted by the writer. The interpretations contain historical references to political events preceding the writer's time, and the series apparently ended with a description of a future ruler who would lead an insurrection that would destroy the power of the Greeks and return the country to Egyptian control. The text then reviews the recent history of Egypt, evaluating each ruler on the basis of how well he adhered to the writer's political and religious views. The text as a whole was probably created by the same sort of oppressed group responsible for the "Oracle of the Potter" and served to articulate the group's distinctive views. The text is thus another example of peripheral prophecy in written form.[85]

84. E. Lobel and C. H. Roberts, *The Oxyrhynchus Papyri*, Part XXII (London: Egypt Exploration Society, 1954) 89–99; Dunand, "L'oracle du potier," 41–67; L. Koenen, "Die Prophezeiungen des 'Topfers,'" *Zeitschrift für Papyrologie und Epigraphik* 2 (1968) 178–209; Ramlot, "Prophétisme," 834–837; Kákosy, "Prophecies of Ram Gods," 345–346, 355–356; and McCown, "Hebrew and Egyptian Apocalyptic Literature," 397–403.

85. For a thorough discussion of the text, see F. Daumas, "Littérature prophétique et exégétique egyptienne et commentaires esséniens," *A la rencontre de Dieu: Mémorial Albert Gelin* (Le Puy: Editions Xavier Mappus, 1961) 203–221. Cf. Ramlot, "Prophétisme," 837–838; McCown, "Hebrew and Egyptian Apocalyptic Literature," 387–392; and Kákosy, "Prophecies of Ram Gods," 355–356.

The stress which all of the Egyptian prophecies place on wisdom
and perception, the court setting of the speaker's activities, and the
predominant political concerns of the texts all suggest that this material was produced by scribes or other members of the Egyptian
royal court. The texts functioned within the central government,
but the precise nature of their function depended on the state
of Egyptian society. As long as the country was under Egyptian
control, the prophecies had social maintenance functions. They
affirmed traditional views of morality and government, sought to
prevent rapid social change, and undergirded government policies.
However, when foreign rulers were in control of the country and
Egyptian court officials found that they no longer had power within
the central government, the same genre of texts functioned peripherally. Through the prophecies the writers attempted to reform the
existing social order and sought to regain their positions at the
center of society.

Although the Egyptian prophecies are not routinely presented as
direct messages from a deity, there is evidence that direct contact
with the divine world did take place in Egypt. Various types of
divination are attested in Egyptian texts, and in particular there are
a number of references to divine oracles. These oracles were given
in response to an inquiry but do not seem to have been surrounded
by the elaborate rituals that were connected with divination in
Mesopotamia. In Egypt a person seeking an oracle would usually
make his request while the god's statue was being carried on a bark
as part of an out-of-doors ritual procession. The petitioner phrased
his question so that it could be answered either yes or no, and then
presented it orally (or occasionally in writing) before the god. The
god replied by forcing his priestly bearers to carry his bark forward
(yes) or backward (no). Sometimes other movements of the divine
statue were interpreted as indications of the god's response. Oracles
of this type were clearly part of the central social structure and
occurred in cultic contexts. Through the oracles the gods dispensed
justice and made decisions that encouraged the stability of Egyptian
society.[86]

86. For a discussion of divination in Egypt, see Leclant, "Éléments pour une étude
de la divination," 1–23. Egyptian oracles are discussed in R. A. Parker, *A Saite
Oracle Papyrus from Thebes* (Providence: Brown University Press, 1962), especially
pp. 35–48 ["Egyptian Oracles," by J. Černý]; Kákosy, "Prophecies of Ram Gods,"
341–356; and A. M. Blackman, "Oracles in Ancient Egypt," *The Journal of Egyptian
Archaeology* 11 (1925) 249–255; 12 (1926) 176–185.

PROPHECY IN PALESTINE AND SYRIA

In spite of the fact that Canaanite prophecy is sometimes thought to have been an important influence on prophecy in Israel, there are actually very few nonbiblical references to Palestinian or Syrian intermediaries, and these references shed little light on the role of prophecy in the societies that were Israel's immediate neighbors.[87] The earliest published reference to Canaanite prophecy occurs in the Egyptian story of Wen-Amon, portions of which reflect conditions in Phoenicia around 1100 B.C.[88] In the relevant portion of the text, Wen-Amon visits the port of Byblos and seeks to remain there until he can settle a matter having to do with some stolen silver. The ruler of Byblos is at first unwilling to allow Wen-Amon to stay, but while the ruler is sacrificing to his gods, the Egyptian god Amon seizes one of the ruler's pages and through him demands that Wen-Amon be permitted to remain in the city (1, 38–40). The Egyptian term used to describe the page's behavior is elsewhere used to indicate possession by a spirit, and the determinative before the term depicts a human in violent motion. This suggests that possession behavior at Byblos involved stereotypical physiological manifestations, although their exact nature cannot be accurately deduced from the text. Although the page was possessed during a ritual, there is no indication that he was acting in any official capacity, and the social function of his message is uncertain. The fact that he is possessed by an Egyptian god rather than a Canaanite deity is reminiscent of peripheral possession, but the role which the inci-

---

87. For discussions of the Canaanite background of Israelite prophecy, see above, ch. 3, n. 1. Much of the evidence on the nature of Canaanite prophecy comes from relatively late Greek and Latin texts, the accuracy of which cannot be determined. See R. de Vaux, "The Prophets of Baal on Mount Carmel," in his *The Bible and the Ancient Near East* (Garden City, N.Y.: Doubleday, 1971) 238–251.

88. The following discussion is based on the recent edition of H. Goedicke, *The Report of Wenamun* (Baltimore: Johns Hopkins University Press, 1975), especially pp. 53–57. Cf. the translation in *ANET*, 25–29. Earlier references to Syrian prophecy may be present in the recently discovered archive from Ebla, where the word *nabi ꜣūtum* is said to occur along with the *mahhû* in cultic contexts (G. Pettinato, "The Royal Archives of Tell Mardikh-Ebla," *BĀ* 39 [1976] 49, "Relations entre les royaumes d'Ebla et de Mari au troisième millénaire, d'après les archives royales de Tell Mardikh-Ebla," *Akkadica* 2 [1977] 21). *Nabi ꜣūtum* is presumably related to Hebrew *nābîꜣ*, the most common title given to the Israelite prophets. However, until the relevant texts are published, nothing can safely be said about the nature or even the existence of intermediaries at Ebla. The existence of prophecy at Ugarit has been argued on the basis of *CTA* 32 (A. van Selms, "CTA 32: A Prophetic Liturgy," *UF* 3 [1971] 235–248). However, no intermediary is actually mentioned in connection with this text, and the text as a whole is too vague to support the argument.

dent plays in advancing the plot of the story suggests that the account has been colored by the perceptions of the Egyptian narrator. It would therefore be unwise to attempt to derive from the story specific details about the nature of Phoenician intermediation.

A more helpful reference to Syrian intermediaries occurs in an Aramaic inscription of Zakir, the king of Hamath and Lu‹ash.[89] The inscription, which is traditionally dated to the end of the ninth century or the beginning of the eighth century B.C., relates that when Zakir was confronted by a powerful coalition of enemy kings that had besieged one of his cities, he "lifted his hand" (prayed) to his god, Ba‹al-Shamayn. The god then answered him (wy‹nny) by means of seers and intermediaries ([b]yd ḥzyn wbyd ‹ddn). Ba‹al-Shamayn promised the king divine aid and foretold the destruction of the enemy coalition. The seers (ḥzyn) mentioned in the text are presumably related to similar figures mentioned in the Hebrew Bible, where the title "seer" (ḥōzeh) is applied to a particular type of Israelite intermediary. The etymology of the word here translated "intermediaries" (‹ddn) is uncertain, but comparative evidence clearly links the root ‹dd with intermediation. The root occurs in Ugaritic in several broken contexts, but in one instance it is probably parallel to a form of ṯwb, "to answer or reply" (CTA 4, col. 3, ll. 10–11). This suggests that ‹dd means "to give a message" or something similar. The root may also appear in Mandaic, although the only occurrence is too obscure to shed any light on the meaning of the word. The root ‹dd may lie behind the personal name Iddo (‹iddô / ‹iddō› / ‹iddô›), which occurs several times in the Hebrew Bible. Some of the figures bearing this name were connected with prophecy, and others played cultic roles. The prophet Zechariah traces his genealogy to Iddo the prophet (nābî› [Zech 1:1; cf. Ezra 5:1; 6:14]). Iddo appears twice in Chronicles as the author of a noncanonical book. In one reference Iddo is called a seer (ḥōzeh [2 Chr 12:15]), while in the other reference he is labeled a prophet (nābî› [2 Chr 13:22]). These two texts may refer to the same individual, who may also have been the ancestor of Zechariah, although there is no direct evidence on this point. A person named Iddo is also known to have been a postexilic priest (Neh 12:4, 16), and the name is given to a Levitical descendant of Gershom (1 Chr 6:6 [6:21]). The evidence thus suggests that Iddo

89. KAI 202; translated in ANET, 655–656.

may have been a family name (and perhaps originally a title) that was used by prophets and priests in postexilic Israel.[90] The root ʿdd may also lie behind the personal name Oded (ʿōdēd / ʿôdēd). In 2 Chr 15:1, Azariah the son of Oded is said to have been possessed by the spirit of God and to have delivered an oracle to Asa, the king of Judah. Much later, in the time of Ahaz, an Israelite prophet (nābîʾ) named Oded delivered a message condemning the Israelites for killing a large number of the inhabitants of Judah (2 Chr 28:8–11). The name Oded thus seems to be connected with prophecy, and if the name is really derived from ʿdd, its participial form suggests that the name may have once been the title of a particular type of Israelite intermediary. This might also explain the problematic Hebrew text of 2 Chr 15:8, where the oracle of Azariah the "son" of Oded is attributed to Oded, who is called a prophet (nābîʾ). The latter designation may be a gloss to explain the older title, which was no longer understood.[91]

Although the Zakir inscription does not indicate the distinctive behavioral characteristics of the ḥzyn and ʿddn, the text does throw considerable light on their social roles. Both types of intermediaries were part of the central social structure and probably carried out their activities in the context of the cult. When the king prayed for divine aid, the intermediaries delivered to him an oracle of reassurance. A cultic setting for the intermediaries' activities may also be suggested by the structure of the inscription itself, which closely follows the pattern of the biblical psalm of thanksgiving (Danklied).[92] Such psalms were presumably sung at cultic ceremonies in which God was thanked for intervening to help an individual or the whole community, and it is conceivable that the text

90. For a discussion of the nature and use of ancestral names in the ancient Near East, see R. R. Wilson, Genealogy and History in the Biblical World (New Haven: Yale University Press, 1977) 114–118.

91. For a more detailed discussion of the intermediaries mentioned in the Zakir inscription, see J. F. Ross, "Prophecy in Hamath, Israel, and Mari," HTR 63 (1970) 1–28; and J. C. Greenfield, "The Zakir Inscription and the Danklied," Proceedings of the Fifth World Congress of Jewish Studies (Jerusalem: World Union of Jewish Studies, 1969) 1. 175–176.

92. For a discussion of the Hebrew psalms of thanksgiving and a study of the form and content parallels between these psalms and the Zakir inscription, see H. Gunkel, Einleitung in die Psalmen (Göttingen: Vandenhoeck & Ruprecht, 1933) 265–292; F. Crüsemann, Studien zur Formgeschichte von Hymnus und Danklied in Israel (Neukirchen-Vluyn: Neukirchener Verlag, 1969) 155–284; Greenfield, "The Zakir Inscription and the Danklied," 178–191; and H.-J. Zobel, "Das Gebet um Abwendung der Not und seine Erhörung in den Klageliedern des Alten Testaments und in der Inschrift des Königs Zakir von Hamath," VT 21 (1971) 91–99.

inscribed on Zakir's stele was originally used in the same way. If so, then the intermediaries may have played some part in the ritual recitation of the text. However, even if this should prove not to be the case, the content of the Zakir inscription alone is sufficient to demonstrate that intermediaries in Syria had social maintenance functions within the central cult.

A final bit of evidence on intermediaries in Palestine comes from an Aramaic inscription discovered at Deir ʿAlla, a site located in modern Jordan. The inscription, which is written on plaster in black and red ink, is poorly preserved, but on archaeological and paleographical grounds it can be assigned an approximate date of 700 B.C. The first line of the text ascribes the contents to Balaam son of Beor, who is called a seer of the gods (ḥzh ʾlhn; cf. also ll. 5–6). According to the text, the gods came to Balaam by night, and at least one of them gave him a disturbing message. The next morning he began weeping because of the message that he had received, and when people inquired about the reasons for his distress, he told them what the gods had said to him. The contents of the divine message are not clear, and the inscription may have originally contained messages received on several different occasions, but the fragments that have been preserved suggest that the gods delivered oracles of doom or even curses against their adversaries. This picture generally agrees with the one found in Numbers 22—24, where Balaam son of Beor is portrayed as a professional curser, who nevertheless delivers blessings to Israel. Both the Deir ʿAlla inscription and the biblical references undoubtedly refer to the same individual, although he may have already been a traditional figure by the time the texts were written.[93]

In spite of the poor condition of the Deir ʿAlla inscription, it may be possible to make a few deductions about the social setting of Balaam's activities. The text indicates that he received his revelations at night, apparently without actively seeking them. The fact that he is given a title suggests that he may have played a central

---

93. The text is published and thoroughly discussed in J. Hoftijzer and G. van der Kooij, *Aramaic Texts from Deir ʿAlla* (Leiden: E. J. Brill, 1976). See particularly pp. 173–192, 268–282. By slightly rearranging some of the fragments, it is possible to reconstruct a more complete version of the first line than the one proposed by Hoftijzer and van der Kooij. According to this reconstruction, the first line could be translated, "Inscription of Balaam son of Beor; he was a man, a seer of (the) gods, and gods came to him by night. . . ." See the review of J. A. Fitzmyer in *CBQ* 40 (1978) 94–95; and the reconstruction proposed in A. Caquot and A. Lemaire, "Les textes araméens de Deir ʿAlla," *Syria* 54 (1977) 193–202.

role in his society, and this suggestion is reinforced by the very fact that his oracles were preserved both at Deir ʿAlla and in the Bible. Furthermore, the Deir ʿAlla inscription was written on a stele which was originally located in what may have been a cult place or a shrine. This hints at a religious function for the oracles and for Balaam himself. Because the gods that spoke to Balaam seem to have been the chief gods of Deir ʿAlla, the seer may have played a role in the central social structure and may have had social maintenance functions. However, these deductions must remain tentative, both because of the fragmentary state of the inscription and because of the role that tradition may have played in shaping the picture of Balaam preserved in the texts.

PROPHECY AND SOCIETY IN THE ANCIENT NEAR EAST

The evidence that we have been able to glean from ancient Near Eastern sources indicates that intermediation in antiquity had some of the same features that are attested in modern societies. Ancient intermediaries sometimes exhibited stereotypical behavior, which was to some extent shaped by their societies. Particularly in Mesopotamia, certain types of intermediaries were required to deliver oracles in specific contexts and were expected to conform to relatively rigid behavioral patterns. This was especially true of central intermediaries, such as the diviner. Like their modern counterparts, ancient Near Eastern intermediaries were related to their societies in complex ways and had a number of different functions. Some intermediaries, such as the Mesopotamian diviners and the Palestinian seers, were part of the central social structure, which they helped to regulate and maintain. Such figures were carefully selected, trained, and supported by the whole society or at least by the ruling elite. On the other hand, some intermediaries, such as the Mesopotamian oracular speakers, were peripheral figures who delivered messages aimed at reforming the political and religious establishments. These individuals were supported by small groups and were tolerated by the larger society only so long as they did not become disruptive. Some peripheral figures were taken seriously when it served the purposes of the rulers, but finally these intermediaries were held in check by the use of social pressure. Their oracles were sometimes tested by the religious establishment, and other subtle control mechanisms were also employed.

The Near Eastern material thus suggests that the relationship between ancient prophets and their societies was fully as complex as the relationship between prophet and society in modern cultures. It is therefore reasonable to suppose that prophecy in Israel exhibited similar complexity. This supposition must now be tested by a comprehensive survey of the biblical evidence.

4

Prophecy in Israel:
The Ephraimite
Tradition

The importance of prophecy in the Ephraimite tradition is indicated by the numerous references to prophetic activity in the literature produced by this tradition. In addition to preserving collections of oracles, the books of Hosea and Jeremiah both contain extensive "biographical" narratives *about* prophets, while prophetic narratives appear regularly throughout the Deuteronomic History. The literature of the Ephraimite tradition therefore sheds a great deal of light on the relationship between prophecy and society in the groups that carried the tradition. These groups presumably supported at least some of the Ephraimite prophets and provided the social base from which prophetic activity was directed to the larger society. In order to determine Ephraimite views on prophecy, we will examine in turn each prophetic figure in the tradition, paying particular attention to the prophet's characteristic behavior, his relationship to a support group, the arena of his prophetic activity, and his various social functions. On the basis of this examination we will then be able to make some generalizations about the relationship between prophecy and society among the Ephraimite groups.

CHARACTERISTIC SPEECH IN THE
EPHRAIMITE TRADITION

Although the prophets of the Ephraimite tradition emerge from the narratives as individuals with distinctive social contexts and

functions, the biblical literature itself does use somewhat stereotypical language to describe the words and actions of these figures and
to speak about prophecy in general. It is difficult to determine precisely when this language became a part of the developing biblical
tradition, and it is possible that the stereotypical features of the text
are the work of the final authors or editors. However, the pervasive-
ness of some of this language suggests that it reflects to a certain
extent the way in which Ephraimites actually talked about
prophecy and the characteristic way in which Ephraimite prophets
themselves talked. Because stereotypical speech is a common feature of most intermediaries, we will survey briefly the biblical evidence on this point before turning to an examination of individual
prophets.

Prophetic Titles

The Prophet (nābî)

The title most frequently given to intermediaries in the Ephraimite tradition is nābî, "prophet." In various nominal forms, this
designation occurs slightly over 200 times in the Ephraimite literature, with the majority of the occurrences being in the
Deuteronomic History (107) and in Jeremiah (87). In contrast, the
title appears only about 30 times in preexilic prophetic literature
outside of the Ephraimite tradition, and of these occurrences 17 are
in Ezekiel, a book which also exhibits other characteristically
Ephraimite features. The title appears sporadically in postexilic
literature and is used especially in Chronicles (33 times), although
some of these occurrences are in passages quoted from Kings.[1]
These statistics suggest that although the title nābî was not the
exclusive property of the Ephraimite tradition, the designation
played an important role in that tradition's view of prophecy.

Unfortunately, the title nābî itself indicates very little about the
characteristics of the figures to whom it was applied. The rare extrabiblical occurrences of the title throw no light on its meaning,
and the etymology of the word nābî itself is uncertain.[2] Nābî is

1. For a discussion of the distribution of the word nābî, see R. Rendtorff,
"Prophētēs : nābî in the Old Testament," *TDNT* 6 (1968) 799–809.
2. The only certain occurrence of the title is in one of the Lachish ostraca, where a
letter is said to have been delivered by "the prophet" (hnb) (Lachish Ostracon No.
3, *KAI* 193:20). For a discussion of this text, see D. W. Thomas, *"The Prophet" in the
Lachish Ostraca* (London: Tyndale Press, 1945); idem, "Again 'The Prophet' in the

probably related to the Akkadian verb *nabû*, "to call, to announce, to name," but it is uncertain whether the form has an active or a passive meaning. *Qātîl* forms in Hebrew are sometimes active, and for this reason *nābî* has been taken to mean "one who calls or announces."[3] However, Hebrew *qātîl* forms can also have passive force, and if this interpretation of *nābî* is accepted, the title would refer to "one who has been called."[4] It is impossible to choose between these two options on the basis of the Hebrew data alone, but Akkadian evidence seems to support a passive interpretation. The Akkadian noun *nabīum*, "one who has been called," appears in royal epithets and in sentence names as early as the Old Akkadian period.[5] If this noun is related to the morphologically similar Hebrew noun *nābî*, then the prophetic title would also designate one who has been called. However, it is no longer possible to determine precisely how the Ephraimites understood this designation.

Because the etymology of the title *nābî* throws little light on the characteristics of this figure, scholars have turned to an analysis of the Hebrew verbal forms derived from the root **nb*. The Hebrew Bible uses this root only in the niphal and hithpael, and both of these forms are assumed to be denominatives of the noun *nābî*. However, the semantic distinction between these two verb forms is difficult to establish, for they often appear together and seem to carry the same meaning (for example, 1 Sam 10:5, 6, 10, 11, 13; Jer 26:20; Ezek 37:9–10). Therefore, most scholars assume that any original distinction between the two forms has been lost, and both are usually translated "to prophesy."[6] When scholars do try to reconstruct the original distinction between the two forms, some varia-

Lachish Ostraca," *Von Ugarit nach Qumran* (BZAW 77, ed. J. Hempel and L. Rost; Berlin: Alfred Töpelmann, 1961) 244–249; and H.-P. Müller, "Notizen zu althebräischen Inschriften I," *UF* 2 (1970) 241–242. The import of the reported occurrence of the title at Ebla can be assessed only after the relevant text has been published. See above, p. 129, n. 88.

3. F. Haeussermann, *Wortempfang und Symbol in der alttestamentlichen Prophetie* (Giessen: Alfred Töpelmann, 1932) 8–10; A. Haldar, *Associations of Cult Prophets among the Ancient Semites* (Uppsala: Almqvist & Wiksell, 1945) 109.

4. W. F. Albright, *From the Stone Age to Christianity* (Garden City, N.Y.: Doubleday, 1957) 303; cf. A. Guillaume, *Prophecy and Divination among the Hebrews and Other Semites* (London: Hodder and Stoughton, 1938) 112–113; Rendtorff, "*Prophētēs*," 796–797; and A. R. Johnson, *The Cultic Prophet in Ancient Israel* (Cardiff: University of Wales, 1944; 2d ed., 1962) 24–25.

5. For the references, see *AHW* 697–698, s.v. *nabīum*.

6. See the survey of H. H. Rowley, "The Nature of Old Testament Prophecy in the Light of Recent Study," *HTR* 38 (1945) 1–38 (=H. H. Rowley, *The Servant of the Lord*, [2d ed.; Oxford: Blackwell, 1965] 95–134; see especially 103–115).

tion of the following semantic development is usually suggested: The hithpael forms, which predominate in the early texts, originally indicated ecstatic activity. The few niphal forms occurring in early texts also seem to have had links to ecstasy, although this is not entirely certain. Soon, however, the niphal came to be associated only with intelligible prophetic speech, while the hithpael continued to be used to describe ecstatic prophetic activity. As the niphal forms became more common in the period of classical prophecy, the meaning of the hithpael gradually merged with that of the more common niphal, until finally the two were used interchangeably.[7]

If this reconstruction is accepted, then it would suggest that the early Israelite prophets were characterized by ecstatic behavior and that this behavior gradually disappeared over the course of Israel's history. However, this view cannot be supported by the biblical evidence. In fact the hithpael of *nbɔ sometimes appears in passages where there are no clear indications of ecstatic behavior, so the occurrences of this form cannot be used to support the notion that ecstasy was the chief characteristic of the early nābîɔs. Rather, the hithpael of *nbɔ should probably be given a more general meaning. On the analogy of forms such as hithḥāl ("pretend to be sick," "act as if you were sick" [2 Sam 13:5]), hitɔabbēlî ("pretend to mourn," "act like a mourner" [2 Sam 14:2]), and lĕhištaggēaɔ ("to act like a madman" [1 Sam 21:16]), it is probable that hitnabbēɔ originally meant "to act like a prophet," "to exhibit the behavior characteristic of a nābîɔ." In contrast, the niphal forms of *nbɔ were probably originally denominatives meaning simply "to prophesy," "to deliver a prophetic oracle." If this was in fact the case, then the verbal forms of *nbɔ do not specify the behavioral characteristics of the nābîɔ. These characteristics can only be determined on the basis of an examination of the behavior of each prophet.

7. For a defense of this semantic development, see Rendtorff, "Prophētēs," 797–799; Haeussermann, Wortempfang und Symbol, 10–11; W. Jacobi, Die Ekstase der alttestamentlichen Propheten (Munich: Bergmann, 1920) 5–6; A. Jepsen, Nabi: Soziologische Studien zur alttestamentlichen Literatur und Religionsgeschichte (Munich: C. H. Beck, 1934) 5–10; and W. F. Lofthouse, " 'Thus Hath Jahveh Said,' " AJSL 40 (1924) 243. A variation of this development is outlined by S. B. Parker ("Possession Trance and Prophecy in Pre-exilic Israel," VT 28 [1978] 271–275), who suggests that the niphal and hithpael forms of *nbɔ both mean "to be in, or to fall into, a possession trance."

The Seer (rō,eh)

The Ephraimite literature applies the title "seer" (*rō,eh*) only to Samuel, and even in this case the use of the title is confined to the old story of Saul's search for the lost asses (1 Sam 9:11, 18, 19). According to this narrative, which may actually reflect old Ephraimite traditions from the time of Saul, the seer was an intermediary to whom people went to ask questions of God. In return for a fee, the seer used unspecified methods to obtain the desired information (1 Sam 9:5–21). This function of the seer is explicitly stated in an explanatory gloss in 1 Sam 9:9, in which later Ephraimite authors interpreted the meaning of the archaic title. The gloss explains that "previously in Israel, thus people said when going to inquire of God, 'come, let us go to the seer'; for the one who is now called a prophet (*nābî,*) was previously called a seer (*rō,eh*)." This explanation indicates that by the glossator's time the title "seer" had ceased to be used and that this figure's function of inquiring of God had been taken over by the prophet. 1 Samuel 9 also suggests that the seer sometimes delivered unsolicited oracles (1 Sam 9:15–20) and that he may have had cultic connections (1 Sam 9:11–14). However, these references to the cult may have been introduced into the narrative because later tradition saw Samuel both as priest and prophet, and they may not actually indicate that other seers operated in cultic contexts.

Outside of the Ephraimite corpus, the seer is mentioned primarily in Chronicles, where the title is again applied to Samuel (1 Chr 9:22; 26:28; 29:29). A seer named Hanani is also said to have delivered a judgment oracle against Asa, king of Judah (2 Chr 16:7–10). This individual is mentioned in the Deuteronomic History as the father of the prophet Jehu (1 Kgs 16:1, 7; cf. 2 Chr 19:2; 20:34), but there is no additional evidence on his characteristic behavior. Seers appear in earlier Jerusalemite literature in Isa 30:10, where they are set in poetic parallelism with "visionaries" (*hōzîm*). However, this reference gives no indication of the characteristics of the seers, and the term may have been included in the text only for poetic reasons.

The biblical evidence thus suggests that seers existed in Ephraim at an early period but that they disappeared shortly after the rise of the monarchy. They seem to have served as channels of communication between God and the people, inquiring of God on behalf of the people and delivering oracles from God to the people. Both of these functions were later taken over by the prophet, who became the primary intermediary within the Ephraimite tradition. The etymology of the title suggests that the seer may have derived his oracles from dreams, visions, or divination, but outside of the account of Samuel's (dream?) experience in 1 Sam 3:2–18 there is little in the texts to indicate the seer's characteristic methods.[8]

The Man of God

The title "man of God" (ʾîš [hā]ĕlōhîm) occurs about sixty-six times in the Ephraimite corpus and is widely attested in extrabiblical literature. The phrase "man of God" should probably be understood to mean "servant of God," and there is some indication that the designation was an honorific title applied to certain members of prophetic groups. However, in the biblical traditions that have been preserved, the man of God is synonymous with the prophet (nābîʾ), and in fact both titles are sometimes applied to the same individual (1 Sam 3:20; 9:6, 7, 8). It is possible that the characteristics of the man of God were originally different from those of the prophet, and the two titles may have been used in different geographical areas, but it is now impossible to separate the two figures.[9]

The "Sons of the Prophets" (bĕnê hannĕbîʾîm)

The use of the title "sons of the prophets" (bĕnê hannĕbîʾîm) is restricted to Ephraimite narratives describing prophetic activity in Israel during the reigns of Ahab, Ahaziah, and Joram (1 Kgs 20:35; 2 Kgs 2:3, 5, 7, 15; 4:1, 38; 5:22; 6:1; 9:1).[10] The title thus seems to have been employed for a relatively brief period of time (ca. 869–

8. For discussions of the seer in Israel see Haeussermann, *Wortempfang und Symbol*, 4–5; Rendtorff, "*Prophētēs*," 809; M. Jastrow, Jr., "Rôʾēh and Ḥōzēh in the Old Testament," *JBL* 28 (1909) 42–56; H. M. Orlinsky, "The Seer in Ancient Israel," *OrAnt* 4 (1965) 153–174; R. Kraetzschmar, *Prophet und Seher im alten Israel* (Tübingen: J. C. B. Mohr, 1901) 19–25; and M. A. Vanden Oudenrijn, "De vocabulis quibusdam, termino *nābîʾ* synonymis," *Bib* 6 (1924–1925) 294–297. It should be noted that most of these studies move beyond the biblical evidence in their attempts to elaborate a picture of the seer's characteristics.

9. For a discussion of the man of God see Rendtorff, "*Prophētēs*," 809; Haldar, *Associations of Cult Prophets*, 126–130; R. Hallevy, "Man of God," *JNES* 17 (1958) 237–244; Vanden Oudenrijn, "De vocabulis quibusdam, termino *nābîʾ* synonymis," 305–309; and N. P. Bratsiotis, "*ʾîsh*," *TDOT* 1 (1977) 233–235.

10. The phrase "son of a prophet" (*ben-nābîʾ*) appears in Amos 7:14 and has often been taken as a singular form of the title "sons of the prophets." Both grammatical and historical considerations weigh against this interpretation, however. We will consider this difficult passage as part of our discussion of Amos.

but you don't discuss it seriously on p. 269

842 B.C.) and is particularly identified with the activities of Elisha. The expression "son of . . ." or "sons of . . ." is frequently used in Semitic to indicate membership in a group or guild, so there is little doubt that "sons of the prophets" was a designation applied to members of some sort of prophetic group.[11] Although loosely structured prophetic bands are attested earlier in Israel's history (1 Sam 10:10; 19:20), the group labeled "sons of the prophets" seems to have had a more rigid structure. As we will see when we analyze the Elijah-Elisha narratives, the group was capable of coordinated social action and had a hierarchical structure. The group was governed by a leader given the title "father" (ʾāb), and upon the death of the leader, the title was transferred to another prophet (2 Kgs 2:12; 6:21; 13:14).[12] Members of the group sometimes lived together (2 Kgs 6:1) and shared common meals (2 Kgs 4:38–41) but were also capable of living independent lives (2 Kgs 4:1).

Little is known of the characteristic behavior of the sons of the prophets. On the basis of 1 Sam 10:5–13, it has been suggested that they were ecstatics, whose incoherent ravings required translation by the prophetic "father."[13] However, the prophets mentioned in this narrative are not given the title "sons of the prophets," so it would be unwise to take the passage as an indication of the behavior of the later group. In addition, the Elisha narratives themselves never portray the sons of the prophets exhibiting ecstatic behavior, so there is really no evidence to indicate that they were ecstatics.[14]

Prophetic Speech Forms

Since the seminal work of Hermann Gunkel, scholars have accumulated a great deal of evidence on the speech patterns that Israelite prophets used to express their messages. These speech

11. For a discussion of the linguistic evidence, see H. Haag, "*Bēn*," *TDOT* 2 (1977) 152–153; J. G. Williams, "The Prophetic 'Father': A Brief Explanation of the Term 'Sons of the Prophets,'" *JBL* 85 (1966) 344; I. Mendelsohn, "Guilds in Ancient Palestine," *BASOR* 80 (1940) 18–19; idem, "Gilds [*sic*] in Babylonia and Assyria," *JAOS* 60 (1940) 68–69.

12. For a discussion of the use of "father" as a title for a group leader, see Williams, "The Prophetic 'Father,'" 344–348; and A. Phillips, "The Ecstatics' Father," *Words and Meanings* (ed. P. R. Ackroyd and B. Lindars; Cambridge: At the University Press, 1968) 183–194.

13. Phillips, "The Ecstatics' Father," 189–194.

14. For a thorough discussion of the title "sons of the prophets," see P. Joüon, "Qu'étaient les 'fils des prophètes,'" *RSR* 16 (1926) 307–312; M. A. Vanden Oudenrijn, "L'expression 'fils des prophètes' et ses analogies," *Bib* 6 (1925) 165–171; and Haldar, *Associations of Cult Prophets*, 134–144.

forms were drawn from all areas of social life and were creatively adapted by the prophets in a variety of ways.[15] For this reason it is difficult to isolate rigid literary genres that are used without variation in the prophetic corpus, and it is even more difficult to uncover a single oracle pattern which is the exclusive property of a single prophet or prophetic tradition. Nevertheless, there is some evidence to suggest that at least one prophetic speech form was characteristic of the Ephraimite tradition, although non-Ephraimite prophets also occasionally employed the form. There is no way to prove that this form actually reflects the stereotypical speech of Ephraimite prophets, but at least the form indicates how Ephraimite writers viewed typical prophetic speech.

In an important analysis of the various forms of prophetic speech, Claus Westermann isolated what he considered to be a basic speech form that originated with the prophets and was not borrowed from other spheres of social life. This form—which he called "the judgment speech to individuals" but which might more accurately be called "the announcement of disaster to individuals"—has roughly the following structure:

A. The commissioning of a messenger.

B. The accusation referring to a specific transgression of the addressee. The transgression mentioned violates a current Israelite law but has not yet been punished. The accusation may be in the form of a question or a declaratory statement and sometimes includes a citation of the words of the addressee.

C. The announcement of judgment based on the accusation and consisting of

    1. the introduction of the announcement by means of phrases such as "thus says the Lord" (*kōh ʾāmar yhwh*), "therefore, thus says the Lord" (*lākēn kōh ʾāmar yhwh*), "for thus says the Lord" (*kî kōh ʾāmar yhwh*), "therefore" (*lākēn*), or *hinnēh;*

    2. the body of the announcement in the form of a direct ad-

15. For a brief history of the form-critical study of the prophetic literature and a survey of recent trends, see J. H. Hayes, "The History of the Form-critical Study of Prophecy," SBLSP 1973, 1. 60–99; W. E. March, "Prophecy," *Old Testament Form Criticism* (ed. J. H. Hayes; San Antonio: Trinity University Press, 1974) 141–177; R. R. Wilson, "Form-critical Investigation of the Prophetic Literature: The Present Situation," SBLSP 1973, 1. 100–127; and G. M. Tucker, "Prophetic Speech," *Int* 32 (1978) 31–45.

dress. The announcement usually has only one part, although it is sometimes expanded in various ways.[16]
It is doubtful that this speech pattern represents the "original" form of prophetic speech, for there are too few clear examples of the form, and there is no solid evidence that it had a formative influence on prophetic speech in general.[17] However, it is instructive to note the passages in which the form occurs. Westermann was able to demonstrate at least traces of the form in the following texts (doubtful examples are in parentheses): 1 Sam 2:27–36; (3:11–14); 13:11–14; 15:10–31; 2 Sam 12; 1 Kgs 11:29–40; 13:1–3; 14:7–14; 17:1; 20:35–43; 21:17–22; 22:13–23; 2 Kgs 1:3–4; 1:6, (16); 20:14–19; 21:10–15; Amos 7:14–17; Isa (7:10–16); 22:15–25; 37:22–30; 38:1 [=2 Kgs 20:1]; 39:3–7 [=2 Kgs 20:14–19]; Jer 20:1–6; 22:10–12, 13–19, 24–27, (28), 30; 28:12–16; (29:21–23); 29:24–32; 36:29–30; 37:17; (Ezek 17:11–21).[18]

This list indicates that the announcement of disaster to individuals is found primarily in the Deuteronomic History. Of the reasonably good examples actually found in prophetic books, the largest number are from prose passages in Jeremiah, where Deuteronomic influence may be involved. Two of the remaining examples (from Isaiah) are duplicates of passages in 2 Kings. When these two examples are eliminated, only three non-Ephraimite examples are left, and of these only one (Amos 7:14–17) can be considered paradigmatic. It therefore appears that Westermann has uncovered a prophetic literary genre that was peculiar to the Ephraimite tradition. This genre at least reflects the Ephraimite writers' views of how prophets spoke and may actually be an indication of the structure of oral prophetic speech in Ephraim.

Prophetic Rhetoric

While it is difficult to isolate whole prophetic speech forms that are exclusively Ephraimite, scholars have long recognized that Ephraimite writers used a distinctive vocabulary. Stereotypical

16. C. Westermann, *Basic Forms of Prophetic Speech* (Philadelphia: Westminster Press, 1967) 137–168.

17. For a more thorough critique of Westermann's work, see Wilson, "Form-critical Investigation of the Prophetic Literature," 114–121.

18. This list is based on Westermann's own analysis (*Basic Forms of Prophetic Speech*, 137). It is possible to question Westermann's interpretation of some of these passages, but to do so does not change the overall pattern of the form's distribution.

Ephraimite speech is particularly visible in Deuteronomy, the Deuteronomic History, and Jeremiah, but there are also traces of it in the Elohistic layer of the Pentateuch and in Hosea.[19] It is therefore not surprising that Ephraimite phraseology also occurs in prophetic oracles and sermons. In Jeremiah in particular, characteristically Ephraimite speech abounds, not only in the prose sections of the book but in the poetic sections as well. To a lesser extent the same is true in Hosea.[20] It is difficult to know how to interpret this evidence. On the one hand, the stereotypical language may simply be the result of consistent editing of the nearly completed biblical text. In this case the linguistic patterns would contribute nothing to our understanding of the actual speech of the prophets. On the other hand, the stereotypical language may indicate that Ephraimite prophets used language that was characteristic of the group that supported them and that they shaped their words and deeds to meet group expectations. If so, then the stereotypical language would indicate that the behavior of Israelite prophets was molded by their support groups in much the same way that contemporary societies influence the behavior of their intermediaries.

The Process of Intermediation

Although Ephraimite sources sometimes speak of prophets receiving divine messages through visions (1 Kgs 22:17–23; Jer 1:11–19), a process which might have involved soul migration, the Ephraimites seem to have regarded spirit possession as the most common means of intermediation. Possession by God's spirit is

---

19. A convenient catalogue of stereotypical Ephraimite phraseology may be found in M. Weinfeld, *Deuteronomy and the Deuteronomic School* (Oxford: At the Clarendon Press, 1972) 320–370.

20. Note particularly the phrases cited in ibid., 350–354, 355–361, 364–370. The "Ephraimite" or "Deuteronomic" phraseology of the Book of Jeremiah has been the subject of a great deal of debate. See, for example, J. P. Hyatt, "The Deuteronomic Edition of Jeremiah," *Vanderbilt Studies in the Humanities* (Nashville: Vanderbilt University Press, 1951) 1. 71–95; J. Bright, "The Date of the Prose Sermons of Jeremiah," *JBL* 70 (1951) 15–35; idem, "The Prophetic Reminiscence: Its Place and Function in the Book of Jeremiah," *Biblical Essays* (Proceedings of the Ninth Meeting of "Die Ou-testamentiese Werkgemeenskap in Suid-Afrika"; Potchefstroom: Pro Rege-Pers, 1966) 11–30; W. L. Holladay, "A Fresh Look at 'Source B' and 'Source C' in Jeremiah," *VT* 25 (1975) 402–412; E. W. Nicholson, *Preaching to the Exiles* (New York: Schocken Books, 1970); H. Weippert, *Die Prosareden des Jeremiabuches* (Berlin: Walter de Gruyter, 1973); and W. Thiel, *Die deuteronomistische Redaktion von Jeremia 1–25* (Neukirchen-Vluyn: Neukirchener Verlag, 1973). We will consider in greater detail some of the problems involved when we examine Jeremiah.

clearly indicated in the following typical Ephraimite descriptions of divine-human communication:

(1) "the hand of the Lord fell upon me" (1 Kgs 18:46; 2 Kgs 3:15; Jer 15:17);[21]

(2) "the spirit rested on them" (Num 11:25–26);

(3) "the spirit of the Lord clothed itself with Gideon" (Judg 6:34).

As we have already noted in our discussion of contemporary intermediation, possession theories are usually characterized by the belief that the possessing spirit takes control of the intermediary and speaks directly through him, with the result that the speech of the intermediary is actually the speech of the spirit. This stress on direct divine speech was also associated with Ephraimite possession theories and is reflected in the tendency to describe prophecy as the reception and delivery of the word of God. This stress on God's words is found to a certain extent in all biblical traditions, but it is especially characteristic of Ephraimite sources and is expressed in several ways.

(1) The oracles of Ephraimite prophets are often introduced by phrases such as "the word of the Lord was to PN" or "the word of the Lord which was to PN" (wayhî dĕbar yhwh ʾel-PN; dĕbar yhwh hāyāh ʾel-PN; hāyāh dĕbar yhwh ʾel-PN; ʾăšer hāyāh dĕbar yhwh ʾel-PN; dĕbar yhwh ʾăšer hāyāh ʾel-PN [1 Sam 15:10; 2 Sam 7:4; 24:11; 1 Kgs 12:22; 13:20; 16:1; 17:2, 8; 18:1; 21:17, 28; 2 Kgs 20:4 (=Isa 38:4); Jer 1:2, 4, 11, 13; 2:1; 13:3, 8; 14:1; 16:1; 18:5; 24:4; 25:3; 28:12; 29:30; 32:6, 26; 33:1, 19, 23; 34:12; 35:12; 36:27; 37:6; 39:15; 42:7; 43:8; 46:1; 47:1; 49:34; Hos 1:1; Zeph 1:1]).[22]

(2) Narratives of the prophetic process frequently use phrases such as "the word of the Lord (delivered) through the agency of PN" (dĕbar yhwh bĕyad PN [1 Kgs 14:18; 15:29; 16:7, 12; 17:16, 24; 19:9; 2 Kgs 1:17; 3:12; 9:36; 10:17; 14:25; 20:19 (=Isa 39:8); 23:16; 24:2; Jer 27:18]).[23]

---

21. For a thorough discussion of this phrase, see J. J. M. Roberts, "The Hand of Yahweh," VT 21 (1971) 244–251.

22. O. Grether, Name und Wort Gottes im Alten Testament (Giessen: Alfred Töpelmann, 1934) 67–68. Outside of the Ephraimite corpus these phrases occur in preexilic texts in Joel 1:1 and Mic 1:1. In addition, there are roughly fifty occurrences in Ezekiel, which has affinities with Ephraimite language and theology.

23. Ibid., 68–69. Outside of the Ephraimite corpus these phrases occur only in a few postexilic texts.

(3) Ephraimite prophets frequently call their audiences to "hear
   the word of the Lord" (1 Kgs 22:19; 2 Kgs 7:1; 20:16 [=Isa
   39:5]; Jer 2:4, 31; 7:2; 9:19; 17:20; 19:3; 21:11; 22:2, 29;
   29:20; 31:10; 34:4; 42:15; 44:24, 26; Hos 4:1).[24]

All of these expressions indicate that the Ephraimites regarded possession involving God's speaking as the normal form of intermediation. This view of the mechanisms of prophecy may have also resulted in stereotypical prophetic language that made heavy use of
words describing divine speech.

THE BEGINNING OF THE EPHRAIMITE
TRADITION

The earliest biblical references to prophecy are embedded in the
Elohistic layer of the Pentateuch, which not only mentions several
prophets but also provides the narrative framework for the Balaam
oracles. Scholars who hold that prophecy did not appear in Israel
until the rise of the monarchy usually consider these Elohistic references to be retrojections from a much later time.[25] This theory is
impossible to test definitively on the basis of our present knowledge
of Israelite religion, but even if the theory should prove to be correct, the Elohistic references to prophecy at least indicate that the
group responsible for the Elohistic material *believed* that prophecy
existed at a very early stage in Israelite history. There is no way to
determine when this belief became a part of the Elohistic tradition,
but there are no good grounds for assuming that the belief was
incorporated only after the rise of the monarchy. The Elohists may
actually have known of prophets in the premonarchical period, and
these figures may have operated within the groups that bore the E

24. This call to hear the word of God is found occasionally in preexilic non-
Ephraimite sources (Isa 1:10; 28:14; Amos 7:16) and appears about ten times in
Ezekiel. For a collection of other phrases containing references to the word of God
and a discussion of the Ephraimite origin of these phrases, see ibid., 69–76.

25. F. M. Cross, *Canaanite Myth and Hebrew Epic* (Cambridge: Harvard University Press, 1973) 223–229; W. F. Albright, "Samuel and the Beginnings of the Prophetic Movement," *Interpreting the Prophetic Tradition* (New York: KTAV, 1969) 149–
176. For other views on the origins of Israelite prophecy, see H. B. Huffmon, "The
Origins of Prophecy," *Magnalia Dei: The Mighty Acts of God* (ed. F. M. Cross et al.;
Garden City, N.Y.: Doubleday, 1976) 171–186; A. Malamat, "Charismatic Leadership in the Book of Judges," *Magnalia Dei*, 152–168; R. Rendtorff, "Reflections on
the Early History of Prophecy in Israel," *Journal for Theology and the Church* 4
(1967) 14–34; V. W. Rabe, "Origins of Prophecy," *BASOR* 221 (1976) 125–128; and S.
Herrmann, *Ursprung und Funktion der Prophetie im alten Israel* (Opladen:
Westdeutscher Verlag, 1976) 44–61.

tradition. Therefore, the Elohistic evidence throws some light on the earliest known Ephraimite views of prophecy, even though the antiquity and historical accuracy of these views can no longer be determined.

The Balaam Oracles

Although the Hebrew Bible never calls Balaam a prophet, the biblical traditions about this enigmatic figure do preserve a few clues about the nature of intermediation among Israel's neighbors and about the Elohist's own distinctive perspectives on prophecy. The recently discovered Balaam oracles from Deir ʿAlla suggest that Balaam may have already been a traditional figure by the time the Hebrews entered the Trans-Jordanian area.[26] It is therefore not surprising to find several different pictures of this figure in the biblical texts. These differing pictures all have a partial resemblance to the description of Balaam found at Deir ʿAlla, and the various biblical views are not mutually exclusive. Still, it is unlikely that an image of the "historical Balaam" can be reconstructed by combining them. Rather, the biblical texts simply present several perspectives on a traditional figure and are an uncertain guide to the actual nature of that figure.

The Balaam narratives in Numbers 22—24 are the product of a complex literary and tradition history. Within the present text at least four major literary units can be isolated.[27] Num 22:41—23:26 and Num 23:28—24:19 contain collections of Balaam oracles set into a narrative framework.[28] These two groups of oracles differ slightly in form and content, and many scholars have attempted to assign them to separate literary sources. These attempts have not

26. See above, pp. 132–133.
27. Our analysis follows the scholarly consensus on the delineation of the major units in Numbers 22–24. However, there is much disagreement about the source analysis of some portions of these units. For a discussion, see M. Löhr, "Bileam, Num 22, 2–24, 25," *AfO* 4 (1927) 85–89; O. Eissfeldt, "Die Komposition der Bileam-Erzählung," *ZAW* 57 (1939) 212–241; S. Mowinckel, "Der Ursprung der Bil-āmsage," *ZAW* 48 (1930) 233–271; L. M. von Pákozdy, "Theologische Redaktionsarbeit in der Bileam-Perikope," *Von Ugarit nach Qumran* (BZAW 77; ed. J. Hempel and L. Rost; Berlin: Alfred Töpelmann, 1961) 161–176; W. Gross, *Bileam* (Munich: Kösel-Verlag, 1974) 13–64; M. Noth, *Numbers* (London: SCM Press, 1968) 171–175; and J. de Vaulx, *Les Nombres* (Paris: J. Gabalda, 1972) 255–264. For slightly different tradition-critical and form-critical approaches, see J. Coppens, "Les oracles de Biléam: Leur origine littéraire et leur portée prophétique," *Mélanges Eugène Tisserant* (Vatican City: Biblioteca Apostolica Vaticana, 1964) 67–78; and D. Vetter, *Seherspruch und Segensschilderung* (Stuttgart: Calwer Verlag, 1974).
28. Num 24:20–24 is usually regarded as a later addition. See Noth, *Numbers*, 171.

been fully convincing, and the archaic character of the poetry in the two collections suggests that they may simply be the product of different oral traditions that cannot now be accurately identified.[29] We will therefore note the pictures of Balaam that can be extracted from the two oracle collections, but we will not attempt to link these pictures to specific biblical sources. The Balaam oracle collections are prefaced in the present text by two narratives, which are to be dated much later than the oracles themselves. The introductory narrative in Num 22:2–21 is usually assigned to E, although most scholars agree that traces of J are to be found in the unit as well. To E's introduction has been added the story of Balaam's talking ass (Num 22:22–35), a story which is usually thought to be from J with a few E additions.

The earliest references to Balaam's characteristic behavior are found in Num 23:28—24:19, a unit which contains two poetic oracles. These oracles, which have been dated as early as the thirteenth century B.C., speak of Israel's favorable future and are both introduced by the following lines:

Oracle (*nĕ᾽um*) of Balaam, Beor's son,
oracle of the man whose eye is true;
oracle of one who hears El's words
and knows the knowledge of Elyon;
who sees (*yeḥĕzeh*) the vision (*maḥăzēh*) of Shaddai,
who falls down but has eyes uncovered (Num 24:3–4, 15–16).[30]

This description suggests that Balaam received his messages while in a state of trance, although outside of his "falling down" his trance behavior is not specified. It is not clear whether his trance was due to possession or soul loss, but in either case he received his messages by "seeing" the gods. The messages obtained through his visions are favorable to Israel and seem to be evaluated positively by the author of the poems.

This particular account of Balaam's behavior has links both with Israelite prophecy and with the descriptions found in the Deir ῾Alla

29. The antiquity of the poetry in Numbers 22–24 is now generally recognized. See W. F. Albright, "The Oracles of Balaam," *JBL* 63 (1944) 207–233; and S. Gevirtz, *Patterns in the Early Poetry of Israel* (Chicago: University of Chicago Press, 1963) 48–71.

30. This translation follows the reconstructed Hebrew text of Albright, who also argues for a thirteenth century date ("The Oracles of Balaam," 216–221, 226). For a discussion of *štm h ῾yn* in Num 24:3, 15, see Albright, "The Oracles of Balaam," 216.

texts. The designation *nēʾum* which is applied to these oracles appears throughout the prophetic literature as a description of the utterances of Israelite prophets.[31] Furthermore, the use of forms of the root *ḥzh* to describe the process of intermediation is also characteristic of some Israelite prophets. Although Ephraimite prophets usually used words having to do with speaking to describe their revelations, intermediaries connected with Jerusalem frequently used forms of the verb *ḥzh*, "to see." The most common use of this verb is in the title *ḥōzeh*, "visionary," which is applied to several Jerusalemite prophets (see, for example, 2 Sam 24:11; 1 Chr 21:9; 25:5; 29:29; 2 Chr 9:29; 12:15; 19:2; 29:25, 30; 35:15; Isa 29:10; Mic 3:7; cf. Isa 1:1; 21:2; 29:11; Amos 1:1; Mic 1:1).[32] The Deir ʿAlla texts also apply the root *ḥzh* to Balaam, who is called a "visionary of the gods" (*ḥzh ʾlhn*) to whom the gods spoke by night. Included among these gods are El and the Shaddai gods and goddesses (I, 1, 5–8; II, 6; cf. Num 24:4, 16).

Numbers 22:41—23:26 also contains two ancient poems set in narrative contexts. However, unlike the oracles in Numbers 24, these utterances do not mention Balaam's characteristic behavior but simply contain a number of references to Balak's unsuccessful attempt to obtain from Balaam a curse against Israel (Num 23:7–10, 18–24). These oracles imply that Balaam was an established intermediary whose services as a professional blesser and curser could be purchased. This picture generally agrees with the one that we have reconstructed from the Deir ʿAlla texts, where there are indications that Balaam was part of the central social structure and perhaps even a formal participant in the cult.[33] Like the oracles in Numbers 24, the ones in Num 22:41—23:26 are apparently evaluated positively by the author of the poems.

The clearest statement of Balaam's characteristic behavior comes not from the old poems but from the narrative framework that the Elohist placed around them. This framework makes it impossible to identify Balaam as an Israelite intermediary, an identification that might be possible on the basis of Numbers 24 alone. Balaam's actions are given a negative interpretation which colors the reader's

31. For studies of this term, see R. Rendtorff, "Zum Gebrauch der Formel *nᵉʾum jahwe* im Jeremiabuch," *ZAW* 66 (1954) 27–37; and F. Baumgärtel, "Die Formel *nᵉʾum jahwe*," *ZAW* 73 (1961) 277–290.

32. We will discuss this point in greater detail when we consider the Jerusalemite prophetic tradition.

33. See above, pp. 132–133.

understanding of the old poems themselves, and in the process the Elohist reveals one of his characteristic ideas about prophecy.[34]

E's introduction to the Balaam oracles develops motifs already found in Num 23:7–10, 18–24. Balak sends a message to Balaam requesting that he curse the Israelites so that they can be defeated in battle. Elaborating a motif present in Num 23:23, the Elohist clearly portrays Balaam as a diviner. The Moabite delegation brings him "fees for divination" (*qĕsāmîm* [Num 22:7]), and he obtains an answer to their request by seeking a revelatory night vision (Num 22:8–13, 19–21). The picture of Balaam as a diviner is reinforced by the introductions to the oracles themselves. In Num 23:1–5, 14–17, Balaam is said to have set up seven altars and conducted sacrifices in order to obtain a divine message. As we have already seen, such procedures were a common feature of Mesopotamian divination.[35]

The Elohist's negative picture of Balaam is further developed in later Ephraimite tradition. In Josh 13:22 Balaam is explicitly called a diviner (*qôsēm*), and his death during the conquest is narrated. From the Deuteronomic perspective Balaam's death would have been seen not as an accident of battle but as the fulfillment of Deuteronomic law. Deuteronomy 18:9–14 explicitly prohibits diviners from serving as intermediaries in Israel. They are an abomination (*tôʿēbāh*) which must not be allowed to exist in the land. It is thus clear that the sort of intermediary represented by the traditional figure of Balaam was not acceptable in Ephraimite circles, where, as we will see, only the prophet (*nābîʾ*) was considered a legitimate intermediary. The Elohist therefore edited the old oracles in such a way as to prevent a positive evaluation of Balaam in spite of the blessings which he delivered to Israel.

Abraham as Prophet

In the Elohist's version of the story of the ancestress in danger, the writer refers to Abraham as a prophet (Gen 20:7).[36] The title *nābîʾ* is

34. For a discussion of the Elohist's negative interpretation of Balaam, see G. W. Coats, "Balaam: Sinner or Saint?" *BR* 18 (1973) 1–9; and H. Donner, "Balaam pseudopropheta," *Beiträge zur Alttestamentlichen Theologie* (ed. H. Donner et al.; Göttingen: Vandenhoeck & Ruprecht, 1977) 112–123.

35. For a discussion of Balaam as diviner, see S. Daiches, "Balaam—A Babylonian Bārû," in his *Bible Studies* (London: Edward Goldston, 1950) 110–119; R. Largement, "Les oracles de Bileʿam et la mantique suméro-akkadienne," *Travaux de l'Institut Catholique de Paris, École des Langues Orientales Anciennes de l'Institut Catholique de Paris: Mémorial du Cinquantenaire* (Paris: Bloud & Gay, 1964) 37–50; and L. Rost, "Fragen um Bileam," *Beiträge zur Alttestamentlichen Theologie*, 377–387.

36. The Elohistic origin of Genesis 20 is rarely questioned. See G. von Rad, *Genesis* (rev. ed.; Philadelphia: Westminster Press, 1972) 226.

not applied to Abraham elsewhere in the Hebrew Bible, and it is not precisely clear why the Elohist employs the title here. However, it is interesting to note that Gen 20:7 explicitly connects the title with intercession. Abimelech's household has apparently been stricken with barrenness because of the endangering of Sarah, and God instructs the king to ask the prophet Abraham to offer an intercessory prayer for the removal of the affliction. Abimelech does this, and Abraham's intercession is successful (Gen 20:17–18). The passage thus suggests that the Elohist considered intercession to be a normal part of the prophet's characteristic behavior.

Israelite Prophets in the Wilderness Period

In addition to providing evidence on foreign intermediaries such as Balaam, Ephraimite sources also describe Israelite prophetic activity during the period of the wilderness wanderings. These descriptions are difficult to evaluate, but at the very least they reflect Ephraimite beliefs about the nature of prophecy.

Prophetic activity in the wilderness is first mentioned in Numbers 11, a chapter with a complex literary and tradition history that has thus far not been completely elucidated. Fragments of several different stories about Israel's murmuring in the wilderness have been woven together, and there is evidence of multiple layers of tradition beneath the present text.[37] The chapter opens with a notice that Israel complained about an unspecified problem and that Yahweh responded to this complaint by sending a fire to burn the outskirts of the camp. Such a judgmental response is typical in cases where Israel's complaints do not involve the actual necessities of life (Numbers 12, 14, 16; cf. Exod 14:10–14; 15:22–25; 16; 17:1–7). The complaints are therefore evaluated by Yahweh (and by the biblical writer) as illegitimate requests. The people then cried out to Moses, who successfully interceded with Yahweh and obtained the removal of the burning. The whole incident is said to explain the place name Taberah, "burning" (Num 11:1–3). The chapter thus opens on a negative note, which is immediately reinforced by the following narrative.

After the story of the incident at Taberah, the editor of this portion of Numbers has included a long, complicated narrative that seems to be composed of at least three different traditions. These traditions

37. For a thorough discussion of the problems involved in separating traditions and sources in Numbers 11, see G. W. Coats, *Rebellion in the Wilderness* (Nashville: Abingdon Press, 1968) 96–115, 124–127.

have been woven together somewhat loosely, but the overall narrative is more or less cohesive and presents a consistent point of view. The narrative opens with the remark that "the rabble" (*hā·sapsup*) had a craving (Num 11:4a). Nothing more is said of this group until the end of the chapter, where the rabble alone receives divine punishment and supplies the reason that the place is named Kibroth-hatta-avah, "the graves of craving" (Num 11:33–35). The larger narrative is thus bracketed by references to craving, and in this way the editor gives the narrative a negative tone.

The main portion of the chapter begins immediately after the reference to the rabble (Num 11:4b) and is essentially a negative version of the story of Yahweh's gift of the quail. A positive version of this story is known from Exodus 16, where it is interwoven with the account of the manna. With the help of this second version of the story, it is possible to reconstruct the account used by the editor of Numbers 11. In Num 11:4b the focus of the narrative suddenly shifts from the cravings of the rabble to the whole people of Israel, who weep because they have no meat to eat and complain that God has given them nothing but manna (Num 11:4b–6). The illegitimate nature of their complaint is underlined by the editor in Num 11:7–9, where the miraculous properties of manna are described, and it is therefore not surprising that God immediately becomes angry at the people's request (Num 11:10). In the original story God's anger probably led directly to an announcement of punishment similar to the one now found in Num 11:18–20, where God promises to send the people meat in such great quantities that they will become thoroughly sick of it. Presumably the original story then concluded with a modified version of the judgment narrative now preserved in Num 11:31–32. The original story was therefore a negative one, which saw the quail as God's judgmental response to the people's illegitimate demand for meat.

Into this negative version of the quail story, the editor has incorporated a second story which has also been preserved in a positive form outside of Numbers 11. Exodus 18:13–27, a passage usually assigned to the Elohist, relates that when Moses became overburdened with judicial responsibilities his father-in-law suggested the appointment of helpers who could handle the easier cases, thus freeing Moses to deal with the difficult ones. This suggestion was accepted and led to the creation of a group of minor judges who shared leadership responsibilities with Moses. At one time this

story was presumably used to justify legal and governmental practices in Ephraim, where legal decisions were apparently made by
local magistrates rather than by a centralized royal judiciary, as was
later the case in Judah (cf. Deut 1:13–15; 16:18).[38]

A positive version of this appointment narrative is still visible in
Numbers 11 in verses that are usually attributed to the Elohist.
Following the people's illegitimate demand for meat and God's
angry reaction, Moses does not share the divine anger, as one might
expect, but he begins to complain that the people are a burden to
him. He asks how he is going to supply all of the people with meat
and implies that God has rashly promised something that Moses
cannot deliver (Num 11:11–15). Moses' complaint seems to ignore
the negative interpretation of the quail incident and rests on the
assumption that the people's demand is a legitimate one which has
received a favorable reply from Yahweh. The tension between the
assumptions of Moses' complaint and the present negatively colored
context of the complaint suggests that the complaint was once attached to a story in which the people made a legitimate request that
required additional work from Moses. The complaint was therefore
appropriate to its context and was answered with a positive response from God. Such a response is now found in Num 11:16–17,
where God agrees to allow seventy elders to share the leadership
burden with Moses. The chosen elders are gathered together at the
tent of meeting, and as a sign of their election they are possessed by
the divine spirit that rested on Moses. As part of their characteristic
possession behavior, they acted like prophets (*wayyitnabbĕʾû*). The
precise nature of this behavior is unclear, but it was obviously recognizable as prophetic behavior, a fact that suggests that prophets in
this period did have certain stereotypical characteristics. In this
case the narrator makes clear that the characteristic behavior was
not a sign that the elders were to become prophets but that their
behavior was an indication of divine appointment (Num 11:24–25).
The whole incident thus has a positive interpretation in the context
of the appointment story. This positive view of possession behavior

38. For a discussion of this interpretation, see B. S. Childs, *The Book of Exodus*
(Philadelphia: Westminster Press, 1974) 321–326; and R. Knierim, "Exodus 18 und
die Neuordnung der Mosaischen Gerichtsbarkeit," *ZAW* 73 (1961) 146–171.
Knierim's view that the passage was used to support Jehoshaphat's judicial reform is
unlikely on the grounds that an Ephraimite tradition would not likely have been
used to support a Judean reform. In this connection it is worth noting that the
Deuteronomic History does not mention the reform.

is reinforced in the Eldad and Medad story, in which the two elders who did not go to the tent of meeting are possessed in the camp and exhibit characteristic prophetic behavior there. Joshua objects to their behavior not because of the behavior itself but precisely because he recognizes it as an indication of divine election and therefore as a potential threat to Moses' authority. Moses meets Joshua's objection by affirming that the elders' behavior is indeed due to possession by Yahweh's spirit and that Yahweh has ordered the sharing of leadership responsibilities (Num 11:26–30). The story thus indicates that the Elohistic groups that originally created the story viewed possession positively and assigned it an important role in authenticating Israelite leaders. This in turn suggests that possession and the prophetic behavior that resulted from it played a role within the central social structure of the Ephraimite groups.

However, the originally positive interpretation of the story of the divine appointment of the elders has been altered by placing the story in its present negative context. By weaving the appointment story into the account of Israel's illegitimate request and the punishment that resulted from it, the editor implies that the appointment of the elders was necessary only because of Israel's sin. The appointment and the prophetic behavior that accompanied it are now interpreted negatively, a fact which implies that the editor did not accept the leadership role of the elders and that he did not look favorably upon the method of their appointment or their behavior. The identity of the editor is unclear, but he may have represented Jerusalemite groups that favored a centralized royal judiciary rather than the Ephraimite system of local judges.[39] If so, then one might also conclude that the Jerusalemites did not accept the charismatic mode of legitimation or the type of prophetic behavior found in Ephraim. However, the accuracy of this conclusion can be established only after additional evidence has been examined.

The second passage bearing on the question of Israelite prophecy in the wilderness period (Numbers 12) is also set in the context of a

39. A Judean reform centralizing the judicial structure and bringing it under royal control is attributed to Jehoshaphat (2 Chr 19:5–11). However, it is impossible to determine whether or not this event led to the negative interpretation of the Elohist's story of the appointment of the elders. For a discussion of Jehoshaphat's reform, see W. F. Albright, "The Judicial Reform of Jehoshaphat," *Alexander Marx Jubilee Volume* (New York: Jewish Theological Seminary, 1950) 61–82; and G. C. Macholz, "Die Stellung des Königs in der israelitischen Gerichtsverfassung," *ZAW* 84 (1972) 157–182; idem, "Zur Geschichte der Justizorganisation in Juda," *ZAW* 84 (1972) 314–340.

murmuring story. Like Numbers 11, Numbers 12 seems to have had a complex editorial history, and it is difficult to link the chapter with any of the regular Pentateuchal sources.[40] However, as we will soon see, the chapter reflects some of the Elohist's characteristic views of prophecy, so it is likely that Ephraimite writers were involved somewhere in the process of the chapter's creation.

Because Numbers 12 deals with Miriam and Aaron's challenge to Moses' authority, the narrative is sometimes said to reflect conflicts between segments of the Israelite priesthood.[41] However, there are several indications that Aaron's name is a later addition to the narrative and that prophecy was the original focus of the story. The unit opens with a third-person-singular feminine verb, a fact which suggests that originally Miriam alone was the one who murmured against Moses (Num 12:1). This suggestion is substantiated by the fact that Aaron plays only a subsidiary role in the following story, which deals primarily with Miriam. She alone is punished for questioning Moses' authority (Num 12:9–10, 14–15), and Aaron's only function in the narrative is to request Moses to intercede with Yahweh on her behalf (Num 12:11–12). It therefore appears that Aaron was included in the story secondarily. If so, then it is unlikely that the story was originally concerned with priestly conflict, for Miriam is nowhere said to have performed priestly functions. However, Miriam is elsewhere said to have been a prophetess (*nĕbîʾāh* [Exod 15:20]), a fact which suggests that the narrative was originally concerned with a dispute over prophetic authority. This suggestion is supported by an analysis of the story itself.[42]

The narrative in its present form begins with the statement that Miriam and Aaron "spoke against" Moses because he married a Cushite woman (Num 12:1). This may be a reference to Moses' marriage to Zipporah (Exod 2:21), although the precise reasons for the dispute are unclear, and the whole matter is immediately dropped. The real point of Miriam and Aaron's complaint appears in Num 12:2, where they ask if God has spoken only through Moses. The issue here seems to be the means by which God communicates with Israel. In the original version of the story, Miriam, as a prophetess, apparently claimed to be a legitimate channel through

40. Coats, *Rebellion in the Wilderness*, 261–264.
41. For this interpretation of the chapter, see in particular Cross, *Canaanite Myth and Hebrew Epic*, 203–204.
42. For an analysis of Numbers 12 in the context of prophecy, see L. Perlitt, "Mose als Prophet," *EvT* 31 (1971) 592–596.

which God could speak to the people, a claim that was denied by
Moses. The problem which gave rise to the original story thus seems
to have been one which plagues any society containing more than
one intermediary: how are the authority claims of the intermediaries to be adjudicated, particularly when they bring conflicting messages from the divine world? In Numbers 12 this problem is
solved by a divine revelation that occurs when the participants in
the dispute are gathered at the tent of meeting (Num 12:6–8). Rather
than denying Miriam prophetic status, the narrative suggests that
prophets are arranged in a hierarchy. Yahweh speaks to prophets
such as Miriam in visions and dreams. In contrast, God speaks to
Moses directly rather than in vague speech. This means that the
words of the prophets may be authentic messages from God but that
when these words conflict with those of Moses, the latter are to be
considered more accurate. The problem of contradictory prophetic
messages is to be solved by accepting the words of Moses, who sees
and hears more clearly than the other prophets. Because Miriam
fails to understand this principle and claims prophetic equality with
Moses, she is punished by Yahweh (Num 12:9–10). Her punishment
is moderated only when Moses intercedes for her (Num 12:13–15).
The story lying behind Numbers 12 thus seems to be the earliest
statement of a view of prophecy that is developed in greater detail
by later Ephraimite sources. There is a hierarchy of prophets, at the
top of which stands the Mosaic prophet, who hears the word of God
directly and whose word is always accurate. In addition to speaking
the true word of God, this prophet also functions as intercessor for
the people.

THE DEUTERONOMIC TRADITION

The most detailed statement of Ephraimite views on prophecy
comes from literature produced by the Deuteronomists. This literature covers the period of the conquest and the entire history of the
monarchy, so the Deuteronomic corpus not only supplies general
information on the relationship between prophecy and society in
Israel but also gives Ephraimite perspectives on the historical development of prophecy. However, from the outset it must be recognized that it is sometimes difficult to place the Deuteronomic evidence into a specific historical context. Although it is generally
agreed that a version of the Deuteronomic History and some portion

of the present Book of Deuteronomy came into existence in the time of Josiah, the Deuteronomic traditions themselves appear to antedate the Josianic period, and it is even possible that there was a pre-Josianic version of the History. The generally recognized links between Elohistic and Deuteronomistic views suggest that the Deuteronomic tradition may be very old indeed, but because of the thorough editing which the Deuteronomic sources have received it is often difficult to isolate the underlying layers of tradition with any certainty. Furthermore, it is clear that the Deuteronomic corpus underwent additional editing after the time of Josiah before reaching its present form. These later editorial layers are also difficult to analyze and are sometimes indistinguishable from earlier Deuteronomic material. Because of the complex character of the Deuteronomic traditions, it will be difficult for us to trace the evolution of Deuteronomic views on prophecy. In most instances we will be able only to uncover a generalized picture of how prophets functioned in Deuteronomic groups, and we will be unable to put this picture in a concrete historical framework.

Moses as Prophet

The only biblical laws that deal with prophecy are found in the Deuteronomic corpus. Deuteronomy 18:9–22 gives several regulations governing intermediaries and promises Israel a series of prophets "like Moses." Scholars have long recognized the importance of this passage for understanding Israelite prophecy, but only in recent years have systematic attempts been made to use the passage to reconstruct a picture of the typical Deuteronomic prophet. Because of the legal and covenantal context of Deut 18:9–22, it has been argued that Ephraimite prophets regularly held the office of "covenant mediator," an office which was traced back to Moses himself. This argument has been advanced in various forms, but it received its classic statement from Hans-Joachim Kraus.[43]

Kraus' argument begins with the observation that in Num 12:6–8 a sharp distinction is made between Moses, who receives God's

---

43. Kraus first developed the concept of the covenant mediator in detail in *Die prophetische Verkündigung des Rechts in Israel* (Zollikon: EVZ, 1957); and he presented his thesis in a revised form in *Worship in Israel* (Richmond: John Knox Press, 1966) 102–112. For earlier statements of the same thesis, see G. Hölscher, "Komposition und Ursprung des Deuteronomiums," ZAW 40 (1922) 204; C. Steuernagel, *Das Deuteronomium* (Göttingen: Vandenhoeck & Ruprecht, 1923) 121; and G. von Rad, "Die falschen Propheten," ZAW 51 (1933) 113.

word directly, and the other prophets, who receive it in an ambiguous and oblique way. This distinction also appears later in the history of prophecy, where true and false prophets are distinguished by the fact that the true prophets receive their messages directly from Yahweh while the false prophets do not (Jer 23:16–40; 1 Kgs 22:13–23). To Kraus this distinction suggests that in Israel there were always certain prophets who were in a category different from that of the normal prophets. Kraus finds support for this suggestion in Deut 18:15–22, where the prophet is discussed in the context of other Israelite officeholders. According to this passage the prophet "like Moses" receives messages directly from Yahweh, while the false prophets do not speak the word of Yahweh at all. Furthermore, these verses ground the Mosaic prophetic office in an incident mentioned in Deut 5:22–23 and in an Elohistic narrative in Exod 20:18–21. In this brief story the people of Israel express their fear at the possibility of confronting Yahweh and request that Moses act as their mediator with Yahweh. Yahweh agrees to the people's request. Moses alone hears the words of the law from Yahweh and then repeats them to the people. According to Kraus, Deut 18:15–22 can be nothing less than an account of the institution of the office of covenant mediator. In addition, because the Book of Deuteronomy itself follows the general pattern of a covenant renewal festival and because Moses is himself said to have read the law to the people during such a festival (Deuteronomy 27), it can be assumed that subsequent Mosaic prophets also operated in cultic contexts. Among the Ephraimite groups at least one prophet in each generation played the Mosaic role and proclaimed the law to the people during the covenant renewal ceremony. After the demise of prophecy, the office was continued by the Levites.

Many scholars have accepted Kraus' views, at least in a modified form, and there is virtually a scholarly consensus affirming the existence of a prophetic covenant mediator in northern Israel.[44] If the

44. See in particular M. Newman, *The People of the Covenant* (Nashville: Abingdon Press, 1962) 46–47, 119; idem, "The Prophetic Call of Samuel," *Israel's Prophetic Heritage* (ed. B. W. Anderson and W. Harrelson; New York: Harper & Row, 1962) 86–97; J. Muilenburg, "The Form and Structure of the Covenantal Formulations," *VT* 9 (1959) 347–365; idem, "The 'Office' of the Prophet in Ancient Israel," *The Bible in Modern Scholarship* (ed. J. P. Hyatt; Nashville: Abingdon Press, 1965) 74–97; idem, "The Intercession of the Covenant Mediator (Exodus 33: 1a, 12–17)," *Words and Meanings: Essays Presented to David Winton Thomas* (ed. P. R. Ackroyd and B. Lindars; Cambridge: At the University Press, 1968) 159–181; and E. W. Nicholson, *Deuteronomy and Tradition* (Philadelphia: Fortress Press, 1967), 58–82.

consensus is correct, then it would have important implications for our understanding of the relationship between prophecy and society in Israel, for the consensus holds that at least one type of prophet regularly occupied an office within the central Ephraimite cult. However, there are several reasons for challenging the consensus. First, Kraus bases his work only on Deut 18:15–22 and does not take into account the larger context of the passage. Yet Deut 18:15, where the Mosaic prophet is first mentioned, depends for its meaning on a contrast between the prophet and the intermediaries mentioned in Deut 18:9–14. The nature of the Mosaic prophet cannot be properly understood without considering this contrast, and for this reason Deut 18:9–22 must be treated as a whole.[45] Second, there is actually no reference in Deut 18:9–22 to the cultic reading of the law. If such a reading were the primary function of the covenant mediator, then one might expect the Deuteronomic writers to have mentioned it explicitly in the passage instituting the office. The periodic reading of the law is mentioned in Deut 31:9–13, but the task is assigned to Levitical priests, not to prophets. Third, Kraus must assume that Israelite prophets *regularly* participated in a covenant renewal ceremony in which their function was to read the law. Outside of Moses and Joshua (who is never called a prophet), the biblical texts never portray prophets in such a role, and there is no good evidence to indicate the existence of a *continuous* cultic office of the sort that Kraus describes. Finally, Kraus' reconstruction is based on certain theories about the role of the covenant in unifying the Israelite amphictyony during the period of the Judges. These theories are currently being challenged, and in particular the amphictyonic hypothesis seems unable to bear the weight that Kraus places upon it.[46] It is therefore clear that Deut 18:9–22 must be reexamined and that the theory of the covenant mediator must be reevaluated.[47]

45. This point has not been recognized by most studies of the Mosaic prophet. Note, however, the comments of Steuernagel, *Deuteronomium*, 121–122; R. P. Merendino, *Das Deuteronomische Gesetz* (Bonn: Peter Hanstein, 1969) 192–199; and N. Lohfink, "Die Sicherung der Wirksamkeit des Gotteswortes durch das Prinzip der Schriftlichkeit der Tora und durch das Prinzip der Gewaltenteilung nach den Ämtergesetzen des Buches Deuteronomium (Dt 16, 18–18, 22)," *Testimonium Veritati: Festschrift für Bischof Wilhelm Kempf* (ed. H. Wolter; Frankfurt: Josef Knecht, 1971) 146.

46. R. E. Clements, *Prophecy and Tradition* (Atlanta: John Knox Press, 1975) 8–14.

47. For general treatments of the unit, see Perlitt, "Mose als Prophet," 596–601; Lohfink, "Sicherung," 146; N. Habel, "Deuteronomy 18—God's Chosen Prophet," *CTM* 35 (1964) 575–582; and B. Chiesa, "La promessa di un profeta (Deut 18, 15–20)," *BeO* 15 (1973) 17–26.

Deuteronomy 18:9–22 forms the climax of a larger unit which begins in Deut 16:18 and which deals with the responsibilities and privileges of various officials within Israel's central social structure.[48] The inclusion of prophets among these officials indicates that in the Deuteronomic vision of the ideal society prophets played a central role. Deut 16:18—18:22 begins with a consideration of judges and other persons concerned with the administration of justice (Deut 16:18—17:13). The laws dealing with justice are quite logically followed by those dealing with kingship (Deut 17:14–20). In contrast to the situation that actually existed in Judah and in Ephraim, the Deuteronomic law holds that the king's power should be severely limited. Apparently the king was not to be involved with the judicial system, which Deuteronomy places under the control of local judges and Levitical priests. Similarly, the king was to be a native Israelite and was forbidden to make foreign alliances or form his own standing army (cf. Deuteronomy 20). The king himself was to be subservient to the law, which was in the keeping of the Levitical priests. There is no indication that the king was allowed to exercise any priestly functions, and to underline this point, the text moves to a consideration of the rights and responsibilities of the Levitical priests (Deut 18:1–8). In this unit the Deuteronomist deals only with the role of the priests in making cultic offerings, but other passages indicate that the priests also played a part in the judicial process (Deut 17:8–13) and were responsible for periodic readings of the law (Deut 31:9–13). In this list of priestly functions there is one striking omission. According to the Deuteronomic point of view, the priests were not to provide any means by which people could contact Yahweh. This seems to be a departure from earlier Ephraimite practice, which assigned priests the responsibility of divining by means of Urim and Thummim (Deut 33:8). Divination also seems to have been a priestly function in Judea, and it is possible that the use of Urim and Thummim continued in Jerusalem in monarchical times (1 Sam 23:9–12; 30:7–8; Num 27:21; Exod 28:30; Lev 8:8; cf. Ezra 2:63 = Neh 7:65). However, this omission of divination from the list of priestly tasks in Deut 18:1–8 is hardly accidental, for the Deuteronomist begins the next unit (Deut 18:9–22) with a consideration of various means by which people might contact Yahweh.

---

48. For an interpretation of the structure of this larger unit, see Lohfink, "Sicherung," 143–155.

The Deuteronomic regulations dealing with prophecy begin with a general command forbidding Israel to follow the abominable practices (*tôʿābōt*) of the nations inhabiting the land that God has promised to Israel.[49] Specific examples of these abominations are then given in the form of a series of participial phrases describing various intermediaries who are not to be allowed to exist in the land (Deut 18:10–11). The titles given to some of these figures are not clearly understood, but the general sense of the titles can be deduced from their context. The list begins with "one who makes his son or his daughter pass through the fire." This phrase is usually thought to denote a type of child sacrifice that was practiced outside of Jerusalem in the Valley of the Son(s) of Hinnom (2 Kgs 23:10; Jer 32:35). However, the interpretation of the phrase is still debated, and it is possible that it actually describes some sort of cultic practice designed to elicit oracles from the (deified) dead.[50] Following this somewhat problematic reference, the list mentions the diviner (*qōsēm qĕsāmîm*), the soothsayer (*mĕʿônēn*), the augur (*mĕnaḥēš*), the sorcerer (*mĕkaššēp*), the charmer (*ḥōbēr ḥāber*), the one who inquires of ghosts (*šōʾēl ʾôb*), the wizard (*yiddĕʿōnî*), and the one who seeks oracles from the dead (*dōrēš ʾel-hammētîm*).[51] With the possible exception of the first, all of the proscribed intermediaries in the list share one common feature. They are all specialists to whom a person may go to seek information from the supernatural realm. They are all channels through which humans can communicate with the divine world.

The Deuteronomic ban on these intermediaries raises the question of how Israel can legitimately contact Yahweh. If the people may not go to priests or to these intermediaries, then what mechanisms are provided for communicating with God? To answer this

49. For a discussion of the concept of "abomination" in Deuteronomy, see J. L'Hour, "Les interdits *to ʿeba* dans le Deutéronome," *RB* 71 (1964) 481–503.

50. For recent discussions, see M. Weinfeld, "The Worship of Molech and of the Queen of Heaven and Its Background," *UF* 4 (1972) 133–154; and M. H. Pope, "Notes on the Rephaim Texts from Ugarit," *Essays on the Ancient Near East in Memory of Jacob Joel Finkelstein* (ed. M. de J. Ellis; Hamden, Conn.: Archon Books, 1977) 166, 170–172, 174.

51. For a discussion of some of these figures, see J. Lust, "On Wizards and Prophets," *Studies on Prophecy* (VTSup 26; Leiden: E. J. Brill, 1974) 133–142; O. Eissfeldt, "Wahrsagung im Alten Testament," *La divination en Mésopotamie ancienne* (Paris: Presses Universitaires de France, 1966) 141–146; A. Caquot, "La divination dans l'ancien Israël," *La divination* (ed. A. Caquot and M. Leibovici; Paris: Presses Universitaires de France, 1968) 1. 83–113; and A. Barucq, "Oracles et Divination," *DBSup* 6. 752–788.

question Deuteronomy promises that in the place of the banned intermediaries God will periodically raise up a prophet "like Moses," that is, a prophet whose behavior and functions are like those of Moses.[52] The people are to listen to this Mosaic prophet rather than to other types of intermediaries (Deut 18:14–15). The Mosaic prophet is therefore the only legitimate channel of communication between Yahweh and the people. God speaks directly to the prophet, who, like Moses, clearly and accurately perceives the word of God (cf. Num 12:6–8) and repeats it to the people. In addition, the people are to go to the prophet when they want to approach Yahweh with questions or requests.

The reason for creating this special type of prophet is supplied by the Deuteronomist in Deut 18:16–19, which refers to an event recorded in the Elohist's account of the giving of the law. According to Exod 20:18–21, after God gave the Ten Commandments to the people, they became terrified because of their direct contact with Yahweh and asked Moses not to let God speak directly to them again. Moses agreed to this request and went alone into God's presence to receive the remainder of the law. This passage undoubtedly reflects early Ephraimite views about the special status of the Decalogue and about Moses' role in the giving of the law, but there is no suggestion that the Elohist intended the narrative to serve as the etiology of an office. However, by the time the Deuteronomist recounts this event in Deut 18:16–19, the Ephraimite tradition has already connected the incident with a particular understanding of the Mosaic prophetic office. Deuteronomy 18:16 implies that the people at Sinai asked for a *prophetic* mediator when they refused to hear the voice of God. According to the Deuteronomic account, this request was made *to Moses* but was answered *by God* (Deut

---

52. The use of imperfect verb forms (*yāqîm, ʾāqîm*) in Deut 18:15, 18 seems to point to a series of prophets rather than to a single prophet. The interpretation of this passage as a reference to a single messianic figure is a late development. See J. R. Porter, *Moses and Monarchy* (Oxford: Basil Blackwell, 1963); W. A. Meeks, *The Prophet-King* (Leiden: E. J. Brill, 1967); and H. M. Teeple, *The Mosaic Eschatological Prophet* (Philadelphia: Society of Biblical Literature, 1957). The notion of a series of Mosaic prophets seems to be contradicted by Deut 34:10–12, where it is said that "a prophet like Moses has not arisen again in Israel." Moses is assigned a unique status for several reasons, including his direct contact with God. However, the glorification of a hero by stressing his incomparability is common in folkloristic death accounts, such as the one in Deuteronomy 34, and the view that Moses was a unique sort of prophet probably developed secondarily as part of a general tendency to portray Moses as a heroic figure. See G. W. Coats, "Legendary Motifs in the Moses Death Reports," *CBQ* 39 (1977) 37–38.

18:17–18). The Deuteronomic writer thus seems to assume that God received the request when it was relayed by Moses. God then gave a response *to Moses*, not to the people directly, and promised a series of prophets who would continue Moses' mediatorial functions. Thus, according to the Deuteronomist, the promise of a series of Mosaic prophets was actually made *at Sinai*, and the somewhat disjointed character of the dialogue in Deut 18:16–19 suggests that the author of the passage already had in mind the image of Moses as the prophetic mediator through whom the people conversed with God.

A more fully developed form of this idea is reflected in Deuteronomy 5, where the Deuteronomist's own version of the giving of the Decalogue is recounted. The Deuteronomist follows the Elohist in the belief that Israel heard the Ten Commandments directly from God before refusing to hear the divine voice again (Deut 5:4). However, the Deuteronomic statement of the course of events apparently reflects the belief that Moses was already acting as a prophetic mediator. In Deut 5:23–27 the people address their complaint to Moses, and in Deut 5:28 it is explicitly stated that Yahweh heard the people's request *when they spoke to Moses*. Again the Deuteronomist seems to assume that Moses relayed the people's request to Yahweh, who replied directly to Moses with a message for the people (Deut 5:28–33).

The importance of the Deuteronomic concept of the prophetic mediator can be seen in Deut 5:5, a verse which is probably a later Deuteronomic gloss. According to this verse, Moses was already acting as a mediator *before* the Decalogue was given, with the result that the people never actually heard the voice of God at all. This statement reflects a fully developed Deuteronomic belief that communication between God and Israel can take place *only* by means of a prophetic intermediary. For the glossator this belief was so important that a statement of it was added to Deuteronomy 5, in spite of the fact that the addition created an apparent contradiction in the text and undermined the earlier Deuteronomic notion of the special status of the Decalogue.[53]

The concept of the Mosaic prophet is further developed in Deut 18:18–22, where this special type of prophet is contrasted with other sorts of prophets. God puts divine words directly into the

53. For an alternative interpretation of Deut 5:4–5, see Childs, *Exodus*, 351–360.

mouth of the Mosaic prophet, who faithfully speaks all of the words
that God has dictated. By implication the Mosaic prophet does not
filter the divine message in any way and does not add or subtract
words. A word from a Mosaic prophet is a word directly from God.
People are therefore required to obey the words spoken by Mosaic
prophets, and God promises divine punishment for people who do
not obey. Similarly, God decrees a death sentence for prophets who
speak words that are not dictated by God or who speak in the name
of other gods.[54] This decree warns future Mosaic prophets not to
embellish the messages which they receive and warns other types
of prophets not to contradict the message of a Mosaic prophet. Finally, the Deuteronomist turns to the question of how to recognize
prophets who are not speaking God's word. Having already noted
that any prophet who speaks in the name of other gods is illegitimate from the start, the Deuteronomist considers the problem of
distinguishing Mosaic prophets, who faithfully relay God's word,
from other prophets, who do not accurately convey what Yahweh
has said. The Deuteronomist's solution to this problem is to say that
prophets whose predictions do not come true are prophets to whom
Yahweh has not spoken. They presumably are speaking only their
own words and will eventually incur divine penalties for this pre-
sumptuousness, but in the meantime the people need not fear such
prophets. By implication, then, Mosaic prophets, who speak only
the pure word of God, always deliver oracles that come true, although the Deuteronomist does not explicitly state this proposition
in this passage. However, the Deuteronomist apparently did not
rule out the possibility that the oracles of prophets to whom Yahweh
had not spoken could also come true. This case is considered in
Deut 13:1–5, where the writer concludes that Yahweh sometimes
tests Israel by allowing the fulfillment of predictions which did not
have a divine origin.

The Deuteronomic concept of the Mosaic prophet thus seems to
have had the following features. This special type of prophet was
authorized by God at Sinai at the request of Israel and served as the
only legitimate link between God and the people. Through the

54. The text does not indicate how the death sentence is to be carried out. However, later Ephraimite texts seem to assume that the sentence would be executed
directly by God, who alone is able to identify a false prophet with any certainty. The
law concerning the false prophet thus resembles traditional laws dealing with witchcraft. We will return to this point again when we consider the problem of false
prophecy.

prophet the people could approach God, and in turn the prophet delivered to the people only the pure word of God. There is no evidence that the prophet's task was restricted to proclaiming or reading the law, and it is probable that the links between the Mosaic prophet and the law are due to the fact that Moses was the archetype both of the prophet and of the lawgiver. The prophet's task seems to have been to deliver to the people *all* words which God placed in his mouth. These words would inevitably come true, thus allowing Israel to distinguish "true" prophets from "false" ones. This concern with false prophets suggests that the Deuteronomists were living in a society in which more than one type of prophet existed and where contradictory oracles were a potential problem. The Deuteronomic concept of the Mosaic prophet helped to solve this problem by providing a clear picture of a true prophet. According to Deuteronomic theory, any prophet who followed the Mosaic pattern was by definition a true prophet whose words could be believed.

The Deuteronomists seem to imply that there will be a series of Mosaic prophets, although there is no indication of a continuous "office." The fact that God "raises up" these prophets implies that they will appear irregularly whenever God feels that Israel needs them. Presumably there was only one Mosaic prophet in any given area at a particular time, although the biblical sources are rather vague on this point. Similarly, there is no indication that the Deuteronomists considered non-Mosaic prophets illegitimate unless their words conflicted with those of a Mosaic prophet. Even though the texts do not suggest that the Mosaic prophet had regular cultic functions, the Deuteronomist clearly intended him to play an important role within Israel's social structure. In the Deuteronomic picture of the ideal state, the prophet was to work along with the judges, kings, and Levitical priests to help maintain the social structure.

Although Deuteronomy 18 is the most detailed theoretical statement of Ephraimite views on prophecy that we have seen so far, it is important to note that the Deuteronomic picture of the Mosaic prophet is a development of older Ephraimite ideas. We have already seen that intercession was a feature of early Ephraimite prophecy. This prophetic function was developed by the Deuteronomist into the notion that the prophet was to replace other intermediaries and was to serve as the only legitimate means by which Israel could communicate with God.[55] Similarly, the Deuteronomist took from the Elohistic tradition reflected in Numbers 12 the idea of a prophetic hierarchy headed by Moses and then generalized the idea so that it could be applied to prophets in later periods. Finally, like the Elohistic creators of Numbers 12, the Deuteronomists faced the problem of conflicting prophetic messages and elaborated earlier Ephraimite views by developing new techniques for dealing with the problem. Deuteronomy 18 thus seems to be a consolidation and development of Ephraimite ideas, which are here given divine legitimation. When we turn to the narratives of the Deuteronomic History, we will see how these ideas are actually reflected in prophetic behavior.

Prophets in the Period of the Judges

There are some indications that the Deuteronomists believed that prophets existed in Israel during the period of the judges, but the texts provide little data on the actual behavior and functions of these figures. In Judg 4:4 Deborah is called a prophetess (*nĕbî³āh*), although it is not completely clear why she is assigned this title.[56] She is portrayed as a judge to whom people came for legal decisions, but there is no indication that she acted as the people's intermediary. However, according to Judg 4:6–7, she did deliver to Barak what appears to be a prophetic oracle commanding the war against Sisera, although the text does not indicate how she obtained this oracle or whether she delivered such messages on more than one occasion. In addition, she seems to have had foreknowledge of the outcome of the battle, but again the writer is vague about how she obtained this information (Judg 4:9). Still, these passages might

---

55. Moses is also portrayed as an intercessor in passages that do not refer to his prophetic functions (Exod 32:11–14, 31–34; 34:9; Num 14:13–19; 21:7; Deut 9:18–10:10; cf. Jer 15:1). Some of these passages antedate Deuteronomy 18 and may indicate that Moses was considered an intercessor before he was considered a prophet. However, it is more likely that he was assigned intercessory functions because of his prophetic status.

56. Commentators usually consider the title to be a Deuteronomic editorial addition, although there are differences of opinion about the significance of the addition. Some have assumed that there were originally two Deborah traditions, one of which portrayed her as a judge and one of which saw her as a prophet. Others have assumed that the title simply represents a retrojection of much later ideas about prophecy. For a thorough discussion of the problem, see W. Richter, *Traditionsgeschichtliche Untersuchungen zum Richterbuch* (Bonn: Peter Hanstein, 1966) 37–39, 42, 44–45, 59–65; and J. Schüpphaus, *Richter- und Prophetengeschichten als Glieder der Geschichtsdarstellung der Richter- und Königszeit* (Bonn: Rheinischen Friedrich-Wilhelms-Universität, 1967) 160–162.

indicate that the Deuteronomists connected prophets with the holy wars of the conquest.[57] If the story of Deborah is actually a reliable guide to the functions of other prophets, then the prophet in this period may have delivered the divine oracle that set the holy war in motion and may have then accompanied the army into battle. After the successful conclusion of the battle, the prophet may have delivered a victory oracle, just as the prophetess Deborah is said to have sung the poetic battle song in Judges 5 and the prophetess Miriam is said to have sung a victory song after the crossing of the Reed Sea (Exod 15:20–21). If prophets actually played such a military role, then it would indicate that they were part of Israel's central establishment during the period of the judges and helped to maintain the society. However, it is important to note that Deuteronomy 18 does not specifically assign the prophet military functions and that Deuteronomy 20 does not mention the prophet in the laws governing the conduct of the holy war. This would suggest that among the Deuteronomic groups the prophet's military activities—if they ever existed at all—were confined to Israel's early history.

Outside of the Deborah story, the only other reference to prophecy in the period of the judges is found in Judg 6:7–10, which records a prophetic message delivered to Israel by an unnamed prophet. Nothing is said about the behavior or social location of this individual, but his message is expressed in stereotypical Deuteronomic language (cf. Judg 2:1–5; 10:11–16). This fact, in addition to the fact that the passage seems to disrupt a standard Deuteronomic narrative pattern, has led many scholars to suggest that it is a later editorial addition. However, even if this is the case, the Deuteronomic phraseology indicates that it is a later *Deuteronomic* editorial addition, so the placement and general shape of the unit still reveal something about the Deuteronomist's view of prophecy.[58]

Throughout the Book of Judges the Deuteronomic writer uses an

---

57. There is ample evidence that some prophets participated in holy wars in later times. For a discussion of the situation in the period of the judges, see F. Stolz, *Jahwes und Israels Kriege* (Zurich: TVZ, 1972) 102–113; P. D. Miller, Jr., *The Divine Warrior in Early Israel* (Cambridge: Harvard University Press, 1973) 156–157; and R. Smend, *Jahweh War and Tribal Confederation* (Nashville: Abingdon Press, 1970) 59–61. On the basis of the early attestations of prophecy in Mesopotamia, there is no reason to doubt that prophets could have existed in Israel at an early period. Similarly, there is no reason to assume that Israelite judges could not have experienced occasional possession and functioned as prophets.

58. Schüpphaus, *Richter- und Prophetengeschichten,* 163; W. Richter, *Die Bearbeitungen des "Retterbuches" in der deuteronomischen Epoche* (Bonn: Peter Hanstein, 1964) 97–109.

almost formulaic narrative pattern to recount the stories about each judge. In this standard pattern Israel does what is "evil in the sight of the Lord," serves the Baals, and forsakes Yahweh. As punishment Yahweh delivers Israel into the power of an oppressor. But when the people cry to Yahweh because of their oppression, God sends a judge to deliver them. The successful efforts of the judge are then narrated, and the land again has rest for a designated number of years (see, for example, Judg 2:11–23; 3:7–11, 12–30; 4:1–3; 5:31). Usually this sequence of events seems to occur automatically, and the writer gives no indication of the mechanisms of the system. However, in Judges 6 the pattern is broken, and the insertion of the prophetic speech in Judg 6:7–10 may reveal the writer's concept of how the redemption process actually worked.

Chapter 6 begins with the standard introductory statement that Israel "did what was evil in the sight of the Lord." God therefore gave the people into the power of Midian, and the writer describes the Midianite oppression in some detail. As expected, the people then cried to the Lord for help (Judg 6:1–6). However, at this point the writer does not recount the sending of a new judge (Judg 6:11) but inserts the narrative about the prophet. In response to the people's cries, Yahweh sends a prophet who in a divine oracle explains to the people why they are being oppressed. This explanation reflects standard Deuteronomic theology and appears elsewhere in the Deuteronomic History. God led Israel out of Egypt and gave them the command not to worship other gods, but Israel refused to listen (Judg 6:10). The prophet does not call for any particular response on the part of the people, but the writer immediately moves to the first of the stories about Gideon, whom Yahweh sent to deliver Israel. By inserting the prophet's message in this way the Deuteronomic writer may be suggesting that God normally responds to the complaints of the people by sending a prophet to explain their misfortune. God speaks only through the prophet and does not act directly. Furthermore, the abrupt beginning of the Gideon story in Judg 6:11 implies that the appearance of the deliverer is somehow connected with the activities of the prophet, although the editor does not explicitly connect the two events. The final shape of the overall unit thus may indicate the editor's belief that in the time of the judges prophets helped to preserve Israel by pointing out the people's violations of the Deuteronomic law. If prophets actually had this function, then it would be another indication that prophets in this period had social maintenance functions within Israel's central social structure.

The Samuel Traditions

Samuel appears in a prophetic role in three narrative complexes, each of which has a complicated tradition and editorial history. Samuel first appears in the story of his prophetic call (1 Sam 3:1— 4:1), a story which is now connected with an account of the rejection of the Elide priesthood and with narratives about the ark. In the second narrative complex, Samuel appears in connection with the establishment of the monarchy (1 Samuel 7—12), while in the third he is involved with Saul's decline and David's rise (1 Sam 13:1–15; 15; 16:1–13; 19:18–24; 28). All of this material now bears the clear stamp of the Deuteronomist, but earlier editorial layers and earlier layers of tradition are sometimes still visible beneath the present text. Some of these layers may represent Ephraimite views that antedate those of the final Deuteronomic editor, while a few stories may preserve earlier traditions that originated in non-Deuteronomic circles. In either case it is sometimes difficult to assign even a relative date to these literary strata and layers of tradition. Similarly, it is doubtful that the same editorial and tradition-historical layers run continuously throughout the Samuel stories. Some individual stories and narrative complexes seem to have had their own unique editorial histories. In addition, there is no convincing evidence to support the notion that each editorial layer portrays a different aspect of Samuel's activities. Rather, all of the editors seem to have been aware that Samuel exercised priestly, prophetic, judicial, and governmental functions. Individual stories or editors may focus on one of these functions, but this cannot be taken to indicate an ignorance of the others.[59] The literary and tradition-historical complexity of the Samuel stories thus makes it virtually impossible to reconstruct an accurate picture of this early prophet. However, this multilayered material can indicate how various groups *perceived* this important figure, and this information can, in turn, be used to reconstruct their views on prophecy in general.

59. For a brief discussion of the complexity of the Samuel traditions, see B. C. Birch, *The Rise of the Israelite Monarchy: The Growth and Development of 1 Samuel 7—15* (Missoula: Scholars Press, 1976) 1–10; cf. J. L. McKenzie, "The Four Samuels," *BR* 7 (1962) 3–18.

The Call of Samuel

The story of Samuel's prophetic call (1 Sam 3:1—4:1) is now prefaced by an account of his miraculous birth (1 Samuel 1) and by several narrative units dealing with the evils of the Elide priesthood (1 Sam 2:12–36). Scholars usually assume that the birth narrative and the anti-Elide narratives originally existed independently and were finally woven together by the writer who also gave the call narrative its present shape.[60] However, even if this assumption accurately characterizes the process by which the present text came into existence, the fact remains that the Deuteronomic writer has molded the original components together in a reasonably coherent way. Furthermore, by arranging the components in their present order the Deuteronomist has indicated how he thought the prophetic process worked at the end of the period of the judges. The final form of 1 Sam 1:1—4:1 can therefore be used to reconstruct the Deuteronomic writer's views on the social and religious roles of the early prophets.

Although the anti-Elide character of 1 Samuel 1—3 is most obvious in 1 Sam 2:12–36, subtle criticisms of Eli himself have also been worked into Samuel's birth narrative (1 Samuel 1). When the barren Hannah is engaged in prayer in the temple at Shiloh, Eli mistakes her for a drunken woman, a fact which suggests that he has lost his religious sensitivity, even if he is not actually dishonest. Nevertheless, when Hannah's barrenness is removed and Samuel is born, she places him in the care of Eli, and the boy performs cultic functions at Shiloh (1 Sam 2:11). Having established the social location of Samuel within the central cult, the writer gives the reader a picture of that cult by including two narratives demonstrating the depravity and dishonesty of Eli's sons (1 Sam 2:12–17). According to the narrator, Eli recognized his sons' abuses, but he was either unwilling or unable to reform them. As a result an unnamed man of God delivered to Eli a judgment oracle foretelling the end of his priestly line and promising the establishment of a righteous priestly house (1 Sam 2:22–36). The text does not give the social background of the man of God, but there is no reason to think that he was not part of

60. For general discussions of the literary and tradition history of these chapters, see I. Hylander, *Der literarische Samuel-Saul-Komplex* (Uppsala: Almqvist & Wiksell, 1932) 9–62; M. Noth, "Samuel und Silo," *VT* 13 (1963) 390–400; H. W. Hertzberg, *I & II Samuel* (Philadelphia: Westminster Press, 1964) 43–44; and H. J. Stoebe, *Das erste Buch Samuelis* (Gütersloh: Gerd Mohn, 1973) 84–88. For discussion of the call itself, see Newman, "The Prophetic Call of Samuel," 86–97.

Shiloh's central social structure. His oracle is said to have been fulfilled after the accession of Solomon, who removed Abiathar from his priestly office in Jerusalem and exiled him to Anathoth (1 Kgs 2:26–27). Abiathar was the son of Ahimelech the son of Ahitub (1 Sam 22:20), and Ahitub was in turn related to the Elides of Shiloh (1 Sam 14:3). If Abiathar was indeed a descendant of Eli, then some form of the oracle now contained in 1 Sam 2:22–36 may have been used either by the Zadokites to explain how they came to be the sole priestly house in the Jerusalem temple or by the descendants of Abiathar to explain why they lost their priestly office. If the oracle originally functioned in the latter way, then it is worth noting that this use of the oracle reflects orthodox Deuteronomic theology. From the Deuteronomist's point of view, the people of Israel, their rulers, and their cities suffer because they violate God's commands.[61]

No matter what the original function of the oracle in 1 Sam 2:22–36, it now marks the transition to the narrative of Samuel's call (1 Sam 3:1—4:1), which again portrays Eli in a negative light and reinforces the judgment against him by repeating it in an elaborated form.[62] In spite of the fact that the call narrative has been shaped for the purpose of developing the anti-Elide theme of the preceding chapters, the account nevertheless contains motifs that are also found in the anthropological evidence that we have examined. The narrative opens with a note that divine words and visions were infrequent in Eli's time (1 Sam 3:1), a remark which not only casts doubt on his cultic effectiveness but also serves to explain why Samuel did not initially recognize the voice of God. Samuel is clearly portrayed as a member of the central religious establishment at Shiloh (1 Sam 3:1), and it was he rather than Eli who slept in the temple, perhaps to seek some sort of revelatory dream (1 Sam 3:2–3). Nevertheless, when God first tried to contact Samuel by calling him, he was uncertain about the proper interpretation of his experience. He replied to the divine call (1 Sam 3:4), but God did not

---

61. For a case analogous to the one in 1 Sam 2:22–36, note that after the account of Jeroboam's installation of a bull image at Bethel, the Deuteronomist inserts a story about an unnamed man of God who delivered a judgment oracle against the altar at Bethel (1 Kings 13). The later destruction of the altar by Josiah is then explained as a fulfillment of this prophecy and as a judgment against the sins of Jeroboam (2 Kgs 23:15–16).

62. For a discussion of the anti-Elide character of 1 Samuel 1—3, see J. T. Willis, "An Anti-Elide Narrative Tradition from a Prophetic Circle at the Ramah Sanctuary," *JBL* 90 (1971) 288–308.

continue to speak. Samuel therefore assumed that Eli had called and went to him. Eli, as a priest, should have immediately been able to supply the proper interpretation of Samuel's experience, but the old man did not understand what had happened. This sequence of events was repeated two more times before Eli finally perceived the real meaning of Samuel's experience and told him the response that was required to bring about a complete revelation of God. The narrative thus reflects the fact that potential intermediaries are not sure how to interpret their initial experiences with the spirits and frequently must visit an established intermediary in order to learn what has actually happened. The established intermediary determines the correct interpretation of events, a process that usually involves forcing the spirit to identify itself. Eli demonstrated his incompetence by not playing his proper role until Samuel's third visit. However, he did finally tell Samuel the proper procedure to follow, and when Yahweh called again, Samuel gave the required response. God then continued speaking and gave a second oracle foretelling the destruction of Eli's priestly line. In this case, Samuel's initial contact with the supernatural realm led him to become an intermediary. God continued to speak to Samuel at Shiloh, and Samuel served as Yahweh's prophet, delivering the divine words to all Israel (1 Sam 3:20—4:1). Furthermore, Samuel was a Mosaic prophet, whose words always came true, and this authenticated him in the eyes of the people (1 Sam 3:19–20).

Our analysis of 1 Sam 1:1—4:1 thus suggests that the Deuteronomist saw Samuel as a priestly member of the central cult who periodically received prophetic oracles. These oracles condemned the cultic establishment because it had departed from the ritual patterns that God had originally set up. Samuel therefore appears as a central prophet with important social maintenance functions. This fact implies that the Deuteronomist believed that central prophets like Samuel existed before the rise of the monarchy and that they were connected with some of the northern sanctuaries. These figures were priests who sometimes acted as prophets, and their social roles were not limited to prophecy. This picture of Samuel as a central intermediary is further developed in the Deuteronomist's later narratives.

Samuel and the Establishment of the Monarchy

The narratives that deal with Samuel's role in the establishment of the monarchy are extraordinarily complex, and there is no general scholarly consensus on how accurately the individual stories reflect historical reality. Older attempts to assign all of the stories either to a "promonarchical source" or to an "antimonarchical source" and then to argue for the historicity of one source or the other are now generally rejected for failing to take into account the complexity of the traditions. However, it is clear that the narratives that have been preserved reflect differing evaluations of the monarchy and of Samuel's role in its establishment.[63] On the basis of literary style and content, the following narrative blocks can be distinguished: (1) 1 Sam 8; 10:17–27; and 12 are generally acknowledged to be from the Deuteronomist and to reflect a negative view of kingship. In our present text these Deuteronomic comments on the founding of the monarchy are preceded by the Deuteronomic account of Samuel's judgeship (1 Sam 7:3–17) and are followed by the beginning of the Deuteronomic history of the monarchy (1 Sam 13:1). These Deuteronomic units serve as a frame for the other narratives dealing with kingship and in this way impose a Deuteronomic perspective on the entire series of stories. It must therefore be assumed that the Deuteronomist gave the overall complex its final shape, but it is not necessary to assume that the Deuteronomist's views are therefore later than the views found in the remainder of the material. The Deuteronomic units may be composed of several editorial or tradition layers and may even represent antimonarchical views existing in Ephraimite circles at the end of the period of the judges.[64] (2) 1 Sam 9:1—10:16 is generally recognized as an early account that presents a favorable view of the monarchy. Such views presumably did exist at the end of the period of the judges, thus permitting the

---

63. For thorough discussions of Samuel's role in the rise of the monarchy, see Birch, *The Rise of the Israelite Monarchy*; A. Weiser, *Samuel* (Göttingen: Vandenhoeck & Ruprecht, 1962); Hylander, *Samuel-Saul-Komplex*, 94–183; Stoebe, *Das erste Buch Samuelis*, 176–181; Hertzberg, *Samuel*, 130–134; O. Plöger, *Die Prophetengeschichten der Samuel- und Königsbücher* (Greifswald: E. Panzig, 1937) 6–11; T. Veijola, *Das Königtum in der Beurteilung der deuteronomistischen Historiographie* (Helsinki: Suomalainen Tiedeakatemia, 1977) 30–99; F. Crüsemann, *Der Widerstand gegen das Königtum* (Neukirchen-Vluyn: Neukirchener Verlag, 1978) 54–84; T. N. D. Mettinger, *King and Messiah* (Lund: C. W. K. Gleerup, 1976) 64–98; T. Ishida, *The Royal Dynasties in Ancient Israel* (Berlin: Walter de Gruyter, 1977) 26–54; J. A. Soggin, *Das Königtum in Israel* (Berlin: Alfred Töpelmann, 1967) 29–57; W. Richter, *Die sogenannten vorprophetischen Berufungsberichte* (Göttingen: Vandenhoeck & Ruprecht, 1970) 13–56; and M. A. Cohen, "The Role of the Shilonite Priesthood in the United Monarchy of Ancient Israel," *HUCA* 36 (1965) 59–98.

64. H. J. Boecker, *Die Beurteilung der Anfänge des Königtums in den deuteronomistischen Abschnitten des I. Samuelbuches* (Neukirchen-Vluyn: Neukirchener Verlag, 1969).

monarchy to be established in the first place, but it is still possible that the account in 1 Sam 9:1—10:16 has been influenced by later monarchical views. (3) 1 Sam 11:1–15 is usually regarded as a third account of the founding of the monarchy, even though the unit's present position in the text implies that the events recounted in the narrative occurred after Saul's anointing. The date and historiographic import of the unit have been the subject of great debate, but there is no reason to doubt that the narrative contains early material.

1 SAM 11:1–15

If 1 Sam 11:1–15 was in fact originally an account of how Saul came to power, then it is clear that the creator of the unit believed that Samuel played almost no role in the process.[65] Rather, the narrative portrays Saul's elevation as the direct result of divine election. The beginning of the story implies that Israel's political system had deteriorated to the point that individual cities and tribes were no longer safe from outside military pressure. Presumably, Samuel, the last of the judges (cf. 1 Sam 7:3–17), was no longer able to contain the Philistines, and in the ensuing political turmoil the Ammonites were able to besiege Jabesh-gilead and impose on it outrageous treaty conditions (1 Sam 11:1–4). When Saul heard of this hopeless situation, "the spirit of God rushed upon Saul," and he himself assumed the leader's role. Using the threatening sign of the dismembered oxen, Saul gathered the tribes under his own leadership and together with Samuel (1 Sam 11:7) went to the relief of Jabesh-gilead. As a result of Saul's victory, all opposition to his kingship ceased (1 Sam 11:12), and Samuel assembled the people at Gilgal to "renew the kingdom." There *the people* made Saul king and made ritual offerings to celebrate the event (1 Sam 11:15).

According to this version of events, Samuel by this time was a weak political leader who had lost his ability to deliver the people. God therefore chose a new leader, who like the earlier judges was

---

65. Some scholars have even argued that Samuel originally played no role in the story at all. See the discussion of Hylander, *Samuel-Saul-Komplex*, 155–159; Birch, *The Rise of the Israelite Monarchy*, 54–55; and Mettinger, *King and Messiah*, 83–87. Because 1 Sam 11:1–15 has frequently been taken as an old, reliable account of how Saul actually became king, Samuel's absence from the story would suggest that he played virtually no role in Saul's accession. For a discussion of the reliability of 1 Sam 11:1–15, see J. M. Miller, "Saul's Rise to Power: Some Observations Concerning 1 Sam 9:1—10:16, 10:26—11:15 and 13:2—14:46," *CBQ* 36 (1974) 165–171; and V. Fritz, "Die Deutungen des Königtums Sauls in den Überlieferungen von seiner Entstehung I Sam 9—11," *ZAW* 88 (1976) 346–362.

inspired by the spirit of God to perform heroic deeds (cf. Judg 14:6, 19; 15:14). Saul's election was thus in keeping with Ephraimite ideas about charismatic leadership. Saul himself did not claim political power, but power was conferred on him by the spirit of God. Although the narrative implies that Saul originally intended only to help the aging Samuel (1 Sam 11:7), the younger man's success resulted in his election to kingship. Samuel's role in the election is unclear, and in the end the people ratified the divine choice of Saul. The narrator thus retains a small role for Samuel but apparently did not recognize his prophetic or priestly status. The identity of the narrator cannot be determined with any certainty, but the general tone of the story suggests that it may have come from an Ephraimite group that supported Saul's kingship by appealing to traditional methods of legitimation. The group apparently did not recognize Samuel as a legitimate prophet and may have also rejected the power claims of the sanctuaries with which Samuel was associated.

1 SAM 9:1—10:16

The account of Saul's election in 1 Sam 9:1—10:16 gives Samuel a more important prophetic role than does 1 Sam 11:1–15, but the narrative stops short of portraying him as a powerful central intermediary.[66] Saul is still the main focus of the narrative and is shown in a favorable light.[67] The man of God, whether originally Samuel or not, plays a subsidiary role. Saul is from an old, wealthy Benjamite family and is the most handsome young man in Israel (1 Sam 9:1–2). He is zealous in pursuing the errand on which he has been sent, and when he is unable to locate the lost asses, he is concerned that his father will begin to worry (1 Sam 9:5). The visit to the man of God is initiated by a servant rather than by Saul, so there can be no suggestion that Saul was in any way responsible for engineering the events that were to follow (1 Sam 9:5–6). The man of God is not portrayed as a powerful charismatic leader, prophet, and priest but as a successful local seer (*rōʾeh*) to whom people come to get information

66. First Samuel 9:1—10:16 appears to have had a complex history of development, and the unity of the passage has been questioned. For a summary of the issues and an evaluation of recent scholarly theories on the unity of the passage, see Miller, "Saul's Rise to Power," 157–161. Arguments for interpreting the passage as a single unit are presented by Birch, *The Rise of the Israelite Monarchy*, 29–42; cf. Mettinger, *King and Messiah*, 64–78.

67. The positive tone of the narrative is generally acknowledged. See Birch, *The Rise of the Israelite Monarchy*, 29, 42.

about the future. Such seers were apparently intermediaries through whom the people could contact God, although by the writer's time this function was performed in Ephraim only by the prophet (1 Sam 9:9). The seer also had cultic functions in the local sanctuary, although the extent and importance of these functions are unclear.

In spite of the fact that the narrative focuses on Saul and portrays Samuel as a relatively unimportant figure, the prophet still plays a clear role in Saul's election. The command to anoint Saul is given to Samuel in a prophetic revelation which indicates that Saul is to be a leader (*nāgîd*) who will save Israel from the Philistines. There is no reference to anointing Saul as king, and there are no negative overtones in Yahweh's message of appointment. Rather, the narrative interprets Yahweh's command to anoint Saul as a gracious reply to the cries of oppressed Israel, and the language used to express this reply is reminiscent of the language used to describe Yahweh's deliverance of Israel from Egypt (1 Sam 9:16; cf. Exod 2:23; 3:7–9). When Saul finally arrives in Samuel's city, the young man reacts modestly to the seer's special treatment (1 Sam 9:21). Samuel then performs the anointing which God had commanded and delivers a prophetic oracle legitimating Saul's election (1 Sam 10:1). Saul's reaction to the actual anointing is not recorded, but his incredulity is implied by the fact that three signs are given to authenticate Samuel's oracle.

The third of these authenticating signs, and the only one whose fulfillment is narrated in detail, throws some additional light on the narrator's views about prophecy. Saul is told that he will encounter a band of prophets exhibiting characteristic prophetic behavior (*mitnabbĕʾîm*). This behavior is not specifically described. However, the fact that the prophets are pictured playing musical instruments suggests that trance may have been involved, for music is frequently used to induce trance. Yet, apparently the prophets are still able to carry out normal human activities, such as walking and performing on musical instruments, and there is no suggestion that the trance state is incapacitating. When Saul encounters this group, the spirit of Yahweh will come upon Saul and he will be changed. The positive nature of this experience is indicated by the fact that the possessing spirit comes from Yahweh and is an indication of divine election (1 Sam 10:5–6). The sign occurs just as Samuel had predicted. When Saul meets the prophetic band, he exhibits its characteristic behavior (*wayyitnabbē> bĕtôkām*). Again the precise nature of this behavior is unspecified, but no negative evaluation is given to it. However, the stereotypical character of Saul's behavior is clear from the fact that his acquaintances are able to recognize his behavior as prophetic. They are surprised at this turn of events, a fact that is said to explain the origin of the question "Is Saul also among the prophets?" Although the reader knows the answer to this question, the bystanders do not, and to obtain an interpretation of Saul's behavior, one person inquires about the "father" or leader of the prophetic band of which Saul seems to be a member (1 Sam 10:10–13).[68] According to the anthropological evidence, this procedure is the one usually followed in cases of unexpected spirit possession. Because in many societies the signs of genuine spirit possession and the symptoms of illness are virtually identical, a professional medium or diviner is frequently consulted for a diagnosis of the affected individual's condition. In this case it is usually assumed that the "father" referred to in the bystander's inquiry is Samuel, although this passage never portrays him as the leader of a prophetic group. In any case, Samuel would certainly be capable of answering the bystander's question. Saul's unusual behavior does not mean that he has become a prophet but that he has received Yahweh's spirit as a sign of election to Israel's leadership.

The individual or group that produced 1 Sam 9:1—10:16 thus seems to have followed the author of 1 Sam 11:1–15 in seeing Saul's election in continuity with the charismatic election of earlier Ephraimite leaders, but there are subtle differences between the two views. First Samuel 9:1—10:16 places a much greater stress on Saul's general suitability for leadership and seems to take pains to counter any accusation that Saul actually sought kingship. The almost polemical character of the narrative on this point suggests a situation in which the legitimacy of Saul's rule was being challenged. Such challenges could have occurred at any time, but they would have been particularly likely to have appeared after David

68. For a grammatical analysis of the two possible answers to the question "Is Saul also among the prophets?" see J. Sturdy, "The Original Meaning of 'Is Saul Also Among the Prophets?'" *VT* 20 (1970) 210–211. The question about the prophets' "father" is difficult to interpret in this context, but there is no doubt that *ʾāb* is the title of the leader of a prophetic group. See Williams, "The Prophetic 'Father,'" 344–348; and Phillips, "The Ecstatics' Father," 183–194. Because there is no reference to any kind of prophetic speech in this passage, Phillips' theory that the prophetic "father" was sought to translate the incoherent ravings of the ecstatics cannot be supported in this instance. Cf. Parker, "Possession Trance," 273–275.

had begun to gather political support.[69] Similarly, the author of 1 Sam 9:1—10:16 places a greater emphasis on Samuel and seems to be more tolerant of prophecy in general than the author of 1 Sam 11:1–15. In 1 Sam 9:1–10:16 the divine spirit that legitimates Saul leads him to exhibit *prophetic* behavior, and the author evaluates this behavior positively. The actual anointing of the new leader is performed by Samuel, who also delivers a prophetic oracle of appointment. However, the author does not see Samuel as a major prophetic leader but as a local seer who is used by Yahweh to legitimate the new ruler. This view of Samuel is sometimes thought to be an accurate description of this early prophet, while more complimentary views are taken to be later attempts to aggrandize him. Although this interpretation cannot be ruled out, the picture of Samuel found in 1 Sam 9:1—10:16 could just as easily be seen as the product of a group which wished to gain popular support for Saul and which therefore did not wish to alienate the groups that accepted the prophetic authority of Samuel.

1 SAM 7; 8; 10:17–27; 12

In the Deuteronomic interpretations of Samuel's role in the rise of the monarchy, he clearly appears as a Mosaic prophet exhibiting all of the characteristics of prophets in the Deuteronomic tradition. Because of the Deuteronomist's skillful editing of the Samuel-Saul narratives, this view now eclipses the other views that we have just discussed.

The Deuteronomic portrait of Samuel begins in 1 Sam 7:3–17, a unit which is usually thought to be concerned with describing Samuel as the last of the judges.[70] Although this is certainly the focus of the narrative, Samuel's prophetic functions are also mentioned, and the author seems to assume that Samuel was both judge and prophet. The unit begins in 1 Sam 7:3 with Samuel delivering to the people a characteristically Deuteronomic exhortation to return to Yahweh and to cease worshiping foreign gods so that Yahweh will deliver Israel out of the power of the Philistines. The people obey the exhortation, and Samuel then acts as intercessor and prays for them (1 Sam 7:4–6). In the face of a new Philistine threat, the repentant people continue to plead with Samuel to intercede,

---

69. Cf. Ishida, *Royal Dynasties*, 42–46, 49–51; Weiser, *Samuel*, 53–61.
70. Birch, *The Rise of the Israelite Monarchy*, 11–21.

and Samuel does so, with the result that the Philistines are routed by Yahweh's direct intervention (1 Sam 7:7–11). The pattern exhibited in the narrative is thus the same one implied in Judg 6:7–10.[71] When foreigners afflict the people, a prophet exhorts them to return to Yahweh. The people listen to the divine word that comes from the prophet and repent. The prophet then intercedes with Yahweh, who sends divine deliverance in some form.

The Deuteronomic version of Saul's rise continues in 1 Samuel 8, where Samuel is still portrayed as Israel's principal leader, although his sons have not been divinely designated as his successors and do not "walk in his ways" (1 Sam 8:1–3). The elders of Israel therefore ask Samuel for a king rather than waiting for God to appoint a successor. Acting as Mosaic prophet, Samuel takes their request to Yahweh (1 Sam 8:4–6). The Lord replies with an oracle that agrees to set up a king but that interprets the people's request as a rejection of Yahweh's rule (1 Sam 8:7–9). Samuel repeats the oracle to the people and elaborates it by describing the burdens which the king will inflict upon the people (1 Sam 8:10–18). This passage seems to look forward to the practices of Solomon and reflects the abuses of royal power which Deut 17:14–20 seeks to prevent.[72] The people refuse to listen to Samuel's warning, and he finally agrees to install a king.

After the insertion of 1 Sam 9:1—10:16, which is now negatively colored because it is preceded by 1 Samuel 7—8, the Deuteronomic editor reinforces the negative image of Saul by recounting a different version of his election (1 Sam 10:17–27). Samuel again delivers to the people a prophetic oracle accusing them of rejecting Yahweh and suggesting that their new king will be a form of richly deserved punishment. Samuel then has Saul chosen by lot. The new king is not said to have been legitimated either by prophetic oracle or by the gift of Yahweh's spirit, and Saul is portrayed in a less than favorable light. He is not the charismatic leader of 1 Sam 11:1–15 but a coward who hides among the baggage as soon as he has been elected. Samuel then gives the people written instructions on the rights and duties of kingship, but not all of the people seem to be willing to accept the new ruler.

71. Richter, *Die Bearbeitungen des "Retterbuches,"* 106–109; Weiser, *Samuel,* 5–24; Veijola, *Das Königtum,* 30–38; Schüpphaus, *Richter- und Prophetengeschichten,* 184–190.
72. R. E. Clements, "The Deuteronomistic Interpretation of the Founding of the Monarchy in I Sam. VIII," *VT* 24 (1974) 398–410.

After 1 Sam 11:1–15, now also colored negatively because of its context, the Deuteronomist inserts a final detailed comment on the election of Saul (1 Samuel 12). Samuel defends his conduct as Israel's leader and then delivers to the people a long characteristically Deuteronomic account of Israel's history, after which the people recognize their sin and ask Samuel to intercede for them. Samuel assures them that he will continue to serve as their intercessor and leaves them with a final exhortation.

The narratives describing Samuel's role in the rise of the monarchy thus reflect different views of the nature and importance of his prophetic activities. It is now difficult to determine which of these views is historically accurate—if indeed any of them are. However, if Samuel was actually an Ephraimite priest who occasionally functioned as a central prophet, as 1 Samuel 3 suggests, then some version of the Deuteronomist's picture of Samuel may turn out to be more historically accurate than the others. According to this picture, Samuel was a member of the central cultic establishment who also functioned as a Mosaic prophet. He served as a means by which the people could contact Yahweh, and his speech and possession behavior followed the expectations of his support group, the people who supported the sanctuaries that he served. As a member of the central religious and political establishments, he invoked Ephraimite tradition to oppose the institution of kingship, which he saw as a threat to Yahweh's rule.[73] The groups which supported Saul quite naturally took a different view of Samuel. From their perspective he was not the central figure pictured by the Deuteronomist, and they seem not to have recognized his prophetic authority. Still, some of Saul's supporters apparently did not wish to alienate Samuel's support group, and they therefore accorded him some measure of prophetic status. However, in the end Samuel and his support group won a qualified victory by deposing Saul and installing David.

The Decline of Saul and the Rise of David

Samuel's prophetic role in bringing about Saul's decline is known to us only from a Deuteronomic narrative which includes some pro-Davidic material that may have come from non-Deuteronomic

73. Cohen, "The Shilonite Priesthood," 59–76.

sources.[74] The picture of Samuel in this narrative is therefore generally similar to the one that we have seen elsewhere in the
Deuteronomist's writings. The Deuteronomic History's official account of Saul's reign begins with an incident that illustrates his
abuse of royal power. Although in this account Samuel is still
clearly portrayed as the priest who controls Israel's central cult,
Saul attempts to usurp Samuel's priestly prerogatives by offering a
sacrifice before a battle. This is a violation of Deuteronomic law,
which gives kings no priestly functions, and Samuel immediately
condemns Saul and predicts the end of his rule (1 Sam 13:5–15).
Soon after this incident, Samuel delivers to Saul an oracle demanding the complete destruction of Amalek. Saul does not obey the
command, and he is immediately condemned by Samuel and rejected by Yahweh (1 Samuel 15).

According to the Deuteronomic account, Samuel then plays a crucial role in the election of David. Responding to a divine command,
Samuel anoints the new king, who is then legitimated by the spirit
of Yahweh. At the same time Yahweh's spirit leaves Saul, who is
tormented by an evil spirit sent from Yahweh (1 Sam 16:1–14).

Samuel appears only one other time in a demonstrably
Deuteronomic passage, the curious tale of Saul's encounter with the
medium at Endor (1 Samuel 28).[75] After Samuel's death, another
Mosaic prophet was apparently not appointed to replace him.
Therefore, when the rejected Saul sought to approach Yahweh
through other types of intermediaries, there was no answer. Without
a Mosaic prophet to serve as a channel of communication through
which Saul could inquire of Yahweh, there was no legitimate way to
obtain divine information. God therefore did not answer Saul either
by dreams, or by other prophets, or by Urim and Thummim (1 Sam
28:6). For this reason Saul sought one of the mediums that he had
banished from the land, a woman at Endor who was able to control
the spirits of the dead. Saul did not attempt to seek information
about the future directly from the medium, for such a thing was not
possible according to the Deuteronomic perspective. Instead he

74. For thorough studies of the narratives of David's rise, see Ishida, *Royal Dynas-
ties*, 55–80; J. H. Grønbaek, *Die Geschichte vom Aufstieg Davids* (Copenhagen:
Munksgaard, 1971); and T. Veijola, *Die ewige Dynastie* (Helsinki: Suomalainen
Tiedeakatemia, 1975).

75. For a discussion of the background of this chapter, see Lust, "On Wizards and
Prophets," 133–142.

had the medium call up Samuel, the last Mosaic prophet, from the land of the dead. Saul then inquired of Samuel concerning the future, and Samuel, a Mosaic prophet who could intercede and perceive God's word more clearly than normal prophets, gave Saul a divine reply, characteristically in the form of a Deuteronomic sermon (1 Sam 28:8–19).

Although the Deuteronomic accounts of Saul's rejection and David's election portray Samuel as a powerful central prophet capable of controlling the course of kingship, the present text contains some indications that this positive Deuteronomic view of Samuel and of prophecy in general was not shared by some of David's supporters. The account of David's rise, which to a certain extent reflects Deuteronomic views, includes two descriptions of prophetic behavior that is evaluated negatively. Because the Deuteronomist tends to evaluate characteristic prophetic behavior positively and because both descriptions are strongly pro-Davidic, it is likely that the two passages in question originated among non-Deuteronomic groups that supported David. According to 1 Sam 18:10–11, an evil spirit which Yahweh had sent possessed Saul and caused him to exhibit characteristic prophetic behavior (*wayyit-nabbē*>). The precise nature of this behavior is unspecified, but it was apparently uncontrolled and violent, leading Saul to attack David with a spear. As is typical in cases of uncontrolled possession behavior, Saul's actions are evaluated negatively, a fact indicated not only by the description of the violence of his behavior but also by its attribution to an evil spirit.

This negative view of characteristic prophetic behavior is further developed in 1 Sam 19:18–24. As a result of Saul's hostility, David was forced to take refuge in Ramah with Samuel, who in this story is clearly portrayed as the head of a group of prophets. When Saul sent messengers to capture David, they approached while the prophets were prophesying (*nibbĕ*>*îm*), and the messengers too began exhibiting characteristic prophetic behavior (*wayyitnabbĕ*>*û*). Two more sets of messengers were sent, and each time the result was the same (1 Sam 19:20–21). The exact nature of the prophetic behavior is unspecified at this point in the narrative, but it incapacitated the messengers and physically prevented them from reaching David. This seems to suggest that the author of the story considered prophetic behavior to be a form of uncontrolled trance. This suggestion is confirmed by the conclusion of the story. Saul himself approached, and he too began to exhibit characteristic prophetic behavior (*wayyitnabbē*). In this case the nature of the behavior is clear: Saul lost control of himself, tore off his clothes, and lay naked and helpless all day and night before Samuel. Saul's behavior on this occasion, the narrator concludes, is the real origin of the saying "Is Saul also among the prophets?" (1 Sam 19:22–24). Here there is no doubt that typical prophetic behavior is evaluated negatively, and because Samuel is the leader of the prophets, he too shares the negative evaluation. Prophetic behavior is seen as uncontrolled and incapacitating. Furthermore, in the overall context of these narratives, the traditional question "Is Saul also among the prophets?" has a new answer. The reader already knows why Saul exhibits stereotypically uncontrolled, violent prophetic behavior. He is possessed by an evil spirit which is driving him mad (1 Sam 18:10–11). The answer to the question is therefore, "No, Saul is no prophet; he is insane."[76] The group responsible for these narratives thus tends to evaluate possession behavior negatively and to consider it a potentially dangerous and uncontrollable type of activity.

The various traditions concerning Samuel's prophetic activity thus portray him in various ways. The Deuteronomic narratives describe him as a typical Mosaic prophet, whose behavior conformed to Ephraimite expectations and who occupied a central role in Israel's religious and political establishments. He was a political leader and priest, who sometimes also acted as a prophet. As a central prophet, he was supported by the groups owing allegiance to certain northern sanctuaries, and he used his prophetic position to preserve and promulgate traditional Ephraimite views. Groups of prophets also seem to have been related to these sanctuaries, so it may be that Samuel was the head of some sort of a central possession cult. Among the groups that supported Saul's kingship, Samuel seems to have played a less central role, although they too seem to have recognized the importance of obtaining his support for the new ruler. Yet, as Saul attempted to consolidate his power, he and the groups that supported him seem to have rejected Samuel's pro-

76. Sturdy ("'Is Saul Also Among the Prophets?'" 211–213) is probably correct in suggesting that this saying originated in pro-Davidic circles and was used to denigrate Saul by calling attention to his "madness." If this was the original use of the saying, then its incorporation into the election narrative in 1 Sam 9:1—10:13 may represent an attempt by Saul's supporters to counter this pro-Davidic propaganda by providing an alternative explanation. For other interpretations, see Parker, "Possession Trance," 278–279; J. Lindblom, "Saul inter Prophetas," *ASTI* 9 (1974) 30–41; and V. Eppstein, "Was Saul Also Among the Prophets?" *ZAW* 81 (1969) 287–304.

phetic claims, a move that may have also been made by some of David's supporters. Still, none of the sources portray Samuel as a peripheral prophet, and they indicate that he retained some measure of political and religious power until his death.

Ahijah of Shiloh

The prophet Ahijah appears twice in the Deuteronomic History (1 Kgs 11:29–39; 14:1–18) and is the first of a series of Ephraimite prophets who appear regularly to deliver divine messages to the kings of Israel and Judah. Although old traditions may lie behind some of the accounts of these prophets' activities, the accounts in their present form bear the clear stamp of the Deuteronomist. As a result, many of these prophets use strikingly similar phrases in their oracles and exhibit behavior that resembles the behavior of earlier Ephraimite prophets.[77] The oracles of these monarchical prophets reflect Deuteronomic theology and usually condemn the kings for not obeying the Deuteronomic law. It is now impossible to determine why so many of these prophets resemble each other. In some cases, the similarities may simply be due to thorough editing by the Deuteronomists, who have imposed their own views about prophecy on earlier prophetic traditions. However, it is not possible to rule out the hypothesis that the Ephraimite monarchical prophets actually shared characteristic speech and behavioral patterns by virtue of having similar support groups that had certain expectations about the way legitimate prophets should act and speak. In this case the Ephraimite prophets of the monarchical period would have resembled each other for the same reason that contemporary intermediaries having the same support group exhibit stereotypical behavior. Support groups exert subtle pressure on their intermediaries to conform to expected behavioral patterns. We will consider this hypothesis in greater detail as we examine the Deuteronomic accounts of Ahijah and his Ephraimite successors.

Ahijah first appears in the Deuteronomic History at the conclusion of a heavily edited account of Solomon's marriages and of the apostasy which accompanied them (1 Kgs 11:1–13).[78] According to the

77. For a thorough study of the language of these prophetic narratives, see W. Dietrich, *Prophetie und Geschichte* (Göttingen: Vandenhoeck & Ruprecht, 1972).

78. The Deuteronomic features of this unit are discussed by J. Gray, *I & II Kings* (2d ed.; London: SCM Press, 1970) 271–274; and M. Noth, *Könige* (Neukirchen-Vluyn: Neukirchener Verlag, 1968) 1. 244–251.

Deuteronomist, Solomon's failure to keep God's commandments led to a divine judgment oracle removing all but one Israelite tribe from the control of Solomon's line. The actual fulfillment of this oracle is set in motion in 1 Kgs 11:29–39, the account of Ahijah's encounter with Jeroboam.[79] Ahijah's background is unclear. He was a Shilonite and thus lived in an old Ephraimite cult center that was associated with Samuel and the Elide priesthood (cf. 1 Kgs 14:2, 4). Although the text does not suggest that Ahijah himself was a priest, he may well have been a descendant of the people who supported Samuel.[80] The characteristic Deuteronomic tone of Ahijah's oracle suggests that he represented the Ephraimite theological views originally preserved at Shiloh and other northern shrines, and it is therefore not difficult to understand why he condemned Solomon. Israel's monarchy under Solomon had become precisely the type of absolutist political institution that Samuel and his supporters had opposed. In addition, Solomon had removed Abiathar, the last of Eli's Shilonite priestly line, from his priestly office and had thus purged Israel's central cult of all Ephraimite influence (1 Kgs 2:26–27). It is therefore probably not an accident that Ahijah met Jeroboam outside of Jerusalem. There is no indication that Ahijah was in any way connected with the Jerusalem cult. Instead, he appears as a peripheral prophet representing the views of a group outside of the central religious establishment. Just as Samuel had done earlier (1 Sam 15:26–31), Ahijah used the symbol of a torn garment to represent the royal authority that had been removed from one king and given to another. Just as Samuel had tried to counter Saul's growing power by anointing David as the new king, so also Ahijah and the group he represented apparently tried to curb the power of Solomon by designating a new king. Unlike Solomon, Jeroboam was an Ephraimite (1 Kgs 11:26) who might therefore be expected to be more supportive of the traditional northern political and religious views that Ahijah represented. The new king was legitimated by means of a prophetic oracle, a traditional Ephraimite

79. First Kings 11:29–39 may contain several editorial layers, but most of the later editing was done in connection with the oracle itself and did not alter the basic picture of Ahijah preserved in the original narrative. For a discussion of the editorial history of the unit, see Dietrich, *Prophetie und Geschichte*, 15–20, 54–55; and J. Debus, *Die Sünde Jerobeams* (Göttingen: Vandenhoeck & Ruprecht, 1967) 3–7.

80. A. Caquot ("Ahhiya de Silo et Jéroboam Ier," *Sem* 11 [1961] 17–27) has suggested that the prophet Ahijah is identical with an Elide priest of the same name in the time of Saul (1 Sam 14:3). This is an attractive suggestion, but chronological problems make it doubtful.

practice that was not followed when Solomon became king (cf. 1 Kgs 1:33–35, 39, 43–46).[81]

The Deuteronomic account of Jeroboam's election thus portrays Ahijah as a peripheral prophet representing traditional Ephraimite theological views. His support group was presumably composed of Ephraimites and may have included some of the priests that had been removed from power by Solomon. By means of prophecy Ahijah sought to change the central social structure and regain for himself and his support group some of the power that the group had lost during Solomon's reign. To enhance the prophet's authority, he is portrayed by the Deuteronomist as a Mosaic prophet, who delivers to the people the pure word of God, which inevitably comes to pass. The Deuteronomist narrates the fulfillment of Ahijah's prophecy in 1 Kgs 12:15 and in this way indicates his prophetic status. This prophecy-fulfillment motif appears throughout the Deuteronomic History and is used to underscore the authenticity of the utterances of the Ephraimite prophets.[82]

Unfortunately, Ephraimite hopes for a reformed monarchy were doomed to frustration. According to the Deuteronomists, Jeroboam immediately committed an unforgivable sin by reviving the old sanctuaries at Bethel and Dan and by instituting a royal cult in which he himself exercised priestly functions (1 Kgs 12:26–33). The Ephraimite groups that had once supported Jeroboam then turned against him. In 1 Kgs 14:1–18 Ahijah again appears as a typical peripheral prophet and delivers an oracle of judgment against Jeroboam's house. Although this unit has undergone considerable Deuteronomic reworking, the basic outlines of the prophet's characteristic behavior are visible in the earliest layers of the text.[83] In 1 Kgs 14:1–18 Ahijah is still at Shiloh, and again there is no indication that he is part of a central cult. Jeroboam sends his wife to inquire of Yahweh through Ahijah, whose miraculous powers are indicated by his foreknowledge of the visit (1 Kgs 14:1–6). Ahijah gives to the woman an oracle for the king, an oracle which has now been ex-

81. For a discussion of Jeroboam's rise to power and Ahijah's role in it, see H. Seebass, "Tradition und Interpretation bei Jehu ben Chanani und Ahia von Silo," *VT* 25 (1975) 175–190; idem, "Zur Königserhebung Jerobeams I," *VT* 17 (1967) 325–333; idem, "Zur Teilung der Herrschaft Salomos nach I Reg 11:29–39," *ZAW* 88 (1976) 363–376.

82. G. von Rad, *Studies in Deuteronomy* (London: SCM Press, 1953) 78–81.

83. Dietrich, *Prophetie und Geschichte*, 51–54, 112–114; H. Seebass, "Die Verwerfung Jerobeams I. und Salomos durch die Prophetie des Ahia von Silo," *WO* 4 (1968) 166–169.

panded to reflect traditional Deuteronomic theological views. Because of Jeroboam's apostasy, his sick child will die, and Jeroboam's line will come to an end (1 Kgs 14:7–16). The fulfillment of both aspects of the prophecy are eventually narrated (1 Kgs 14:17–18; 15:29).[84]

Shemaiah

In contrast to Ahijah, Shemaiah is portrayed by the Deuteronomists as a Judahite who exhibits none of the familiar characteristics of the Ephraimite prophets (1 Kgs 12:21–24).[85] The Deuteronomist says nothing about Shemaiah's background except that he delivered his oracle in Jerusalem, and his characteristic behavior is not described. However, a Judahite tradition preserved in Chronicles shows Shemaiah prophesying in the Jerusalemite royal court and condemning the people for abandoning Yahweh. When the people repent, the prophet delivers to them a qualified oracle of forgiveness. Outside of Shemaiah's prophetic activities, he is also said to have been the author of a chronicle of Rehoboam's reign (2 Chr 12:5–15). Thus the Chronicler suggests that Shemaiah was a member of the central religious establishment in Jerusalem. The Deuteronomist, however, says only that he delivered to Rehoboam an oracle warning the king not to go to war with Israel (1 Kgs 12:21–24).

The Man of God from Judah and the Prophet at Bethel

First Kings 13:1–32 contains a coherent but somewhat curious story about an unnamed man of God from Judah who delivered an oracle against Jeroboam's altar at Bethel and who was subsequently destroyed as the result of an encounter with an old prophet. In its present form the unit cannot be earlier than the time of Josiah, whose reforms are predicted in 1 Kgs 13:2. The reference to Josiah and the fact that the fulfillment of the prediction is explicitly narrated in 2 Kgs 23:16 are sometimes taken as indications that the whole story is a *vaticinium ex eventu* and therefore a late

84. At the final redactional level the oracle is broadened to include all of Israel rather than just the house of Jeroboam (1 Kgs 14:16). The fulfillment of this dimension of the oracle is found in 2 Kgs 17:21–23.

85. In the LXX (1 Kgs 12:24 o) Shemaiah replaces Ahijah as the prophet responsible for the election of Jeroboam, but this is certainly a late Judahite view. For a discussion of the LXX material, see Debus, *Sünde Jerobeams*, 55–90; and Seebass, "Die Verwerfung Jerobeams I.," 179–182.

Deuteronomic creation. However, several tensions between this story and the account of Josiah's reform suggest that older traditions lie behind the present form of 1 Kings 13. In 1 Kgs 13:2 the man of God predicts only that Josiah will defile the altar at Bethel by sacrificing on it the priests of the high places and by burning human bones on it. This prediction is then authenticated by means of a sign: the altar will be torn down, and its ashes will be poured out (1 Kgs 13:3). This sign immediately occurs (1 Kgs 13:5), thus guaranteeing the future fulfillment of the prophecy itself. Yet, according to 2 Kings 23, Josiah's reforms did not correspond perfectly with what is predicted in 1 Kings 13. Josiah did indeed fulfill the prophecy of 1 Kgs 13:2 by burning human bones on the altar at Bethel (2 Kgs 23:16). However, he also pulled down the altar and pulverized the stones (2 Kgs 23:15). The actual destruction of the altar itself is not part of the original prediction but is the sign whose immediate fulfillment is recorded in 1 Kgs 13:5. The fact that 2 Kgs 23:16 improbably speaks of burning bones on the altar after it has already been pulverized (2 Kgs 23:15) suggests that the reference to Josiah's destruction of the altar has been added to 2 Kings 23 by an editor who wrongly interpreted the sign of 1 Kgs 13:3 as part of the prediction in 1 Kgs 13:2. Furthermore, whereas 1 Kgs 13:2 predicts that Josiah will sacrifice the priests of the high places *on the altar at Bethel,* 2 Kgs 23:20 says that Josiah slew the priests *on the altars of high places* throughout the land. These discrepancies between 1 Kings 13 and 2 Kings 23 suggest that in 1 Kings 13 the Deuteronomist has edited an earlier story to make it into a prediction of Josiah's reforms but that the editorial process has not obliterated all traces of the original narrative.[86]

The picture of the man of God presented in 1 Kings 13 follows typical Deuteronomic lines, although it is impossible to know whether this picture was part of the original story or is the result of later Deuteronomic editing. In either case the picture can be as-

---

86. For attempts to reconstruct the traditions behind the chapter, see Noth, *Könige,* 1. 291–295; Gray, *Kings,* 318–323; Dietrich, *Prophetie und Geschichte,* 114–120; A. Jepsen, "Gottesmann und Prophet," *Probleme biblischer Theologie: Gerhard von Rad zum 70. Geburtstag* (ed. H. W. Wolff; Munich: Chr. Kaiser Verlag, 1971) 171–182; E. Würthwein, "Die Erzählung vom Gottesmann aus Juda in Bethel," *Wort und Geschichte: Festschrift für Karl Elliger zum 70. Geburtstag* (ed. H. Gese and H. P. Rüger; Kevelaer: Butzon & Bercker, 1973) 187–188; and M. A. Klopfenstein, "1. Könige 13," *Parrēsia: Karl Barth zum achtzigsten Geburtstag* (Zurich: EVZ-Verlag, 1966) 646–672. Unfortunately, the nature of the evidence makes it difficult to reconstruct with any certainty the tradition-history of 1 Kings 13.

sumed to represent Ephraimite views on prophecy. In its present context 1 Kings 13 immediately follows the Deuteronomist's account of Jeroboam's cultic activities. To prevent people from going to Jerusalem, the king revived the old northern shrines at Dan and Bethel, where he set up bull images, installed a non-Levitical priesthood, and instituted a new cultic calendar. He thus created central royal shrines for his newly established kingdom, and by performing cultic rites at Bethel he claimed priestly status for himself (1 Kgs 12:26–33). These moves were unacceptable to the Deuteronomists, who maintained that Jerusalem was still Israel's central shrine. In addition, the Deuteronomists followed a different cultic calendar, forbade royal participation in the cult, and required that all priests be Levites. From the Deuteronomic point of view, Jeroboam was inciting people to worship other gods and had overstepped the bounds of royal power. Seen in this context, the man of God from Judah appears as a peripheral intermediary who comes to the northern central sanctuary to reform it. Nothing is said about the social location of this figure, and in an older version of the story he might have been a representative of the central cult in Jerusalem.[87] However, in the present narrative he represents a Deuteronomic point of view and exhibits the characteristics of Ephraimite prophets. The word which he speaks against the altar (1 Kgs 13:2) ultimately comes true (2 Kgs 23:16), and the sign which he predicts occurs immediately (1 Kgs 13:3, 5). In addition he relays to God the king's request for healing and is successful in restoring his dried-up hand (1 Kgs 13:4, 6). The man of God is thus a true Deuteronomic prophet who serves as the channel through which God's word comes to the people and through which the people's requests are relayed to God.

In its present form the first episode of 1 Kings 13 concludes with the man of God stating the conditions which God had imposed on the man's prophetic activities. He was not to eat, drink, or return by the way in which he came. The original reason for these restrictions is unclear, but they now serve as the introduction to the second episode in the chapter, the encounter with the old prophet at Bethel. If this episode ever had an independent existence outside of 1 Kings 13, its original function is unclear. However, as a sequel to the

87. Since the time of Wellhausen, some scholars have seen in the story a reflection of the work of Amos. See most recently J. L. Crenshaw, *Prophetic Conflict* (Berlin: Walter de Gruyter, 1971) 41–42. However, this theory rests on very little evidence.

first episode it serves to raise another of the Deuteronomist's central concerns: how to identify the word that God has not spoken (cf. Deut 18:20–22). The social location of the old prophet at Bethel is not clearly specified. He apparently did not attend the sacrifice, so there is no indication that he had cultic functions. The fact that he is called an *old* prophet might imply that he once had cultic responsibilities at Bethel before the centralization of the cult in Jerusalem, but there is nothing else in the text to suggest this. If the plural ("his sons") is read in 1 Kgs 13:11–12, then the prophet might be seen as the head of a prophetic group, perhaps the head of what was formerly a central possession cult at Bethel. However, the singular ("his son") of the MT does not require this interpretation. Thus the man of God and the prophet look very much alike, and it is not impossible that they came originally from similar backgrounds. The man of God from Judah reflects a Deuteronomic point of view and might have been related to the northern priestly group that had been part of the central cult in Jerusalem but that had been exiled to the southern city of Anathoth. The old prophet might have remained in Bethel, where some of the older northern traditions were still being preserved. In any case, the confrontation between the two is clearly portrayed as a confrontation between two intermediaries of the same type. In this sense their meeting resembles the contests sometimes held between shamans to determine which is the strongest. The old prophet from Bethel apparently sets out to see whether or not the man of God from Judah is a true prophet. Because the Deuteronomists believed that an intermediary who was not a true prophet could still give a sign that subsequently occurred (cf. Deut 13:1–2), other methods had to be used to authenticate prophets. The old prophet may have intended to see if the man of God could recognize a false oracle. The prophet deliberately lies to the man of God, delivering a message that countermands the man of God's own divine instructions (1 Kgs 13:14–19). The man of God fails to recognize the lie and violates God's command. The prophet then receives a message from God condemning the man of God for his infidelity. However, ironically this message also authenticates the man of God, for it tells the old prophet that the man of God had told the truth about receiving from God an oracle with an accompanying prohibition (1 Kgs 13:16, 20–22). The prophet therefore realizes that the judgment oracle against Bethel will come true and throws in his lot with the man of God (1 Kgs 13:26–32).

If the issue lying behind this episode is the question of false prophecy, then the message of the story was pertinent only to an audience of prophets, not to an audience of ordinary people.[88] The "moral" of the story is that prophets who receive divine messages should obey those messages, even in the face of contradictory oracles. Just as the prophet is to speak all that Yahweh tells him (Deut 18:18), so also the prophet is to believe in the authenticity of his own revelation. Because this sort of exhortation is appropriate only to a group of prophets, it is likely that the story lying behind 1 Kings 13 was originally addressed to a group of prophets who were faced with prophetic messages that contradicted their own. This sort of prophetic conflict will become more common in the later history of Ephraimite prophecy.

Jehu

The Deuteronomist's picture of the prophet Jehu the son of Hanani resembles that of Ahijah in 1 Kings 14, although Jehu is less clearly assigned the usual attributes of an Ephraimite prophet. He is said to have received an oracle against the Israelite king Baasha, but the actual delivery of the oracle is not reported. Still, the oracle itself reflects Deuteronomic theology and in part is virtually the same as Ahijah's oracle against Jeroboam (1 Kgs 16:4 = 1 Kgs 14:11). The oracle is fulfilled against Baasha's house in 1 Kgs 16:11–13, thus underlining the truth of Jehu's message. The Deuteronomist therefore seems to have considered Jehu a peripheral prophet operating in the north. However, the Chronicler places Jehu in Jerusalem and shows him delivering a Deuteronomic-style oracle to Jehoshaphat (2 Chr 19:2–3). The Chronicler also attributes to Jehu a history of Jehoshaphat's reign (2 Chr 20:34). Jehu's father Hanani is said to have been a visionary (*ḥōzeh* [2 Chr 19:2]) and may have been the same figure who delivered an oracle against Asa, the king of Judah (2 Chr 16:7–10). This figure is given the old title "seer" (*rōʾeh* [2 Chr 16:7, 10]), although it is not clear what the Chronicler understood this title to mean. The Chronicler thus seems to have understood Jehu as a Jerusalemite prophet like Shemaiah, who was part of the central religious establishment. However, it is now impossible to determine whether the Chronicler's view or

88. Crenshaw (ibid., 46) correctly recognizes the story's concern with false prophecy but overlooks the specialized character of the story's function.

the Deuteronomist's view is correct, if indeed either of them is accurate.[89]

The Prophets of the
Elijah-Elisha Traditions

Unlike many of the prophetic stories in the Deuteronomic History, the Elijah-Elisha narratives reveal little obvious Deuteronomic editing. Rather, the Deuteronomists appear to have taken earlier Ephraimite traditions about prophecy in northern Israel during the reigns of Ahab and his successors (ca. 869–786 B.C.) and then incorporated those traditions into the History with a minimum of editorial comment. The Elijah-Elisha narratives therefore reflect characteristic Ephraimite views about the nature and function of prophecy but do not usually express these views in stereotypical Deuteronomic language.[90]

The present Elijah-Elisha narratives are composed of a number of originally independent stories, some of which may have been combined into larger units before being incorporated in the Deuteronomic History. For purposes of analysis these stories may be divided into three groups.

(1) Stories about Elijah's prophetic activities. Included in this group are the accounts of the prophet's rain-making activities (1 Kgs 17:1; 18:1–2a, 16–17, 41–46); the contest on Mount Carmel (1 Kgs 18:19–40); the theophany on Mount Horeb (1 Kgs 19:3b, 8b, 9–12, 13); the incident of Naboth's vineyard (1 Kgs 21:1–9, 11–20); and the oracle against Ahaziah (2 Kgs 1:2–8, 17a). To these stories have been added various tales of the prophet's supernatural powers and of the miraculous ways in which he was protected and fed (1 Kgs 17:2–6, 7–16, 17–24; 18:1a, 2b–15; 19:4a, 5–8; 2 Kgs 1:9–16). The stories and tales now found in 1 Kings 17—19 may have circulated as a collection before being taken into the Deuteronomic History. The Elijah traditions as a whole have been linked to the

89. First Kings 16:7 seems out of place because it repeats a version of Jehu's oracle against Baasha after the king's death has already been narrated (1 Kgs 16:6). For a discussion of the relation of 1 Kgs 16:7 to the oracle in 1 Kgs 16:2–4, see Seebass, "Tradition und Interpretation," 175–179; and Dietrich, *Prophetie und Geschichte,* 9–10.

90. The northern origin of the Elijah-Elisha traditions is seldom questioned, not only because of the northern setting of the stories themselves but also because of their distinctive vocabulary. See the discussion of C. F. Burney, *Notes on the Hebrew Text of the Books of Kings* (Oxford: At the Clarendon Press, 1903) 207–209.

Elisha traditions through the account of the call of Elisha (1 Kgs 19:19–21), which sees Elisha as the prophetic successor of Elijah. This link, if not historical, probably at least antedates the Deuteronomist.[91]

(2) Stories about Elisha. Included in this group are a series of originally unrelated miracle stories and *legenda* demonstrating the prophet's supernatural powers (2 Kgs 2:19–22, 23–25; 4:1–7, 8–17, 18–37, 38–41, 42–44; 6:1–7; 8:1–6).[92] In the present text these stories are introduced by an account of the transfer of prophetic authority from Elijah to Elisha (2 Kgs 2:1–18). To this series of stories a number of other narratives have been added. These additional stories have various characteristics. Some are didactic legends (2 Kings 5) and treat Elisha's dealings with the Syrians (2 Kgs 5; 6:8–23; 8:7–15). Others deal with the prophet's encounters with various Israelite kings (2 Kgs 3:4–27; 6:24—7:20; 9:1–10; 13:14–19).[93] The historical background of the Elisha stories is not always clear, and in the present text they do not seem to be arranged in a chronological sequence.[94]

(3) Stories of individual prophets. The originally independent stories of Micaiah ben Imlah (1 Kings 22) and of several anonymous prophets (1 Kgs 20:13–43) have been woven into the Elijah stories. Although these individual prophetic stories are

91. This analysis of the Elijah traditions follows G. Fohrer, *Elia* (2d ed.; Zurich: Zwingli-Verlag, 1968) 33–55. For slightly different analyses and additional discussions of the problems involved, see O. H. Steck, *Überlieferung und Zeitgeschichte in den Elia-Erzählungen* (Neukirchen-Vluyn: Neukirchener Verlag, 1968) 5–31, 40–53; Plöger, *Prophetengeschichten*, 16–22; O. Eissfeldt, "Die Komposition von I Reg 16:29—II Reg 13:25," *Das Ferne und Nahe Wort: Festschrift Leonhard Rost* (BZAW 105; ed. F. Maass; Berlin: Alfred Töpelmann, 1967) 49–58; and A. Jepsen, "Elia und das Gottesurteil," *Near Eastern Studies in Honor of William Foxwell Albright* (ed. H. Goedicke; Baltimore: Johns Hopkins University Press, 1971) 291–306. For an exhaustive study of the Deuteronomic editing of the Elijah traditions, see G. Hentschel, *Die Elija-erzählungen* (Leipzig: St. Benno-Verlag, 1977) 9–274; cf. Fohrer, *Elia*, 53–55; and R. Smend, "Das Wort Jahwes an Elia," *VT* 25 (1975) 525–543.

92. For a discussion of the proper classification of these stories, see A. Rofé, "The Classification of the Prophetical Stories," *JBL* 89 (1970) 427–440; idem, "Classes in the Prophetical Stories: Didactic Legenda and Parable," *Studies on Prophecy* (VTSup 26; Leiden: E. J. Brill, 1974) 143–164.

93. For analyses of the Elisha traditions, see Plöger, *Prophetengeschichten*, 22–29; Gray, *Kings*, 465–471; H.-C. Schmitt, *Elisa* (Gütersloh: Gerd Mohn, 1972); and H. Schweizer, *Elischa in den Kriegen* (Munich: Kösel-Verlag, 1974).

94. For a discussion of the historical background of the Elisha stories, see J. M. Miller, "The Elisha Cycle and the Accounts of the Omride Wars," *JBL* 85 (1966) 441–454.

now set in the reign of Ahab, they may have initially involved other kings.[95]

The complex tradition-history of the Elijah-Elisha stories and in particular their miraculous and legendary character make it difficult to determine the reliability of their picture of the nature and functions of Ephraimite prophecy. However, in making a judgment on this question it is important to note that form-critically diverse stories coming from various historical backgrounds nevertheless reflect the same characteristic views of prophecy that we have seen in other Ephraimite texts. At the very least this suggests that the Elijah-Elisha stories were created and/or shaped by groups that held common opinions about the behavior and social roles of prophets.

The Elijah Traditions

1 KINGS 17—19

The majority of the Elijah stories are found in 1 Kings 17—19, a complex unit composed of a number of originally independent narratives. In their present form these narratives are tied together in two ways. First, an earlier account of Elijah's role in the alleviation of a drought has been expanded to serve as the matrix for several other stories. The description of the increasing severity of the drought now serves as an appropriate background for two stories dealing with the way in which Elijah was fed during the time of deprivation (1 Kgs 17:2–6, 7–16), and the second of these stories in turn leads to a third involving the same characters (1 Kgs 17:17–24). The drought also motivates the meeting between Elijah and Obadiah (1 Kgs 18:2–15). The account of the removal of the drought now provides a setting for the story of the contest on Mount Carmel and the slaughter of the prophets of Baal (1 Kgs 18:19–40), and the drought narrative finally concludes with the bringing of rain (1 Kgs 18:41–46). In the present text this expanded and relatively cohesive drought narrative has been woven together with an account of Elijah's escape from the wrath of Jezebel after the killing of the Baal prophets. The description of the prophet's flight leads naturally to

---

95. For analyses of these stories and discussions of the historical problems, see Schmitt, *Elisa*, 42–51; Miller, "The Elisha Cycle," 441–447; and J. M. Miller, "The Rest of the Acts of Jehoahaz," *ZAW* 80 (1968) 337–342.

the story of the theophany on Mount Horeb and the call of Elisha (1 Kgs 19:1–21).

However, for our purposes, the more important unifying principle in these chapters is the second, the motif of the persecution of Elijah.[96] In addition to providing a background for some of the stories, this motif also clearly portrays Elijah as a peripheral prophet who operated on the fringes of the Israelite royal court. The prophet is pictured as an ardent opponent of Baal worship, a lonely figure who used prophecy to condemn the religious establishment and to advocate reforms resembling those demanded by the Deuteronomists. Because of his outspoken opposition to the official Israelite cult, he was suppressed and even persecuted by Jezebel, whom the narratives describe as a royal patron of Baal worship.[97]

The persecution motif is implied at the very beginning of 1 Kings 17, where God commands the prophet to hide himself (1 Kgs 17:3). However, the motif is not developed until 1 Kgs 18:3b–4, which describes Jezebel's active persecution of the prophets of Yahweh (cf. 1 Kgs 18:13), who by implication operated outside of the official royal cult. As we have already seen, repressive measures of this type are usually taken by a society only when its peripheral intermediaries make obviously unacceptable demands or engage in behavior that threatens the integrity of the social structure. Such a volatile situation is described in detail in the account of the contest on Mount Carmel (1 Kgs 19:19–40). This narrative not only illustrates Elijah's peripheral social functions but also describes some of his characteristic prophetic behavior and paints a clear picture of his prophetic opposition, the Baal prophets of Israel's central cult.[98]

In the narrative of the incident on Mount Carmel, the contest is described as a confrontation between Elijah, a peripheral prophet, and the prophets of Baal and Asherah, who enjoy royal protection and are part of the central religious establishment (1 Kgs 18:19).

96. A thorough discussion of later literary and theological developments of the motif of the persecution of the prophets is provided by O. H. Steck, *Israel und das gewaltsame Geschick der Propheten* (Neukirchen-Vluyn: Neukirchener Verlag, 1967).

97. It is possible that in an earlier version of these narratives Ahab rather than Jezebel was Elijah's chief opponent. See the discussion of Hentschel, *Die Elijaerzählungen*, 69; and Steck, *Überlieferung*, 29.

98. For thorough discussions of this narrative, see R. de Vaux, "The Prophets of Baal on Mount Carmel," in his *The Bible and the Ancient Near East* (Garden City, N.Y.: Doubleday, 1971) 238–251; H. H. Rowley, "Elijah on Mount Carmel," *Men of God* (London: Thomas Nelson, 1963) 37–65 (= *BJRL* 43 [1960–61] 190–219); and H. Seebass, "Elia und Ahab auf dem Karmel," *ZTK* 70 (1973) 121–136.

Elijah opens the contest by delivering a sharp challenge to the religious establishment. He demands that the people choose between Yahweh and Baal, a choice that will also involve supporting either Elijah and the type of Yahweh worship that he represents or the prophets of Baal, who are the intermediaries of the god of the central cult. Choosing Yahweh will necessarily involve rejecting Baal and will result in the destruction of the entire central cult. To help the people make their decision, Elijah sets up a contest which operates on two levels. On the divine level the contest is between Yahweh and Baal. However, on the human level the contest is between the gods' intermediaries. According to the guidelines that Elijah establishes, the contest is to determine which of the parties is the most effective intercessor. The one who is successful in obtaining a divine answer will be accredited as a genuine intermediary, and his god will be recognized as a true god. The peculiar stress on intercession that lies at the heart of the contest is reminiscent of the Ephraimite view of prophecy, which sees the prophet as a channel through which people can communicate with Yahweh. However, the standard Ephraimite view of the prophetic intercessor differs from the one found in 1 Kings 18 in one important respect. Whereas the stereotypical Ephraimite prophet relays requests from the people to Yahweh, the intercessory function mentioned in 1 Kings 18 only involves the prophet's ability to contact the deity and to obtain a divine response. The prophet does not relay any message from the people.

The contest takes place according to Elijah's instructions, and from the standpoint of the narrative the outcome is inevitable from the start. Baal is no god, and his intermediaries therefore cannot be genuine intermediaries. For this reason they are unsuccessful in their attempts at intercession. They exhibit their stereotypical possession behavior (*wayyitnabbĕʾû* [1 Kgs 18:29]), performing a characteristic dance and slashing themselves with knives (1 Kgs 18:26, 28). Their behavior is violent but not uncontrolled, for they are still capable of coherent speech (1 Kgs 18:26). On the other hand, Yahweh *is* God, and Elijah demonstrates his own genuine prophetic status by eliciting a divine response (1 Kgs 18:23–38). He does this by performing a series of ritual acts, the precise significance of which is unclear (1 Kgs 18:31–35). There is no indication that they were part of the normal worship of Yahweh or that Elijah regularly had cultic functions. The rituals are also unusual in that they take place at a Yahweh altar on Mount Carmel, a procedure that is at variance with the Deuteronomic view that Yahweh could legitimately be worshiped only at the central sanctuary in Jerusalem. Nevertheless, in spite of the apparently unorthodox character of the ritual God responds favorably to it. As a result, the people turn again to Yahweh and reject the central cult. Having proven the prophets of Baal not to be genuine prophets, Elijah imposes on them the penalty demanded by Deuteronomic law (Deut 18:19–22; 13:1–5). He slaughters all of the prophets of Baal. Even with the support of the people, violent activities such as murder are not viewed as acceptable behavior for peripheral prophets, for such acts destroy the social fabric and may lead to the disintegration of the whole society. Jezebel quite naturally seeks to reverse the damage by trying to harass and destroy Elijah (1 Kgs 19:1–3). However, Elijah escapes to Mount Horeb.

In the account of the theophany on Horeb (1 Kgs 19:9–18), the narrator underlines yet another aspect of the characteristic Ephraimite view of prophecy. Elijah is clearly portrayed as a prophet *like Moses.* The account of the theophany contains a number of interpretive difficulties, not the least of which is the doublet in 1 Kgs 19:9b–10 and 1 Kgs 19:13b–14.[99] The highly symbolic character of the narrative also raises questions about the historicity of the incident.[100] Yet, no matter how these difficulties are resolved, the fact remains that the author of the account unambiguously stresses the links between Elijah and Moses.[101] After being divinely prepared for the journey to Horeb, Elijah apparently fasted during the forty days and nights required to reach the sacred mountain (1 Kgs 19:4–8). In a similar way, when Moses received the Law, he did not eat or drink during the forty days and nights that he spent on the

99. For discussions of the unity and literary history of 1 Kgs 19:9–18, see E. Würthwein, "Elijah at Horeb: Reflections on I Kings 19:9–18," *Proclamation and Presence: Old Testament Essays in Honour of Gwynne Henton Davies* (ed. J. I. Durham and J. R. Porter; London: SCM Press, 1970) 152–166; J. J. Stamm, "Elia am Horeb," *Studia Biblica et Semitica Theodoro Christiano Vriezen* (Wageningen: H. Veenman, 1966) 327–334; R. A. Carlson, "Élie à l'Horeb," *VT* 19 (1969) 416–439; K. Seybold, "Elia am Gottesberg," *EvT* 33 (1973) 3–18; and J. K. Kuntz, *The Self-Revelation of God* (Philadelphia: Westminster Press, 1967) 147–154.

100. Cf. the assessments of Fohrer (*Elia,* 67–68); Gray (*Kings,* 373–374); and Steck (*Überlieferung,* 90–130).

101. The similarities between Moses and Elijah are obvious and have long been recognized. See Seybold, "Elia am Gottesberg," 10; Fohrer, *Elia,* 55–57; and R. P. Carroll, "The Elijah-Elisha Sagas: Some Remarks on Prophetic Succession in Ancient Israel," *VT* 19 (1969) 400–415.

mountain (Exod 24:18; 34:28). When Elijah reached Horeb, he found shelter in the cave (*hammě ʿārāh* [1 Kgs 19:9]), perhaps the same rocky cleft where Moses hid to protect himself from the glory of Yahweh (Exod 33:22–23). In response to Yahweh's question, Elijah complained that he had fled to the mountain because the people had forsaken the covenant, destroyed Yahweh's altars, and killed all of the rest of Yahweh's prophets (1 Kgs 19:10, 14). The prophet's situation was similar to that of Moses, who alone went to Horeb to receive the law and then returned to find that the people had forsaken Yahweh and were worshiping a molten calf. This apostasy on the part of the people forced Moses to return to the mountain, where he pleaded with Yahweh on their behalf and experienced a theophany that preceded the giving of a new set of laws (Exodus 32—34).[102] Finally, both Elijah and Moses experienced theophanies that are described in strikingly similar terms, and both theophanies culminated in a divine message (Exodus 19; 1 Kgs 19:11–12).

However, for the purposes of our inquiry, it is important to note that 1 Kgs 19:9–18 does not simply portray Elijah as a Mosaic prophet who is one of a long line of such prophets. Rather, the author of the passage links a critical period in Elijah's career with a *specific* incident in Moses' life: the giving of the Law at Horeb. By making this link the author reveals his understanding of the nature and authority of prophecy during the period of Elijah's prophetic activity.

In the overall context of the Elijah stories in 1 Kings 17—19, the theophany at Horeb occurs at a low point in the prophet's career.[103] In spite of his victory in the contest on Mount Carmel, Elijah appears not to have had the sort of support group necessary for his survival as an intermediary. This lack of social support is implicit in the persecution motif and in the narratives now contained in 1 Kings

---

102. In the light of this parallel it is interesting to note that the apostasy mentioned by Elijah in 1 Kgs 19:10, 14 is also the result of the illicit worship of bovine cult images. The Deuteronomic Historian ultimately traces the sins of Ephraim to Jeroboam's revival of the bull cult at Dan and Bethel (1 Kgs 12:26–33). In the opinion of the Deuteronomists, this act led to the sort of unorthodox worship that was condemned by Elijah and that finally brought about the destruction of Samaria.

103. Some scholars have actually suggested that the account of the theophany belongs *before* the contest on Mount Carmel because Elijah's depression in 1 Kgs 19:10, 14 is inappropriate after the great victory described in 1 Kgs 18:36–40 (Jepsen, *Nabi*, 63). This suggestion overlooks the sociological implications of the prophet's triumph.

17—18, where Elijah is consistently portrayed as a solitary figure operating outside of the context of an organized group. As the anthropological evidence indicates, peripheral prophets in such situations have little chance of survival, and Elijah's chances are not improved by the outcome of the contest. He wins the contest and the support of the people present, but he also commits a mass murder that threatens the existence of the central cult and the integrity of the establishment. Societies will not tolerate such actions, and as a result the crown seeks to repress Elijah and presumably also the few supporters that he had managed to collect. Clearly, he needs to regain some sort of social support and to bolster his authority in order to justify the major social, political, and religious changes that he has set in motion. The narrative of the theophany at Horeb has precisely this function, and if the present narrative or an earlier version of it was actually in use during Elijah's lifetime, the account presumably served to lend additional divine support to the prophet's words and deeds.

The account of the theophany enhances Elijah's authority in two ways. First, by portraying him as a Mosaic prophet, the text assigns Elijah a status which is superior to that of his prophetic contemporaries. As a prophet like Moses, Elijah's word always comes true (cf. 1 Kgs 17:16, 24), and his actions are based on a unique relationship to Yahweh. Second, the theophany itself confers new status on Elijah and by extension on all future Mosaic prophets. Elijah's authority is the authority of Moses, and the prophet's word is a divine word, fully comparable to the Torah, the Law given to Moses at Horeb. The prophet's new status is made clear by the structure of the narrative. When Elijah complains of his isolated state, Yahweh responds with a theophany resembling the one experienced by Moses. Elijah receives a new prophetic word, spoken directly by God to the prophet (1 Kgs 19:11–12). When Elijah again complains, Yahweh reassures the prophet and lends new authority to his message. He is to continue the traditional Ephraimite prophetic practice of anointing new kings and is to bring about even greater social upheaval than he caused with his slaughter of the Baal prophets. He will anoint Hazael as king of Syria and Jehu as king of Israel, thus bringing a violent end to the Omride line and at least temporarily obliterating the worship of Baal (2 Kgs 9:21—10:31). Elijah will also anoint Elisha as the next Mosaic prophet (1 Kgs 19:15–17). Furthermore, the narrative makes Elijah aware of his support group:

seven thousand Israelites who have not accepted the central Baal cult (1 Kgs 19:18). The narrative thus lends divine support to Elijah's past activities and helps to justify the even more radical prophetic actions that are to come.

1 KINGS 21

In contrast to 1 Kings 17—19, where Elijah is the primary concern of the narratives and where Deuteronomic editing is minimal, the story of Naboth's vineyard (1 Kings 21) pays little attention to the prophet and describes his brief appearance in stereotypical Deuteronomic terms.[104] After Jezebel arranges the murder of Naboth so that his vineyard can be seized by Ahab (1 Kgs 21:1–16), Elijah appears at the command of Yahweh and condemns this abuse of royal power. The prophet's original oracle may have simply predicted Ahab's death (1 Kgs 21:19), but this oracle has now been expanded by the Deuteronomic editors to include Ahab's royal line as well as his queen. In words that are strikingly close to those used in similar circumstances by Ahijah (1 Kgs 14:7–11) and Jehu the son of Hanani (1 Kgs 16:1–4), the prophet foretells the destruction of the Omride dynasty and the death of Jezebel (1 Kgs 21:20–24). In the present version of the Elijah stories, the threat against Ahab is fulfilled in 1 Kgs 22:38, while the prophecies against Ahab's line and against Jezebel are repeated by an unnamed prophet in 2 Kgs 9:7–10 and finally fulfilled in 2 Kgs 9:22–26, 30–37 and 2 Kgs 10:1–17. Thus the narrative portrays Elijah as a typical peripheral Mosaic prophet, who seeks to curb the excesses of the monarchy and whose word inevitably comes true.

2 KGS 1:2–17

The narrative of the encounter between Elijah and Ahaziah also reflects characteristic Ephraimite views about prophecy, although there is little evidence of Deuteronomic editing.[105] After falling and sustaining a serious injury, Ahaziah sent messengers to inquire of

104. For discussions of the literary history of 1 Kings 21 and the Deuteronomic picture of Elijah that the chapter contains, see Gray, *Kings*, 433–436; Steck, *Über-lieferung*, 33–77; Hentschel, *Die Elija-erzählungen*, 14–43; J. M. Miller, "The Fall of the House of Ahab," *VT* 17 (1967) 307–324; P. Welten, "Naboths Weinberg (1. Könige 21)," *EvT* 33 (1973) 18–32; B. D. Napier, "The Omrides of Jezreel," *VT* 9 (1959) 366–378; H. Seebass, "Der Fall Naboth in 1 Reg. XXI," *VT* 24 (1974) 474–488; and A. Jepsen, "Ahabs Busse," *Archäologie und Altes Testament: Festschrift für Kurt Galling* (ed. A. Kuschke and E. Kutsch; Tübingen: J. C. B. Mohr, 1970) 145–155.
105. Hentschel, *Die Elija-erzählungen*, 10.

(*drš*) Baalzebub, the god of Ekron.[106] This move ran counter to Deuteronomic theology in two ways. First, by seeking an oracle from a foreign god, the king rejected Yahweh, the true god of Israel. Second, the inquiry presumably would have required patronizing one of the intermediaries banned by Deut 18:9–14 instead of going to Elijah, the Mosaic prophet through whom one should seek oracles from Yahweh. Because of these violations of Deuteronomic law, Elijah confronts the royal messengers with an oracle of judgment against the king. The messengers return and inform the king of their encounter with the prophet, whose distinctive dress is described (2 Kgs 1:8). In what is presumably a hostile act, the king sends a group of soldiers to Elijah, who is miraculously protected (2 Kgs 1:9–16). The story ends with a reference to the fulfillment of Elijah's prophecy (2 Kgs 1:17).

The various stories about Elijah thus present a relatively consistent picture of his characteristic behavior, his social location, and his social functions. Both the Deuteronomists and the creators of some of the earlier Elijah narratives saw him as a peripheral prophet who used prophecy in an attempt to reform Israel's central cult, which had been infiltrated by the worship of Baal. Elijah's support group seems to have consisted of a small number of Ephraimites who remained faithful to the same sorts of Yahwistic religious views that later found expression in the writings of the Deuteronomists. Elijah's characteristic behavior was that of a Mosaic prophet, who delivered the pure word of Yahweh to the people and who on occasion interceded for them. As a Mosaic prophet, his word always came true, and his attempts at religious reform were ultimately successful. However, his work had the effect of completely disrupting the central cult and the general social structure, and for this reason various unsuccessful attempts were made to suppress his activities. To counter these attempts there were moves to enhance the authority of Elijah and his prophetic successors. As part of this process the prophetic word was elevated to the status of Torah, with the result that the prophet was assigned as much authority as Moses.

---

106. For a discussion of the meaning of *drš* and the other technical terms used in the process of intercession, see C. Westermann, "Die Begriffe für Fragen und Suchen im Alten Testament," *KD* 6 (1960) 2–30; and O. G. de la Fuente, *La busqueda de Dios en el Antiguo Testamento* (Guadarrama: Publicaciones de la Fundacion Juan March, 1971) 17–42.

The Elisha Traditions

Although the Elisha narratives resemble the Elijah stories in certain respects, the two prophetic figures are portrayed in slightly different ways. While Elijah is usually described as a traditional Ephraimite peripheral prophet, even in non-Deuteronomic narratives, Elisha is said to have occasionally exhibited behavior that was not stereotypically Ephraimite and to have had a wider range of social functions than his predecessor.

The distinctive characteristics of Elisha begin to emerge even in the legends, which demonstrate the prophet's miraculous powers but otherwise shed little light on his prophetic activities (2 Kgs 2:1–18, 19–22, 23–25; 4:1–7, 8–17, 18–37, 38–41, 42–44; 6:1–7; 8:1–6). Some of these stories portray Elisha as the head of a prophetic group called "the sons of the prophets," and indeed some of the stories grow out of the group's common life (2 Kgs 4:1–7, 38–41, 42–44[?]; 6:1–7; cf. 2:3, 5, 7, 15). As we have already noted, this group seems to have had a definite structure, with some members living and eating communally (2 Kgs 6:1; 4:38–41). Group members did not all live in the same city but carried out their activities in various locations (2 Kgs 2:3, 5, 7) and were capable of acting as individual prophets (2 Kgs 9:1). Although there are indications that Elisha and the sons of the prophets had some minimal support within Ephraimite society (2 Kgs 4:8–17, 42–44), they appear primarily as peripheral prophets like Elijah, whose prophetic status was transferred to Elisha (2 Kings 2). Seen from a sociological perspective, the sons of the prophets closely resemble members of a peripheral possession cult. Although there is no direct evidence on this point, members of the group were presumably peripheral individuals who had resisted the political and religious policies of the Ephraimite kings and who had therefore been forced out of the political and religious establishments. After having prophetic experiences, these individuals joined the group, which was under the leadership of Elisha. In the group they found mutual support and were encouraged to use prophecy to bring about changes in the social order. In addition to supporting its regular members, the group also functioned as Elisha's support group and may well have been responsible for preserving and elaborating the legends about him.

As long as the Omride dynasty survived, Elisha and the sons of the prophets seem to have opposed it. This opposition is reflected in several of the stories that deal with Elisha's prophetic activities. In 2 Kgs 3:4–27, which is set during a Moabite rebellion against Israel, the king of Israel enlists the aid of the king of Judah to put down the rebellion. During the campaign, the Judahite king requests that an inquiry be made through a prophet of Yahweh in order to determine the proper course of military action. In spite of the valiant efforts of Elijah, who tried to remove all of the Baal prophets from the central cult and restore the worship of Yahweh, there are apparently no Yahweh prophets available in the royal court. Elisha is therefore summoned, and even the king of Israel recognizes that Elijah's successor is a true prophet. Elisha meets the king's request for intercession by refusing to cooperate, suggesting that the king rely on the Baal prophets. After further royal pressure, Elisha finally relents and agrees to make an inquiry for the sake of the king of Judah. The prophet induces possession by having a minstrel play and then predicts victory for Israel because of Yahweh's divine aid. The story in its present form clearly illustrates Elisha's peripheral status and also reflects the traditional Ephraimite notion that only a Mosaic prophet can effectively inquire of Yahweh. By virtue of inheriting Elijah's position, Elisha is now the only available Mosaic prophet, and his authority must be acknowledged, even by the apostate Israelite king.[107]

Elisha's opposition to the Omride dynasty is given a different expression in 2 Kgs 8:7–15, which describes the prophet playing a role in the internal politics of Israel's enemies, the Syrians. When Benhadad, the king of Syria, becomes sick, he sends Hazael to Elisha to request that he inquire of Yahweh concerning the outcome of the sickness. Elisha agrees to this procedure and foretells the death of Benhadad, the accession of Hazael, and the destruction that Syria will cause in Israel. Acting on Elisha's advice, Hazael lies about the result of the inquiry and gives to Benhadad an oracle predicting his recovery. Hazael then murders Benhadad and becomes king. In this way Elisha indirectly brings about the accession

---

107. The incident recounted in 2 Kgs 3:4–27 is strikingly similar to the one found in 1 Kings 22. For further discussion of 2 Kgs 3:4–27 and the role that prophetic inquiry plays in the narrative, see Schmitt, *Elisa*, 32–37; Schweizer, *Elischa in den Kriegen*, 17–210; and B. O. Long, "2 Kings III and Genres of Prophetic Narrative," *VT* 23 (1973) 337–348. The account of the transfer of prophetic authority from Elijah to Elisha (2 Kings 2) is treated in detail in A. Schmitt, *Entrückung—Aufnahme— Himmelfahrt* (Stuttgart: Katholisches Bibelwerk, 1973) 47–151.

of Hazael, which Elijah had earlier been told to accomplish by anointing (1 Kgs 19:15). However, Elisha engineers the transition of power by using his prophetic abilities. As a Mosaic prophet he is able to inquire of Yahweh and to obtain the valid oracle that encourages the murder. In the process, the prophet helps to hasten the downfall of the Omrides by using his powers in the service of Israel's enemies.[108]

Elisha's opposition to the Omrides reaches its peak in 2 Kgs 9:1–10. This narrative illustrates clearly both the prophet's peripheral role and his continuity with earlier Ephraimite prophets. Again acting to obey the divine command given to Elijah on Mount Horeb (1 Kgs 19:16) and reviving the old Ephraimite practice of the prophetic anointing of kings, Elisha instructs one of the sons of the prophets to anoint Jehu king of Israel. The prophet finds Jehu with the commanders of the army and takes him aside to perform the anointing. In a perfectly coherent oracle, the prophet predicts Jehu's accession, the destruction of the house of Ahab, and the death of Jezebel (2 Kgs 9:6–10). This oracle, which has certainly been shaped by the Deuteronomists, repeats the prophecy that Elijah delivered to Ahab in 1 Kgs 21:23–24, 29. When Jehu returns to his companions, they ask him what the madman (*měšuggāʿ*) said. Jehu responds by trying to change the direction of the conversation, suggesting that the prophet's message was either inconsequential or unintelligible (2 Kgs 9:11).[109]

This exchange between Jehu and his companions illustrates a situation that frequently exists in societies having peripheral intermediaries. The symptoms of spirit possession usually resemble those of illness or insanity, and when a person exhibits these symptoms the society must determine the true cause of the person's behavior. Usually this determination is made by a specialist, and in societies having peripheral possession cults accredited intermediaries are usually involved. If they decide that the person in question is actually possessed by a spirit, then the individual is taken into the cult and recognized as a genuine intermediary. However, the society as a whole may not agree with this evaluation.

108. For a discussion of the role of the inquiry motif in shaping 2 Kgs 8:7–15, see B. O. Long, "The Effect of Divination upon Israelite Literature," *JBL* 92 (1973) 494–497.

109. For a thorough discussion of the literary structure and historical background of 2 Kgs 9:1–10, see Schmitt, *Elisa*, 19–31; and Miller, "The Fall of the House of Ahab," 307–324.

While the larger society may tolerate cult members, it may still hold the opinion that they are mentally ill rather than possessed. In the case of Elisha and his group, the Ephraimite political establishment apparently did not usually see their behavior as the result of genuine possession. Rather, they were considered madmen, whose messages, however intelligible, could be safely ignored.

However, in this case the commanders take the prophet's message seriously. They proclaim Jehu king, and he sets about reforming the political and religious establishments along the lines demanded by Elisha and his support group, the Ephraimites loyal to the traditional Yahwistic faith. The prophecy of Elisha's disciple is fulfilled, and Jehu becomes king (2 Kgs 9:22–26, 30–37; 10:1–14). Joining forces with the religiously orthodox Rechabites, the new king finishes the task begun by Elijah. Jehu slaughters *all* of the worshipers of Baal and thus destroys the central religious establishment (2 Kgs 10:15–27). What he put in its place is not clear, but the retrospective judgment of the Deuteronomists suggests that he did not institute Yahweh worship of the Deuteronomic type (2 Kgs 10:28–31).[110]

Regardless of the opinion of the Deuteronomists, the peripheral prophets represented by Elisha apparently took on new functions after Jehu's accession. Although these prophets may not have made a complete transition from peripheral prophecy to central prophecy, they at least adopted a more positive attitude toward the government and performed social maintenance functions for the crown. The sons of the prophets are not mentioned after Jehu's accession, and it may be that the group disbanded once their religious views ceased to be at odds with those of the central cult. In any case, several of the narratives that are to be dated during and after Jehu's reign illustrate that Elisha himself cooperated with the government. In 2 Kgs 6:8–23, during a war with Syria, Elisha is said to have used his prophetic powers to obtain information from the secret strategy meetings of the Syrians. When the Syrians attempt to surround the prophet and cut off the flow of information, he is protected by a heavenly army that blinds the would-be captors. In 2 Kgs 6:24—7:20, a complex unit that probably includes a number of originally independent stories, the prophet counters the hostility of the Israel-

110. Elisha's role in bringing about the accession and reform of Jehu is discussed in M. Sekine, "Literatursoziologische Beobachtungen zu den Elisaerzählungen," *Annual of the Japanese Biblical Institute* 1 (1975) 39–62.

ite kings by delivering an oracle predicting a break in the Syrian siege of Samaria (2 Kgs 6:32—7:2). God directly intervenes to end the siege, and the prophet's word is vindicated (2 Kgs 7:5–6, 17–20).[111] Finally, in 2 Kgs 13:14–19 the dying Elisha instructs the Israelite king to perform a symbolic act to insure the defeat of Syria. The prophet delivers a victory oracle to insure an Israelite triumph.[112]

The Elisha narratives thus suggest that the prophet began his career as a peripheral prophet in the classic Ephraimite mold. He was head of a peripheral possession cult, and, at least in the opinion of the Deuteronomic editors, he functioned as a Mosaic prophet by virtue of succeeding Elijah. He delivered oracles that invariably came true, and as a prophetic intercessor he inquired of Yahweh on behalf of the people. By means of prophecy Elisha continued to work for changes in the political and religious establishments, even though those changes would require the destruction of the old social order. However, unlike many peripheral prophets, Elisha's attempts at reform were at least partially successful. He then moved closer to the political establishment and took on social maintenance functions, particularly in military contexts.

Stories of Individual Prophets

The stories of prophetic activity now found in 1 Kings 20 and 22 raise a number of literary and historical problems. Some of the narratives appear to have had a complex literary history before they were incorporated in the Deuteronomic History, and it is now difficult to reconstruct the pre-Deuteronomic versions of the stories with any certainty. In addition, the historical background of the stories is disputed, and many scholars want to date some or all of the narratives after the accession of Jehu.[113] This uncertainty about the date of the stories is unfortunate, for it precludes accurate dating of the rather clear picture of prophetic activity that they present.

111. For a detailed analysis of 2 Kgs 6:24—7:20, see Schweizer, *Elischa in den Kriegen*, 309–406.

112. The story of Elisha's miraculous healing of Naaman (2 Kings 5) is difficult to date with any certainty. The picture of the prophet reflected in the story has some affinities with the one found in 2 Kgs 6:8–23 and 6:24—7:20, so the incident may have occurred after Jehu's accession. In any case, the narrative sheds little light on Elisha's relationship to the Israelite court. See Gray, *Kings*, 467–468.

113. Arguments for redating the narratives are presented in ibid., 414–418; Miller, "The Elisha Cycle," 441–447; and idem, "The Rest of the Acts of Jehoahaz," 337–342.

1 KINGS 20

In its present form, 1 Kings 20 contains accounts of two battles between Syria and Ephraim. The text is not a unity and may contain several originally unrelated stories, although it is now impossible to determine when they were joined in their present sequence. There is little evidence of Deuteronomic editing in the chapter except in vv. 35–43, where the theological perspective and the narrative links with 1 Kgs 13:11–32 betray the hand of the Deuteronomist.[114] Yet, in spite of the chapter's complex literary history, the overall narrative presents a relatively cohesive account of two military encounters (1 Kgs 20:1–21, 22–34) and a prophetic reaction to the Israelite king's conduct during one of the battles (1 Kgs 20:35–43).

The prophetic figures mentioned in 1 Kings 20 all seem to have played a role in the war against Syria, although their social locations and functions may have been somewhat different. In 1 Kgs 20:13–14, an unnamed prophet delivers to the Israelite king three oracles concerning the coming battle. It is unclear whether this prophet was a member of the central government or was one of the peripheral prophets connected with Elijah and Elisha. However, regardless of the intermediary's normal social location, on this particular occasion he cooperates with the royal establishment. His first utterance is a victory oracle delivered to the Israelite king, although there is no indication that it was the result of a formal royal inquiry about the outcome of the battle. However, the second and third oracles are given in answer to the king's questions, although there is no suggestion that a formal cultic inquiry was involved.

The second encounter with the Syrians opens when the prophet (presumably the same one mentioned in 1 Kgs 20:13–14) delivers a warning to the Israelite king, exhorting him to prepare for the next Syrian attack, which will come in the spring (1 Kgs 20:22). When the actual battle begins, the Israelites, who are greatly outnumbered, are visited by a man of God, who prophesies an Israelite victory (1 Kgs 20:26–28). Both the prophet and the man of God play a role in the conduct of the war, although there is no indication that they acted in an official capacity or that their oracles were in response to a cultic inquiry.

The last intermediary mentioned in 1 Kings 20 appears in the

114. For a discussion of the various attempts that have been made to analyze the literary history of 1 Kings 20, see the discussion of Schmitt, *Elisa*, 46–51.

prophetic story in 1 Kgs 20:35–43 and is portrayed somewhat differently from the other intermediaries in the chapter. He is said to
have been one of the sons of the prophets (1 Kgs 20:35) and seems to
have functioned outside of the royal establishment. This is the only
reference to the sons of the prophets apart from the Elisha narratives, and this fact, together with the story's interest in relationships
between prophets, suggests that an earlier version of the narrative
may have been carried by the prophetic group during the time of
Elisha and then incorporated in 1 Kings 20 in a revised form by the
Deuteronomists. However, regardless of the origin of the story, it
now follows logically from the account of Ahab's lenient treatment
of the captive Syrian king, Benhadad (1 Kgs 20:30–34). One of the
sons of the prophets asks another member of his group to strike him.
When the second prophet refuses, the first delivers a judgment oracle to his reluctant brother, who is immediately killed by a lion (cf. 1
Kgs 13:20–25). The prophet then asks a third member of the group
to strike him, and the man does so. The prophet covers his forehead
with a bandage and then meets the king on the road. The use of the
bandage suggests either that the prophet wished to hide a characteristic mark that indicated his membership in the prophetic group
or that he was personally known to Ahab and wished to disguise
himself (cf. 1 Kgs 20:41). In any case, the king does not recognize
the prophet, who uses a ruse similar to the one employed by Nathan
(2 Samuel 12) and lures Ahab into pronouncing judgment upon
himself. The king's own verdict is repeated by the prophet in an
oracle condemning the king for violating the prescriptions of the
holy war. The prophet thus appears to have been a peripheral intermediary who used prophecy to advocate his group's views on the
proper conduct of a holy war.

1 KINGS 22

The story of Micaiah ben Imlah (1 Kgs 22:1–38) is one of the most
complete pictures of Ephraimite prophetic activity to be found in
the Deuteronomic History. The text reveals little late Deuteronomic editing, except perhaps in v. 38b, and there is no reason
to doubt that the bulk of the narrative was already a coherent
unit before being incorporated in the Book of Kings. Portions of
the unit, particularly vv. 19–23, may have been added after the
remainder of the story was complete, but it is not necessary to posit

a long editorial history behind the present text.[115] Even if some portions of the narrative are secondary additions, the whole unit is well-integrated and presents a consistent story.

In its present form, 1 Kgs 22:1–38 presents a picture of prophets having similar behavioral characteristics but different social functions. The first prophets mentioned in the chapter appear in the context of preparations for a military campaign. The Israelite king enlists the aid of Jehoshaphat, the king of Judah, to recapture Ramoth-gilead from Syria. However, before the expedition begins, the Judean king requests that an inquiry be made of Yahweh to determine the proper course of action. Such inquiries were regularly performed before battle (cf. Ezek 21:21–23), and the king of Israel therefore goes to his court prophets, who functioned within the central social structure. These prophets were apparently Yahweh prophets and must have shared central maintenance functions with the Baal prophets mentioned in 1 Kings 18. The king phrases his inquiry in the form of a question designed to elicit a yes or no answer, a procedure well-attested in Mesopotamian divination rituals. The prophets respond with a favorable oracle exhorting the king to reclaim Ramoth-gilead. However, the king of Judah is still not satisfied and requests that another Yahweh prophet be consulted. The king of Israel reluctantly agrees to summon Micaiah ben Imlah, who is clearly portrayed as a peripheral prophet. He lives outside of the royal court and in the past has delivered oracles critical of the central government. From the perspective of the author of the narrative, Micaiah is a Mosaic prophet, like Elijah, and as such is superior to normal prophets. He is capable of making an accurate inquiry and delivering a true oracle. While Micaiah is

---

115. Arguments for the essential literary integrity of the narrative are presented by Gray, *Kings*, 414–418, 444–445; cf. E. Haller, *Charisma und Ekstasis* (Munich: Chr. Kaiser Verlag, 1960); and J. A. Montgomery and H. S. Gehman, *A Critical and Exegetical Commentary on the Books of Kings* (Edinburgh: T. & T. Clark, 1951) 336. Attempts to argue for the composite character of the unit have recently been made by E. Würthwein ("Zur Komposition von I Reg 22:1–38," *Das Ferne und Nahe Wort*, 245–254), F. L. Hossfeld and I. Meyer (*Prophet gegen Prophet* [Fribourg: Schweizerisches Katholisches Bibelwerk, 1973] 27–36), Schmitt, (*Elisa*, 42–45), and Hentschel (*Die Elija-erzählungen*, 10–13). Of these attempts, the most convincing is Würthwein's suggestion (followed by Schmitt, Hossfeld, and Meyer) that 1 Kgs 22:19–23 was added secondarily to the rest of the narrative. Even so, there is no reason to follow Hossfeld and Meyer, who use parallels between 1 Kgs 22:19–23 and Isaiah 6 to argue that the Kings addition was made at a late date in Jerusalem and was based on Isaiah's call vision. The lines of literary dependence, if they existed at all, could just as easily have run in the other direction.

being summoned, the court prophets continue to exhibit their characteristic possession behavior (*wĕkol-hannĕbîʾîm mitnabbĕʾîm* [1 Kgs 22:10]). The precise nature of this behavior is not indicated in the text, but it must have included coherent speech, for the prophets continue to repeat their victory oracle. One of them, Zedekiah ben Chenaanah, also performs a symbolic action to reinforce the group's oracle and then delivers his own oracle, which is expressed in the same stereotypical prophetic language used by other Yahweh prophets.

When the royal messenger reaches Micaiah, the messenger strongly suggests to the prophet that he agree with the opinion of the other prophets and deliver a favorable oracle. As a genuine Mosaic prophet, who speaks only the pure word of Yahweh, Micaiah replies that he will speak only what God commands him to speak. Nevertheless, when the Israelite king inquires of Yahweh through Micaiah by asking him the same question that was asked of the other prophets, Micaiah echoes their response and replies with a favorable oracle. He expresses his oracle in virtually the same words that the court prophets had used, a fact which may indicate that such oracles followed a stereotypical pattern. Yet, because Micaiah's oracle is uncharacteristically positive, the king of Israel exhorts the prophet to say only what God has told him. The prophet complies by repeating the horrific vision that he had actually seen. According to Micaiah's vision, the Israelites were to be defeated and scattered without a royal leader.

This first vision report is followed by a second, which does not answer the king's original inquiry but accuses the other prophets of speaking falsely. Micaiah recounts a vision of a meeting of Yahweh's divine council. On this particular occasion the subject under discussion was the method that might be used to entice Ahab to go into battle against Ramoth-gilead so that he would be killed. A solution to the council's problem was provided by a spirit who volunteered to be a lying spirit (*rûaḥ šeqer* [1 Kgs 22:22]) in the mouth of Ahab's prophets. Micaiah thus accounts for the favorable oracle of the court prophets by claiming that they are possessed not by Yahweh's spirit but by a destructive spirit of deception.

Micaiah's tactic is the functional equivalent of the witchcraft accusation that is used in many modern societies to control obstreperous intermediaries. By making (or threatening to make) a witchcraft accusation, the accuser exerts overt pressure on an intermediary, for in most societies convicted witches are killed or ostracized. Witchcraft accusations therefore lead to the disruption of the social order and are usually employed only in unstable societies and in situations where the tensions between peripheral and central groups have become unbearable. Micaiah's deceptive-prophecy accusation is capable of functioning as a witchcraft accusation because of the peculiar view of the Mosaic prophet that was held by Micaiah and the Ephraimite support group that preserved the account of his activities. According to Ephraimite ideology, Mosaic prophets were characterized by the fact that they spoke only the pure word of God. In contrast, prophets who tampered with the divine word that they received or who spoke a word that God did not dictate were considered presumptuous and were condemned to death by the Deuteronomic Law (Deut 18:18–20). Micaiah's charge is therefore not simply an expression of contempt for his opponents but an accusation of a capital crime. If Micaiah's charge is taken seriously, the result will be a rift in the social structure and a sundering of the social links between the two parties involved. His accusation must therefore be seen against the background of the social tensions that existed between peripheral and central prophets and their respective support groups. By accusing his opponents of false prophecy, Micaiah not only seeks to discredit their oracles but also attempts to destroy the religious establishment.

When accusations of this sort are made by a peripheral prophet without a strong support group, they are difficult to sustain against the social pressure of the majority of the society. It is therefore not surprising that Zedekiah responds to Micaiah's threat by making a counter-accusation. Zedekiah claims to be possessed by Yahweh's spirit, a claim which implies that Micaiah has not been possessed at all. This confrontation is a classic encounter between two intermediaries having opposing messages and conflicting authority claims. Because their messages are expressed in the same stereotypical language, there is no obvious way for the society to adjudicate their claims. Social factors therefore play a role. The prophet with the strongest support group becomes dominant and represses the prophet with weaker support. In this case, the counter-accusation by Zedekiah is enough to settle the argument. The Israelite king orders Micaiah imprisoned until the conclusion of the battle.

The Deuteronomists, however, had another criterion for adjudicating prophetic disputes. According to Deuteronomic theology, the genuine prophet is the one whose word comes true (Deut 18:21–22). This test is not usually applicable at the time the prophecy is given but can only be applied retrospectively. The narrative thus continues with an account of Micaiah's vindication. The Israelite king follows the advice of his court prophets. As a result, he is slain in battle and Micaiah is proven to be a true prophet. Yet, it is important to note that the sensitive Ephraimite hearer or reader of the story could have predicted its conclusion long before the end. Throughout the story, Micaiah exhibits the distinctive behavior of a Mosaic prophet, one whose oracles *inevitably* come true. For someone who accepts the Ephraimite ideology, there is therefore no doubt about the outcome of conflict between prophets. The Mosaic prophet will invariably win, and people who do not accept this fact are to be condemned.

Our examination of the prophets of the Elijah-Elisha traditions suggests that Ephraimite prophecy during this period was a complex phenomenon. Various types of prophets existed, and each had distinctive behavioral characteristics and social functions. Certain prophets had social maintenance functions within the royal court. Some of these figures were Baal prophets, while others represented Yahweh, but it is difficult to determine whether these two types of prophets functioned in the central cult at the same time. Each type seems to have had characteristic behavior patterns, although the texts do not preserve much evidence on this point. Along with the various types of central prophets, peripheral prophets also existed in Ephraim at this time. These intermediaries were supported by peripheral groups that retained the old Yahwistic faith in the face of royal political and religious abuses. Through prophets such as Elijah and Elisha, these groups attempted to reform Ephraimite society and restore older social and religious values. During the time of Elisha, a peripheral group of prophets was formally organized, and this group played a role in overthrowing the Omride dynasty and at least temporarily ridding the land of Baal worship. When Jehu's reform occurred, some peripheral prophets, including Elisha, apparently took on social maintenance functions. However, conflicts between central and peripheral groups continued to exist, and false-prophecy accusations were sometimes used to suppress prophetic opponents.

Jonah

In 2 Kgs 14:25–27 there is a brief reference to Jonah the son of Amittai, to whom the Book of Jonah is also attributed (Jonah 1:1). The reference implies that Jonah was active in Ephraim, where he is said to have delivered an oracle to Jeroboam II. Nothing can be said about the prophet's characteristic behavior or about his social location. In spite of the fact that he delivers a positive oracle to the king, there are no grounds for assuming that Jonah was part of the royal court. The Deuteronomic Historian recounts the fulfillment of Jonah's oracle concerning the restoration of Israel's borders, and by this means the writer may intend to link Jonah with earlier Ephraimite prophets whose words were fulfilled by Yahweh, but Jonah is not explicitly portrayed as a Mosaic prophet. The link with other Ephraimite prophets may be strengthened by the fact that Jonah's Judahite contemporary, Amos, condemns the same border expansion that Jonah here supports (Amos 6:13–14). An oblique reference to Amos's prophecies of the destruction of Samaria may also be found in 2 Kgs 14:27, where the Deuteronomic Historian comments that Yahweh *did not* threaten to destroy Ephraim.[116] If 2 Kgs 14:25–27 is to be understood as a subtle polemic against the activities of Amos, then Jonah may have been involved in a prophetic conflict with the Jerusalemite establishment, but no conflict of this sort is actually mentioned in the text.

Isaiah

In 2 Kings 18—20, the story of Sennacherib's siege of Jerusalem and its aftermath, the Deuteronomic Historian presents several accounts of the prophetic activities of Isaiah. These chapters are important for our inquiry not only because they afford a rare glimpse of prophetic activity in Jerusalem but also because their tradition history can be traced with a reasonable degree of certainty. We can therefore see how Deuteronomic perceptions of Isaiah changed over a period of time and how later non-Deuteronomic writers viewed the same figure. By carefully examining the various layers

---

116. F. Crüsemann, "Kritik an Amos in deuteronomistischen Geschichtswerk," *Probleme biblischer Theologie,* 57–63. While Crüsemann is certainly correct in seeing in 2 Kgs 14:27 a polemic against a prophetic judgment oracle, his suggestion that the unnamed prophet was Amos would be strengthened if Amos were actually quoted or mentioned in the text.

of tradition that deal with the siege, we can gain some insight not only into a single prophet but also into the differing concepts of prophecy held by the biblical writers.

The biblical accounts of Sennacherib's siege of Jerusalem are now found in 2 Kings 18—19 (much of which has been incorporated secondarily in Isaiah 36—37) and in 2 Chr 32:1–22. It has long been recognized that the Deuteronomic narrative of the siege is not a unity, and most scholars distinguish three major literary units within the present text: (1) 2 Kgs 18:13–16 (the so-called annalistic account); (2) 2 Kgs 18:17—19:9a, 36—37; and (3) 2 Kgs 19:9b–35.[117] All three of these units in their present form seem to be the work of the Deuteronomist, although all of the traditions within the units may not have originated in Deuteronomic circles or been carried by the same Deuteronomic groups. Lying behind all three of the units is a complex tradition history, but because only the latter two deal with Isaiah, we will limit our discussion to them.

Second Kings 18:17—19:9a, 36–37 and 2 Kgs 19:9b–35 are essentially two different accounts of the same historical event. Although both draw from common traditions about the siege, each account has a distinctive perspective on this incident and each views Isaiah's role somewhat differently. In 2 Kgs 18:17—19:9a, the bulk of the narrative consists of a rambling speech by the Assyrian official, the Rabshakeh. Although the speech is ostensibly directed to the Judean king, Hezekiah, in fact many of its arguments are aimed at the people of Jerusalem. The Assyrian argument has a number of turns in it, but its general strategy is to question Hezekiah's political and religious policies. His attempts to seek help from Egypt are ridiculed (2 Kgs 18:21), and his religious reforms—which were generally in line with Deuteronomic theological views—are misinterpreted as a rejection of Yahweh (2 Kgs 18:22, 25). Finally, the Rabshakeh speaks directly to the people and warns them not to trust Hezekiah, even though the king assures them of Yahweh's help (2 Kgs 18:28–35).

---

117. The discussion that follows depends heavily on the thorough tradition-historical analysis of B. S. Childs (*Isaiah and the Assyrian Crisis* [London: SCM Press, 1967] 69–111), who also provides references to earlier scholarly treatments. Although scholars generally agree in their delineation of the different literary units in 2 Kings 18—19, there is still much debate over the historical accuracy of the different accounts of the siege. Childs's great contribution to this debate has been to demonstrate that all of the accounts are the products of a complex history of tradition. They therefore provide more insight into the perceptions of the bearers of the traditions than into the actual course of events.

In the face of the Assyrian threats, Hezekiah reacts calmly and piously. He goes into mourning and visits the temple, although he does not pray there for the deliverance of Jerusalem. Rather, he sends an official delegation to the prophet Isaiah asking *him* to intercede with Yahweh and to pray for the salvation of the city. Isaiah's prayer is not recorded in the text, but he delivers to the messengers an oracle of assurance for Hezekiah (2 Kgs 19:1-7).

The picture of Isaiah's activities in this account clearly reflects traditional Ephraimite views. The prophet is portrayed as the only legitimate channel of communication between God and the people. The king recognizes Isaiah's special status and goes to the prophet in order to contact Yahweh. In this respect, Hezekiah follows Deuteronomic law (Deut 18:15-22), just as he did in his religious reforms. Isaiah's oracle reassures the king and thus implies that his present Deuteronomically oriented course of action is correct and will be rewarded. Like all true prophets, Isaiah's prophetic word comes true (2 Kgs 19:36-37), and Hezekiah's policies are validated.

Although Isaiah's characteristic behavior in this story conforms to standard Deuteronomic views about prophecy, one unusual feature of the story should be noted. While most of the Ephraimite prophets that we have examined up to this point have been peripheral prophets, in this account there is no suggestion that Isaiah played such a role. The king turns to the prophet as a matter of course and even sends an official delegation to request intercession. The narrative thus implies that Isaiah was an important figure in Jerusalem, who was regularly involved in the workings of the government. Although there is no suggestion that Isaiah played a role in the cult, he is certainly portrayed as a central prophet with social maintenance functions.

However, there are reasons to question the historical accuracy of some parts of this picture, and in particular Isaiah's close conformity to the Deuteronomic model of the ideal prophet is suspect. The Book of Isaiah itself never portrays the prophet as an intercessor, and, as we will soon see, other accounts of his involvement in the siege reduce or eliminate his intercessory role. It is therefore probable that the picture of Isaiah found in 2 Kgs 18:17—19:9a, 36-37 has been edited in such a way as to portray Isaiah as a typical Deuteronomic prophet. The probability of Deuteronomic editing is strengthened by the overall message of the whole account, which comes close to describing Hezekiah as an ideal Deuteronomic king.

After following the Deuteronomic theology by reforming the cult of Yahweh and by breaking Judah's ties with foreign powers, Hezekiah is faced with a crisis which challenges his rule. He consults a central prophet, who successfully intercedes with Yahweh, and the king is vindicated. The message to future kings is clear. The king who follows the Deuteronomic theology will be strengthened and preserved, by supernatural means if necessary. In the narrative both king and prophet play the roles laid out for them in the Deuteronomic system and thus provide an object lesson for future kings. It is therefore probable that the account of the siege found in 2 Kgs 18:17—19:9a, 36–37 is composed of old traditions that have been reworked by the Deuteronomists to present an ideal picture of king and prophet functioning in a state governed by Deuteronomic principles. Yet, in spite of the apparent polemical function of the present form of the narrative, it may also contain some historical data. If Hezekiah did indeed institute reforms similar to those demanded by the Deuteronomists, then he may well have voluntarily limited his royal power and allowed typical Ephraimite prophets to function within the central government.[118] However, it is not certain that Isaiah played such a role or that his behavior actually met Deuteronomic expectations. Rather, the Deuteronomic writers may have taken a traditional story about the siege, a story containing references to Isaiah, and then reworked it in accordance with Deuteronomic views about the nature and functions of prophecy.

The second Deuteronomic account of the siege, now found in 2 Kgs 19:9b–35, differs greatly from the first one that we have just discussed. While the first narrative focuses on the speech of the Rabshakeh and is concerned with the validity of Hezekiah's religious and political policies, the second narrative emphasizes the role of the king in the salvation of the city. In the second account the Rabshakeh's speech has been condensed so that it deals with only one issue: the ability of Yahweh to save Jerusalem. The Assyrian king sends a message to Hezekiah warning him not to trust in

---

118. Although it has sometimes been argued that there is little historical value in the accounts of Hezekiah's reforms, most contemporary scholars accept the historiographic reliability of the biblical material. See, for example, H. H. Rowley, "Hezekiah's Reform and Rebellion," *BJRL* 44 (1961–62) 395–461 (= H. H. Rowley, *Men of God* [London: Thomas Nelson, 1963] 98–132); and F. L. Moriarty, "The Chronicler's Account of Hezekiah's Reform," *CBQ* 27 (1965) 399–406. W. Zimmerli ("Jesaja und Hiskia," *Wort und Geschichte*, 199–208) even argues that because of Hezekiah's reforms Isaiah became a member of the royal court and actually played the supportive role ascribed to him in the texts.

Yahweh and implying that God will not be able to keep the city or its king from destruction (2 Kgs 19:9b–13). The message strikes at the very heart of the Jerusalemite royal theology, which held that Yahweh had elected Jerusalem and the Davidic royal line in perpetuity (2 Samuel 7), with the result that both the city and the dynasty were inviolable.[119] In the face of this threat, Hezekiah *himself* goes to the temple and delivers an elaborate intercessory prayer, instead of going to a prophetic intercessor as the Deuteronomic law requires. Hezekiah's prayer has the typical structure of a complaint psalm and closely resembles the prayer given by David when the dynastic promise was first made (2 Sam 7:18–29) and the prayer given by Solomon at the dedication of the temple (1 Kgs 8:22–53). More important, the structure and language of Hezekiah's prayer recall the late prayers found in Jer 32:16–25, 2 Chr 20:5–12 (also delivered by a Judahite king in the temple), Neh 9:6–37, and Dan 9:3–19. This fact suggests that the entire unit, in its present form, comes from a very late stage in the development of the Deuteronomic tradition and is probably to be dated to the postexilic period.[120]

When Hezekiah finishes his prayer, he receives an oracle from Isaiah. There is no indication that the king sought an oracle from the prophet, and in fact the divine words are introduced with the remark that they have been given in response to the king's prayer, not to an intercessory prayer by Isaiah (2 Kgs 19:20). The oracle itself, which may be a secondary addition to the narrative, does not give a word of assurance to the king but reaffirms Yahweh's promise to Jerusalem. The arrogant Assyrian king is in fact only an instrument of Yahweh and will be destroyed for not recognizing the power of God (2 Kgs 19:21b–28).

As was also the case in 2 Kgs 18:17—19:9a, 36–37, the account in 2 Kgs 19:9b–35 portrays Isaiah as a central prophet. However, here the similarity between the two accounts ends. In the second account Isaiah helps to maintain the social order by reiterating the old Jerusalemite theology of the inviolability of Zion, not by vindicating the Deuteronomic policies of the king. Furthermore, in the

---

119. For discussions of the Jerusalemite royal theology, see Cross, *Canaanite Myth and Hebrew Epic*, 241–265; J. H. Hayes, "The Tradition of Zion's Inviolability," *JBL* 82 (1963) 419–426; and J. Schreiner, *Sion-Jerusalem, Jahwes Königssitz* (Munich: Kösel-Verlag, 1963).

120. For a more detailed discussion of the date of the unit, see Childs, *Isaiah and the Assyrian Crisis*, 99–100.

second account Isaiah has no intercessory functions. Thus, even though the narrative itself is Deuteronomic, its picture of prophetic activity differs from the one usually found in Ephraimite sources. This very fact suggests the historical reliability of the picture, and it is probable that 2 Kgs 19:9b–35 contains an old Jerusalemite account that has been reworked by a postexilic Deuteronomic editor. This probability is enhanced by the decidedly Jerusalemite theological coloring of the narrative and by the links between Isaiah's oracle and similar oracles found in the Book of Isaiah. Furthermore, the picture of prophetic activity found in this account is similar to the one found in the story of Hezekiah's sickness (2 Kings 20). Here too Isaiah seems to be an important figure with free access to the king. The prophet appears unbidden and announces that Hezekiah will die because of his sickness (cf. the analogous Deuteronomic story in 1 Kgs 14:1–18). The king then prays directly to Yahweh, who responds in a favorable oracle delivered through Isaiah (2 Kgs 20:2–6).[121] After the king's recovery, Isaiah suddenly appears again to condemn Hezekiah for his political policies toward Babylon (2 Kgs 20:12–19). The picture of Isaiah found in 2 Kgs 19:9b–35 thus may be a relatively accurate reflection of the behavior and functions of this Jerusalemite prophet.[122] If so, then we may conclude that he was a central prophet who was part of the Jerusalemite establishment. To maintain that establishment he delivered oracles that regulated social change by reaffirming traditional values and religious views.

This reconstruction of Isaiah's prophetic activities is consistent with the last of the accounts of the siege, which is now found in 2 Chr 32:1–22. This account comes from Jerusalemite rather than from Deuteronomic circles, and although it is basically a conflation of the accounts in Kings, it reflects the Chronicler's interests and attitudes toward prophecy. In this late version of the siege, Isaiah plays almost no role. He prays along with the king for the salvation of the city, but the long oracle of 2 Kgs 19:21b–28 is omitted, as is the Deuteronomist's account of the prophet's role in curing Hezekiah's sickness. This suggests that the Chronicler recognized Isaiah as a central prophet but did not attach as much importance to

---

121. In the following account of the sign that Isaiah delivers to authenticate his oracle (2 Kgs 20:8–11), the prophet's behavior more closely resembles that of a typical Ephraimite prophet, although intercession is still not involved.

122. Zimmerli, "Jesaja und Hiskia," 205–208.

prophecy as did the Deuteronomist. We will return to this point when we discuss prophecy in Chronicles.

Our survey of the various traditions about Isaiah's role in the siege thus indicates differing perceptions of his prophetic activity. Furthermore, these perceptions can be placed in a rough chronological sequence. The earliest Deuteronomic account (2 Kgs 18:17—19:9a, 36–37) portrays Isaiah as a central prophet with the behavioral characteristics of typical Ephraimite prophets. He serves as a spokesman for the Deuteronomists' theological views, and his appearance in the narrative may indicate that prophets having stereotypical Ephraimite characteristics actually played a role in the Jerusalemite establishment during the time of Hezekiah. A much later Deuteronomic account of the siege (2 Kgs 19:9b–35) shows the prophet in a different light. He is still a central figure, but he does not exhibit stereotypical Deuteronomic prophetic behavior. He is now subordinate to the king and is a spokesman for the Jerusalemite royal theology. If this picture is an accurate indication of the role that prophets actually played in Jerusalem, then the presence of the picture in a Deuteronomic narrative must indicate that by the postexilic period the Deuteronomists had accepted certain aspects of the Jerusalemite prophetic ideology. The latest account of the siege (2 Chr 32:1–22) suggests the disappearance of the Deuteronomist's characteristic views of prophecy and a decline in the whole institution of prophecy, at least in the circles represented by the Chronicler.

Huldah

The two biblical accounts of the reforms of Josiah (2 Kgs 22:1—23:30; 2 Chronicles 34—35) differ markedly in their presentation of the chronology and scope of the reforms, but both agree in their portrayal of the prophetess (nĕbîʾāh) Huldah.[123] According to the Deuteronomic account (2 Kgs 22:8—23:3), which is essentially followed by the Chronicler (2 Chr 34:14–32), Hilkiah the priest found a book of the law in the temple while repairs were being made on the building in Josiah's eighteenth year. Hilkiah gave the book to Shaphan the scribe, who reported the discovery to Josiah and read the book in the king's presence. When Josiah heard the words of the book, he tore his garments and instructed Hilkiah, Shaphan,

---

123. For a discussion of the essential differences between the two accounts, see Nicholson, *Deuteronomy and Tradition*, 8–17.

Ahikam the son of Shaphan, Achbor, and Asaiah the king's servant to inquire of Yahweh concerning the words of the book. It is clear from the tone of Josiah's command that he was not simply seeking additional information about the contents of the book. Rather, he was worried because the people had not obeyed the laws contained in the book and were therefore in danger of being punished by Yahweh. The king thus appears to have been trying to intercede with Yahweh in order to avert a divine judgment. Following Josiah's instructions, the royal messengers visited Huldah, who is said to have been the wife of Shallum, a member of Josiah's court. In response to the delegation's inquiry, the prophetess delivered a judgment oracle phrased in stereotypical Deuteronomic language. According to the oracle, the people had not obeyed the Deuteronomic prescriptions and were therefore to suffer the evils mentioned in the book. However, the penitent king, who initiated the inquiry, was to be spared witnessing the destruction of the nation. When Huldah's oracle was delivered to the king, he gathered the priests, prophets, and people, read the book to them, and made a covenant with Yahweh to follow the laws contained in the book. Then, at least according to the Deuteronomic account, Josiah began a series of sweeping religious reforms.

In this story of the finding and validation of the lawbook, Huldah clearly appears as a central prophet exhibiting the behavioral characteristics typical of Ephraimite intermediaries. She is part of the royal court, and her importance is indicated by the fact that an official delegation of high-ranking government officers is sent to inquire through her. Josiah apparently recognizes her as a Mosaic prophet, who is capable of interceding with Yahweh. In keeping with Deuteronomic ideas about the proper functions of Mosaic prophets, her oracle validates the book, revives old Ephraimite religious traditions, and sets in motion the Deuteronomistic reform.[124]

Although the nature and function of Huldah's prophetic activities are clear in the narrative, the historical accuracy of the narrative itself is difficult to assess. The account of Josiah's reforms now found in Kings bears the clear stamp of the Deuteronomist, who has constructed the narrative in such a way as to focus attention on Josiah, the ideal Deuteronomic ruler.[125] In this respect the account closely

124. Second Kings 23:2 implies that there were other prophets in Jerusalem during Josiah's reign, but nothing can be said of their behavior or social functions.
125. N. Lohfink, "Die Bundesurkunde des Königs Josias," *Bib* 44 (1963) 265–280; J. R. Lundbom, "The Lawbook of the Josianic Reform," *CBQ* 38 (1976) 295–302.

resembles the earlier story of Hezekiah's actions during the siege of Jerusalem (2 Kgs 18:17—19:9a, 36–37). In both stories the Judean king (Hezekiah/Josiah) receives threatening news (the message of the Rabshakeh/the words of the book of the law). The news causes the king to tear his clothes and to send an official delegation to inquire of Yahweh through a central prophet (Isaiah/Huldah). The inquiry leads to an oracle that vindicates the Deuteronomically influenced actions of the king and underlines his piety. One might therefore suspect that the picture of Huldah found in 2 Kings 22 is simply the creation of the Deuteronomist. If so, then it would be reasonable to doubt that prophets in the time of Josiah had the typically Deuteronomic behavioral characteristics and functions ascribed to Huldah.

However, this skeptical evaluation of the biblical picture of Huldah must be questioned because of the Chronicler's version of the reform. While the Chronicler's own theological interests are obvious in the portions of his narrative dealing with Josiah's passover (2 Chr 35:1–19), the remainder of the account reflects no obvious tendenz. The Chronicler may thus be a more reliable guide to the chronology of Josiah's reign than the Deuteronomist, who seems to have arranged the Kings account to suggest that the Deuteronomistic lawbook was responsible for the reform.[126] If the Chronicler's version of the reform is accepted as the more accurate of the two, then it is possible not only to vindicate the biblical picture of Huldah but also to set it into a historical context that is more comprehensible than the one supplied in Kings.

According to 2 Chronicles 34, Josiah began his reform in his eighth year, ten years before the finding of the book in the temple. The king's motives are not specified in the narrative, and they may have been political as well as religious, but there is no doubt that his reforms followed the general lines laid down in the Deuteronomic

---

126. It is also possible to correlate the Chronicler's version of the reform with the political fortunes of Assyria during Josiah's reign. This fact, plus the lack of theological tendenz in most of the Chronicler's account, has recently led an increasing number of scholars to accept its essential accuracy. For discussions of the reliability of the Chronicler's account, see Nicholson, *Deuteronomy and Tradition*, 9–14; T. Oestreicher, *Das Deuteronomische Grundgesetz* (Gütersloh: C. Bertelsmann, 1923) 39–69; A. Bentzen, *Die Josianische Reform und ihre Voraussetzungen* (Copenhagen: P. Haase, 1926) 15–27; F. M. Cross and D. N. Freedman, "Josiah's Revolt against Assyria," *JNES* 12 (1953) 56–58; and L. Rost, "Josias Passa," *Theologie in Geschichte und Kunst: Walter Elliger zum 65. Geburtstag* (ed. S. Herrmann; Witten: Luther-Verlag, 1968) 169–175.

theology.[127] We have already suggested that this theology was simply the crystallization of older Ephraimite views, and we have seen advocates of these views on the periphery of Israelite society since the time of Solomon. They seem to have inspired the reform of Hezekiah and were presumably known in Jerusalem, so it is not difficult to understand how Josiah might have been influenced by them.[128] If the present Book of Deuteronomy is an accurate indication of the theology that inspired Josiah, then it is reasonable to suppose that he not only purified the cult and eliminated syncretistic worship but also restructured his government according to the Deuteronomic ideals expressed in Deuteronomy 16—18. This would have meant limiting the priestly and political powers of the king (Deut 17:14–20), restructuring the judicial system (Deut 16:18–20; 17:8–13), incorporating a Mosaic prophet into the central social structure (Deut 18:9–22), and allowing Levitical priests to participate freely in the central cult in Jerusalem (Deut 18:1–8).

Some of Josiah's reforms were more extensive than those demanded by Deuteronomy, so it is not certain that he instituted precisely the sort of political system that the book requires. However, there is some evidence that he did make changes in the Jerusalemite religious establishment to make it conform more closely to Deuteronomic expectations. Huldah is clearly portrayed as a typical Mosaic prophet who is an integral part of the royal court, and she may well have become a central prophet as the result of the king's early reforms. Furthermore, it is tempting to speculate that Hilkiah the high priest was originally a peripheral Levitical priest who was installed in the central cult in accordance with Deuteronomic requirements. Several individuals bearing the name Hilkiah are mentioned outside of 2 Kings 22—23, and most of them have Levitical connections (1 Chr 6:30; 26:11; Neh 12:7, 21). More important, Jeremiah, who was active during the time of Josiah, is said to have had a father named Hilkiah. Both father and son were members of the priestly groups at Anathoth (Jer 1:1), the city to which Abiathar

127. For a discussion of the possibility that Josiah's reforms were motivated by political considerations, see Nicholson, *Deuteronomy and Tradition*, 9–14; and Cross and Freedman, "Josiah's Revolt," 56–58. A different set of motives is suggested by W. E. Claburn, "The Fiscal Basis of Josiah's Reforms," *JBL* 92 (1973) 11–22.

128. For an exploration of the religious traditions that might have prompted Josiah's reforms, see Lundbom, "The Lawbook of the Josianic Reform," 293–302; L. Rost, "Zur Vorgeschichte der Kultusreform des Josia," *VT* 19 (1969) 113–120; and W. Dietrich, "Josia und das Gesetzbuch," *VT* 27 (1977) 13–35.

and his fellow Ephraimite priests were exiled by Solomon (1 Kgs 2:26–27). Although some scholars deny that Jeremiah's father and the priest who found the lawbook are the same individual, there are no compelling reasons for such a denial.[129] It may well be, then, that Hilkiah was an Ephraimite priest who entered the Jerusalemite cult as a result of Josiah's reforms.

However, Hilkiah may not have been the only individual with Ephraimite connections who was involved in the later discovery of the lawbook in the temple. It is worth noting that Huldah's husband, Shallum, bears the same name as Jeremiah's uncle, whose family owned hereditary property in Anathoth (Jer 32:7). If the two individuals are identical—and there is no particular reason to deny this—then Huldah herself may have had connections with the bearers of the Ephraimite traditions. If so, then her stereotypical speech and behavior simply reflect the expectations of her support group and are not completely the result of Deuteronomic editing.[130] In addition, Shaphan and his family may have had Ephraimite ties, although the only available evidence is inferential. He and his sons seem to have been involved in the reform, and his sons later supported Jeremiah, whose oracles reflect the Deuteronomic point of view (Jer 26:24; 29:3; 36:10–12).

The biblical evidence thus suggests that several individuals having Deuteronomic connections were members of the royal court in the time of Josiah. At least one of these figures was a prophet, and one may have been a Levitical priest. If they became part of the central establishment when Josiah began his reform, then they were perhaps responsible for "finding" the book of the law, which revived old Ephraimite traditions and encouraged the continuation of the reforms that Josiah had already begun.[131]

---

129. A convenient summary of the various scholarly positions on this issue is provided by H. H. Rowley, "The Early Prophecies of Jeremiah in their Setting," in his *Men of God* (London: Thomas Nelson, 1963) 138.

130. This is not to deny that her oracle in its present form has been reworked by the Deuteronomists to take into account the fall of Jerusalem. For a thorough discussion of the oracle, see Dietrich, "Josia und das Gesetzbuch," 25–29.

131. This reconstruction assumes that there were two stages to the reform. Only the second stage was inspired by the discovery of the lawbook (Nicholson, *Deuteronomy and Tradition*, 9–17). The question of the precise contents of the lawbook and its relation to the present Book of Deuteronomy need not concern us here. For discussions of the problem, see Nicholson, *Deuteronomy and Tradition*, 18–36; J. Lindblom, *Erwägungen zur Herkunft der Josianischen Tempelurkunde* (Lund: C. W. K. Gleerup, 1971); and the literature cited above, n. 128.

The Prophets and the Fall of
Samaria and Jerusalem

The prophetic narratives that we have discussed up to this point give a relatively clear indication of the stereotypical behavior and social functions of Ephraimite prophets. However, before we turn to a brief examination of the writing prophets of the Ephraimite tradition, we should note two general statements of the role that prophets played in Israel. Both of these statements come from a late period in the history of the Deuteronomic tradition, and both are pure representations of Deuteronomic theological views. In 2 Kgs 17:7–18 the Deuteronomic Historian departs from his narrative and inserts a theological reflection on the reason for the fall of Samaria. In essence the writer concludes that the nation was destroyed because the king and the people ignored the Deuteronomic theology. Among other things, they ignored the prophets and visionaries, who had been sent to warn the people to repent.[132] Instead, the people turned to diviners and sorcerers, who were not legitimate intermediaries (2 Kgs 17:13, 17).

In a similar passage seeking to explain the fall of Jerusalem, the Historian repeats his observations. The city was destroyed because of the sins of Manasseh, who violated the Deuteronomic prescriptions even more than had his predecessors. He too relied on various types of mediums, in direct violation of Deuteronomic law (2 Kgs 21:6; cf. Deut 18:10–11). He ignored the prophets whom Yahweh sent, and they finally delivered a judgment oracle against the city and the nation (2 Kgs 21:10–15).

Both of these passages reinforce the picture of prophetic activity that we have drawn from the prophetic narratives themselves. According to Deuteronomic ideology, the prophets were the only legitimate means of communication between God and the people. No other intermediaries were allowed. Through the prophets the people could contact Yahweh, and in turn the prophets delivered to the people the word of Yahweh, judging them, saving them, or exhorting them to repent. The prophets, however, were ignored, and throughout most of the history of the monarchy they remained

---

132. This is one of the few positive references in the Deuteronomic corpus to a visionary (ḥōzeh). The reference may have been included to show the Deuteronomists' approval of Jerusalemite intermediaries, such as Isaiah, who bore this title and who had theological views compatible with those of the Deuteronomists.

on the periphery of the society, never influencing it enough to prevent its final destruction.

WRITING PROPHETS IN THE
EPHRAIMITE TRADITION

Biblical scholars have sometimes been reluctant to admit that there was any continuity between Israel's great writing prophets and the earlier prophets described in the Deuteronomic History. The reasons for this reluctance are not always clear, but it has led to various attempts to distinguish the two types of intermediaries. Some scholars have assumed that the writing prophets represented purer forms of religion and ethics than did their predecessors. Others have claimed that the early prophets were ecstatics or participated in the cult, while the writing prophets did not. However, none of the traditional attempts to distinguish the two types of prophets has been totally convincing, and most scholars today recognize some sort of continuity in the history of Israelite prophecy.

This continuity has been described in various ways, but it is usually thought to have been ideological and/or linguistic. Attempts to trace ideological continuity have often appealed to the vague notion of a "prophetic tradition" or even a "prophetic office" in which all Israelite prophets participated. Individual prophets drew their ethical sensitivities and theological insights from the tradition, and as a result prophets throughout Israel's history shared a distinctive "prophetic theology." Taking another tack, linguistic explanations for prophetic continuity have tried to account for shared vocabulary and speech patterns by assuming some sort of literary influence. Thus, for example, parts of Jeremiah are said to resemble the Deuteronomic History either because Jeremiah himself knew the Book of Deuteronomy and consciously copied its literary style or because his writings were edited by the same writers responsible for the History.

There is undoubtedly some truth in both of these approaches to the problem of continuity. Certainly the prophets were influenced by the various theological traditions in Israelite society, although it is doubtful that there was ever a single "prophetic tradition." Similarly, some prophets may have consciously or unconsciously copied the words of their predecessors, and the presence of secondary editing in the prophetic books must be acknowledged. However, the

anthropological material that we have examined suggests that sociological factors may have also been involved in the continuity of
Israelite prophecy. We have seen that prophets cannot exist without
some sort of support group and that all of the prophets within a
single group respond to subtle group pressures to make their behavior conform to group expectations. Two prophets may speak and act
in a similar way and may express similar points of view because
they are both members of the same support group. Thus, the links
between some of Israel's writing prophets and the earlier nonwriting prophets may be explained by assuming that they shared the
same basic support group. With this thesis in mind, we will now
examine briefly the writings of Hosea and Jeremiah, two prophets
usually considered to be within the Ephraimite tradition. We will
be looking not only for evidence on their characteristic behavior but
also for some indication of the nature of their support groups and
social functions.[133]

Hosea

The Book of Hosea furnishes little information on the prophet's
relationship to his society, but enough data can be gleaned from the
text to permit a few tentative conclusions. The superscription of the
book tells us only that Hosea was the son of Beeri, who is otherwise
unknown, and that he prophesied during the reign of Jeroboam
II.[134] However, the introductory phrase, "the word of Yahweh
which was to Hosea" (*debar-yhwh ăšer hāyāh >el-hôšēa* ‹ [Hos 1:1]),
is a standard Ephraimite formula that is used to describe spirit possession, so from the very beginning of the book Hosea is linked with

133. For a more detailed discussion of the continuity between Israel's early
prophets and the writing prophets, see R. R. Wilson, "Early Israelite Prophecy," *Int*
32 (1978) 3–16. Cf. Clements, *Prophecy and Tradition*, 24–57; and the very different
approach of M. Haran, "From Early to Classical Prophecy: Continuity and Change,"
VT 27 (1977) 385–397.

134. The superscription of Hosea, like the superscriptions of the other prophetic
books, was added by a later editor, presumably a Deuteronomist. There is no particular reason to question the traditional date of Hosea's activity in Ephraim, although
the references to Judean kings are not chronologically accurate. For a discussion of
the superscription, see H. W. Wolff, *Hosea* (Philadelphia: Fortress Press, 1974) 3–6.
Note also the more general discussion of G. M. Tucker, "Prophetic Superscriptions
and the Growth of a Canon," *Canon and Authority* (ed. G. W. Coats and B. O. Long;
Philadelphia: Fortress Press, 1977) 56–70. Hosea's much discussed marriages tell us
nothing about his social location or about his characteristic behavior. They indicate
only that he used striking symbolic actions. Attempts to portray Hosea as a priest,
farmer, member of a prophetic guild, or member of the "wisdom movement" lack
support in the text and are not convincing (G. Fohrer, *Introduction to the Old Testament* [Nashville: Abingdon Press, 1968] 419).

the Ephraimite prophetic tradition.[135] Although the prophet is never portrayed delivering an oracle in a specific geographical area, it is safe to assume that he carried out his activities in Ephraim. Most of his oracles are directed at the northern kingdom, and Judah is rarely mentioned.[136] Furthermore, most of the places that Hosea refers to in his speeches are located in the north: Samaria (Hos 7:1; 8:5–6; 10:5, 7; 14:1); Bethel (Hos 4:15; 5:8; 10:5; 12:5); Gilgal (Hos 4:15; 9:15; 12:12); the Valley of Achor (Hos 2:17); Adam (Hos 6:7); Ramah, Gibeah (Hos 5:8); and Gilead (Hos 6:8; 12:12).

The similarities between the language of Hosea and the language of the Deuteronomic History have long been noted, although they have usually been explained by suggesting that Hosea's prophecies influenced later Deuteronomic writers. However, on the basis of the anthropological material, it would be more plausible to suggest that Hosea's characteristic possession behavior included using the stereotypical language expected by his Ephraimite support group. This suggestion is strengthened by the fact that the closest verbal links between Hosea and the Deuteronomic literature occur in expressions of the Deuteronomic theology, precisely the sort of material one might expect to have been included in oracles delivered by a possessed prophet. Thus, for example, both Hosea and Deuteronomy use similar language to condemn worship on the high places (Hos 4:13; Deut 12:2) and to describe the folly of worshiping idols (Hos 8:6; 13:2; 14:4; Deut 4:28; 28:36, 64; 31:29; 2 Kgs 19:18). Both also use the same idioms to speak of breaking Yahweh's covenant with Israel (Hos 6:7; 8:1; Deut 17:2; cf. Josh 23:16; Judg 2:20; 2 Kgs 18:12). The love of Yahweh plays an important role both in the theology of Hosea and in the theology of the Deuteronomists, and in both theologies the errant people are exhorted to seek (*bāqaš*) Yahweh and to return (*šûb*) to God (Hos 5:15—6:1; Deut 4:29–30).[137] Although some of these linguistic parallels may indeed be the result of later editing, it is reasonable to assume that most of

135. See above, pp. 145–146.

136. The references to Judah in Hosea are usually thought to be secondary additions, perhaps the work of a Judean editor. Leaving the question of the editor aside, it is probably safe to assume that some of the references to Judah were added after the fall of Samaria, when the book was reinterpreted to make it relevant to a new historical context. However, there is no reason to deny that Hosea might have been interested in Judah and its future relations with Israel, so some of the references to Judah may come from the prophet himself. For a discussion of this question, see R. E. Clements, "Understanding the Book of Hosea," *RevExp* 72 (1975) 417–419.

137. For a detailed listing of the links between Hosea and the Deuteronomic literature, see Weinfeld, *Deuteronomy and the Deuteronomic School*, 366–370.

them indicate that Hosea was a member of a group that followed Ephraimite theological and political traditions and that during possession he used the group's stereotypical language.[138]

Just as Hosea seems to have had linguistic and theological affinities with the Ephraimite tradition, so he also seems to have held an Ephraimite view of prophecy. Like other Ephraimites, he regarded Moses as a prophet. Furthermore, Hosea seems to have accepted the Deuteronomic notion that in each generation Yahweh raised up a Mosaic prophet to lead the people, just as Moses had led them in the wilderness: "By a prophet Yahweh brought Israel up from Egypt, and by a prophet he was guarded" (Hos 12:14 [Eng. 12:13]; cf. 12:11 [Eng. 12:10]).

The characteristic Ephraimite concept of the Mosaic prophet who serves as an intermediary between God and the people may also be reflected in Hosea's frequent use of language drawn from legal disputations. This language undoubtedly originated in the trials that were held in the city gate, but because of the original function of the language it would have been ideally suited for use in expressing the dialogues between God and the people that were carried on through Mosaic prophets. Although the Book of Hosea never provides a picture of a Mosaic prophet functioning as a divine-human intermediary, the book does preserve several dialogues in which the prophet speaks both the words of God and the words of the people. In Hos 8:1–3 the prophet's oracle begins with the words of Yahweh, who calls the people to prepare for war against the enemy. The impending battle is seen as a judgment on the people because they have broken Yahweh's covenant (Hos 8:1).[139] The prophet then quotes the people, who are apparently attempting to intercede with God in order to avoid the threatened invasion: "My God, we Israel know thee" (Hos 8:2). However, the people's plea is followed immediately by a second judgment oracle, which by implication is God's response to their request. The judgment cannot be averted, and the people must suffer (Hos 8:3). A more detailed divine-human dialogue takes place in Hos 5:15—6:6. At the beginning of the dialogue, the prophet speaks the words of Yahweh, who threat-

138. Hosea may have also shared the early Ephraimite view that kings could be chosen only by Yahweh and that hereditary kingship was not permissible (Hos 8:4–6). In addition, Hosea seems to have followed the Ephraimite tradition in seeing the shrines at Dan and Bethel as illegitimate sanctuaries (Hos 8:5; 13:2).

139. It is unlikely that Hos 8:1 is addressed to the prophet rather than to the people. See the discussion of Wolff, Hosea, 133–134.

ens to withdraw from the people until they acknowledge their guilt and again seek God (Hos 5:15). The divine threat is immediately followed by a quotation from the people, who direct to God a penitential psalm stating their faith that when they return to Yahweh the Lord will also return to them (Hos 6:1–3). Although the psalm itself may have originated in the cult, the text does not indicate the setting in which the people actually recited it. However, the people's attempt to appease Yahweh is not effective. The prophet speaks again the words of God, who expresses despair at Israel's apostasy. Israel's actions are said to have prompted Yahweh to slay the people with divine words delivered by the prophets (Hos 6:4–6). The prophets are clearly portrayed here as the intermediaries who deliver God's pure, effective words to the people. This description recalls the Deuteronomic concept of the Mosaic prophet, into whose mouth God sets divine words and who is to deliver those words unaltered to the people (Deut 18:18).

An additional passage that throws light on Hosea's concept of prophecy is found in Hos 9:8, where the prophet is called the watchman (ṣōpeh) of Ephraim. This image, which was adopted by later prophets, is not clearly defined here, but it presumably implies that Hosea understood the prophet to be a figure who stood between God and the people and who was to protect the people by warning them of approaching danger. Hosea's use of the image of the watchman may thus be another expression of the Ephraimite concept of the prophetic mediator.[140]

The Book of Hosea gives no explicit picture of the prophet's function in Ephraimite society, but it is safe to infer that he was a peripheral prophet who delivered his divine messages to the central society in an attempt to reform it. The book gives no indication that he was a member of the political or religious establishments, and his words provide a sharp challenge to Ephraim's prevailing political and religious views. In addition, there are hints that he was opposed by the majority of the society and supported only by a minority group accepting the Deuteronomic point of view. In the difficult and textually corrupt oracle in Hos 9:7–9, Hosea apparently quotes the people as saying that "the prophet (hannābîʾ) is foolish (ʾĕwîl)

140. The theological background of Hosea's conception of prophecy, as well as the general source of his theological and political views, is discussed in detail in H. W. Wolff, "Hoseas geistige Heimat," *TLZ* 81 (1956) 83–94 (=H. W. Wolff, *Gesammelte Studien zum Alten Testament* [Munich: Chr. Kaiser Verlag, 1964] 232–250). Cf. Wolff, *Hosea*, xxiii–xxix.

and the man possessed by the spirit (ʾîš hārûaḥ) is insane (mĕšuggā ʿ)" (Hos 9:7).[141] Language of this type is frequently used by the establishment to characterize peripheral prophets whose claims are not accepted. The symptoms of spirit possession are capable of being understood either as an indication of genuine intermediation or as a sign of mental illness. The latter evaluation indicates that the society refuses to recognize the possessed individual as a divine intermediary. Hos 9:7 thus suggests that at least some of the society did not recognize Hosea as a genuine prophet but considered his possession behavior, whatever it included, to be an indication of illness. The identity of Hosea's opponents is implied in the next two verses, where the prophet continues by complaining that although the prophet is the watchman of Ephraim, he is now ineffective. "A trap is upon all his paths, and there is hostility in the house of his God" (Hos 9:8). This statement suggests that the group that refused to recognize Hosea's authority and that prevented him from functioning as a prophet was connected with the central cult. The obscure reference to those who "corrupt themselves as in the days of Gibeah" (Hos 9:9) may further identify the opponents as Levitical priests functioning in the northern sanctuaries, but textual difficulties in the verse make its interpretation uncertain.[142] The location of Hosea's opposition within the central religious establishment is also suggested by Hos 4:4–6, where Hosea accuses the priests and prophets of not carrying out their proper functions. For this reason God will make these central intermediaries ineffective and will prevent them from doing further damage to the people. The prophets mentioned in the oracle were presumably central prophets attached to the royal court or to one or more of the northern sanctuaries. Hosea clearly does not recognize their prophetic authority, presumably because their behavior and their theological and political views differed from his own.

The Book of Hosea thus suggests that Hosea was a peripheral prophet whose characteristic words and deeds followed stereotypical Ephraimite patterns. He was presumably supported by the groups that carried the Ephraimite traditions, and later incarnations of these groups must have preserved and edited his writings. The editorial additions made by these groups quite naturally used typi-

141. For a discussion of the text and translation of this verse, see Wolff, Hosea, 150–151, 156–157.
142. Ibid., 157–158.

cal Deuteronomic language. Because some of the Deuteronomists were in Judah and recognized Jerusalem as the only place where Yahweh could legitimately be worshiped, they made editorial additions that mention the southern kingdom. The book thus became the first collection of prophetic writings to be preserved by the Deuteronomists and became a permanent part of the tradition in which later Ephraimite prophets participated.

Jeremiah

Literary and Historical Problems

Links between Jeremiah and the Deuteronomic corpus were recognized long before the rise of critical biblical scholarship, and the linguistic and theological similarities between the two may have led the rabbis to credit Jeremiah with the authorship of Kings (*b. B. Bat.* 14b–15a). Modern scholars have followed their predecessors in seeing Deuteronomistic language and theology throughout Jeremiah, but there has been much debate over the literary and historical processes that led to the inclusion of this material in the book.[143] For our purposes it is not necessary to explore this problem in detail, but before we can consider Jeremiah's relationship to his society we must at least adopt a working hypothesis on the book's literary history.

Scholars have long agreed that Jeremiah is not a literary unity. Since the fundamental work of Sigmund Mowinckel, most critics have recognized three basic types of material in the book. These types (which Mowinckel designated A, B, and C) have usually been assigned different dates and regarded as the work of different authors. According to Mowinckel's analysis, which most subsequent scholars have accepted with only minor modifications, the A material consists of poetic oracles from Jeremiah himself. These oracles are now scattered throughout Jeremiah 1—25. The B material is composed of biographical narratives that were written in Egypt by Baruch sometime between 580 and 480 B.C. B is found mostly in Jeremiah 26—29, 36—44, although there are fragments of Baruch's narratives elsewhere in the book. The C material has close linguistic and theological affinities with the Deuteronomic History and was probably added to the book by a Deuteronomistic editor in the

143. For a brief history of research on the Deuteronomistic features of Jeremiah, see Nicholson, *Preaching to the Exiles*, 20–32.

postexilic period. C is now found throughout the book and is mixed with both A and B. According to Mowinckel, C can be detected in Jer 3:6–13; 7:1–8:3; 11:1–5, 9–14; 18:1–12; 21:1–10; 22:1–5; 25:1–11a; 27; 29:1–23; 32:1–2, 6–16, 24–44; 34:1–22; 35:1–19; 39:15–18; 44:1–14; 45. To this basic body of material later editors added collections of poetic and prose promises (Jeremiah 30—33), a series of oracles against foreign nations (Jeremiah 46—51), and a historical appendix (Jeremiah 52).[144]

Although Mowinckel's basic literary analysis has continued to enjoy widespread support in the scholarly community, recent studies have challenged his conclusions about the authorship and dating of the B and C material. Gunther Wanke has carefully analyzed Mowinckel's B material and concluded that it is composed of two different sources. Chapters 26—28 and 36 were perhaps actually written by Baruch, but chapters 37—44 were written at Mizpah by someone in Gedaliah's administration. This unknown author was interested in showing the impact of Jeremiah's prophetic calling on his personal life.[145] Helga Weippert has subjected the alleged Deuteronomic vocabulary of C to a thorough contextual study and has demonstrated that C's language is in many instances closer to A than to the postexilic layers of the Deuteronomic History. Weippert's analysis suggests that C was a prosaic development of A and was the work of Jeremiah himself.[146] Expanding Weippert's conclusions, other scholars have suggested that C was produced by Jeremiah's disciples or by an exilic editor.[147] Somewhat similar conclusions have been reached by E. W. Nicholson, who has shown that both B and C have links to Deuteronomic language and theology and that both are also related to A. Nicholson sees B and C as attempts of the Jeremiah tradition to apply the prophet's oracles to a new historical situation.[148]

At this stage in the scholarly debate it is difficult to draw firm

---

144. S. Mowinckel, *Zur Komposition des Buches Jeremia* (Oslo: Jacob Dybwad, 1914) 20–21, 24, 31, 40–45.

145. G. Wanke, *Untersuchungen zur sogenannten Baruchschrift* (Berlin: Walter de Gruyter, 1971). Cf. K.-F. Pohlmann, *Studien zum Jeremiabuch* (Göttingen: Vandenhoeck & Ruprecht, 1978).

146. H. Weippert, *Die Prosareden des Jeremiabuches;* cf. Holladay, "A Fresh Look at 'Source B' and 'Source C,' " 408–412.

147. W. Thiel, *Die deuteronomistische Redaktion von Jeremia 1—25.*

148. Nicholson, *Preaching to the Exiles,* 56, 134–135. Linguistic and theological features appearing in all three types of Jeremiah material have also been noted by others. See, for example, T. W. Overholt, "Remarks on the Continuity of the Jeremiah Tradition," *JBL* 91 (1972) 457–462; and Hyatt, "The Deuteronomic Edition of Jeremiah," 71–95.

conclusions about the literary history of Jeremiah, but current research suggests the following tentative reconstruction. The A material includes the poetic oracles of Jeremiah himself. These oracles are difficult to date with any certainty, but they seem to come primarily from two historical periods. A few oracles, now found mainly in Jeremiah 1—6, seem to come from the beginning of Jeremiah's prophetic activity and are probably to be dated during Josiah's reign (ca. 627–622 B.C.). However, most of the oracles come from the reign of Jehoiakim (609–598 B.C.) and are now scattered throughout Jeremiah 7—25.[149] The B material should probably be assigned to two different authors. As Wanke has suggested, Jeremiah 26—28, 36 may come from Baruch, although the distinctive Deuteronomic coloring of some of this material may indicate that the author stood in the Ephraimite tradition. Jeremiah 37—44 also has Ephraimite links, although the vocabulary and style of the author differ from those of the author of Jeremiah 26—28, 36. The fact that Jeremiah 37—44 focuses on the personal aspects of Jeremiah's prophetic activity suggests that the author was a prophet or at least had a special interest in prophecy. All of the B material was probably produced between the beginning of Jehoiakim's reign and Jeremiah's death, although later editing cannot be ruled out. The C material seems to be a prose form of Jeremiah's poetic speeches and apparently reflects the Ephraimite language and thought of Jeremiah's time. C is therefore difficult to date. Although some of C may come from Jeremiah himself, it seems more reasonable to assign most of this material to his Ephraimite followers, who presumably shared some of his characteristic speech patterns. Parts of C may have been produced during the prophet's lifetime, but exilic or even postexilic disciples may have reformulated his oracles to make them speak to new historical situations. Thus, the overall picture of Jeremiah suggests a book produced over a period of time by Ephraimite authors who supported Jeremiah and shared with him certain linguistic and theological traditions but who also had distinctive literary styles.[150]

Jeremiah's Personal Background

The superscription of the Book of Jeremiah identifies the prophet as the son of Hilkiah and as a member of one of the priestly families at Anathoth, the city which according to tradition was given to the

149. J. Bright, *Jeremiah* (Garden City, N.Y.: Doubleday, 1965) lxix.
150. Cf. J. Bright, "The Date of the Prose Sermons of Jeremiah," 15–29.

descendants of Levi (Josh 20:18) and to which Abiathar and his Ephraimite priestly relatives had been exiled by Solomon (1 Kgs 2:26–27). Jeremiah is thus clearly portrayed as one of the priestly descendants of Abiathar and therefore as a member of one of the Levitical groups that carried the old Ephraimite traditions and were involved in Josiah's reforms. In addition, as we have already suggested, Jeremiah's father, Hilkiah, may have even been the same priest who found the Deuteronomistic lawbook in the temple. However, even if Jeremiah's father is not to be identified with Josiah's high priest, there are other indications that some of the prophet's relatives were involved in Josiah's reform and that in Jeremiah's own time they were still occupying high positions in the political and religious establishments in Jerusalem.[151] We have already seen that Jeremiah's uncle, Shallum, owned hereditary property at Anathoth. He was thus presumably a member of one of the Levitical priestly groups there, as was Jeremiah. The prophet's uncle may have also been the husband of Huldah, the prophetess of whom Josiah inquired concerning the book found in the temple (2 Kgs 22:14), although this is by no means certain.[152] In any case, the Book of Jeremiah clearly indicates that some of the descendants of the prophet's uncle held priestly and administrative offices in the Jerusalem temple. Shallum's son Maaseiah was a keeper of the threshold in the temple during the reign of Jehoiakim (Jer 35:4) and may have been the same individual who, along with Shaphan, was sent by Josiah to initiate repairs on the temple (2 Chr 34:8). One of Maaseiah's sons, Zephaniah, was a priest (Jer 21:1; 37:3) who, according to Jer 29:25–26, held an administrative position in the temple. Another of Maaseiah's sons, Zedekiah, was apparently a prophet who was taken to Babylon during the first deportation (Jer 29:21). Jeremiah thus seems to have been related not only to the priestly bearers of the Ephraimite traditions but also to members of the central political and religious establishments. These individuals presumably assumed their positions during the reign of Josiah, who was supportive of the Deuteronomic position. Therefore, there can be no doubt that members of the Anathoth priesthood constituted the initial support group for Jeremiah's prophetic activities.

151. I owe many of the following observations to S. Dean McBride, who has reconstructed Jeremiah's family background in his unpublished paper, "Jeremiah and the 'Men of ⟨Anatot.'"

152. First Chronicles 5:38–39 (Eng. 6:12–13) lists an individual named Shallum as the father of Hilkiah. However, it is doubtful that this individual is to be identified with Jeremiah's uncle.

However, even though Jeremiah came from a priestly family, there is no reason to suppose that he himself ever performed priestly functions, either at Anathoth or in Jerusalem. The Deuteronomists in Jeremiah's time probably would not have recognized the legitimacy of worship outside of Jerusalem, so it is doubtful that the Anathoth priests would have maintained a local cult. Similarly, the Deuteronomic law does not *require* that all Levites function as priests at the central sanctuary. Deuteronomy simply states that any Levite living in Israel *may* come to the central sanctuary and offer sacrifices if he so chooses (Deut 18:6–8). The law demands that Levites be treated in the same way as the sanctuary's resident priests, but no compulsory priestly service is imposed on local Levites.

Jer 1:2 explicitly states that Jeremiah began his prophetic activity in the thirteenth year of Josiah. This date has been challenged on various grounds, and attempts have been made to emend or reinterpret it. However, it is difficult to ignore the unambiguous statement of the text, and even if the verse is assigned to a much later editor, there are no grounds for questioning its historical accuracy.[153] If the Chronicler's dates for Josiah's reform are accepted, then Jer 1:2 implies that Jeremiah began to prophesy after the first stage of the reform had begun in Josiah's eighth year but before his eighteenth year, when the discovery of the book in the temple initiated the reform's second stage. Although Jeremiah is said to have been from Anathoth, his prophetic activities seem to have been carried on in Jerusalem.

Jeremiah's Characteristic Behavior

The Book of Jeremiah begins with a typical Ephraimite superscription indicating that the prophet received his revelations when he was possessed by Yahweh's spirit. Only rarely is Jeremiah said to have had visions (Jer 4:23–26), and in some cases even the visions are attributed to the divine word that came to him (Jer 1:4, 9, 11, 13). There are some indications that Jeremiah's possession behavior included a form of trance with observable physiological features (Jer 4:19–21), although there are no indications that his trances were uncontrolled.[154] While possessed he was apparently still capa-

---

153. T. W. Overholt, "Some Reflections on the Date of Jeremiah's Call," *CBQ* 33 (1971) 165–184.

154. For an early statement of this view, see Hölscher, *Die Profeten*, 274–275.

ble of intelligible speech, so there is no way to determine whether or not his oracles were delivered while he was in trance.

There are some indications that Jeremiah's possession behavior involved stereotypical language. His vocabulary has clear links with the characteristically Ephraimite speech of the Book of Deuteronomy (particularly Deuteronomy 32), and his oracles also have linguistic affinities with Hosea.[155] This situation has sometimes been explained by assuming that Jeremiah knew and consciously quoted Deuteronomy and Hosea or that his words were later edited by the Deuteronomists. While these possibilities cannot be ruled out, it is also conceivable that Jeremiah's possession behavior included the use of the stereotypical language of his support group, the Ephraimite priests at Anathoth.

In addition to using stereotypical Ephraimite language, there is some evidence that Jeremiah's oracles followed patterns already present in the Ephraimite tradition. Several of Jeremiah's speeches are composed of the following sequence of elements: (1) a question about the reasons for Israel's condition after judgment; (2) an answer explaining in typical Deuteronomic terms the sins that brought about the judgment; (3) a repetition of the circumstances that gave rise to the question (Jer 5:19; 9:11–15 [Eng. 9:12–16]; 16:10–13; 22:8–9). This pattern is also found in Deut 29:21–27 [Eng. 29:22–28] and 1 Kgs 9:8–9 and is a variant of the familiar Deuteronomic *Kinderfrage*-pattern, in which the child asks his parents a question, and the parents provide an explanation followed by a repetition of the state of affairs that prompted the question (Deut 6:20–25; Josh 4:6–7, 21–24; Exod 12:26–27; 13:14–15).[156] Although literary dependence cannot be ruled out as an explanation for the occurrences of this pattern, it is also possible that Jeremiah consciously or unconsciously used the pattern because it was part of the stereotypical behavior expected by his support group.

Scholars have long noted that Jeremiah's theology is similar to that of the Deuteronomists, although the degree of similarity cannot now be determined due to the thorough way in which the

---

155. For detailed lists of these linguistic links and discussions of their implications, see Holladay, "A Fresh Look at 'Source B' and 'Source C,' " 410; H. H. Rowley, "The Prophet Jeremiah and the Book of Deuteronomy," *Studies in Old Testament Prophecy* (ed. H. H. Rowley; Edinburgh: T. & T. Clark, 1950) 157–174; J. P. Hyatt, "Jeremiah and Deuteronomy," *JNES* 1 (1942) 156–173; Weinfeld, *Deuteronomy and the Deuteronomic School*, 359–361; and K. Gross, *Die literarische Verwandtschaft Jeremias mit Hosea* (Leipzig: Robert Noske, 1930) 1–19.

156. Nicholson, *Preaching to the Exiles*, 59–66.

Deuteronomic corpus was edited in the postexilic period. Like the Deuteronomists, Jeremiah demanded faithfulness to Israel's covenant with Yahweh and condemned the worship of other gods, worship on the high places, and any attempt to ignore the ethical and cultic demands of the covenant. Furthermore, Jeremiah followed the Deuteronomists in seeing Yahweh's judgment as the result of Israel's repeated covenantal abuses and the people's refusal to heed the warnings to repent that Yahweh persistently sent through the prophets. We have already seen this theology in the Deuteronomic explanation for the fall of Samaria (2 Kgs 17:13–18), and examples appear throughout the Book of Jeremiah (Jer 7:25–26, 32–34; 15:4–11; 26:4–6; 29:17–19; 35:15–17; 36:1–31; 44:4–6).[157]

Jeremiah's links with the Ephraimite tradition are apparent not only in his language and theology but also in his concept of his prophetic role. A number of scholars have pointed out that in the prophet's call he was not simply appointed as a prophet but he was specifically designated a *Mosaic* prophet.[158] In reply to Jeremiah's objection to Yahweh's original call, God touches the prophet's lips and declares, "I have put my words in your mouth" (Jer 1:9). This phrase is almost identical to the one used in Deut 18:18, where Yahweh says of the promised Mosaic prophet, "I will put my words in his mouth." As a Mosaic prophet, Jeremiah is told to speak only the divine word that God gives: "Whatever I command you, you shall speak" (Jer 1:7); "say to them everything that I command you" (Jer 1:17). Similar instructions were also given to Moses and his prophetic successors: "He shall speak to them all that I command him" (Deut 18:18). It is, of course, impossible to know whether Jeremiah actually quoted the words of Deuteronomy in describing his call or whether the quotations were added by later editors in the Jeremiah tradition. In either case, the call narrative places the prophet clearly in the distinctive Ephraimite prophetic tradition. As a Mosaic prophet, he is to speak the pure word of God to the people, who are required to obey the word that comes through such a prophet.

157. Ibid., 57–58.
158. K. Gouders, " 'Siehe, ich lege meine Worte in deinen Mund,' " *Bib Leb* 12 (1971) 162–186; P. E. Broughton, "The Call of Jeremiah," *AusBR* 6 (1958) 41–43; W. L. Holladay, "The Background of Jeremiah's Self-understanding," *JBL* 83 (1964) 155–161; idem, "Jeremiah and Moses: Further Observations," *JBL* 85 (1966) 17–27; and J. M. Berridge, *Prophet, People, and the Word of Yahweh* (Zurich: EVZ-Verlag, 1970) 26–62.

However, the Ephraimite view of prophecy also assigns the Mosaic prophet the task of serving as a means by which the people can contact Yahweh. The prophet is to serve as their intercessor and mediator. Jeremiah himself apparently saw intercession as part of the task of the true prophet, for according to Jeremiah 27 he used the concept in a dispute with the Jerusalemite prophets. In Jer 27:16–17 he warns the people not to listen to these prophets, who are predicting the return of the sacred vessels from Babylon, and he accuses them of lying. He then proposes a test to determine the validity of their prophetic claims. He challenges them to intercede with Yahweh for the return of the vessels. Their success would indicate that they are indeed Mosaic prophets, for only such a prophet can be a successful mediator according to the Ephraimite prophetic ideology (Jer 27:18). The narratives describing the final days of the siege indicate that in this critical period the king himself recognized Jeremiah's status as a Mosaic prophet and sent official delegations to request him to intercede with Yahweh on behalf of the city. However, Jeremiah's efforts to avert the impending destruction were not successful, and God responded with additional judgment oracles (Jer 21:1–10; 37:3–10; 42:1–22).

In the light of Jeremiah's belief that intercession was part of his prophetic task, it is striking that there is little evidence of intercessory activity in the prophet's oracles. Only in Jer 4:9–10 does the prophet attempt to intervene with Yahweh on behalf of the people, and even in this case there is no indication that the people requested the intercession. An explanation for this strange state of affairs is found in a striking series of passages in which Yahweh actually forbids the prophet to intercede for the people.[159] In Jer 7:16–17 God warns Jeremiah not to pray for the people, for their sins are so great that intercession cannot be effective. The same theme is repeated in Jer 11:14–17, where Yahweh again prohibits intercession because of the persistent sins of the people. Finally, in Jer 14:1—15:4 a number of earlier oracles have been secondarily woven together to indicate the effects of this limitation of the prophet's role. The entire unit bears the superscription "the word of the Lord which came to Jeremiah concerning the drought" (Jer 14:1), and the first section of the unit is a clear description of the devastation brought about by a drought (Jer 14:2–6). This descrip-

---

159. For a discussion of these passages, see G. C. Macholz, "Jeremia in der Kontinuität der Prophetie," *Probleme biblischer Theologie*, 306–334.

tion is followed immediately by a prayer of repentance from the people. In stereotyped cultic phrases Israel confesses its sins and appeals to God for relief (Jer 14:7–9). However, instead of receiving a positive response from Yahweh, the prayer is followed immediately by a judgment oracle (Jer 14:10). The dialogue between God and the people has been interrupted. Yahweh no longer listens to the people's requests. The reason for this situation appears in Jer 14:11–12, where God directs Jeremiah not to pray for the people. The juxtaposition of the units implies that the people did not address God directly in the prayer in Jer 14:7–9 but channeled their request through Jeremiah, the Mosaic prophet. Yahweh's prohibition of intercession thus explains the unexpected judgmental response in Jer 14:10. However, in spite of God's command, Jeremiah attempts to defend the people by claiming that they have been misled by the Jerusalemite prophets, who continue to advocate the royal theology of the inviolability of Zion (Jer 14:13). To this attempted defense Yahweh responds that the Jerusalemite prophets are lying and that they do not have a genuine divine word. According to Deuteronomic law (Deut 18:19–20), prophets who speak without actually being commanded by God to do so deserve death, and people who do not recognize the falseness of their words must also be punished. God therefore decrees that the lying prophets shall be destroyed by sword and famine, while the people who listened to them will also be judged (Jer 14:14–16).[160] Following a lament by Jeremiah over the destruction caused by the judgment (Jer 14:17–18), the editors have inserted another prayer of repentance and petition from the people (Jer 14:19–22). Like the first prayer, this one is followed by a reiteration of God's refusal to listen. Jeremiah is told that even if Moses and Samuel were to intercede on behalf of Israel, Yahweh would not relent. As we have already seen, Moses and Samuel were paradigmatic intercessory prophets in the Ephraimite tradition, and God's refusal to listen even to them indicates the seriousness of Israel's plight. The dialogue between God and Israel that would normally be carried on through a Mosaic prophet has now become a monologue. Because of their sins the people are no longer allowed to communicate with God through the prophet. Communication now moves in only one direction, from

160. At this point the judgment ceases to be described as a drought and is portrayed as an impending military disaster. Shifts of this sort indicate the originally separate origin of the oracles in the unit.

God to the people. Thus Jeremiah is told that when the people come to him, they are to be given only a word of judgment, the only word which God will now speak to them (Jer 15:1–4).

The passages that we have just examined suggest that although Jeremiah believed intercession to be a part of his prophetic task, from the reign of Jehoiakim until the fall of Jerusalem Jeremiah was forbidden to play that part of the Mosaic prophet's role. It is impossible to determine whether these passages come from Jeremiah himself or from later editors, but in either case the reason for their inclusion is not too difficult to deduce. Jeremiah apparently saw himself as a Mosaic prophet, and this perception was certainly shared by his support group and by the later Deuteronomic tradition. As a Mosaic prophet Jeremiah delivered oracles that inevitably came to pass, and certainly the truth of his judgment oracles was confirmed when Jerusalem fell to the Babylonians. However, as a Mosaic prophet Jeremiah should have also interceded with Yahweh for the salvation of the city. Yet, the fact that the city fell implied that the prophet's intercessions had not been effective, and this in turn cast doubts on his status as a Mosaic prophet. Thus, after the fall of Jerusalem, Jeremiah's supporters, and perhaps Jeremiah himself, faced the problem of explaining the apparent ineffectiveness of his attempts at intercession. The solution to the problem was found in the notion that Yahweh had forbidden Jeremiah to exercise the Mosaic prophet's intercessory function. The prophet's oracles were thus arranged to suggest that the ban on intercession and God's refusal to listen were both part of the judgment brought about by the people's past refusal to listen to the warnings that God had delivered through the prophets. Because the people had refused to listen to the divine words delivered through the Mosaic prophet, God refused to listen to the requests that the people presented through the Mosaic prophet. The divine-human dialogue ceased, at least until the judgment had taken place.

The background of this broken dialogue between God and Israel is suggested by the way that some of Jeremiah's early oracles have been arranged in the present text. It is uncertain whether this arrangement is the work of Jeremiah or a later editor, but in either case it seems to reflect the characteristically Ephraimite idea that God and the people communicate through the prophet.[161] One of

161. Nicholson, *Preaching to the Exiles*, 59–77. For examples of divine-human dialogue in Jeremiah, see B. O. Long, "Two Question and Answer Schemata in the Prophets," *JBL* 90 (1971) 129–139.

the clearest examples is found in Jer 6:16–30, a unit which begins with Yahweh calling the people through the prophet. They are exhorted to seek the "ancient paths" (presumably the old Ephraimite traditions) and to walk in those paths. However, the people refused to do so (Jer 6:16). Yahweh then established prophetic watchmen to stand between God and the people and to warn them of the approaching judgment. However, the people refused to be warned (Jer 6:17). Yahweh therefore delivers a judgment oracle against the people, threatening them with unspecified punishment (Jer 6:18–21). To this oracle has been added a second that delineates the judgment more clearly. The people will be attacked by an enemy from the north (Jer 6:22–23). To this oracle the people respond with a lament (Jer 6:24–26). However, Yahweh does not continue the dialogue by replying to them but instead directs a private word to Jeremiah, confirming his prophetic status and reaffirming the divine judgment on rebellious Israel (Jer 6:27–30). The final shape of the whole unit thus suggests a gradual disintegration of the divine-human dialogue that is carried on through the prophets. This process finally results in the divine prohibition on intercession described in later chapters.

Jeremiah's Social Functions

When the various types of Jeremiah material are examined from a chronological standpoint, the evidence suggests that Jeremiah's relationship to his support group and his relationship to the whole society changed gradually during the course of his prophetic activity. If we accept the Chronicler's chronology for Josiah's reforms, then, as we have already noted, Jeremiah must have begun to prophesy after the reforms had already begun.[162] This fact, plus the fact that he was related to the priestly group whose theology inspired the reform, might suggest that he was a central prophet who worked within the religious establishment along with Hilkiah, Shaphan, and the rest of the reformers. However, nothing in the book supports this suggestion.[163] Rather, all of the evidence indi-

162. For a discussion of the historical context of Jeremiah's early oracles, see H. H. Rowley, "The Early Prophecies of Jeremiah in Their Setting," 198–234 (*Men of God*, 133–168).
163. The attempt of H. G. Reventlow (*Liturgie und prophetisches Ich bei Jeremia* [Gütersloh: Gerd Mohn, 1963]) to show that Jeremiah was involved in the cult has not been accepted by most scholars. See the critique of J. Bright, "Jeremiah's Complaints: Liturgy, or Expressions of Personal Distress?" *Proclamation and Presence*, 189–214.

cates that Jeremiah functioned as a peripheral prophet with respect to the people and the Jerusalemite establishment. His peripheral status is clearly suggested in the vision report in Jer 1:13–19. According to this report, immediately after Jeremiah's call he was told the judgment message that he was to deliver. He was also warned to expect opposition to his message but was promised divine strength to ward off the people's attacks.

Jeremiah thus seems to have begun his activities as a peripheral prophet attempting to reform the society by urging the people to repent and to follow the traditional Ephraimite prescriptions. The people are condemned for rejecting Yahweh, who had brought them from Egypt and given them the land (Jer 2:4–7). In particular, the priests and kings are reminded of their past transgressions, and the prophets are accused of prophesying by Baal, an offense punishable by death acccording to Deuteronomic law (Jer 2:8–9; cf. Deut 13:1–5). In this early period Jeremiah's oracles actually seem somewhat optimistic. Although he condemns the people in characteristically Deuteronomic terms, his speeches almost represent God as pleading with the people and expressing disappointment at their rejection. Nevertheless, Jeremiah clearly spoke of the possibility of immediate judgment because of the past and present sins of the people. The nature of the judgment is still not precisely clear. Sometimes it is unspecified (Jer 2:35; 4:23–28), while at other times it is seen as a devastating drought (Jer 3:3) or as an invasion by an enemy from the north (Jer 4:29; 5:15–17; 6:1–8, 22–23). Still, Jeremiah apparently believed that the judgment could be averted if the people repented and sincerely returned to Yahweh. The prophet therefore issued to them a call to return (Jer 3:12–14, 22–25) and suggested that repentance would bring God's forgiveness (Jer 3:15–18; 4:1–4).[164]

Jeremiah's activities during this period immediately raise the question of his relationship to Josiah's reform.[165] As a Levitical priest, Jeremiah should have supported the reform, and yet, with the possible exception of Jer 15:16, the book gives no indication that Jeremiah even knew of the reform, much less supported it. In fact, most of his early speeches are designed to condemn the same

164. For a study of the role of repentance in Jeremiah's prophecies, see T. M. Raitt, A *Theology of Exile* (Philadelphia: Fortress Press, 1977) 35–45.

165. For a summary of scholarly discussions of this problem, see Rowley, "The Early Prophecies of Jeremiah," 198–234 (*Men of God*, 133–168).

abuses that Josiah was supposed to have corrected. The solution to this apparent problem is probably to be found in the fact that the reform was neither as pervasive nor as Deuteronomic as 2 Kings 22—23 suggests.[166] We have already noted that the Chronicler ascribes to Josiah reforms not demanded by the Book of Deuteronomy. This fact, plus Josiah's apparent political motives, may have led orthodox Deuteronomists to believe that there was still room for improvement. In addition, even if Josiah was successful in quickly carrying out a reform of Israel's official political and religious institutions, a longer period of time would probably have been required for the reform to penetrate all levels of society. The rapidity with which even the official reforms were neglected after Josiah's unexpected death suggests that they were not as pervasive as the Deuteronomic History indicates (cf. Ezekiel 8). We may thus suspect that Jeremiah's early oracles were designed to continue the reforms that had been begun by Josiah. In this effort he was presumably supported by his fellow Levitical priests at Anathoth, some of whom may have already gained positions in the central Jerusalemite establishment because of Josiah's acceptance of their views. Hilkiah and the family of Shaphan, among others, may have been in this category. However, we may also suspect that if Levitical priests did enter the central establishment they soon became more conservative and less willing to advocate radical social and religious change. The anthropological evidence indicates that central intermediaries tend to favor carefully controlled changes that maintain the stability of the social order and preserve the society's continuity with traditional religious, political, and social views. Deuteronomists who had become part of the establishment would thus have become increasingly annoyed at Jeremiah's prophecies and may have felt that his sharply worded oracles would alienate members of the establishment who supported Josiah's continuing reforms. Eventually, these Deuteronomists within the government may have convinced Jeremiah to stop prophesying in order to allow the internal reforms to work. In any case, after a brief initial period of activity Jeremiah seems to have lapsed into silence until sometime during the reign of Jehoiakim.

The feelings of optimism which Jeremiah may have experienced during the Josianic reformation had apparently faded by the time he resumed his prophetic activity. The theological views that Jeremiah

166. Hyatt, "Jeremiah and Deuteronomy," 159–161.

and the Deuteronomists advocated had made some inroads into the Jerusalemite establishment, and by the time of Jehoiakim some supporters of the Deuteronomic position may have still occupied important positions in the central bureaucracy. However, from the orthodox Deuteronomic perspective of Jeremiah, religious conditions in Israel had worsened considerably after Josiah's death. A few members of the establishment seem to have been convinced of the truth of the Deuteronomic message, but the people as a whole had not been willing to listen. The repentance which Jeremiah had called for during Josiah's reform did not occur. People continued to worship other gods besides Yahweh, and the pagan cult practices which Josiah had removed from the land and from the temple in Jerusalem reappeared. Furthermore, political conditions had continued to deteriorate. After Josiah's death, the possibility of a Babylonian attack steadily increased. Against this background of deteriorating religious and political conditions, Jeremiah began delivering increasingly harsh oracles which stressed the judgment that would come on the people because of their sins. The call to return, which appeared in his early oracles, is rare in the speeches from this period, and his words paint increasingly dark and graphic pictures of Jerusalem's fate. It is therefore not surprising that public opposition to his message increased. As Jer 14:13–16 indicates, most of the people in Jerusalem continued to believe that nothing was really wrong. Yahweh still dwelled in the temple in Jerusalem, and as long as the divine presence remained in the city, it could never be captured. This view was articulated publicly by the Jerusalemite prophets, who, as members of the central establishment, maintained the stability of the central social structure by proclaiming the traditional royalist doctrine of the perpetual election of the dynasty and the city. They continued to support the inviolability of Zion even during the final siege of the city.

During the reign of Jehoiakim, Jeremiah's support group was presumably composed of fellow Levitical priests who shared his analysis of the religious situation, and the group may have also included members of the general population who had become convinced of the truth of the prophet's message. However, there is evidence that sometime during this period he was ostracized by at least part of his support group. This rejection by his fellow Levitical priests is reflected in some of Jeremiah's "complaints." In a poetic oracle in Jer 11:18–20, the prophet reveals his shock at learning that people have been trying to kill him. The identity of the plotters is not clear in this oracle, which closes with Jeremiah's plea for vengeance on his adversaries. However, the prose oracle in Jer 11:21–23 leaves no doubt about their identity. The oracle is directed against "the men of Anathoth, who seek your life, and say, 'Do not prophesy in the name of the Lord, or you will die by our hand' " (Jer 11:21). Yahweh delivers a death sentence against them and promises to punish the men of Anathoth for their crimes (Jer 11:22–23). This same group of opponents may have provoked some of Jeremiah's other complaints, although his adversaries are not elsewhere explicitly identified (cf. Jer 18:18; 20:11).

Jeremiah's rejection by "the men of Anathoth" is sometimes thought to indicate that the prophet's immediate family became enraged at his harsh message and therefore sought to silence him. However, it is also possible that the "men of Anathoth" are to be identified as some of Jeremiah's priestly relatives who were still occupying important positions in Jerusalem's religious establishment.[167] If so, then the reason for their opposition to Jeremiah is suggested by Jer 7:1—8:3, which may be taken as a fair representation of Jeremiah's message during the reign of Jehoiakim. According to this account, Jeremiah was told to deliver a "sermon" in the gate of the temple. His message to the people is expressed in typical Deuteronomic language and reflects orthodox Deuteronomic theology. After warning the people not to rely on the Jerusalemite belief that the presence of Yahweh's temple would protect the city, Jeremiah exhorts them to reform their conduct. If they do so, then the prophet implies that they will be allowed to continue to dwell in Jerusalem (Jer 7:1–7). He then turns his attention to the temple itself and to the cult. The people are condemned for worshiping other gods, a clear violation of the Deuteronomic law, and then coming to the temple to claim Yahweh's protection. Jeremiah stresses that God's willingness to dwell in the temple depends on the people's willingness to keep their covenant with Yahweh and to observe its demands. To illustrate this point, Jeremiah reminds the people of the fate of the old shrine at Shiloh, where Yahweh had been worshiped before the shrine was destroyed and the center of worship moved to Jerusalem. Because of the people's persistent refusal to listen to Yahweh's call, Jeremiah now predicts that the

167. I owe this interpretation to S. Dean McBride.

Jerusalemite temple will be destroyed just as God destroyed the sanctuary at Shiloh (Jer 7:8–15).

Jeremiah's "temple sermon" must have struck the people of Judah as a harsh indictment of their central cult, but his words would have had an even stronger impact on his Levitical relatives—including his cousins, the priests Maaseiah and Zephaniah—who had joined other Anathoth priests in participating in the Jerusalemite religious establishment. For them Jeremiah's reference to Shiloh would have carried a powerful message. According to Ephraimite tradition, their ancestor Abiathar's loss of priestly status in Jerusalem was interpreted as the fulfillment of a prophetic judgment oracle against the priestly line of Eli (1 Kgs 2:26–27; cf. 1 Sam 14:3; 22:20). The tradition maintained that the Elide line came to an end and Shiloh was destroyed because of the corruption of the Ephraimite priestly house, not because of the sins of the people (1 Sam 2:27–36; 3:12–14; 5:10–18). For Jeremiah's fellow Levites who were serving the religious establishment, his reference to Shiloh would have evoked the disastrous consequences of their ancestors' participation in a corrupt central cult.

We may thus suspect that by the time of Jehoiakim Jeremiah had come to believe that Levites who were still participating in the increasingly corrupt Jerusalemite central cult had violated their Deuteronomic theological principles. In spite of any intentions they may have had to reform the establishment from their position within the central social structure, Jeremiah seems to have turned against his priestly colleagues, thus earning for himself their active opposition. The prophet was rejected by at least portions of his original support group, and his resultant feelings of isolation may be reflected in his increasingly bitter complaints, in which he regrets his prophetic call and finally accuses God of deception and coercion (Jer 12:1–4; 15:10–18; 18:19–23; 20:7–12, 14–18). However, Yahweh refuses to relieve Jeremiah of his prophetic responsibilities and exercises over him the same sort of "tyranny" experienced by many possessed individuals (Jer 12:5–6; 15:19–21; 20:9, 11). Jeremiah therefore continued to deliver judgment oracles against the political and religious establishments and did not spare his former Levitical supporters.

However, by the time of Zedekiah, just before the fall of the city, opposition from the prophet's own "family" seems to have lessened. According to the accounts of Jeremiah's activities in this period, the members of his family who remained in the service of the temple no longer actively opposed him, and he even seems to have had some supporters within the central establishment. In Jer 21:1–2 and 37:3, Jeremiah's priestly cousin Zephaniah is sent to ask the prophet to intercede for the salvation of the city, and there is no suggestion of animosity between them, even though Jeremiah replies to the request by repeating his indictment against the city. Although Zephaniah's priestly colleague Pashhur is credited with having Jeremiah beaten and put in the stocks, there is no indication that Zephaniah participated in this incident (Jer 20:1–6). Similarly, in Jer 29:24–32 Zephaniah is said to have received a harsh letter from Shemaiah saying, "Yahweh has made you priest instead of Jehoiada the priest so that in the house of Yahweh you might be in charge of every madman (*mĕšuggā ʿ*) and everyone who acts like a prophet (*mitnabbē ʾ*), so that you might put him in the stocks and the collar. Now why have you not rebuked Jeremiah of Anathoth who is prophesying to you?" (Jer 29:26–27). This letter indicates that Shemaiah did not recognize Jeremiah's prophetic authority and interpreted his typical possession behavior as an indication of madness. However, the letter also indicates Zephaniah's reluctance to curb Jeremiah's activities. Even after receiving the letter, Zephaniah does not take any action against the prophet but shows the letter to him. As a result Jeremiah writes a new letter to the exiles, accusing Shemaiah of false prophecy (Jer 29:29–32).

There are also indications that Jeremiah enjoyed the support of other members of the royal establishment, particularly the family of Shaphan, who had earlier been involved in Josiah's reform (2 Kgs 22:3–14). When Jeremiah spoke against the temple, the Jerusalemite priests and prophets accused him of having committed a capital crime. At their instigation a trial was held before the princes, and after an inconclusive hearing, during which precedents were cited on both sides of the issue, Jeremiah was finally rescued by Ahikam, one of Shaphan's sons who had also been involved in Josiah's reform (Jer 26:1–24). Later, Elasah, another of Shaphan's sons, and Gemariah, a son of Hilkiah, delivered Jeremiah's letter to the exiles (Jer 29:3). Finally, the account of the reading of Jeremiah's scroll (Jeremiah 36) suggests that some members of the royal court took his words seriously. After Jeremiah's message had been dictated to Baruch the scribe, he read the scroll publicly in the temple in the chamber of Gemariah, the son of Shaphan. By allowing his chamber to be used for this purpose Gemariah showed some support for Jeremiah, and indeed when Gemariah's son Micaiah heard the scroll's message, he brought word to the princes, two of whom (Elnathan the son of Achbor and Gemariah himself) had had relatives involved in Josiah's reform. The princes then ordered Baruch to read the scroll to them, and when they heard it, they were apparently impressed by its contents. After first hiding Jeremiah and Baruch for their own safety, the princes had the scroll read before Jehoiakim. Unlike his father Josiah, Jehoiakim refused to listen to this statement of the Deuteronomic position, and he burned the scroll as it was read, in spite of the attempts of Elnathan, Delaiah, and Gemariah to prevent its destruction. All of these narratives suggest that Jeremiah was not without friends in the Jerusalemite establishment, and even after the destruction of the city he remained in the care of Gedaliah, who was the son of Ahikam and the grandson of Shaphan (Jer 39:13–14; 40:5–6).

In spite of the fact that some members of Jeremiah's support group were members of the central establishment, he remained a peripheral prophet. After he began to prophesy again in the reign of Jehoiakim, tensions between the prophet and his society grew progressively worse. As the fall of the city approached, Jeremiah became increasingly convinced that the disaster could not be avoided, and he advised the people not to resist the Babylonians (Jer 27:11; 37:6–10; 38:2–3). The establishment viewed the prophet's activities as treasonous, and his opponents sought to kill him (Jer 38:4). However, although the prophet was beaten and imprisoned, Zedekiah would not permit Jeremiah's execution (Jer 37:15–21; 38:4–6, 16).

As social conditions continued to deteriorate, Jeremiah appears to have become increasingly vehement in his opposition to the Jerusalemite prophets. These central intermediaries, who supported the Jerusalemite royal theology, grounded their oracles in orthodox Jerusalemite traditions, and as the fall of the city approached, they could legitimately point to Yahweh's miraculous intervention to save Jerusalem in the time of Hezekiah. Although Jeremiah had long been convinced that these prophets were misleading the people (Jer 5:12–13, 30–31; 6:13–14; 8:10–11; 14:13–16), he seems to have increased his use of false-prophecy accusations in his latter years. Just as witchcraft accusations multiply in modern societies when unstable conditions make social fragmentation inevitable, so the political and religious tensions of Jeremiah's time seem to have given rise to a flurry of false-prophecy accusations. As we have already seen, in the Deuteronomic tradition false prophecy is punishable by death (Deut 18:20), so a false-prophecy accusation has the same function that a witchcraft accusation does in modern societies. The accusation is an effective means of countering the claims of an opponent, but the use of this tactic normally creates irreparable rifts in the social fabric.

Some of Jeremiah's false prophecy oracles have been collected in Jer 23:9–40, and narratives of Jeremiah's encounters with Jerusalemite prophets have been preserved in Jeremiah 27—28.[168] The oracles, which are both in prose and in poetry, were probably delivered at different times, but for the most part they reflect Jeremiah's Ephraimite ideology. The prophets who support the inviolability of Zion are accused of speaking visions of their own minds rather than the true word which Yahweh has spoken (Jer 23:16–17). The prophets have not stood in the divine council as Ephraimite prophets do (cf. 1 Kgs 22:19–23) but have spoken ineffective words that did not achieve any results (Jer 23:18, 21–22). Unlike Mosaic prophets such as Jeremiah, the Jerusalemites have relied on dreams and have copied words from one another instead of speaking the direct word of Yahweh, which can always be recognized because of its effectiveness (Jer 23:25–32; cf. Num 12:6–8; Deut 18:21–22). Finally, Jeremiah rejects the characteristic language of the Jerusalemite prophets and looks forward to the day when the typical Deuteronomic prophetic terminology will again be used. People will no longer come to a prophet or a priest and ask for a "burden" (maśśāʾ), a particular type of oracle that may have been characteristically Jerusalemite (Jer 23:33; cf. Isa 13:1; 14:28; 15:1; 17:1; 19:1; 21:1, 11, 13; 22:1; 23:1; 30:6; Ezek 12:10; Nah 1:1; Zech 9:1; 12:1; Mal 1:1; 2 Chr 24:27).[169] Anyone who continues to use this terminology will be punished. Instead, the people will again use the dialogic terminology favored by Jeremiah. People shall ask the prophet, "what has Yahweh answered (ʿānāh)" or

---

168. For recent thorough discussions of these chapters and of the question of false prophecy in general, see Crenshaw, *Prophetic Conflict*, 49–61; T. W. Overholt, *The Threat of Falsehood* (London: SCM Press, 1970); T. Seidl, *Texte und Einheiten in Jeremia 27—29* (St. Ottilien: EOS, 1977); Hossfeld and Meyer, *Prophet gegen Prophet*, 57–113; I. Meyer, *Jeremia und die falschen Propheten* (Freiburg: Universitätsverlag, 1977); and Berridge, *Prophet, People, and the Word of Yahweh*, 32–38.

169. We will explore this point in greater detail when we discuss the characteristic speech of the Jerusalemite prophetic tradition.

"what has Yahweh spoken (*dibber*)" (Jer 23:34–40; cf. Deut 18:17–22; Jer 1:7, 17; 23:21; 1 Sam 7:9; 1 Kgs 18:37).

A classic example of prophetic confrontation is found in Jeremiah 27—28. Following Yahweh's command, Jeremiah puts on a yoke and then delivers several oracles advocating the necessity of submitting to the yoke of the king of Babylon (Jer 27:1–11). To Zedekiah, the prophet also directs exhortations not to listen to the Jerusalemite prophets who are offering contrary advice. According to his usual pattern, Jeremiah accuses them of lying and of being unable to intercede effectively with Yahweh (Jer 27:12–18). Sometime later, Hananiah, a prophet from Gibeon, confronts Jeremiah in the temple and delivers an oracle that is diametrically opposed to Jeremiah's earlier oracle. Hananiah's behavior is exactly the same as that of Jeremiah, and both prophets use the same forms of speech. In addition, the conflicting oracles are both rooted in orthodox Yahwistic traditions. Jeremiah's prophecies are informed by the Ephraimite tradition, while Hananiah's words reflect the Jerusalemite theology of the inviolability of Zion (Jer 28:1–4). The incident is thus a clear example of conflicting prophetic claims which cannot be adjudicated on the basis of the prophets' words or deeds. Rather, the observer can decide which of the prophecies to believe only if he has already recognized the authority of one prophet or the other. For the author of the narrative and for Deuteronomic readers, the choice is obvious, for the Ephraimite theological tradition in which they stood considered Jeremiah to be a Mosaic prophet, who by definition heard the divine word more clearly than other prophets. In cases of prophetic conflict, the Mosaic prophet's oracles could therefore be considered more accurate than those of other prophets (cf. Num 12:6–8). For this reason, Jeremiah replies to Hananiah's challenge by invoking the Deuteronomic principle that the words of Mosaic prophets invariably come true while those of false prophets do not (Deut 18:21–22). Jeremiah cites a whole line of (presumably Ephraimite) prophets whose predictions of disaster had been fulfilled. In contrast, prophets of salvation were still waiting for the fulfillment of their oracles. Without directly claiming to be a Mosaic prophet, Jeremiah thus places his oracle in the tradition of past Mosaic prophets whose words had proven to be true (Jer 28:5–9). After the confrontation with Hananiah, Yahweh spoke to Jeremiah a second time and repeated his original judgment oracle. On the basis of this reassurance, Jeremiah finally confronted Hananiah and accused him of false prophecy. In keeping with Deuteronomic law, Jeremiah then delivered a death sentence to Hananiah, and in the same year the sentence was carried out, presumably by Yahweh (Jer 28:12–17).

CONCLUSIONS

Our survey of the literature produced by the Ephraimite tradition has yielded a relatively coherent picture of the characteristic behavioral patterns of Ephraimite prophets and has provided some insight into the relationship between prophecy and society at various stages in Israel's history. The biblical evidence suggests that within the groups that bore the Ephraimite tradition there were fairly clear ideas about acceptable prophetic behavior. Although these ideas undoubtedly developed over a long period of time, there are enough similarities between the early and late layers of the tradition to suggest long-term continuity as well as change. It will therefore be helpful at this point to summarize the characteristic features of the Ephraimite view of prophecy.

The biblical evidence seems to indicate that prophets related to the groups that bore the Ephraimite traditions used stereotypical speech patterns and employed a distinctive vocabulary. The prophets' use of language presumably conformed to the expectations of their support groups, which believed that when prophets were genuinely possessed by Yahweh they spoke in certain characteristic ways. For the most part stereotypical prophetic language seems to have reflected the normal speech of the prophets' social matrix, although certain speech patterns may have been used only by prophets.

In addition to using stereotypical language, Ephraimite prophets also seem to have exhibited certain standard behavioral patterns. The model for prophetic behavior was the Mosaic prophet, who served as a channel of communication between God and the people. The Mosaic prophet delivered to the people the true word of Yahweh, which was inevitably effective. The people also went to the prophetic intercessor when they wished to make requests of Yahweh. The prophet was thus considered a central figure in Israelite society, for he was the only legitimate means of communication between God and the people. With the exception of priests, other types of intermediaries were prohibited. Non-Mosaic prophets were permitted to exist, but they were always inferior to the prophet "like Moses," whose word was to be obeyed in cases of prophetic conflict.

The social functions of Ephraimite prophecy seem to have changed over the course of Israelite history. The narratives of early prophetic activity show prophets such as Abraham, Moses, and Samuel playing a central role in their societies. These individuals were political as well as religious leaders, and their prophetic activities had important social maintenance functions. In addition, these early Ephraimite prophets seem to have had cultic functions, which were not clearly distinguished from their prophetic functions. However, after the rise of the monarchy, Ephraimite prophets seem to have functioned primarily on the periphery of society. With a few notable exceptions, they became spokesmen for the characteristic social, political, and religious views of their Ephraimite support groups and used prophetic authority to attempt to change the central social structure both in Ephraim and in Judah. They apparently ceased to play a role in the central cult and had no voice in governmental affairs. This situation seems to have continued until the fall of Jerusalem, the event which marks the end of distinctively Ephraimite prophetic activity. When prophecy emerges again after the exile, it has a form somewhat different from the one that existed in the preexilic period.

5

Prophecy in Israel: The Judean Traditions

In contrast to the Ephraimite tradition, which provides a number of narratives that can supply information on the relationship between prophets and their societies, the Judean traditions furnish little material from which to construct a picture of prophecy in Judah. Prophetic narratives are found in only a few of the Judean prophetic books, and many of the Chronicler's accounts of prophetic activity simply duplicate the ones found in Kings. This scarcity of narratives about prophets is itself interesting and may indicate that prophecy did not play an important role in the life of the groups that carried the Judean traditions. However, the dearth of specific narrative material means that most of our information on prophecy and society in Judah must be gleaned from the prophetic writings themselves. Unfortunately, these sources are highly complex and difficult to interpret, and as a result they yield little firm data.

In addition to recognizing the scarcity of helpful sources of information, the student of Judean prophecy must also face the question of the unity of the Judean prophetic tradition itself. While many contemporary scholars recognize the continuity of the Ephraimite prophetic tradition, there is less consensus on the coherence of the Judean traditions.[1] Although many of the Judean prophets seem to have shared a belief in certain features of the Jerusalemite royal

---

1. Note, however, the comments of O. H. Steck, "Theological Streams of Tradition," *Tradition and Theology in the Old Testament* (ed. D. A. Knight; Philadelphia: Fortress Press, 1977) 191–212.

theology, these figures also have individual characteristics that are difficult to locate within a particular tradition. In general the Judean prophets do not resemble each other in the same way that Ephraimite prophets do, and in the end the Judeans may be linked together only by the fact that their behavior is not characteristically Ephraimite. It is therefore likely that the Judean prophets did not share the same support group, and for this reason we may have to speak of Judean prophetic *traditions* rather than a Judean prophetic *tradition*.

In the light of the problems that we have just described, it is clear that any significant study of the relationship between prophecy and society in Judah must involve a thorough analysis of all of the relevant prophetic writings. Such a detailed treatment cannot possibly be undertaken in a single chapter, but rather than simply ignoring the Judean traditions we will briefly summarize the conclusions that can safely be drawn on the basis of our present knowledge of the prophetic books. By sacrificing depth for breadth we can at least consider all of Israel's prophets, and we will then be able to sketch the outlines of a social history of Israelite prophecy. However, it must be recognized that this approach renders our analysis of the Judean material highly tentative. Future studies will have to be undertaken to refine the analysis, and these studies may lead to major modifications in our conclusions.

CHARACTERISTIC SPEECH IN THE JUDEAN TRADITIONS

Prophetic Titles

The Visionary (ḥōzeh)

The title "visionary" (ḥōzeh) is a participle of the verb ḥāzāh, "to see" or "to have a vision." The majority of the occurrences of the verb and its nominal derivatives are in visionary contexts, so we may safely assume that the ḥōzeh was one who obtained revelations through visions.[2] The title is employed primarily by Judean authors and is almost always given to individuals who can be identified as

---

2. Statistics on the occurrences of ḥāzāh and its derivatives are supplied by A. Jepsen, *Nabi: Soziologische Studien zur alttestamentlichen Literatur und Religionsgeschichte* (Munich: C. H. Beck, 1934) 45.

Judeans. In Amos 7:12 the prophet Amos is called a visionary by the northern priest Amaziah, and in Mic 3:7 the title is apparently applied to advocates of the Jerusalemite royal theology (cf. Mic 3:5). Isaiah twice uses the title in speaking of prophets in Jerusalem (Isa 29:10; 30:10).[3] According to the Judean traditions reflected in Chronicles, visionaries were particularly active in Judah around the time of the united monarchy (1 Chr 21:9; 25:5; 29:29; 2 Chr 9:29; 12:15; 19:2; 29:25, 30; cf. 2 Sam 24:11), although the prophetic books themselves indicate that these intermediaries were still present in Judah in later times (cf. 2 Chr 33:18; 2 Kgs 17:13).

If the evidence of the Chronicler is reliable, then it is clear that the visionary was a central intermediary. Gad is explicitly called the "visionary of David" (2 Sam 24:11; 1 Chr 21:9) or the "visionary of the king" (2 Chr 29:25). Gad's central status is further implied by the fact that he is said to have been the author of an official chronicle of David's reign (1 Chr 29:29) and to have played a role in the establishment of temple worship (2 Chr 29:25). Heman and Jeduthun are also given the title "visionary of the king" and together with Asaph are assigned roles in the organization of the Levitical singers (1 Chr 25:5; 2 Chr 29:30; 35:15). Official archival activity is attributed to the visionary Iddo, who is said to have collected some of his visions dealing with the acts of Solomon and Jeroboam (2 Chr 9:29) and to have written a chronicle of the reign of Rehoboam (2 Chr 12:15). Although the Chronicler's portrayal of these visionaries as organizers of temple worship is of doubtful historical accuracy, there is no reason to doubt that they were part of Judah's central social structure.

It is impossible to determine whether or not the visionary had distinctive behavioral characteristics. The fact that in Mic 3:7 the word "visionaries" appears in poetic parallelism with the word "diviners" (*qōsĕmîm*) might be taken as an indication that the visionary used divination to obtain his oracles. However, this evidence is of doubtful value, for Jerusalemite authors also pair visionaries with prophets (*nĕbî'îm*) and seers (*rō'îm*) (Isa 29:10; 30:10; cf. Ezek 13:23; 22:28). In fact, Gad is called both a visionary and a prophet (1 Sam 22:5; 2 Sam 24:11; 1 Chr 29:29; 2 Chr 29:25). This use of titles suggests that Judean authors did not clearly distin-

---

3. In Isa 28:15 the poetic parallelism indicates that *ḥōzeh* must be a synonym of *bĕrît*, "covenant," "agreement."

guish the various types of intermediaries, so it is doubtful that any of these figures exhibited distinctive behavior.[4]

The Prophet (nābîʾ)

As we have already noted, the use of the title "prophet" (nābîʾ) to designate intermediaries is a characteristic of the Ephraimite tradition. However, the title was also occasionally used by Judahite authors. In the preexilic period the title was employed by Isaiah (5 times), Amos (4 times), Micah (3 times), and Ezekiel (17 times). After the exile several Judean authors used the title, but outside of the 33 occurrences in Chronicles and the 12 occurrences in Zechariah, it is relatively rare. Except for Ezekiel, whose use of the title is not typical of other Judahite authors, southern writers seem to have applied the designation nābîʾ to figures within the central social structure. Thus Isaiah lists the prophet along with the judge, diviner, and various military officers as one of the leaders of Judah and Jerusalem (Isa 3:2). Elsewhere, the prophet is linked with the elder, the priest, and the seer (Isa 9:14 [Eng. 9:15]; 28:7; 29:10), all of whom are members of the Jerusalemite establishment. However, Judahite authors do not seem to have associated any sort of distinctive behavior with the prophet. We have already noted the Judahite tendency to equate the prophet and the visionary, and Jerusalemite prophets are also associated with visions and divination (Mic 3:5–7).

The Diviners

Various types of diviners seem to have functioned within Judah's central social structure in the preexilic period. We do not need to comment on these intermediaries in detail, but it is important to note the attitude of the Jerusalemite prophets toward them. While Ephraimite prophets condemned all types of diviners and considered prophets to be the only legitimate intermediaries (Deut 18:9–11, 14; 2 Kgs 17:17), some of the Jerusalemite prophets may have accepted the existence of diviners as a matter of course. Thus, although Isaiah occasionally rejects diviners (Isa 2:6), he sometimes

4. For a more detailed discussion of the visionary and his Judean setting, see H. M. Orlinsky, "The Seer in Ancient Israel," *OrAnt* 4 (1965) 153–174; M. Jastrow, Jr., "Rôʾēh and Ḥôzēh in the Old Testament," *JBL* 28 (1909) 50–56; M. A. Vanden Oudenrijn, "De vocabulis quibusdam, termino nābîʾ synonymis," *Bib* 6 (1924–1925) 297–305; F. Haeussermann, *Wortempfang und Symbol in der alttestamentlichen Prophetie* (Giessen: Alfred Töpelmann, 1932) 7–8; and Z. Zevit, "A Misunderstanding at Bethel: Amos VII 12–17," *VT* 25 (1975) 785–790.

seems to tolerate their presence within the establishment. For example, in Isa 3:2 he lists the diviner (*qōsēm*) among the leaders of Judah and does not question that arrangement. Similarly, Ezekiel sees divination as a prophetic task, and although he condemns the Jerusalemite prophets for divining lies, he does not suggest that divination is not an appropriate prophetic function (Ezek 22:28). In a similar way, Micah criticizes the prophets because they divine only for money (Mic 3:11), but he does not explicitly reject the process of divination. In Mic 3:5–7 the prophet also speaks against intermediaries who link the content of their oracles to the type of payment they receive, but he does not object to the fact that the intermediaries obtain oracles through visions and divination. This situation changes in the literature of the postexilic period, when Jerusalemite authors apparently followed the Deuteronomists in seeing divination only in a negative light (Isa 44:25; 47:9, 12; 57:3; Zech 10:2).[5]

Prophetic Speech Forms

Although individual Judahite prophets had distinctive prose and poetic styles, there is little evidence of a typical prophetic rhetoric that was shared by all southern intermediaries. However, two lines of evidence suggest that Judahite prophets may have delivered oracles structured according to stereotypical patterns. First, as we have already noted, the term *maśśā>* may have designated a distinctive type of oracle associated with Judean prophets. Our analysis of Jer 23:33–40 has suggested that this term was part of the characteristic vocabulary of Jerusalemite prophets, who delivered *maśśā>*s to people who came seeking a word from Yahweh. This suggestion is supported by the fact that when the word *maśśā>* is used to designate a type of oracle, the term always appears in the writings of Judahite prophets or with reference to their activities.[6] The term is usually used to introduce an oracle or a collection of oracles (Isa 13:1; 14:28; 15:1; 17:1; 19:1; 21:1, 11, 13; 22:1; 23:1; 30:6; Nah 1:1; Hab 1:1; Zech 9:1; 12:1; Mal 1:1). When the term is not employed in

5. For a more thorough discussion of divination in Israel, see A. Baruq, "Oracle et Divination," *DBSup* 6 (1960) 752–788.

6. A possible exception may be found in 2 Kgs 9:25, where *maśśā>* seems to refer to the oracle that the Ephraimite prophet Elijah delivered against Ahab (1 Kgs 21:19). However, the syntax of 2 Kgs 9:25 makes the meaning of *maśśā>* uncertain, and the word may not actually designate an oracle. See the discussion of P. A. H. de Boer, "An Inquiry into the Meaning of the Term *maśśā>*," *Oudtestamentische Studiën* 5 (1948) 212–213.

this way, it refers in general to the Jerusalemite prophets' words and deeds (Ezek 12:10; Lam 2:14; 2 Chr 24:27). This pattern of usage may indicate that the word *maśśā᾽* designated a specialized oracle that was peculiar to Judah.

Unfortunately, once the Judean background of the term *maśśā᾽* has been pointed out, little else can be said with any certainty about the structure or function of this type of oracle. *Maśśā᾽* is a nominal form of the verb *nāśā᾽*, "to lift up," "to bear," "to carry." In a number of contexts *maśśā᾽* clearly means "burden," and for this reason it has been argued that the term was secondarily applied to a prophetic oracle because it was both a "burden" laid on the prophet and a "burden" laid by the prophet on the people. Alternatively, *maśśā᾽* is said to refer to an oracle that the prophet "lifts up" or "calls out" (cf. 2 Kgs 9:25).[7] However, neither of these explanations says anything about the structure or function of the *maśśā᾽*. The frequent use of the word *maśśā᾽* to introduce oracles against foreign nations (Isa 13:1; 14:28; 15:1; 17:1; 19:1; 21:1, 11, 13; 23:1; Nah 1:1) has been taken to mean that the term originally designated the divine word which the prophet uttered as part of the ritual of the holy war.[8] If so, then the term would point to the Judahite prophet's role as a central intermediary responsible for maintaining the social structure. Yet, even if *maśśā᾽* was originally the official designation for the oracles against foreign nations that the prophet delivered in military or cultic contexts, this restricted use of the term must have disappeared fairly early in Israel's history. Although collections of oracles against foreign nations occur primarily in the writings of Judahite prophets (Amos 1—2; Isaiah 13—23; Ezekiel 25—32; contrast Jeremiah 46—51), not all of these collections are introduced by the word *maśśā᾽* (cf. Amos 1:2—2:16), and even in Jerusalemite sources the word is applied to individuals as well as nations (Ezek 12:10; Isa 30:6; 2 Chr 24:27). Similarly, if the *maśśā᾽* ever had a distinctive structure, that structure must have degenerated by the time the extant oracles against foreign nations were produced. The examples

---

7. For recent discussions of the meaning of *maśśā᾽*, see M. Saebø, *Sacharja 9–14* (Neukirchen-Vluyn: Neukirchener Verlag, 1969) 137–144; and S. Erlandsson, *The Burden of Babylon* (Lund: C. W. K. Gleerup, 1970) 64–65.

8. Saebø, *Sacharja 9–14*, 138–140; B. Margulis, "Studies in the Oracles against the Nations" (Ph.D. dissertation, Brandeis University, 1975) 202–220; R. E. Clements, *Prophecy and Tradition* (Atlanta: John Knox Press, 1975) 69–72; J. H. Hayes, "The Usage of Oracles against Foreign Nations in Ancient Israel," *JBL* 87 (1968) 81–92; D. L. Christensen, *Transformations of the War Oracle in Old Testament Prophecy* (Missoula: Scholars Press, 1975).

that have been preserved contain a number of distinct prophetic speech forms and do not exhibit a common literary structure.[9] The evidence thus permits but does not require the assumption that *maśśā᾽* was originally a Judahite term for oracles against foreign nations. Such oracles may have had a characteristic structure and may have been delivered by central prophets as part of the ritual associated with the holy war. If so, then the *maśśā᾽* would be an early example of a stereotypically Judahite prophetic speech pattern.

A second line of evidence also hints that some Jerusalemite prophets may have delivered oracles structured according to stereotypical patterns. Since the pioneering work of Sigmund Mowinckel, most scholars have acknowledged that certain types of prophets played a regular role in the Jerusalem cult. Some of the psalms contain divine speeches, usually in the first person singular, that closely resemble prophetic oracles (for example, Psalms 2, 12, 46, 50, 60, 62, 68, 75, 81, 82, 87, 89, 91, 95, 108, 110, 132). Some of these speeches pertain to the election and protection of the king and the city of Jerusalem and therefore contain the sorts of words one might expect from a central prophet with social maintenance functions. Mowinckel interpreted these psalms as an indication that prophets had regular roles in the cult, particularly in the special rituals celebrating the enthronement of the king and the election of the city.[10] Further evidence for prophetic involvement in the cult may come from the individual psalms of lament, in which the psalmist suddenly ends his complaint and expresses his faith that Yahweh will respond favorably (Psalms 6, 22, 28, 31, 34, 66). This striking shift in the tone and content of the psalm has been ex-

9. D. L. Petersen, "The Oracles against the Nations: A Form-critical Analysis," *SBLSP* 1975, 1. 48–56.

10. S. Mowinckel, *Psalmenstudien III: Kultprophetie und prophetische Psalmen* (Oslo: Jacob Dybwad, 1923) 1–29; idem, *The Psalms in Israel's Worship* (Nashville: Abingdon Press, 1962) 2. 53–73. Mowinckel also suggested that some of the writing prophets were connected with the cult, a suggestion that we will discuss in detail when we consider these figures. Mowinckel's basic views have been accepted to a certain extent by a number of scholars, although there has been much debate about the degree to which the writing prophets were involved in the ritual. See A. R. Johnson, *The Cultic Prophet in Ancient Israel* (Cardiff: University of Wales, 1944; 2d ed., 1962) 3, 74–75; H. H. Rowley, "Ritual and the Hebrew Prophets," *JSS* 1 (1956) 338–360 (=idem, *From Moses to Qumran* [New York: Association Press, 1963] 111–138); L. Sabourin, *The Psalms* (Staten Island, N.Y.: Alba House, 1969) 1. 46–49; H. Gunkel, *Einleitung in die Psalmen* (Göttingen: Vandenhoeck & Ruprecht, 1933) 361–381; and H. H. Rowley, *Worship in Ancient Israel* (London: SPCK, 1967) 144–175.

plained by assuming that a priest or prophet delivered an oracle of assurance to the worshiper at the completion of his lament. This oracle then called forth the statement of faith that ends the psalm.[11]

In addition to evidence found within the Psalter itself, the so-called prophetic liturgies (Mic 7:7–20; Isaiah 33; 59:1–4, 9–20; 61; 62; Habakkuk) are sometimes thought to have originally been used by prophets in cultic contexts.[12] Furthermore, as we will soon see, the Chronicler speaks of prophecy within the Jerusalem cult and even attributes the organization of the cult to prophetic inspiration (1 Chr 15:19; 25:1, 5; 2 Chr 20:14–17; 29:25, 30; 35:15). According to the Psalter itself, some of the prophetic figures mentioned by the Chronicler were also authors of psalms (Asaph: Psalms 50, 73–83; Jeduthun: Psalms 39, 62, 77; Heman: Psalm 88). Although the Chronicler's picture of prophetic involvement in the cult probably reflects the details of cultic organization in the postexilic period, there is no reason to suspect that cultic prophecy itself is a late innovation.

The biblical evidence thus indicates that some Jerusalemite prophets carried out their activities in the context of the cult. The precise nature of this cultic involvement is unclear, but if the prophets participated in temple rituals, then their words and deeds were presumably governed to a certain extent by the requirements of the liturgy.[13] If the prophets received their oracles while possessed by Yahweh's spirit, then possession may have been required at specified points in the proceedings. The oracles themselves may have had a traditional form, and the prophets' words may have even been spelled out in detail in the instructions for the ritual. If so, then the speech of these cultic prophets would have followed stereotypical patterns that met the expectations of the prophets' support groups.

The Process of Intermediation

While the Ephraimite prophetic tradition described the process of intermediation in terms of the word which God spoke to the

11. Sabourin, *The Psalms*, 47; J. Begrich, "Das priesterliche Heilsorakel," *ZAW* 52 (1934) 81–92.

12. H. Gunkel, "The Close of Micah: A Prophetical Liturgy," in his *What Remains of the Old Testament* (London: George Allen & Unwin, 1928) 115–149; idem, "Jesaia 33, eine prophetische Liturgie," *ZAW* 42 (1924) 177–208; K. Elliger, *Die Einheit des Tritojesaia* (Stuttgart: W. Kohlhammer, 1928) 15–20, 24–28.

13. Mowinckel, *The Psalms in Israel's Worship*, 57–58; Rowley, *Worship in Ancient Israel*, 166–167.

prophet, Judean authors seem to have stressed the visual aspects of divine-human communication. Although the Judeans also occasionally describe Yahweh speaking to the prophet, more often they refer to the vision which the prophet saw. Even when a divine word is mentioned, the prophet is often said to have *seen* the word (Amos 1:1; Mic 1:1). We have already noted that the visionary (*ḥōzeh*) was a characteristically Judean type of intermediary, and references to visions often appear in the superscriptions of Judean prophetic books (Amos 1:1; Isa 1:1; Mic 1:1; Hab 1:1; Obad 1; Ezek 1:1; Nah 1:1; all but Ezek 1:1 use a verbal or nominal form of *ḥāzāh*, "to have a vision"). Outside of the superscriptions, forms of the verb *ḥāzāh* are also used to describe the process by which the prophet received his oracles (Isa 2:1; 13:1; 30:10; Ezek 7:26; 12:23–24, 27; 13:6, 7, 8, 9, 16; Zech 13:4; Joel 3:1 [Eng 2:28]). It is also worth noting that extensive "call visions" appear only in the books of Judean prophets (Isaiah 6; Ezek 1:1—3:27) and that other types of visions play a major role in Jerusalemite prophecy (Amos 7:1–9; 8:1–3; 9:1–4; Ezekiel 8—11, 37, 40—48; Zechariah 1—8). The evidence thus suggests that although Ephraimite prophets also saw visions, the visionary method of divine-human communication was particularly common in Judah.

Like the Ephraimites, Judean prophets seem to have received their visions when they were possessed by Yahweh's spirit. Spirit possession is clearly indicated by phrases such as "the hand of the Lord was upon me" (Ezek 1:3; 3:14, 22; 8:1; 33:22; 37:1; 40:1; Isa 8:11), which usually introduce prophetic visions. The language of possession is particularly noticeable in Ezekiel, where almost every word and action of the prophet is attributed to the spirit: "the spirit entered into me" (Ezek 2:2); "the spirit lifted me up . . . and brought me in visions" (Ezek 8:3; cf. 8:7, 14, 16; 11:1, 24; 37:1); "the spirit of the Lord fell upon me" (Ezek 11:5). Joel also attributed prophecy to the gift of Yahweh's spirit (Joel 3:1 [Eng 2:28]).

The History of Characteristic Prophetic Speech in Judah

The biblical evidence that we have just surveyed suggests that the possession behavior of Judean prophets may have included the use of stereotypical speech patterns. The use of the title "visionary" (*ḥōzeh*) is a characteristic of Judean authors and may have originally been applied to intermediaries with distinctive speech and behavior. The term *maśśā*ʾ may have been used to designate some sort of characteristically Judean oracle, and prophets in the Jerusalemite cult may have used set liturgical phrases in their prophecies. The Judean prophets routinely obtained their revelations through visions, which were received when the spirit of Yahweh possessed the intermediaries. Judean writers thus frequently employ forms of the verb *ḥāzāh,* "to have a vision," when they are describing the prophetic process. It is not out of the question that some or all of these characteristic features of Judean prophecy are the result of thorough editing by Judean authors. However, the anthropological evidence indicates that we may not rule out the possibility that these features point to stereotypical possession behavior on the part of Judean prophets. If so, then we may assume that they were consciously or subconsciously making their behavior conform to the expectations of their Judahite support groups. In order to be taken seriously by their society, the prophets acted and spoke in the way that the society expected prophets to act and speak.

However, for our purposes it is important to put the evidence on Judean prophetic speech patterns into a historical perspective. When this is done, then it becomes clear that characteristically Judean speech patterns seem to have become less common in the exilic and postexilic periods. The characteristic Judean intermediary, the visionary, survived the exile, but as early as the time of Isaiah this figure seems to have lost his distinguishing features. Thereafter, the visionary is equated with other types of intermediaries, and his unique characteristics are no longer obvious. In the postexilic period, in the writings of the Chronicler, the title is still used, but the common Ephraimite title "prophet" (*nābîʾ*) is more prominent in the literature. Similarly, if the *maśśā*ʾ was ever a characteristically Judean oracle with a clearly defined structure, this type of oracle must have lost its distinguishing characteristics by the time the present exemplars of the genre were created, presumably in the late preexilic or postexilic period. In the same vein, the evidence for prophetic involvement in the cult is strongest in late sources such as the Chronicler, although the existence of cultic prophecy in the preexilic period is highly probable. The evidence thus suggests that prophecy in Judah may have lost some of its distinctively Judean features after the exile. At the same time, exilic and postexilic Judean sources describe prophecy in terms that in the preexilic period were associated primarily with the Ephraimite tradition. We will assess the importance of this observation when we consider the history of prophecy in Israel.

THE BEGINNING OF THE JUDEAN TRADITIONS: GAD AND NATHAN

Gad is the earliest prophet who can be clearly located within the Judean traditions. Although there is little evidence on his characteristic speech and behavior, the texts strongly suggest that he was a Judean who played a role in Jerusalem's central social structure during the reign of David. Gad is usually called "the visionary (*ḥōzeh*) of David" or "the visionary of the king" (2 Sam 24:11; 1 Chr 21:9; 2 Chr 29:5; cf. 1 Chr 29:29), a designation that relates Gad both to the Judean prophetic traditions and to the royal court. Gad is also called a prophet (*nābî* [1 Sam 22:5; 2 Sam 24:11]), and in fact the earliest reference to Gad refers to him as a prophet rather than as a visionary, a title that is not applied to him before David's accession. This might suggest that Gad was originally a prophet and that he functioned as a visionary only after David's rise to power. Support for this suggestion can be found in the two extant stories about Gad's activities. In the first story, Gad appears as one of David's associates and helps the future king to escape from Saul (1 Sam 22:5). Gad's native city is not mentioned, but the narrative suggests that he was one of the Judeans who supported David during his conflicts with Saul (1 Sam 22:1–2). If so, then with respect to Saul's government Gad must have functioned as a peripheral prophet who was supported by the southern groups that recognized David's claims to power. However, it is important to note that the texts never explicitly portray Gad as a peripheral prophet. In 1 Sam 22:5 he gives political advice but does not deliver oracles.

In contrast to the first story of Gad's activities, the second one clearly shows him playing an important central role in David's government. Toward the end of David's life, he took a census of Israel, a move that he later regretted. After he had prayed to Yahweh and asked for forgiveness, God sent a message through Gad allowing the king to choose his own punishment. There is no indication that David addressed his prayer through the prophet, but the judgment oracle seems to have come to the prophet without prior warning. After the judgment had been suspended, Gad again appeared unbidden and delivered an oracle instructing David to build an altar on the threshing floor of Araunah in Jerusalem (2 Sam 24:1–25). This oracle legitimates the future site of the temple and may have suggested to the Chronicler that Gad played a role in establishing and legitimating the organization of the Jerusalemite cult (2 Chr 29:25). In any case, it is important to note that Gad's oracle essentially contradicts Nathan's earlier oracle (2 Samuel 7), which had rejected the concept of a permanent place of worship in Jerusalem. If Gad indeed spoke as a central intermediary representing the southern groups that supported David, then it may be that his oracle and David's earlier wish to build a temple (2 Sam 7:2) both reflect Judean views about the proper organization of worship.[14] If so, then this story portrays Gad as a central intermediary using prophecy to maintain the society by calling the people back to old Judean traditions.

In contrast to Gad, Nathan is always called a prophet (*nābî>* [2 Sam 7:2; 12:25; 1 Kgs 1:8, 10, 22–23, 32, 34, 38, 44, 45; Ps 51:2 (Eng. 51:1); 1 Chr 17:1; 29:29; 2 Chr 9:29; 29:25]). He is clearly pictured as a member of the royal court who played an important role in maintaining the stability of David's government. Unfortunately, the biblical texts provide no specific information on Nathan's background. He appears for the first time in 2 Samuel 7 as an established member of David's court, and nothing is known of the prophet's earlier activities. However, there are hints that Nathan may have originally been an Ephraimite prophet. He is always given the title *nābî>*, a title which is used primarily by the Ephraimite tradition. Furthermore, the descriptions of Nathan's activities suggest that at least in retrospect he was seen as a typical northern prophet. In 2 Sam 7:2 the king expresses to the prophet a desire to build a temple for Yahweh. Although there is no suggestion that David is making a formal request of Yahweh through the prophet, Nathan nevertheless replies with a word of encouragement for the king (2 Sam 7:3). Only later does a divine word come to Nathan prohibiting the building (2 Sam 7:4–17). Nathan's oracle, which is duly delivered to the king, lays the groundwork for the Jerusalemite royal theology, although the oracle also reflects Deuteronomic vocabulary and theological

14. For a somewhat similar theory and a discussion of all of the passages dealing with Gad, see H. Haag, "Gad und Nathan," *Archäologie und Altes Testament: Festschrift für Kurt Galling* (ed. A. Kuschke and E. Kutsch; Tübingen: J. C. B. Mohr, 1970) 135–143; Jepsen, *Nabi*, 94–99; and O. Plöger, *Die Prophetengeschichten der Samuel- und Königsbücher* (Greifswald: E. Panzig, 1937) 12–14.

interests.[15] The account can thus be taken as an illustration of the divine-human dialogue that was carried on through Ephraimite prophets, who advocated the Deuteronomist's theological views. Nathan may also be portrayed as an Ephraimite prophet in 2 Sam 12:1–15, where dialogic features are also in evidence. At the beginning of the story God sends Nathan to David, and the prophet tells David the story of the poor man's ewe lamb. David's emotional condemnation of the rich man in the story is followed immediately by Nathan's judgment oracle, which recounts David's rise to kingship. The oracle contains Deuteronomic language and theology and clearly reflects the traditional Ephraimite view that the king's power is limited by Yahweh's law (cf. Deut 17:14–20).[16] After hearing the oracle, David addresses a confession to Nathan and through him to Yahweh. Nathan replies with a second oracle tempering the king's punishment.

The picture of Nathan found in 2 Samuel thus suggests that he was considered an Ephraimite, at least by later Deuteronomic writers and editors. If in fact he did come from the north, then he may have entered the Jerusalemite establishment at the same time that David installed the northern priest Abiathar (2 Sam 8:17). Just as David chose one priest from the north (Abiathar) and one from the south (Zadok), so he may have chosen one prophet from the north (Nathan) and one from the south (Gad). In any case, Nathan became an establishment prophet under David and in this position used prophecy to maintain the stability of the social structure. He prevented a departure from the Ephraimite traditions when he opposed the creation of a permanent sanctuary in Jerusalem, and he criticized the king for the Bathsheba incident, which violated Ephraimite principles, endangered the stability of the monarchy, and

15. For a thorough discussion of the Deuteronomic features in 2 Samuel 7, see F. M. Cross, *Canaanite Myth and Hebrew Epic* (Cambridge: Harvard University Press, 1973) 249–264; and D. J. McCarthy, "II Samuel 7 and the Structure of the Deuteronomic History," *JBL* 84 (1965) 131–138. The presence of Deuteronomic language in 2 Samuel 7 does not necessarily mean that Nathan's oracle itself is only a late editorial creation. As we have already noted, Deuteronomic language and theology may simply be the crystallization of earlier Ephraimite linguistic patterns and theological views. If so, then there is no reason to doubt that the core of 2 Samuel 7 goes back to the Davidic period. For various reasons, most scholars now accept the authenticity of at least the core of the oracle, although there is still much debate about what was included in the core. See the survey of T. N. D. Mettinger, *King and Messiah* (Lund: C. W. K. Gleerup, 1976) 48–61.

16. For a discussion of the Deuteronomic features of 2 Sam 12:1–15, see H. Seebass, "Nathan und David in II Sam 12," *ZAW* 86 (1974) 207–208.

called into question the validity of the dynastic oracle.[17] Nathan's identification with the Ephraimite traditions may also help to explain his later opposition to Adonijah's kingship (1 Kings 1), for Adonijah was a Judahite who was born while David was ruling Judah at Hebron (2 Sam 3:4–5). In the struggle over the succession, Nathan disagreed with his fellow Ephraimite Abiathar, who supported Adonijah (1 Kgs 1:7), and Nathan himself supported Solomon, who was born in Jerusalem and who did not have close ties with the south. As a direct result of Nathan's pressure on the aging David, the king designated Solomon as his successor and ordered his anointing. Solomon's elevation to kingship was presided over by Zadok the priest, representing Judah, and Nathan the prophet, representing the old Ephraimite tradition of the prophetic anointing of the king. After this event, which would have alienated Nathan from the priestly group represented by Abiathar, the prophet seems to have played no further role in governmental affairs, although later tradition credits him with writing official chronicles of the reigns of David and Solomon and with helping organize the Jerusalemite cult (1 Chr 29:29; 2 Chr 9:29; 29:25).

PREEXILIC WRITING PROPHETS IN THE JUDEAN TRADITIONS

Amos

Any attempt to describe Amos's characteristic prophetic behavior and social functions is hampered not only by the fact that most of the evidence is concentrated in two passages (Amos 1:1; 7:10–17) but also by the fact that the book appears to have had a long and complex history of transmission.[18] Although scholars disagree about the details of this history, it is generally acknowledged that a basic collection of Amos's oracles has been supplemented by several editors, whose identities are not precisely clear. Some of these

---

17. The reasons for Nathan's opposition to the temple have often been discussed, but the available evidence prevents our drawing firm conclusions on this question. However, most scholars attribute the prophet's action to a combination of religious and political motives. Convenient summaries of the scholarly discussion on this point are provided by Mettinger, *King and Messiah*, 48–50; T. Ishida, *The Royal Dynasties in Ancient Israel* (Berlin: Walter de Gruyter, 1977) 81–84; and R. E. Clements, *God and Temple* (Philadelphia: Fortress Press, 1966) 57–62.

18. For a survey of the literary history of the book, see H. W. Wolff, *Joel and Amos* (Philadelphia: Fortress Press, 1977) 106–113.

editors may have been the prophet's own disciples, and Deuteronomic editing has also been detected.[19] It is unfortunate that the two passages containing most of the evidence on Amos's activities are widely thought to be editorial additions, although there is much scholarly disagreement about the origin of these additions. To be sure, it is possible that later editors may have preserved an essentially accurate picture of the prophet's behavior. However, the available evidence does not permit this possibility to be tested, so the accuracy of any reconstructed picture of Amos must remain in doubt. In the end, it may be that we must content ourselves with a traditional portrait of the prophet rather than a historically accurate picture of his activities.[20]

Certain features of the Book of Amos might suggest that the prophet should be placed in the Ephraimite tradition rather than in one of the Judean traditions, but in each case the evidence is far from conclusive. As we have already noted, Amos's oracles sometimes employ forms of prophetic speech that are usually found in Ephraimite sources, although the oracles do not reflect stereotypical Ephraimite rhetoric.[21] Like Mosaic prophets, Amos also seems to have functioned as an intercessor (Amos 7:2–3, 5–6). However, his intercessory activities are the result of his own initiative and do not fit the Ephraimite pattern in which the *people* go to the prophet to seek intercession.[22] Finally, Amos's oracles against Ephraim and particularly against the royal cult at Bethel (for example, Amos 4:4–5; 5:4–7; 6:1–3; 7:10) seem to be consistent with the theological views of the Deuteronomists, but many of the characteristic features of the Deuteronomic theology are lacking. The links between Amos and Ephraim may thus be more apparent than real, and it is probably best to accept the traditional view that Amos was a Judahite who prophesied in the north.

According to the book's superscription (Amos 1:1), which admittedly may be composed of several editorial layers, Amos was a resident of the Judean city of Tekoa, where he was one of the *nōqĕdîm*.

---

19. Ibid., 112–113; W. H. Schmidt, "Die deuteronomistische Redaktion des Amosbuches," *ZAW* 77 (1965) 168–193.

20. S. Wagner, "Überlegungen zur Frage nach den Beziehungen des Propheten Amos zum Südreich," *TLZ* 96 (1971) 653–670.

21. A convenient summary of Amos's speech forms is provided by Wolff, *Joel and Amos*, 91–100.

22. W. Brueggemann, "Amos' Intercessory Formula," *VT* 19 (1969) 385–399. Brueggemann's discussion also demonstrates the Judean background of some of the prophet's language.

This title is a clue to Amos's occupation and therefore to his social status and perhaps to the arena of his prophetic activity, but unfortunately the precise meaning of the title is unclear. Outside of this passage, the title *nōqēd* appears only in 2 Kgs 3:4, where it is applied to the king of Moab. Because the king is said to have paid to Ahab a tribute consisting of 100,000 lambs and the wool of 100,000 rams, the title *nōqēd* is usually taken to mean "shepherd," a meaning which is supported by Akkadian cognates and by the rare term *bōqēr*, "shepherd," which is applied to Amos in Amos 7:14. However, the picture is complicated by the fact that the title *nqd / nqdm* occurs several times in the Ugaritic texts in conjunction with various priests and governmental officials. In *CTA* 6:vi 55 the tablet is said to have been dictated by "Attani-puruleni, chief of the priests (*khnm*), chief of the *nqdm*," and the *nqdm* appear elsewhere in lists of cultic and political personnel (*CTA* 71:71; 82:B 12).[23] On the basis of this evidence it has been suggested that Amos was an official in the Jerusalem cult, and attempts have been made to find support for this view elsewhere in Amos's oracles.[24] However, outside of the title *nōqēd*, the evidence for Amos's cultic background is not conclusive, and even the title itself does not require a cultic interpretation. It therefore seems prudent to conclude that Amos may have been a government employee who was responsible for a fairly sizable herd of sheep, or, alternatively, that he was an independent sheep owner with a large herd.[25] In either case he seems likely to have been a member of the Judean upper classes, if he was not actually a part of the political or religious establishments in Jerusalem.

This picture of Amos as a member of the Judean establishment is

23. For discussions of the meaning of the title *nōqēd*, see A. S. Kapelrud, *Central Ideas in Amos* (Oslo: Oslo University Press, 1961) 5–7; and S. Segert, "Zur Bedeutung des Wortes *nōqēd*," *Hebräische Wortforschung: Festschrift zum 80. Geburtstag von Walter Baumgartner* (VTSup 16; Leiden: E. J. Brill, 1967) 279–283.

24. M. Bič, "Der Prophet Amos—Ein Haepatoskopos," *VT* 1 (1951) 293–296; E. Würthwein, "Amos-Studien," *ZAW* 62 (1949–50) 10–52; A. H. J. Gunneweg, "Erwägungen zu Amos 7, 14," *ZTK* 57 (1960) 1–16; H. G. Reventlow, *Das Amt des Propheten bei Amos* (Göttingen: Vandenhoeck & Ruprecht, 1962); G. Farr, "The Language of Amos, Popular or Cultic?" *VT* 16 (1966) 312–324; H. Gottlieb, "Amos und Jerusalem," *VT* 17 (1967) 430–463.

25. R. Smend, "Das Nein des Amos," *EvT* 23 (1963) 404–423; S. Lehming, "Erwägungen zu Amos," *ZTK* 55 (1958) 145–169; A. Murtonen, "The Prophet Amos—A Hepatoscoper?" *VT* 2 (1952) 170–171; H. J. Stoebe, "Der Prophet Amos und sein bürgerlicher Beruf," *Wort und Dienst* 5 (1957) 160–181; H. W. Wolff, *Amos the Prophet* (Philadelphia: Fortress Press, 1973) 1–5.

reinforced to a certain extent by two other passages in the book. In Amos 1:2—2:16 the prophet condemns Israel, Judah, and some of the surrounding nations for various offenses. Outside of the oracle against Judah (Amos 2:4–5), which may be a secondary addition, the remaining oracles all share the fact that they deal with treaty violations by nations which were part of the old Davidic empire. Amos apparently still considers that treaty to be in effect, and he thus maintains what was probably a common Judean view, that the disintegration of the Davidic empire was the result of illegal rebellions by Judah's treaty partners.[26]

A second indication of Amos's Judean background can be seen in the difficult account of the prophet's encounter with Amaziah, the priest of the royal sanctuary at Bethel (Amos 7:10–15). After informing Jeroboam II that Amos has been predicting the death of the king and the exile of the people, Amaziah orders Amos to leave the country. The priest calls Amos a visionary (*ḥōzeh*), the characteristic Judahite title applied to central intermediaries, and tells him to return to Judah, where visionaries are normally active (Amos 7:12–13). Amos's reply is difficult to interpret because of the ambiguity of the syntax, but he apparently denies that he is a prophet (*nābîʾ*) or the son of a prophet (Amos 7:14–15).[27] He thus uses a characteristically northern word when speaking to Amaziah, but Amos's meaning is unclear. He may be rejecting the northern designation for an intermediary and the understanding of prophecy that accompanied it but tacitly accepting the title "visionary." Alternatively, Amos's reply may indicate that he does not recognize a distinction between visionaries and prophets and that he rejects the idea of a permanent social role implied by both terms. In this case he would be saying that he was not a regular member of Judah's religious establishment but rather an individual who had been temporarily possessed by Yahweh's spirit. In any event, the exchange suggests that Amos did indeed come from the south and that his behavior had certain

26. G. E. Wright, "The Nations in Hebrew Prophecy," *Encounter* 26 (1965) 236; J. Mauchline, "Implicit Signs of a Persistent Belief in the Davidic Empire," *VT* 20 (1970) 287–303.

27. For a thorough discussion of the syntax of Amos's reply, see H. H. Rowley, "Was Amos a Nabi?" *Festschrift Otto Eissfeldt* (ed. J. Fück; Halle: Max Niemeyer, 1947) 191–198. See also the more recent treatments of Smend, "Das Nein des Amos," 416–418; Lehming, "Erwägungen zu Amos," 145–169; Gunneweg, "Erwägungen zu Amos 7, 14," 1–16; S. Cohen, "Amos *Was* a Navi," *HUCA* 32 (1961) 175–178; J. D. W. Watts, *Vision and Prophecy in Amos* (Grand Rapids: Eerdmans, 1958) 9–12, 32–35; Wolff, *Joel and Amos*, 307–316; and Zevit, "A Misunderstanding at Bethel," 783–790.

characteristic features that led Amaziah to identify Amos as a visionary.

The evidence that we have collected thus suggests that Amos was a member of the Judean establishment, although probably not part of the central cult in Jerusalem. When he was possessed by Yahweh's spirit, he went to Israel, where he delivered oracles reflecting the language and theological concepts of his Judean tradition. The identity of his support group is unclear, although if he did function as a central prophet in the south, then he may have been supported by members of the Judean establishment. However, he clearly functioned as a peripheral prophet in the north, where he tried to reform the social and religious systems along Judahite lines. His prophecies aroused opposition from the northern establishment and from the general population (Amos 5:10, 13; 6:9–10; 7:10–13, 16–17), and his hearers refused to recognize his prophetic authority. For this reason he was deported, thus effectively ending his career as a peripheral prophet. He may have then functioned as a central prophet in Judah, although there is no direct evidence on this point.

Isaiah of Jerusalem

In spite of the complex literary history of Isaiah 1—39, there can be no question about the prophet's links with the Jerusalemite traditions. In his oracles he employs typically Judean words and phrases, and there are clear literary and theological similarities between Isaiah and Amos. More important, one of the major foci of Isaiah's theology is the Jerusalemite royal ideology of the election of the city and the election of the Davidic house. Zion plays a central role in the book and is considered the place that Yahweh established as a permanent dwelling for the divine presence (Isa 2:2–4; 6:1; 8:18; 14:32; 18:7; 28:16; 31:9). Isaiah accepts the idea of the election of the Davidic line and then expands it to include the concept of the Davidic messiah (Isa 16:5; 9:6 [Eng. 9:7]).[28]

28. For a discussion of the Jerusalemite background of Isaiah's language and theology, see H. L. Ginsberg, "Isaiah in the Light of History," *Conservative Judaism* 22 (1967) 1–18; T. C. Vriezen, "Essentials of the Theology of Isaiah," *Israel's Prophetic Heritage: Essays in Honor of James Muilenburg* (New York: Harper, 1962) 128–146; J. Schreiner, *Sion-Jerusalem, Jahwes Königssitz* (Munich: Kösel-Verlag, 1963), 243–270; and D. Jones, "The Traditio of the Oracles of Isaiah of Jerusalem," *ZAW* 67 (1955) 226–246. Verbal and theological links between Amos and Isaiah are discussed by F. C. Fensham, "Common Trends in Curses of the Near Eastern Treaties and *kudurru*-Inscriptions Compared with Maledictions of Amos and Isaiah," *ZAW* 75 (1963) 155–175; and R. Fey, *Amos und Jesaja* (Neukirchen-Vluyn: Neukirchener Verlag, 1963) 7–104.

Yet, in spite of the ease with which Isaiah can be related to the Jerusalemite traditions, it is difficult to locate the prophet in the context of Jerusalemite society. The superscription of the book (Isa 1:1) places the prophet in the Jerusalemite prophetic traditions by referring to his prophecies as a vision (*ḥāzôn*), but the title "visionary" (*ḥōzeh*) is not applied to him.[29] Isaiah's father, Amoz, is otherwise unknown, so there is no evidence that the prophet inherited a priestly or prophetic position.[30] There is some support for the traditional scholarly view that Isaiah was an upper-class Jerusalemite who grew up in the city. The prophet seems to have known and had access to members of the royal court (Isa 8:2; 22:15–16), and he apparently had no difficulty gaining an unofficial audience with the king (Isa 7:3). The location of Isaiah within Jerusalem's central social structure may also be suggested by the "wisdom" language that he sometimes uses.[31] At the very least this language may indicate that the prophet was educated at the royal court or in the temple, although our knowledge of Israelite "wisdom circles" is not presently sophisticated enough to permit us to assume that there was a Jerusalemite "wisdom group" of which Isaiah was a member.[32]

In addition to seeing Isaiah as part of the central social structure, some scholars have argued that he was actually a cultic prophet.[33] These arguments are usually based on the prophet's temple vision (Isaiah 6) and on his general upper-class Jerusalemite background, but the book provides insufficient evidence to establish a cultic setting for his activities. It therefore seems best to accept the traditional view that Isaiah was an upper-class Jerusalemite who was part of the city's central social structure but not necessarily a part of its religious establishment.

29. Isaiah's wife is said to have been a prophetess (*nĕbîˀāh* [Isa 8:3]), but there is no indication that Isaiah bore the title "prophet" (*nābîˀ*). See the discussion of A. Jepsen, "Die Nebiah in Jes 8:3," *ZAW* 72 (1960) 267–268.

30. The relatively late seal bearing the name "Amoz the scribe" (*ˀmṣ hspr*) cannot refer to Isaiah's father and so cannot be used to support the argument that Isaiah was a scribe. Cf. R. T. Anderson, "Was Isaiah a Scribe?" *JBL* 79 (1960) 57–58.

31. For a discussion of Isaiah's "wisdom" background, see J. Fichtner, "Jesaja unter den Weisen," *TLZ* 74 (1949) 75–80; and J. W. Whedbee, *Isaiah and Wisdom* (Nashville: Abingdon Press, 1971).

32. See the recent discussion of R. N. Whybray, *The Intellectual Tradition in the Old Testament* (Berlin: Walter de Gruyter, 1974). An upper-class background for some wisdom language has recently been suggested by B. W. Kovacs, "Is There a Class-Ethic in Proverbs?" *Essays in Old Testament Ethics* (ed. J. L. Crenshaw and J. T. Willis; New York: KTAV, 1974) 171–189.

33. S. Mowinckel, *Jesaja-Disiplene* (Oslo: H. Aschehoug, 1926) 10–16, 137–139; I. Engnell, *The Call of Isaiah* (Uppsala: Lundequist, 1949).

The linguistic and theological links between Amos and Isaiah suggest that Isaiah may have been part of a prophetic tradition in which the intermediaries' characteristic behavior included the use of stereotypical speech. However, there is not enough evidence to permit an elaboration of this suggestion, and it may be that Isaiah's speech simply reflects his general social background. Outside of the form and content of the prophet's oracles, the book throws no light on his characteristic behavior. He received his revelations through visions (Isa 1:1; 2:1; 6; 13:1), presumably obtained when he was possessed by Yahweh's spirit (cf. Isa 8:11), but nothing is said about his actions during possession.

The Book of Isaiah provides little insight into the prophet's social functions, but the available data suggest that his relationship to his society may have changed during the course of his prophetic activities. In the oracles delivered between the time of his call and the Syro-Ephraimite War (736 B.C.), now found primarily in Isaiah 1—5, the prophet condemns the leaders and the people for social and cultic abuses, while still holding out the hope of salvation for the truly penitent. It is usually assumed that such critical oracles could be delivered only by someone outside of the central social and religious establishments and that Isaiah must have therefore been a peripheral prophet during this period. However, the anthropological evidence shows that central intermediaries are capable of criticizing their societies and advocating social change. Central intermediaries are usually interested in *orderly* change rather than rapid change, and for this reason they frequently interpret change as a return to traditional values. In fact Isaiah sometimes sees change in precisely this way (Isa 1:26), so it is not out of the question that Isaiah's early oracles were delivered from within the establishment and that Isaiah was functioning as a central prophet.

A similarly ambiguous picture comes from the narratives describing Isaiah's activities during the Syro-Ephraimite War (Isa 7—8; 9:7–20 [Eng. 9:8–21]; 17:1–6; 28:1–4).[34] On the one hand, the prophet resembles a central prophet advocating social stability by reaffirming the old Jerusalemite traditions. As Ahaz is preparing the defenses of the city to withstand a possible siege, Isaiah approaches him and chides him for taking matters into his own hands rather

---

34. For a thorough discussion of these oracles, see W. Dietrich, *Jesaja und die Politik* (Munich: Chr. Kaiser Verlag, 1976) 60–99; and F. Huber, *Jahwe, Juda und die anderen Völker beim Propheten Jesaja* (Berlin: Walter de Gruyter, 1976) 10–34.

than trusting in the Jerusalemite theology of the inviolability of Zion. The king is told that his opponents will soon be destroyed and that he need not fear them (Isa 7:1–9). Only when the king refuses to follow the traditional theology does the prophet deliver judgment oracles against him (Isa 7:10–25; 8:5–8). Yet, in spite of these oracles, Isaiah functions as a central prophet by uttering condemnations of Israel's enemies (Isa 8:1–4; 9:7–20 [Eng. 9:8–21]; 17:1–6; 28:1–4) and by promising the restoration of an ideal Davidic king after the judgment (Isa 9:1–6 [Eng. 9:2–7]).

On the other hand, these narratives suggest that Isaiah's support group was not inside the central establishment and that he himself was experiencing opposition to his activities. According to Isa 8:11–12, sometime during this period Yahweh delivered to Isaiah a private oracle warning him not to follow popular opinion about the war. This warning implies that Isaiah was advocating a minority view and that he was being pressed to change his message. Immediately after this, the prophet orders his prophecies to be bound and sealed so that they could be preserved for future generations that might accept their truth.[35] Here Isaiah's support seems to come from a group of disciples on the periphery of society (Isa 8:16–23 [Eng. 8:16—9:1]). The narrative suggests that Isaiah was a peripheral prophet with a small support group. Because of social opposition, the group withdraws into itself, and the prophet's public activities cease until the reign of Hezekiah. If this picture of Isaiah is historically accurate, then the prophet may have ceased to be a central prophet sometime during the reign of Ahaz and may have moved into a peripheral relationship with the Jerusalemite establishment.[36]

Before Isaiah's last major period of activity, in Hezekiah's reign during the Assyrian crisis of 701 B.C., he seems to have prophesied only briefly during Hezekiah's early years. In Isa 14:28–31 the prophet is said to have delivered an oracle against Philistia, and other oracles against the nations may have been given during the same period (Isaiah 18; 20). Because the delivery of oracles against foreign nations seems to have been a function of central Jerusalemite

35. Jones, "Traditio," 226–246.

36. This shift in the prophet's function may be related to the fact that the prophet's "call" narrative is found in Isaiah 6 rather than at the beginning of the book. For a discussion of the function of the call narrative, see B. O. Long, "Prophetic Authority as Social Reality," *Canon and Authority* (ed. G. W. Coats and B. O. Long; Philadelphia: Fortress Press, 1977) 3–20.

prophets, these passages may suggest that Isaiah moved back into the center of Jerusalemite society during the reign of Hezekiah. This suggestion is supported by the Deuteronomic narratives that have been inserted in Isaiah 36—39 in order to describe the prophet's activities during the Assyrian crisis. As our previous discussion has noted, these narratives present different pictures of Isaiah's role in the crisis, but he is clearly portrayed as a central prophet. It may be, then, that Hezekiah's reforms provided the types of changes that Isaiah had earlier sought and that he again took on social maintenance functions within the central society. He continued to advocate the Jerusalemite theology, but he maintained that Yahweh's election of the city did not imply the impossibility of judgment on the people. This modified version of the Jerusalemite ideology may have aroused the opposition of other prophets, who were claiming that the people were safe because Yahweh was in the city (Isa 28:7–13; 29:10). This opposition may have again led the prophet and his group to withdraw onto the periphery of the society (Isa 30:8–14).

Micah

The current state of scholarly research on the Book of Micah does not permit us to draw any firm conclusions about the social dimensions of the prophet's activities. The editorial history of the book is still a matter of great debate, and for this reason it is not even possible to determine with any certainty which portions of the book are from Micah and which are the work of later editors.[37] However, many scholars still hold the traditional opinion that the authentic words of Micah are to be found in chapters 1–3, while chapters 4–5 and chapters 6–7 are later additions. It has recently been demonstrated that chapters 6 and 7 have clear linguistic and theological links with the Deuteronomic tradition, although it is impossible to determine whether these chapters represent actual oracles from a northern prophet who was active before the fall of Samaria or whether they are the work of later Deuteronomic editors.[38] In either case, these chapters, including the "prophetic liturgy" in Mic 7:8–20, cannot be the work of Micah of Moresheth. Chapters 4 and 5 also reflect editorial activity, some of it late. Portions of these chapters

37. A convenient summary of recent research on Micah is provided by K. Jeppesen, "New Aspects of Micah Research," *Journal for the Study of the Old Testament* 8 (1978) 3–32.

38. A. S. van der Woude, "Deutero-Micha: Ein Prophet aus Nord-Israel?" *NedTTs* 25 (1971) 365–378.

have verbal and theological links with other prophetic books, but there are particularly strong connections with Isaiah, including an entire oracle (Mic 4:1–3) which is quoted from Isa 2:1–3.[39] There are several ways to explain the connections between Micah and 4–5 and Isaiah. First, one might maintain that the chapters actually come from Micah, who was influenced by Isaiah. This would seem unlikely, but the possibility cannot be ruled out. Second, taking a cue from the anthropological literature, one might suggest that both Micah and Isaiah used stereotypical Judean speech patterns. However, this suggestion seems unlikely given the fact that the Isaiah connections appear mostly in Micah 4—5 rather than in Micah 1—3, where most scholars locate the original Micah material. Third, one might suggest that Isaiah himself exerted so much influence on Judean prophecy that later prophets, like the one whose words are contained in Micah 4—5, used Isaiah's characteristic speech as part of their own stereotypical possession behavior. Finally, one might simply assume that both Isaiah and Micah were edited by the same group. Because both Isaiah and Micah exhibit an overall editorial structure in which judgment and promise oracles alternate, the latter possibility seems to be the most probable of the four. This means that the original oracles of Micah are most likely to be found in chapters 1–3, although a few may also be embedded in chapters 4–5.

On the basis of Micah 1—3, little can be said about the prophet's social location or functions. If the superscription (Mic 1:1) is accurate, he was from Moresheth in the southern part of Judah. He prophesied during the reigns of Jothan, Ahaz, and Hezekiah (c. 750–687 B.C.), and in fact Jer 26:18 quotes one of Micah's oracles, which is said to have been delivered to Hezekiah. Micah presumably carried out his activities in Jerusalem, although the oracles in Micah 1—3 give no indication that he was part of the Jerusalemite political or religious establishments. On the basis of the superscription and the content of the oracles, scholars usually assume that the prophet was an elder at Moresheth or one of the rural upper class.[40]

39. B. Renaud, *Structure et attaches littéraires de Michée IV–V* (Paris: J. Gabalda, 1964) 37–74.

40. A. Weiser, *Das Buch der zwölf Kleinen Propheten* (Göttingen: Vandenhoeck & Ruprecht, 1963) 229–230; W. Rudolph, *Micha—Nahum—Habakuk—Zephanja* (Gütersloh: Gerd Mohn, 1975) 22—24; L. C. Allen, *The Books of Joel, Obadiah, Jonah, and Micah* (Grand Rapids: Eerdmans, 1976) 240–241; J. L. Mays, *Micah* (Philadelphia: Westminster Press, 1976) 15–17; Jeppesen, "New Aspects," 5.

Attempts have been made to link Micah with Jerusalemite cultic traditions, but these attempts have not generally been successful when based on Micah 1—3 alone.[41]

The evidence thus suggests that Micah functioned as a peripheral prophet in Jerusalem, where he leveled a devastating attack on Israel's ruling elite. He condemns the great landowners (Mic 2:1–5; 3:1–4), the priests (Mic 3:11), and the princes (Mic 3:1; 3:11). Particularly notable are Micah's oracles against the prophets and diviners (Mic 2:6–11; 3:5–8; 3:11; cf. 4:9–14).[42] These figures appear to have been central prophets who were advocating the Jerusalemite theology of the inviolability of Zion (Mic 2:6; 3:5, 11) and thus opposing Micah's judgment oracles (Mic 2:6). Micah accuses the prophets of lying (2:11) and claims that he is possessed by Yahweh's spirit while they are not (Mic 3:8). Rather, they give favorable oracles in return for money (Mic 3:5, 11), and for this reason the prophets will eventually be punished (Mic 3:6–7). The sharp tone of Micah's speeches suggests that the Jerusalemite establishment was unwilling to recognize his prophetic claims. As a result, he may have turned to false-prophecy accusations in an attempt to curb his prophetic opposition. This move presumably led to a breakdown in the social structure and in this case to the suppression of Micah, but there is no evidence on this point.

Nahum

Scholars are in general agreement that the Book of Nahum must be seen against a cultic background, either as the product of a prophetic group or as a liturgy that was actually used in the Jerusalem cult.[43] Although there are difficulties connected with un-

---

41. W. Beyerlin, *Die Kulttraditionen Israels in der Verkündigung des Propheten Micha* (Göttingen: Vandenhoeck & Ruprecht, 1959); R. Vuilleumier, *Michée, Nahoum, Habacuc, Sophonie* (Neuchâtel: Delachaux et Niestlé, 1971) 90–92.

42. These passages are thoroughly analyzed by A. S. van der Woude, "Micah in Dispute with the Pseudo-Prophets," *VT* 19 (1969) 244–260.

43. Since the work of Mowinckel (*Jesaja-Disiplene*, 56–61), scholars have usually connected Nahum with the cult. However, there have been debates about whether or not the book itself was used in liturgical contexts. For a discussion of this issue and a summary of the older positions, see H. Schulz, *Das Buch Nahum* (Berlin: Walter de Gruyter, 1973) 111–134. Cf. R. Hentschke, *Die Stellung der vorexilischen Schriftpropheten zum Kultus* (Berlin: Alfred Töpelmann, 1957) 173. The attempt of J. Jeremias (*Kultprophetie und Gerichtsverkündigung in der späten Königszeit Israels* [Neukirchen-Vluyn: Neukirchener Verlag, 1970] 11–55) to deny that the book had any cultic connections is based both on a questionable literary analysis of the book and on a misconception about the nature of a central intermediary. Jeremias argues

derstanding the book as a genuine liturgy, there can be no doubt that Nahum was a central prophet related to the Jerusalemite tradition. The superscription characterizes the entire book as a *maśśā*ᵓ, a title that originally may have been used in Jerusalemite prophetic circles to describe oracles against foreign nations. The book is further called a vision (*ḥāzôn*), a word that was also at home in the southern prophetic traditions (Nah 1:1).[44]

Cultic motifs and language are found throughout the book.[45] If the text actually reflects Nahum's speech and is not simply a scribal composition, then we may assume that the prophet's characteristic possession behavior included the use of stereotypical speech that met the expectations of his support group, the Jerusalemite religious establishment. As a central prophet Nahum helped to preserve the social structure by expressing the nationalistic values of the royal cult. His oracles against Nineveh thus have both political and religious implications, for his words help to maintain the whole social structure, not just the cult.[46]

As a central intermediary Nahum might have carried out his activities in any number of locations, including the royal court and the temple itself. The fact that his support group was drawn from the Jerusalemite religious establishment does not necessarily imply that he himself actually participated in temple rituals or that his activities were confined to the temple. He could have functioned equally well in the central government or even in the army. Therefore, until we know more about the actual social location of central Jerusalemite intermediaries, it would be wise to stress Nahum's central social functions and to avoid circumscribing the arena of his activities.

---

that in fact Nahum delivered oracles against Judah and for this reason cannot have been a cult prophet, for such prophets only delivered salvation oracles. The anthropological evidence clearly shows that central intermediaries are quite capable of uttering judgment oracles and calling for social change, as long as that change is controlled and carefully regulated so as to prevent social upheaval. Therefore, if Nahum did indeed deliver oracles against Judah, as Jeremias claims, then the prophet could easily have done so in a cultic context.

44. Comparisons between Nahum and the Near Eastern treaty curses have also shown that Nahum followed the Judean prophets Amos and Isaiah in utilizing phrases and images drawn from stereotypical Near Eastern descriptions of disaster. See K. J. Cathcart, "Treaty Curses in the Book of Nahum," *CBQ* 35 (1973) 179–187.

45. A. Haldar, *Studies in the Book of Nahum* (Uppsala: Lundequist, 1947).

46. For a discussion of the political implications of Nahum's oracles, see N. K. Gottwald, *All the Kingdoms of the Earth* (New York: Harper & Row, 1964) 229–233.

Habakkuk

Like Nahum, the Book of Habakkuk is usually thought to have originated in cultic circles. The first section of the book (Hab 1:1— 2:4) closely resembles a liturgy, and some scholars have even suggested that the whole unit was composed by the prophet for use as part of a ritual asking for God's help in time of trouble. The second section of the book (Hab 2:5–20) contains five or six oracles against an unspecified enemy. Some of this material resembles the oracles against foreign nations, which some scholars have tried to see against a cultic background. Finally, the book closes with a psalm which includes performance instructions and which has linguistic ties to the Psalter (Habakkuk 3). The literary features of the book thus suggest that the author had close connections with the cult, even if he did not participate regularly in the ritual.[47]

Outside of the literary characteristics of the book, there are several other indications that the prophet functioned within Jerusalem's central religious establishment. The superscription (Hab 1:1) characterizes the book as a maśśāʾ, a term which was perhaps originally used by Judean authors to designate oracles against foreign nations. Habakkuk is called a prophet (nābîʾ), but like other Judean prophets he is said to have "seen" (ḥāzāh) his oracles. As one might expect, the language of the third chapter of the book has close affinities with the biblical psalms. The first two chapters also contain some echoes of Psalms, but most of the language reflects wisdom and prophetic influences. Judean prophets are heavily represented, and, as we have already noted, "wisdom language" may have had links with the royal court.[48]

The evidence thus indicates that Habakkuk is to be located within one of the Judean prophetic traditions. He was undoubtedly a central prophet in Jerusalem, who had social maintenance functions within the religious establishment, although it is not necessary to assume that he participated regularly in temple rituals. Like many central intermediaries, he may have been required to produce

---

47. Detailed arguments for the cultic background of Habakkuk have been presented by a number of scholars. For a recent example, see Jeremias, *Kultprophetie*, 55–110. An exhaustive survey of the debate on the relationship of the book to the cult may be found in P. Jöcken, *Das Buch Habakuk* (Cologne: Peter Hanstein, 1977) 313–400.

48. P. Humbert, *Problèmes du livre d'Habacuc* (Neuchâtel: Secrétariat de l'Université, 1944) 80–248; D. E. Gowan, "Habakkuk and Wisdom," *Perspective* 9 (1968) 157–166.

oracles on specified occasions, and for this reason he may have actively sought or induced visions (Hab 2:1). He helped to insure the stability of the society by articulating Israel's traditional faith and by uttering oracles against the people's enemies. His support group was presumably part of the religious establishment, and there is no indication of opposition to his message. However, there are hints in the book that Habakkuk was worried about the failure of his oracles to come true. He is instructed to write down his visions so that future generations may remember them, and he is told by Yahweh that fulfillment of the visions will occur only in the future. Yahweh exhorts the prophet and through him the people not to lose hope and assures them that the events foreseen in the visions will finally take place (Hab 2:2–3). These words of assurance may indicate that the prophet's support group was beginning to question his prophetic authority because the fulfillment of his oracles had been delayed. Still, there are no hints that the prophet was actually in danger of losing the support of his group.

Zephaniah

Zephaniah's Judean credentials are established in the superscription of the book, where a linear genealogy traces the prophet's lineage through three intervening ancestors to Hezekiah. It has sometimes been argued that the prophet's ancestor could not have been Hezekiah king of Judah.[49] However, such an argument is not convincing. The genealogy is abnormally long, and we must therefore assume that the writer of the superscription included it for a particular purpose. Linear genealogies of this type have only one function: to ground in the past an individual's claims to power, property, or position. For the functioning of the genealogy, the most important name is the earliest, the name of the person from whom prestige or power is inherited.[50] The Hezekiah mentioned in the prophet's genealogy must therefore have been an individual whose authority, prestige, or position Zephaniah wished to claim. For the carriers of the biblical traditions, such an individual could only have

---

49. A. S. Kapelrud, *The Message of the Prophet Zephaniah* (Oslo: Universitetsforlaget, 1975) 43–45; Rudolph, *Micha*, 258–259; E. Sellin, *Das Zwölfprophetenbuch* (2 / 3d ed.; Leipzig: A. Deichert, 1930) 414, 419; cf. J. Heller, "Zephanjas Ahnenreihe," *VT* 21 (1971) 102–104.

50. For a general discussion of the function of linear genealogies, see R. R. Wilson, *Genealogy and History in the Biblical World* (New Haven: Yale University Press, 1977) 37–48.

been King Hezekiah, who was responsible for reforms resembling those demanded in Deuteronomy. Zephaniah, prophesying in the time of another great reformer, Josiah, thus bolstered his prophetic authority by tracing his royal lineage back to the earlier reforming king. With this move the prophet placed himself solidly within the Jerusalemite royal establishment, and we might reasonably guess that Zephaniah was a central prophet during the reign of Josiah. However, the evidence presented by the book indicates a more complex picture, for while Zephaniah clearly stands within the Jerusalemite traditions, he also has some intriguing connections with the Deuteronomic tradition.

Scholars have long noted Zephaniah's affinities with Jerusalemite prophetic and cultic traditions. At points the theology of Zephaniah resembles that of Isaiah, and in particular Zephaniah's ideas about the Day of Yahweh (Zeph 1:7—2:3) develop those found in Amos, Isaiah, and Micah. The vocabulary of Zephaniah has roots within the Jerusalemite tradition, and in his words there are echoes of Judean prophets such as Isaiah and Amos. Zephaniah's language also reflects some knowledge of the cult, and both in vocabulary and in ideology his words have close links with Psalms.[51] The language and theology of the book suggest that Zephaniah was indeed a central prophet who was a part of Israel's political and religious establishments, although there are no indications that he had a regular role in temple rituals.[52] As a central intermediary Zephaniah used the language expected by his establishment support group and delivered oracles reaffirming the old Judean traditions. He also delivered oracles against foreign nations (Zeph 2:4—3:8), a task usually performed in Judah by central prophets.

However, this picture of Zephaniah as a central prophet is complicated by the fact that the book has certain unexpected Deuteronomic features. Unlike other Judean prophetic books, Zephaniah does not open with a reference to a vision which the prophet has seen. Rather, the superscription begins with the formula, "the word of Yahweh which was to Zephaniah" (Zeph 1:1). As we have already noted, this formula is found at the beginning of Ephraimite prophetic books and reflects a typical Ephraimite em-

---

51. The evidence for Zephaniah's Jerusalemite background is conveniently summarized by Kapelrud, *Zephaniah,* 56–72. Cf. G. Gerleman, *Zephanja* (Lund: C. W. K. Gleerup, 1942) 118–119.
52. Kapelrud, *Zephaniah,* 51–55.

phasis on the word of Yahweh. Furthermore, throughout the book Zephaniah condemns political and religious practices similar to those condemned by Jeremiah. Zephaniah speaks out against idolatrous priests, the worship of Baal, and the worship of other gods (Zeph 1:4–6). Members of the establishment—officials, judges, prophets, and priests—are criticized for misconduct in office (Zeph 3:3–5). Only the king is not included in the list. Jerusalem itself is accused of refusing to listen to the chastening word of the prophet and of not trusting in Yahweh (Zeph 3:1–2). These oracles often employ terms that seem to have Ephraimite origins, and there are strong links with the language of Jeremiah, Hosea, and the Deuteronomic History.[53]

Although it might be possible to explain these Deuteronomic features by assuming that the Deuteronomists edited Zephaniah as they did Micah, the thorough mixing of Deuteronomic and Jerusalemite features in the book seems to rule out this possibility. It is therefore preferable to suggest that Zephaniah was influenced to a certain extent by Josiah's reform. Zephaniah's references to cultic abuses in Jerusalem are usually taken to indicate that the prophet was active before Josiah's reforms began. However, our analysis of Jeremiah has suggested that the reforms began earlier and were less thorough than the Deuteronomic account indicates. Thus Zephaniah may well have been part of the reform movement, but unlike Jeremiah, Zephaniah carried out his reforming activities within the context of the establishment. Such reform activities are not impossible for central intermediaries, particularly when changes are made slowly and are seen as a return to older and more authentic traditions. The Deuteronomists presented their program in precisely this way and portrayed Josiah's reforms as a direct result of his return to old Israelite principles contained in the Mosaic lawbook found in the temple. We may thus theorize that Zephaniah was a central prophet in Jerusalem at the time the reforms began and that he, unlike some of his colleagues (cf. Zeph 3:4), was convinced by the Deuteronomic program, a process that may have been facilitated by his descent from the earlier reforming king, Hezekiah. The prophet thus continued to carry out his central maintenance

---

53. See the references collected by ibid., 56–72. Zephaniah's links with Deuteronomic tradition make it difficult to sustain Gerleman's thesis (*Zephanja*, 100–128) that the prophet was a disciple of Isaiah who opposed the Deuteronomic reforms.

functions, but the language which was part of his stereotypical possession behavior was modified slightly to meet the expectations of the Deuteronomists. He thus claimed support from both the Deuteronomic reformers and from the Jerusalemite establishment, and in his theology and personal behavior he synthesized the Jerusalemite and Deuteronomic traditions.

Ezekiel

Although the present Book of Ezekiel is the product of a long and complex literary history, it is still possible to reconstruct at least a hazy picture of the prophet's behavioral characteristics and social functions.[54] The introduction of the book identifies Ezekiel as a priest, who was exiled to Babylon during the first deportation (Ezek 1:1–3). He was thus a Zadokite, with deep roots in the priestly traditions of the Jerusalemite establishment. The prophet's priestly background is clearly reflected in his language, which has close ties with the Holiness Code (Leviticus 17—26) and with other Jerusalemite literature. Zadokite theological views appear throughout Ezekiel's oracles and are particularly noticeable in his vision of the restored temple (Ezekiel 40—48).[55]

The spirit of Yahweh plays an important role in the book, and it is safe to assume that the prophet received his visions when he was possessed by Yahweh's spirit.[56] The spirit entered the prophet at his call (Ezek 2:2) and thereafter possessed him periodically, giving him oracles and visions and occasionally transporting him from place to place (see, for example, Ezek 3:14–15, 22, 24; 8:1, 3; 11:1, 5, 24; 33:22; 37:1; 40:1–2). Ezekiel's possession behavior is often bizarre and may have included trance, although there are no specific descriptions of his trance behavior (cf. Ezek 3:15).[57] It may

---

54. The discussion that follows is based primarily on the fundamental tradition-historical analysis of W. Zimmerli, *Ezechiel* (Neukirchen-Vluyn: Neukirchener Verlag, 1969).

55. The linguistic and theological evidence on Ezekiel's Zadokite background has been conveniently collected by Zimmerli, *Ezechiel*, 24*–31*, 66*–79*. See also K. W. Carley, *Ezekiel among the Prophets* (London: SCM Press, 1975) 62–65; J. Bowman, "Ezekiel and the Zadokite Priesthood," *Transactions of the Glasgow University Oriental Society* 16 (1955–1956) 1–14; and J. D. Levenson, *Theology of the Program of Restoration of Ezekiel 40—48* (Missoula: Scholars Press, 1976).

56. For a discussion of the importance of the spirit in Ezekiel, see W. Zimmerli, "The Message of the Prophet Ezekiel," *Int* 23 (1969) 134–136; and Carley, *Ezekiel*, 13–37.

57. For a discussion of Ezekiel's trance behavior, see Carley, *Ezekiel*, 6–8, 71–76; E. C. Broome, Jr., "Ezekiel's Abnormal Personality," *JBL* 65 (1946) 277–292; and

well have involved using the sort of stereotypical speech that was expected by his Zadokite support group. However, some of the descriptions of the prophet's strange behavior are better interpreted as literary devices than as accurate accounts of his actions.[58] His surrealistic behavior in his visions (cf. Ezek 8:8–10; 11:13) probably falls into this category, and his "dumbness" (Ezek 3:24–27; 24:27; 33:21–22) may have theological and literary functions within the overall redactional structure of the book.[59] In particular, the prophet's detailed symbolic acts (Ezekiel 4—5) are likely to be the product of literary activity, for they are too complex to have been comprehensible, and some of them are physically impossible.

On the basis of the evidence that we have discussed up to this point, one might reasonably assume that Ezekiel, like most of his Jerusalemite predecessors, was a central prophet who played an important role in the exilic community. However, other evidence in the book points in another direction. Although Ezekiel's language and theology clearly reflect his Zadokite background, there are also a number of Deuteronomic characteristics in the book. As we have already noted, Ezekiel follows the Ephraimites in placing great stress on the word of Yahweh as the means by which prophetic revelations are given, and in fact the characteristic Deuteronomic formula "the word of the Lord came to me" occurs forty-five times in the book.[60] In addition, there are a number of striking theological and linguistic links between Ezekiel and Jeremiah that have long puzzled scholars.[61] Most important, the few extant descriptions of Ezekiel's actual prophetic activity seem to portray him as a characteristically Ephraimite Mosaic prophet to whom the people come to inquire of Yahweh. In Ezek 14:3 and 20:1 the elders of Israel are said to have come to the prophet to "seek" (*drš*) Yahweh (cf. Ezek

---

C. G. Howie, *The Date and Composition of Ezekiel* (Philadelphia: Society of Biblical Literature, 1960) 69–84.

58. On the literary character of much of the book, see Zimmerli, *Ezechiel*, 104–114.

59. R. R. Wilson, "An Interpretation of Ezekiel's Dumbness," *VT* 22 (1972) 91–104.

60. W. Zimmerli, "The Special Form- and Traditio-historical Character of Ezekiel's Prophecy," *VT* 15 (1965) 515–516.

61. For a comprehensive listing and discussion of the Ephraimite elements of Ezekiel, see M. Burrows, *The Literary Relations of Ezekiel* (Ph.D. dissertation, Yale University, 1925) 19–28, 44–47; J. W. Miller, *Das Verhältnis Jeremias und Hesekiels sprachlich und theologisch Untersucht* (Assen: Van Gorcum, 1955); Zimmerli, *Ezechiel,* 62–79; and Carley, *Ezekiel,* 8–12, 48–62.

8:1; 33:30–33). On both occasions the prophet is forbidden by Yahweh to allow the inquiry, and instead Ezekiel is told that he can only deliver words of judgment to the people. This divine refusal to permit prophetic intercession remains in effect until the fall of Jerusalem, after which Yahweh promises to permit the resumption of the prophet's intercessory role (Ezek 36:37–38). This situation immediately calls to mind Jeremiah's experiences before the fall of the city. Like Ezekiel, Jeremiah was also forbidden to intercede for the people (Jer 11:14–17; 14:11–12; 15:1; 21:1–2; 37:1–10; 42:1–6). As part of the judgment, the Mosaic prophet's intercessory functions were restricted, thus allowing the judgment to take place. The evidence therefore suggests that Ezekiel was seen, at least by later tradition, as a typical Ephraimite prophet, and it is possible that Ezekiel himself also held the same view.

The Ephraimite features that appear throughout Ezekiel might be explained by assuming that the book received Deuteronomic editing sometime in the postexilic period. However, this explanation is unlikely because the Ephraimite features are an integral part of the book at all redactional levels. It is not possible to isolate a specifically Deuteronomic editorial layer. For this reason it is preferable to assume that Ezekiel was influenced by the Deuteronomic reform movement before he was exiled to Babylon. However, rather than becoming a total convert to the Deuteronomic position, he seems to have attempted to make his own personal synthesis of the Zadokite and Deuteronomic positions. This synthesis is reflected in his oracles. In Ezekiel 6—7 the prophet follows the Deuteronomic line that the judgment on Jerusalem is inevitable because of the past sins of the people, but this notion is expressed in Jerusalemite language. In Ezekiel 16 and 23 he develops an originally Ephraimite image (cf. Hosea 2; Jeremiah 2—3) to make the same theological point, but again the language is Jerusalemite rather than Deuteronomic. A similar phenomenon can be seen in Ezekiel 20, where the prophet expands on the Deuteronomic notion that Israel was being punished for past sins. The theology has Deuteronomic features but is slanted toward Zadokite concerns, particularly the role of the law. In a curious mixture of Deuteronomic and Zadokite views, Ezekiel interprets some of Israel's laws as God's judgment on the people because of their past sins (Ezek 20:11–26).

The individualistic character of Ezekiel's views makes it unlikely that he could have functioned as a central prophet in the exilic community. Rather, the evidence suggests that he was a peripheral prophet whose views were largely rejected by the orthodox Zadokite community. Strong opposition to the prophet's message is implied by several features of the book. The account of the prophet's call (Ezek 1:1—3:15) is much more highly developed than most prophetic call narratives, and this stress on his call may have been intended to enhance his authority. Moreover, the call narrative is studded with references to the rebelliousness of the people and with warnings to the prophet not to be intimidated by his opposition (Ezek 2:3–8; 3:7–11). Ezekiel is told to eat a scroll containing Yahweh's words and is warned to speak all of them to the people (Ezek 2:9–10; 3:1–3, 10–11). In order to save his own life, the prophet is required to deliver God's words to the people, even if they will not listen (Ezek 3:16–21). The role of the spirit in the book may also reflect attempts to enhance Ezekiel's authority. Ezekiel rarely does anything of his own free will. Rather, he delivers only the word that comes to him and does only what the spirit leads him to do. The message conveyed by this picture of the prophet is that God, not Ezekiel himself, is responsible for everything that the prophet does and says.[62]

It is likely that Ezekiel's prophecies made little impact on his society, which must have become increasingly hostile because of his harsh words. This opposition may have caused Ezekiel to curtail his public activities and to turn to writing as a way of expressing his views. Many of his oracles are too complex to have been delivered orally, and they show signs of much editorial reworking.

Ezekiel's support group cannot be identified with any certainty, but he presumably gathered around him fellow Zadokites who had also been influenced by the Deuteronomic reforms. A reference to this group may appear in Ezek 23:45, where it is said that righteous men (ʾănāšîm ṣaddîqîm) will participate in the final judgment on sinful Israel. Such language is often used by oppressed peripheral groups that feel themselves to be the only faithful people remaining in their society, and they sometimes see themselves suffering vicariously for the larger society (cf. Ezek 5:1–4). Ezekiel's support group presumably was responsible for preserving and editing his oracles, although he himself may have also been involved in the editorial process. As resistance to the group's views intensified, it

62. Cf. Carley, *Ezekiel*, 67–69.

may have withdrawn even further from the society and turned in an apocalyptic direction. The apocalyptic material in Ezekiel 38—39 may have been added at this time in order to give the group hope that its reconstruction program (Ezekiel 40—48) would eventually be realized. However, the group's expectations were not fulfilled, and the reconstruction took a form very different from the one that the Ezekiel group had desired.

Conclusions

The biblical evidence on the social dimensions of Judean prophecy in the preexilic period throws more light on the functions of the prophets than on their characteristic behavior. Many of the prophets, although by no means all of them, apparently carried out their activities within the central social structure, where they helped to maintain social stability. As part of this task they preserved ancient religious traditions, reinterpreted them to bring about controlled social change, and delivered oracles against Israel's enemies. Although these prophets worked within the establishment, the precise physical location in which they worked is unclear. Some of them may have been attached to the temple, where they took part regularly in specific rituals. Others may have been part of the royal court, where they served as advisers to the king. According to the anthropological data, central intermediaries can perform their functions in a number of different settings, and we may suspect that the same thing was true of central prophets in Judah.

The biblical sources provide little insight into the behavioral characteristics of preexilic Judean prophets. Many of them seem to have used language that was at home in Jerusalem, but there is not enough data to prove that all Judean prophets talked and acted in roughly the same way when they were possessed. Except in the case of Ezekiel, there is no indication that trance was a regular part of their characteristic possession behavior. On the whole, their behavior seems to have been unremarkable and completely controlled. This description of their behavior correlates well with the picture of central intermediaries provided by the anthropological material. Because central intermediaries are part of the established social structure, they are more rigidly controlled by their support groups than are peripheral intermediaries. Unusual and erratic possession behavior is not tolerated, and central intermediaries are expected to adhere closely to social expectations. However, it would be wise not to read too much into the fact that the biblical sources have little to say about the behavior of Judean intermediaries. The silence of the sources may simply indicate that Judean authors did not place much emphasis on prophecy.

EXILIC AND POSTEXILIC WRITING PROPHETS IN THE JUDEAN TRADITIONS

The biblical texts of the exilic and postexilic periods tell us virtually nothing about the behavior or social functions of the prophets who were active after the exile. If the preexilic Judean writing prophets are only vaguely discernible in the texts, then the exilic and postexilic prophets are all but invisible. The little available data on the postexilic prophets can be briefly summarized.

Obadiah is presumed to have prophesied after the fall of Jerusalem, although the exact date of the book is still a matter of debate. The superscription indicates that the prophet received his oracles through a vision (*ḥāzôn*), and this fact suggests that he may have been in the tradition of the Jerusalemite central prophets. This suggestion is supported by the contents of the book itself, which consists of a collection of oracles against Edom. It has been argued that the oracles have been arranged in the form of a liturgy and that therefore Obadiah was a cult prophet, but there is little real evidence on this point. The question of the prophet's tradition-historical setting is complicated by the fact that much of the book has strong linguistic affinities with other oracles against Edom, particularly Jer 49:7–16. However, the oracles in Jeremiah may themselves be a secondary addition, so the linguistic parallels cannot be used to place Obadiah in the Deuteronomic tradition.[63]

The prophetic activity of Haggai can be dated precisely to a few months in the year 520 B.C., when he delivered several oracles concerning the temple reconstruction, priestly purity, and the future kingship of Zerubbabel (cf. Ezra 5:1; 6:14). Haggai's concern with the temple has sometimes been taken as an indication that he

63. H. W. Wolff, "Obadja—Ein Kultprophet als Interpret," *EvT* 37 (1977) 273–284; idem, *Obadja, Jona* (Neukirchen-Vluyn: Neukirchener Verlag, 1977) 3–7; G. Fohrer, "Die Sprüche Obadjas," *Studia Biblica et Semitica Theodoro Christiano Vriezen* (Wageningen: H. Veenman, 1966) 81–93; J. D. W. Watts, *Obadiah* (Grand Rapids: Eerdmans, 1969) 19–27; and W. Rudolph, *Joel—Amos—Obadja—Jona* (Gütersloh: Gerd Mohn, 1971) 295–298.

was a cult prophet or a priest, but there is no clear evidence for either of these views. The prophet's interest in the proper conduct of worship might suggest that he was a central prophet in one of the Judean traditions. However, the theology of the book has roots both in the Jerusalemite traditions and in preexilic Deuteronomic tradition. Haggai is called a prophet (*nābî*), but his behavior has no links with the Deuteronomic concept of the prophet. Haggai's support group was presumably composed of people who shared his views on the building of the temple and the regulation of the cult. However, this group cannot be clearly identified. The tone of the oracles suggests a polemic against other views that were current at the time, but it is not certain whether Haggai played the role of a peripheral prophet or a central prophet in these debates.[64]

The so-called First Zechariah, the author of Zechariah 1—8, began to prophesy in the same year as Haggai and is also connected with the building of the temple (Ezra 5:1; 6:14). Zechariah's genealogy (Zech 1:1) identifies him as the grandson of Iddo. Many scholars claim that the genealogy is in error and that Zechariah was really the son of Iddo, as Ezra 5:1 and 6:14 indicate. If Iddo is to be identified with the priest mentioned in Neh 12:4, 16, then it would indicate that Zechariah came from a priestly family and that he may have been a priest himself. However, another interpretation of the genealogy is also possible. The title "prophet" (*nābî*) in Zech 1:1 follows the name Iddo in the genealogy but is usually understood to apply to Zechariah. Yet, the title could also apply to Iddo, and in fact the Chronicler mentions an earlier intermediary named Iddo. This figure is called both a visionary (*ḥōzeh* [2 Chr 9:29; 12:15]) and a prophet (*nābî* [2 Chr 13:22]) and is clearly portrayed as an important official in the Jerusalem court in the early monarchical period. If Zechariah's genealogy intends to connect the prophet with this early figure, then a number of names must have been omitted. However, such omissions are common in linear genealogies, and in Akkadian texts from the Persian period there are a number of examples of three-generation genealogies in which the third name is not the grandfather of the first person in the line but a much earlier

---

64. W. Rudolph, *Haggai—Sacharja 1–8—Sacharja 9–14—Maleachi* (Gütersloh: Gerd Mohn, 1976) 21–23; K.-M. Beyse, *Serubbabel und die Königserwartungen der Propheten Haggai und Sacharja* (Stuttgart: Calwer Verlag, 1972) 50–51; W. A. M. Beuken, *Haggai—Sacharja 1–8* (Assen: Van Gorcum, 1967) 27–83, 184–229; P. R. Ackroyd, *Exile and Restoration* (Philadelphia: Westminster Press, 1968) 153–170; T. Chary, *Les prophètes et le culte à partir de l'exil* (Tournai: Desclée, 1955) 118–159.

ancestor. Such "family" name patterns are also attested in Aramaic, so it is not out of the question that Zechariah's genealogy in Zech 1:1 mentions his father and then skips over a number of generations to the important prophet / visionary of Solomon's time.[65] If the genealogy is interpreted in this way, then the book's superscription would serve the purpose of enhancing Zechariah's authority by connecting him with an early Jerusalemite prophet. However, no matter which interpretation of the genealogy is accepted, the book's superscription clearly places the prophet within the central social structure and links him closely with the Jerusalemite traditions. This link is reinforced by the fact that most of Zechariah's oracles come from visions, a means of revelation often found in Judean prophetic circles. This evidence, together with the content of the visions themselves, seems to place Zechariah in the Jerusalemite prophetic traditions.

However, at least two passages in the book indicate that Zechariah's behavior had Deuteronomic characteristics. In Zech 1:2–6, Zechariah delivers an oracle that clearly reflects Deuteronomic language and theology. The people are repeatedly exhorted to return to Yahweh and not to be like their ancestors, who ignored the prophetic call to return and were subsequently destroyed. A second reflex of the Deuteronomic prophetic tradition can be seen in Zech 7:1–7, where the people come to make an inquiry of Yahweh concerning the proper procedure for fasting. However, instead of going to a priest, which would have been the normal procedure in the Jerusalemite tradition, or going to a Mosaic prophet, which would have been the practice in the Ephraimite tradition, the people go to both the priests *and* the prophets. The people's inquiry is answered by Yahweh, who speaks through the prophet (Zech 7:8–14). This passage seems to indicate that the Ephraimite and Judean views of appropriate prophetic activity had merged by the early postexilic period.[66]

Nothing is known of Joel's social location, characteristic behavior,

---

65. For a discussion of telescoping in linear genealogies and a treatment of the Babylonian evidence, see Wilson, *Genealogy and History*, 32–36, 114–118.

66. Ackroyd, *Exile and Restoration*, 171–217; Rudolph, *Haggai*, 61–62, 66–71; Beyse, *Serubbabel*, 67–70; Chary, *Prophètes*, 118–159; K. Seybold, *Bilder zum Tempelbau* (Stuttgart: KBW, 1974); L. G. Rignell, *Die Nachtgesichte des Sacharja* (Lund: C. W. K. Gleerup, 1950); M. Bič, *Die Nachtgesichte des Sacharja* (Neukirchen-Vluyn: Neukirchener Verlag, 1964); A. Petitjean, *Les oracles du Proto-Zacharie* (Paris: J. Gabalda, 1969); J. Jeremias, *Die Nachtgesichte des Sacharja* (Göttingen: Vandenhoeck & Ruprecht, 1977).

or social functions. Because of the liturgical patterns that underlie the book and because of the prophet's use of cultic language, it has often been assumed that he was a cult prophet of some sort. The prophet has made heavy use of earlier prophetic books, and whole sayings and phrases are sometimes quoted in Joel's work. The major citations come from the writings of Judean prophets (Obad 17 = Joel 3:5; Isa 13:6; Ezek 30:2–3 = Joel 1:15; Amos 1:2 = Joel 4:16; Zeph 1:14–15 = Joel 2:1–2), but Ephraimite influences can also be seen in Joel's theology and vocabulary.

The answer to the question of Joel's social functions depends largely on how the editorial history of the book is analyzed. The liturgical and tradition-historical features of the book suggest that Joel may have functioned as a central prophet. However, if "proto-apocalyptic" material is detected in the book, then the author would have to be placed in the context of a peripheral apocalyptic group.[67]

Not even the name of the author of Malachi is known, and the book sheds no light on the nature of his prophetic activities. The writer's cultic interests have led some scholars to suggest that he was involved in the cult. If so, then Malachi might have been a central intermediary. On the other hand, the harsh criticism of the priesthood in chapters 1 and 2 calls to mind a peripheral prophet with a priestly background and a desire to reform the religious establishment. The book cannot easily be placed in a single prophetic tradition, for the writer seems to have been influenced both by Judean and by Ephraimite traditions.[68]

Although the exilic and postexilic prophetic books tell us little about the behavior and social functions of individual *prophets,* this literature does imply certain things about the nature of *prophecy* in the postexilic period.[69] First, it is clear that the authors of the late prophetic books were worried about the problem of prophetic authority. Our study of the anthropological sources has shown that

---

67. Wolff, *Joel and Amos,* 4–15; O. Plöger, *Theocracy and Eschatology* (Richmond: John Knox Press, 1968) 96–105; A. S. Kapelrud, *Joel Studies* (Uppsala: A.-B. Lundequistska Bokhandeln, 1948); G. W. Ahlström, *Joel and the Temple Cult of Jerusalem* (Leiden: E. J. Brill, 1971).

68. Rudolph, *Haggai,* 247–251; J. A. Fischer, "Notes on the Literary Form and Message of Malachi," *CBQ* 34 (1972) 315–320; E. Pfeiffer, "Die Disputationsworte im Buche Maleachi," *EvT* 19 (1959) 546–568; G. Wallis, "Wesen und Struktur der Botschaft Maleachis," *Das ferne und nahe Wort: Festschrift Leonhard Rost* (ed. F. Maass; Berlin: Alfred Töpelmann, 1967) 229–237.

69. For an elaboration of the following discussion, see D. L. Petersen, *Late Israelite Prophecy* (Missoula: Scholars Press, 1977) 1–53.

prophets must have some sort of support group in order to survive. They must have at least part of the society recognize and encourage their prophetic claims. Without this sort of communal support, the prophets cannot continue to exist. The question of prophetic authority thus becomes a crucial one, and prophets who experience resistance from their societies must find some way of regaining social support. Our analysis of Ezekiel has shown that the problem of prophetic authority was already a concern in the preexilic period, and certain features of the late prophetic literature suggest that this concern intensified after the exile. For example, the curious structure of Zechariah's visions may be an attempt to assure the reader of the truth of the prophet's message. Rather than following the earlier prophetic practice of describing visions whose meaning is obvious to the hearer or reader (Jer 4:23–26), Zechariah's visions are full of obscure symbolism that he is apparently incapable of interpreting. For this reason a heavenly messenger appears within the vision itself in order to interpret its meaning (see, for example, Zech 1:9, 19; 2:2; 4:4). Both the vision and its interpretation are divinely given, thus assuring their authenticity and removing the possibility that the prophet might have misunderstood what he had seen.

The increase in prophetic anonymity in the late period may also be the result of concern over prophetic authority. A number of the late prophetic writings are simply added on to earlier books, and in this way the anonymous author claims the authority of an earlier prophet who lived in a time when prophetic authority was still recognized. This device has been used by Second Isaiah, Third Isaiah, Second Zechariah, and Third Zechariah, among others. The tendency in this period to edit an existing prophetic book rather than create a new book may also reflect an attempt to gain support from the past. The increase in prophetic anonymity also accounts for the late tendency to write prophetic oracles rather than deliver them orally. Anonymous prophecy cannot be oral, but a newly written prophetic oracle can be anonymously circulated in written form or added to an existing book. As the late prophets made increasing use of writing to deliver their oracles, public prophetic activity presumably became rare, and this situation may help to account for the lack of information on prophetic behavior in the late period. Another device used by late prophets to enhance their authority was the reuse of earlier prophetic oracles. We have noted that some late authors make extensive use of quotations and in this way claim the authority of the quotations' original prophetic sources. It should be noted that for the most part the late prophets did not draw their earlier material from only one prophetic tradition. Rather, they used language and concepts from traditions that had been distinct in the preexilic period.[70]

A second feature of late prophecy was an increase in the polemical use of prophecy. Careful analyses of some of the late prophetic literature have uncovered traces of disputes between conflicting political and religious factions. To date, the precise identity of these factions is unclear, but some of them seem to have used prophecy to advance their own views and to oppose the views of opponents.[71]

Finally, late Israelite prophecy is marked by an increased use of apocalyptic imagery. Zechariah and Joel both exhibit this feature, particularly in late editorial layers. At the same time, postexilic authors seem to have added apocalyptic material to earlier prophetic books such as Isaiah and Ezekiel. The increased use of apocalyptic images suggests that the prophets themselves were part of groups that were beginning to move in an apocalyptic direction. They were presumably becoming more and more isolated from the central social structure and were beginning to formulate their own apocalyptic programs.

JUDEAN PROPHECY AND THE CHRONICLER

Although a comprehensive treatment of the Chronicler's view of prophecy must await a thorough reexamination of the Levitical priesthood, it will be useful for our purposes to sketch the outline of the picture of prophetic activity that the Chronicler presents.[72] As we have already noted, prophets play an important role in the Chronicler's view of society. In this sense his thoughts on the proper social functions of prophecy are similar to those of the Deuteronomists, who placed a Mosaic prophet within the central social structure of their ideal state (Deuteronomy 16—18). Accord-

70. On this point, see W. Zimmerli, "Prophetic Proclamation and Reinterpretation," *Tradition and Theology in the Old Testament*, 69–100.

71. Plöger, *Theology and Eschatology;* M. Smith, *Palestinian Parties and Politics That Shaped the Old Testament* (New York: Columbia University Press, 1971); P. D. Hanson, *The Dawn of Apocalyptic* (Philadelphia: Fortress Press, 1975).

72. The best recent treatment of prophecy in Chronicles is Petersen, *Late Israelite Prophecy,* 55–87. Petersen's work has provided the starting point for much of the discussion that follows. See also the older work of A. C. Welch, *The Work of the Chronicler* (London: Oxford University Press, 1939) 42–54.

ing to the Chronicler, prophetic involvement in Israel's central social structure began at the very beginning of the monarchy. He
accepts the Deuteronomist's account of the legitimation of David by
Nathan (1 Chronicles 17) and the legitimation of the temple site by
Gad (1 Chronicles 21) but then expands the role of these early
figures. According to the Chronicler, Nathan and Gad joined David
in organizing the Levites (2 Chr 29:25) and were also responsible,
along with Samuel, for the official chronicles of David's reign (1 Chr
29:29). Later chronicles were also produced by prophets (2 Chr
9:29; 12:15; 13:22; 20:34). It is interesting that in the accounts of
these early prophets, the Chronicler does not assign separate functions to the prophet (*nābîʾ*) and the visionary (*ḥōzeh*). Both are seen
as legitimate parts of the central social structure.

According to the Chronicler, prophets not only legitimated the
monarchy but also provided advice to kings throughout Israel's history. The Chronicler repeats the Deuteronomist's stories of prophetic activity during the monarchy and adds some oracles and
prophets not included in the Deuteronomic History. In 2 Chr
12:5–6 a second oracle by Shemaiah is given in the context of a war,
and the prophets Azariah, Hanani, and Jehu are included in the history for the first time (2 Chr 15:1–7; 16:1–9; 19:2–3). One of the most
interesting of the Chronicler's additions occurs in 2 Chronicles 20,
where there is a complete picture of a prophet functioning in his
social setting. In the face of a sudden Moabite attack, Jehoshaphat
follows traditional Judean practice by praying directly to Yahweh
for divine aid. In response to the prayer, the spirit of Yahweh comes
upon Jahaziel, an Asaphite Levite, who delivers an oracle of assurance to the king and the people. The king then exhorts the people to
believe the prophets, and the holy war begins with the Levitical
singers going before the army. In this instance the prophet plays a
central role in maintaining the stability of the society, as do the
Levites, from whose ranks the prophet came.

The connection between prophets and Levites seems to have
been an important one for the Chronicler. As we have already noted,
the entire Levitical organization was established under prophetic
authority, and Levites functioning within the central social structure became prophets when they were possessed by Yahweh's
spirit. In addition, the Chronicler's description of the activities of
the Levites speaks of them as prophesying to the accompaniment of
musical instruments (1 Chr 25:1). Heman, the king's visionary, was

the head of one of the Levitical groups (1 Chr 25:4–8), and the Chronicler seems to have equated prophets and Levites (2 Chr 34:30). The evidence thus seems to indicate that the Chronicler considered prophecy to be a legitimate part of the cult so long as prophetic activity occurred among the Levitical priests as they were fulfilling their assigned functions.

CONCLUSIONS

Our survey of literature produced by the Judean traditions has yielded a picture far less cohesive than the one that we discovered in Ephraimite literature. For the most part, Judean prophets appear to have had fewer stereotypical behavioral characteristics than their northern counterparts, and this fact may indicate that the Judeans had no standard model for prophetic behavior. Although they used the distinctive term "visionary" to characterize their intermediaries and stressed the vision as the normal mode of revelation, the southerners did not associate any distinctive behavior with the visionary, whom they often equated with other types of intermediaries, such as the prophet and the diviner. Similarly, we found little evidence that Judean prophets used stereotypical speech as part of their possession behavior. The *maśśāʾ* seems to have been a peculiarly Judean type of utterance, but we were able to detect no standard structure for the oracle. Judean prophets tended to share a common language dealing with the cult and the Jerusalemite theology, but this language was not limited to prophets. It therefore appears that the possession behavior of Judean prophets was not distinctive and that their speech during possession was relatively normal. They simply reflected the regular speech of their support groups.

In contrast to our examination of characteristic Judean prophetic behavior, our consideration of the social functions of Judean prophets has been more fruitful. We were able to uncover several different kinds of functions, but for the most part the Judeans seem to have operated within the central social structure in order to assure orderly change and the preservation of the old traditions. Some of these central prophets may have played a regular role in the temple rituals, but many did not. The location of their prophetic activity is unclear, but they may have been at home in the royal court. Throughout the history of Judean prophecy there seem to have been occasional peripheral prophets. Some of these figures, like Isaiah, may have oscillated between peripheral and central functions, while others may have begun and ended their prophetic careers on the edges of Judean society. In the preexilic period some of the peripheral prophets seem to have been former central prophets who were influenced by the Deuteronomic reform. This situation changed in the postexilic period, when Judean and Deuteronomic types of prophecy became thoroughly mixed. After this blending of the traditions, individual prophets appeared less frequently, except in the reconstructed temple, where Levitical priests carried on prophetic activities. Gradually prophecy seems to have disappeared and to have been replaced by apocalyptic.

6

Toward a History
of Prophecy
in Israel

The writing of a complete history of Israelite prophecy would require a detailed study of the literary and tradition history of the prophetic corpus, a thorough examination of the theology of the prophets, and a systematic consideration of the sorts of sociological questions that we have been discussing. It is clear that Old Testament research has not yet progressed to the point that a definitive history of prophecy can be produced. Many of the relevant issues are still the subject of scholarly debate, and the scarcity and complexity of the data may prevent achieving enough of a consensus to construct even a tentative history. However, our examination of the relationship between prophecy and society in Israel does have some implications for future historians of prophecy, and for this reason we will attempt a historical synthesis of the evidence that we have uncovered. The tentative nature of this synthesis must be emphasized. Further research may modify our interpretations of existing data, and new material or more sophisticated research methods may suggest a different synthesis. Even if our interpretation of the biblical evidence proves to be correct, it may be possible to synthesize that evidence in more than one way. Nevertheless, at this point in our study it will be helpful to attempt to set our research into a general historical context.

Any attempt to synthesize the data that we have collected must take into account several factors that have emerged from our inquiry.

(1) Our examination of preexilic Ephraimite prophecy suggests a close correlation between the various social functions of Ephraimite prophets and the changing social status of the northern Levitical priesthood originally connected with Shiloh. We have seen that prophets seem to have played a central role in Israelite society in the premonarchical period but took on peripheral functions after the rise of the monarchy. The only major exceptions appear during the reigns of Hezekiah and Josiah, when prophets of the Ephraimite type (Isaiah[?], Huldah) seem to have been a part of the central establishment. These shifts in the function of Ephraimite prophecy correspond roughly to what we know of the history of the Shiloh priesthood. Shiloh seems to have been a major shrine in the pre-monarchical period and served as a base of operations for Ephraim's political and religious leaders. However, just before the rise of the monarchy the sanctuary itself ceased to be an important cult center, and the ark, the northern symbol of Yahweh's presence, was re-moved from Ephraimite control. At the same time, the Shiloh priests temporarily lost their positions at the center of Ephraim's religious life. Indeed, this branch of the northern priesthood was almost destroyed when Saul slaughtered the priests at Nob (1 Sam 22:11–19), but one of the priests, Abiathar, escaped and sought the protection of David. When David later brought the ark to Jerusalem, Abiathar was installed as one of two high priests in the central cult, thus reestablishing the religious power of the northern priesthood. However, this situation did not continue beyond the time of Sol-omon, who exiled Abiathar to Anathoth and gave control of the temple to the Zadokites (1 Kgs 2:26–27, 35). Thereafter, the de-scendants of Abiathar seem to have remained on the periphery of the Jerusalemite religious establishment. In addition, after the estab-lishment of the northern kingdom, they played a peripheral role in Ephraim as well, for Jeroboam installed non-Levitical priests at the principal shrines (1 Kgs 12:31). Only during the reigns of Hezekiah and Josiah did the Ephraimites regain any influence in Jerusalem. Both of these kings instituted reforms that were consistent with the old Ephraimite theology, and descendants of Abiathar may have regained some of their former religious authority. The close correla-tion between the shifting functions of Israelite prophets and the social status of one branch of the Ephraimite priesthood supports our earlier hypothesis that this Levitical group formed the support group for the Ephraimite prophets. If, as we have assumed, these

particular Levites also carried the Ephraimite / Deuteronomic traditions, then it is not difficult to understand why prophets play such a prominent role in Ephraimite literature.

(2) In spite of the fact that preexilic Ephraimite prophecy played a peripheral role in Israelite society, the Ephraimite view of prophecy now dominates the biblical material. The Deuteronomists have contributed the only laws dealing with prophecy (Deut 13:1–5; 18:9–22), and the accounts of preexilic Israelite history are filled with stories about Ephraimite prophets. In addition, many of the writings produced by Judean prophets appear to have received Deuteronomic editing sometime in the exilic or postexilic period.

(3) Ephraimite prophecy remained a distinct religious phenomenon roughly until the exile. Thereafter, Ephraimite prophetic characteristics start to appear in material produced by the Judahite establishment. Postexilic literature reflects a mixture of Ephraimite and Judean views of prophecy, and individual prophets can no longer be assigned to one tradition or the other on the basis of language or behavior.

(4) The narratives describing prophetic activity immediately before the exile point to increasing numbers of disputes between rival prophets and to escalating tensions between the prophets and their societies. These tensions seem to have continued into the exilic and postexilic periods, when there is evidence of conflict between opposing theological and political factions. The existence of major tensions between prophet and society suggests a decline in prophetic authority and Israel's growing unwillingness to tolerate prophetic activity.

(5) In prophetic literature of the postexilic period, the prophets themselves become markedly less visible than was the case in preexilic sources. As a result, we can say almost nothing about the behavioral characteristics of these late figures, and in some cases we do not even know their names (Second Isaiah; Malachi). Coupled with this loss of visibility is a growing reliance on writing for the purpose of communicating prophetic messages.

(6) At approximately the same time that prophetic activity became less common, apocalyptic activity seems to have increased. Proto-apocalyptic features appear in the late prophetic literature, and collections of apocalyptic material have been added to earlier prophetic books such as Isaiah and Ezekiel.

Taking these factors into consideration, we may now suggest a tentative historical synthesis of the biblical evidence.

THE ORIGINS OF ISRAELITE PROPHECY

Although there is not much biblical data on the origins of Israelite prophecy, the Ephraimite tradition assumes that as early as the patriarchal period prophets carried out social maintenance functions within the central social structure of the Israelite tribes. There is no particular reason not to accept the accuracy of the Ephraimite view. The evidence from Mesopotamia indicates that prophecy existed in Amorite areas, on the fringes of the Babylonian and Assyrian empires. Furthermore, the earliest Mesopotamian prophets are attested in the same area and in the same period usually associated with the Israelite patriarchs. It is therefore not unreasonable to suggest that prophecy may have existed in some Israelite groups during the patriarchal period. It is not possible to determine the accuracy of the Ephraimite description of these early prophets, but they may have played the central roles assigned to them by the later narratives. As members of the central social structure the prophets presumably had the task of unifying the society and regulating social change, and this task may have also included cultic and political responsibilities. Prophets such as Miriam and Deborah may have also played a role in the conquest and may have had official functions in the conduct of holy wars.

The accounts of Israelite life during the period of the judges suggest that in Ephraim central prophets were connected with some of the sanctuaries. With the exception of Samuel, these prophets do not seem to have been priests, and their role in the cult is unclear. The Samuel narratives suggest that by this time the behavior of some of the prophets already reflected the model of the Mosaic prophet. Prophets such as Samuel played crucial roles in both the political and religious establishments, which were directed by the divine words that the prophets occasionally delivered. Their authority was acknowledged by the society, which constituted their support group. In turn, the prophets articulated the views of the group and behaved in ways that met group expectations. The prophets were therefore able to regulate social, political, and religious change and thus preserve social stability. Even the major political shift from tribal autonomy to monarchical government was accomplished relatively smoothly because a Mosaic prophet legitimated the appointment of the king. The concept of the prophet as an intermediary who delivered to the people the word of God may have originally been connected with the special functions of the *nābî̠*, although there is little evidence on this point. However, some of the prophets of this period also served as intercessors, a function which the Ephraimite tradition saw as a special characteristic of the Mosaic prophet. Intercession in Ephraim seems to have originally been associated with the *rō̠eh*, who was a specialist in providing the people with access to Yahweh. By the time of Samuel the speaking and intercessory functions seem to have resided in the same individual, and as a result the title *rō̠eh* ceased to be used shortly after the rise of the monarchy. In Ephraimite circles the title *nābî̠* was applied to Mosaic prophets who combined both functions, but the title was also given to individuals who were not intercessors.

The origins of Judean prophecy are even less clear than those of Ephraimite prophecy. The characteristic Judean intermediary, the *ḥōzeh*, is first attested at the end of the period of the judges, and we may assume that this figure was originally at home among the southern groups that supported David. In this connection it is worth noting that the title *ḥōzeh* is attested outside of Israel, so this particular type of intermediary may have been a foreign import. From the beginning the *ḥōzeh* seems to have been part of the central Judean establishment, which he helped to support by delivering divine words that he received in visions. A type of *nābî̠* also seems to have existed in the Judean groups supporting David, and like the *ḥōzeh* this figure seems to have had social maintenance functions. The Judean *nābî̠s* apparently did not share the intercessory functions of the northern Mosaic prophets, and it may be that in Judah intercession was strictly a priestly prerogative.

THE DEVELOPMENT OF THE PROPHETIC TRADITIONS

With the establishment of the Davidic monarchy, prophets became a part of the royal court in Jerusalem. Just as David unified the cult by installing two high priests, one from Ephraim and one from Judah, so he may have also brought Ephraimite and Judean prophets into the central social structure. In any case, it is clear that

Jerusalemite prophets in this period had social maintenance functions. Indeed, the foundation of the Jerusalemite royal theology—the perpetual election of the Davidic line and the city of Jerusalem—was laid by Nathan's prophetic oracle (1 Samuel 7), while the prophet Gad legitimated the future site of the temple (2 Sam 24:18). However, being part of the royal court did not prevent the prophets from criticizing the king, the government, or the cult. These central intermediaries had the responsibility of maintaining the stability of the social structure, and they therefore promoted orderly change and opposed anything that threatened social equilibrium. Nathan thus probably confronted David not only because of the immorality of the Bathsheba incident but because the king's actions had endangered the stability of the throne and the continuity of the dynasty, a fact which the Throne Succession Narrative clearly illustrates.

After the reign of Solomon, a shift seems to have taken place in the social functions of some Ephraimite prophets. At this point the Ephraimite and Judean prophetic traditions diverge, and each develops a characteristic view of appropriate prophetic behavior. Not long after Abiathar and his priestly house were exiled to Anathoth, Ephraimite prophets again appeared and began advocating traditional northern political and theological views. These prophets may have been supported by Abiathar's group, which was composed of Levites originally connected with Shiloh. Some of these Levites, like Abiathar, were also priests, but after Solomon removed them from power they became a peripheral social group. Based originally at Anathoth, not far from Jerusalem, the group was able to maintain some links with the royal court, while at the same time staying in contact with other Levites who had remained in the north rather than joining Abiathar in David's sanctuary. The group thus reflected orthodox Ephraimite theological traditions, but because of its experience in Jerusalem, this particular Levitical group developed a distinctive form of theology that coupled northern traditions with qualified support of the Davidic dynasty and an acceptance of Jerusalem as the central sanctuary. The traditions that were created and preserved by this group later developed into what is usually called the Deuteronomic theology.

After its expulsion from Jerusalem, the peripheral Levitical group at Anathoth seems to have begun almost immediately to attempt to recapture some of its lost power and social status. The group sought to change the central social structure in order to bring it in line with orthodox Ephraimite views, and as part of this process some members of the group began receiving prophetic revelations which were directed at the establishment. The oracles of these peripheral prophets quite naturally reflected the language of their support group, and their behavior also conformed to the model of the Mosaic prophet. The prophets articulated the group's frustrations and advocated its reform program. The group's first attempt to regain religious power involved supporting the division of Solomon's kingdom. A prophet who was presumably connected with the group, Ahijah of Shiloh, followed the traditional Ephraimite practice of using a prophetic oracle to legitimate the king whom Yahweh had chosen. The selection of a new king and the division of David's empire were explained as a judgment on Solomon because of his unacceptable religious policies (1 Kgs 11:29–40). It is possible that by this move the Levitical group hoped to regain power by becoming part of the central religious establishment in a restored Ephraimite kingdom governed by traditional northern principles. If so, then the group's hopes were dashed when Jeroboam set up shrines at Dan and Bethel and restored the old bull cult, presided over by non-Levitical priests. This action was absolutely unacceptable to the Anathoth group, which suddenly found itself on the periphery of the budding Ephraimite state as well as on the periphery of the Judean royal establishment. The group therefore began to direct its reform efforts against the north as well as the south, and as part of this process prophets were used to present the group's message to the larger society. The story of the anonymous man of God from Judah (1 Kgs 13:1–10) has certainly been shaped by late Deuteronomic editing, but it nevertheless may be an accurate reflection of the type of peripheral prophetic activity carried on by prophets supported by the Anathoth Levites. From this point on, a series of peripheral prophets delivered oracles demanding the reform of both the northern and the southern kingdoms, and it is likely that the prophets supported by the Anathoth group were soon joined by prophets supported by northern Levitical groups that shared many of the views of their southern colleagues. Like the Levites at Anathoth, the northern Levites were shut out of the Ephraimite religious establishment when Jeroboam installed a non-Levitical priesthood. Although the northern Levitical groups may have had their own distinctive theological and political views, these Levites shared with the Anathoth group both the fundamental features of the Ephraimite traditions and the desire to reform the establishment along traditional Ephraimite lines. Many of the prophetic stories in the Deuteronomic history may reflect the activities of peripheral prophets supported by these northern Levitical groups. Elijah, Elisha, and Micaiah ben Imlah, among others, may be examples of such prophets.

After the northern kingdom had been firmly established, prophets again seem to have played a role within the central establishment. These prophets did not exhibit the same sort of behavior found among the Ephraimite prophets, for the central prophets naturally responded to the expectations of different support groups. Some of the prophets were possessed by Baal rather than by Yahweh, and even the Yahweh prophets carried out their mandate to maintain the stability of the northern social structure. This included supporting the syncretistic cult that had developed at the northern sanctuaries, particularly at Bethel. The activities of the northern central prophets thus brought them into direct conflict with the peripheral prophets supported by the Levitical groups. Accounts of these prophetic conflicts have been preserved in the Elijah stories and in 1 Kings 22.

Although the peripheral prophets supported by various Levitical groups maintained constant pressure on the northern establishment, only in the reign of Jehu were the prophets even moderately successful in their reform efforts. The north finally fell to the Assyrians, an event that the Deuteronomic Historian attributed to the failure of the northern kings to pay attention to the words of the prophets whom Yahweh had sent (2 Kgs 17:13–14; cf. 17:21–23). However, in the south the reform efforts of the prophets fared somewhat differently. Particularly during the reigns of Hezekiah and Josiah, the cult and perhaps also the government were reformed along Ephraimite lines. Under Josiah it is even possible that the Levites at Anathoth again became part of the central Jerusalemite establishment, where a few of them remained until the fall of the city.

Yet, with these exceptions, reform efforts in the south met with hostility from the political and religious establishments. Particularly after the death of Josiah, the government tried to suppress peripheral prophets such as Jeremiah, whose harsh oracles continued to demand radical reforms. Confrontations also developed between peripheral prophets supported by Levitical groups and central prophets who were part of the Jerusalemite establishment. Central prophets seem to have existed in Jerusalem since the time of David. Although some of them may have had cultic functions, it is not certain that all of them did. However, all of the central prophets sought to maintain social stability by regulating social change and by articulating the values that bound the society together. For this reason the prophets advocated the Jerusalemite royal theology, which was the cornerstone of Judahite life. To be sure, some of the Jerusalemite prophets, such as Isaiah, were capable of criticizing the society's official views and warned against the excesses of the Jerusalemite theology. Nevertheless, many of the prophets seem to have been uncritical advocates of the Jerusalemite traditions. This naturally brought the Jerusalemites into sharp conflict with the Ephraimite peripheral prophets. The Book of Jeremiah provides a clear picture of these prophetic confrontations, and the book suggests that inter-prophetic strife grew more violent as social conditions deteriorated. Jeremiah finally resorted to false-prophecy accusations in an attempt to suppress his prophetic opponents, but his efforts were unsuccessful. Judah was finally destroyed, and again the Deuteronomists traced the destruction to the failure of the king and the people to follow the Ephraimite reform program.

THE MIXING OF THE TRADITIONS

After the fall of Jerusalem, Israel's political and religious situation underwent a radical change. The Jerusalemite royal theology, which to the end had maintained the inviolability of Zion, had suffered a serious blow. Furthermore, the central prophets who had supported that theology had been proven to be unreliable. In contrast, the Ephraimite views advocated by the peripheral prophets provided an acceptable explanation for the disaster. Yahweh had punished the nation for breaking the divine covenant and refusing to listen to prophetic calls to repent. The people and the king were themselves to blame for the disaster. In addition, the Ephraimite prophets themselves had demonstrated the truth of their judgment oracles and had thus enhanced their prophetic authority.

The sudden shifts in the fortunes of the groups bearing the Ephraimite and Judean traditions must have had practical social, political, and religious implications for the daily lives of the Israelites in exile. Although we know almost nothing about the life of the exilic community, we may suppose that Deuteronomic views gathered increasing popular support during the exile, while support for the former Jerusalemite establishment must have decreased. This situation would have created problems for members of the establishment when an opportunity came to return to the land. Lacking sufficient popular support, they may have turned to the Deuteronomists, without whose help reconstruction efforts were not likely to succeed. We do not know precisely what occurred at this time, but the religious situation of the early postexilic period suggests that some sort of bargain was struck between the Deuteronomic representatives of the old Levitical priesthood and the Zadokite bearers of the Jerusalemite traditions. Compromises were apparently made on both sides. Many Zadokite features of the cult remained intact in the postexilic reconstruction, but in return for this concession, the Deuteronomists were allowed a free hand in editing the growing corpus of biblical literature. The Deuteronomic interpretation of Israel's preexilic history thus became the official account, to be challenged only much later by the Jerusalemite perceptions of the Chronicler. A prominent place in the Deuteronomic History was given to the activities of Ephraimite prophets, and some of the writings of the Jerusalemite prophets received Deuteronomic editing. Parts of the Deuteronomic reform program were instituted, and in particular Levites were allowed to participate in the Jerusalemite cult. Still, the Levites were not granted total equality with the Zadokite priests, as Deuteronomy had originally demanded.

The exilic mixing of the Deuteronomic and Jerusalemite traditions is reflected in the prophetic literature of the postexilic period and in the writings of the Chronicler. The theological views of the prophets of this period are an amalgam of positions that had been distinct in the preexilic period. The distinctive characteristics of Ephraimite and Judean prophets disappear. Peripheral prophecy also seems to decline, and many prophets play a role in the central political and religious establishments.

THE DECLINE OF PROPHECY AND THE
RISE OF APOCALYPTIC

In spite of the apparent success of the Deuteronomists, prophecy of all types seems to have gone into a period of decline in the postexilic period. The postexilic prophets resorted to various authority-enhancing devices in their writings and relied increasingly on the written word rather than the spoken word. More stress was placed on the prophetic message itself and on the divine origin of that message, and at the same time the person of the prophet receded into the background so that no fallible human intermediary separated the divine word from the reader. As a result, the late prophetic books are virtually devoid of prophetic narratives, and we can deduce little about prophetic behavior in this period.

Ironically, the reason for this state of affairs may be found in the Deuteronomic concept of prophecy, which dominated the thinking of the early postexilic period. According to the Deuteronomic position, true prophets were those whose oracles were effective and whose predictions came to pass. This principle had initially enhanced the status of Deuteronomic prophets such as Jeremiah, whose warnings of disaster had been fulfilled. However, the prophets also gave promise oracles, and in spite of the return from exile and the rebuilding of the temple, many of the promises remained unfulfilled. This situation may have led some prophetic support groups to try to explain the apparent failure of the promises to materialize. Daniel 9:1–2, 24–27 may be an example of this process. However, for the general population the delay in the fulfillment of the preexilic and exilic prophetic promises simply raised doubts about the authority of the prophets themselves, doubts that were reinforced by the unfulfilled oracles of the Jerusalemite prophets. For this reason, people may have grown increasingly unwilling to acknowledge the authority of prophets of any sort, and, lacking the necessary social support, the prophets ceased to exist.

However, the same factors that contributed to the demise of prophecy may have also spurred the development of apocalyptic. The political and religious compromises that were forged during the exile and implemented in the postexilic period were not entirely successful in uniting the Israelite community. The compromises were not accepted by some groups, which attempted to maintain the purity of their preexilic views. One may thus suspect that some Levitical groups did not accept the compromises because they represented a shift away from pure Deuteronomic orthodoxy. Similar opinions may have been held by some of the Zadokites, and the late prophetic literature suggests the existence of various warring factions struggling over a multitude of social, political, and religious issues. Still, the political and religious establishments remained in the hands of the architects of the compromises, and as a result dissenting groups were pushed onto the edges of Israelite society and were deprived of access to the centers of power. As we have already seen in our study of the anthropological literature, such conditions can provide fertile ground for the growth of apocalyptic groups. It is likely that such groups were formed in increasing numbers in the postexilic period. Groups of various sorts of dissatisfied individuals must have been drawn together by catalytic agents capable of articulating group frustrations and providing a plan detailing their solution. Such plans would naturally have reflected the characteristic speech of the groups that produced them and would have drawn on the traditions preserved by the groups. Groups of dissatisfied priests would have used priestly language to express their apocalyptic programs and would have drawn on the priestly traditions. Groups of former government officials would have used the "wisdom" language of the royal court, and groups rooted in the prophetic traditions would have used characteristically prophetic language. The fact that apocalyptic material appears in a few of the prophetic books suggests that in the postexilic period some of the groups carrying the prophetic traditions began to develop in an apocalyptic direction. Some of these groups may have been composed of Levites who were dissatisfied with the exilic compromises. Because genuine prophets were becoming rare, the groups seem to have turned to the prophetic literature, which they had helped to preserve, and sought there the divine guidance that would enable them to survive their time of deprivation. Disturbed by the failure of some of the prophetic promises to be realized, group members may have set the promises into an apocalyptic context so that the fulfillment could be expected only in "the world to come." Some of the prophetic support groups of the preexilic and exilic periods may have thus become apocalyptic groups in the postexilic period. In terms of sociological structure, peripheral prophetic support groups and apocalyptic groups are closely related to each other, so it is not difficult to understand how one might have developed into the other. However, the metamorphosis of prophetic support groups into apocalyptic groups marks the demise of genuine prophetic activity in Israel. Without support even in congenial peripheral groups, the prophets could not continue to exist, and Israelite prophecy came to an end.

Select Bibliography

Ackroyd, P. R. *Exile and Restoration*. Philadelphia: Westminster Press, 1968.

Ahlström, G. W. *Joel and the Temple Cult of Jerusalem*. Leiden: E. J. Brill, 1971.

Beattie, J., and Middleton, J., eds. *Spirit Mediumship and Society in Africa*. New York: Africana Publishing Corporation, 1969.

Belo, J. *Trance in Bali*. New York: Columbia University Press, 1960.

Berger, P. L. "Charisma and Religious Innovation: The Social Location of Israelite Prophecy." *ASR* 28 (1963) 940–950.

Bourguignon, E. "The Self, the Behavioral Environment, and the Theory of Spirit Possession." In *Context and Meaning in Cultural Anthropology*, edited by M. E. Spiro, pp. 39–60. New York: Free Press, 1965.

Bright, J. "The Date of the Prose Sermons of Jeremiah." *JBL* 70 (1951) 15–35.

Burridge, K. *New Heaven, New Earth*. New York: Schocken Books, 1969.

Carley, K. W. *Ezekiel among the Prophets*. London: SCM Press, 1975.

Clements, R. E. *Prophecy and Tradition*. Atlanta: John Knox Press, 1975.

Crenshaw, J. L. *Prophetic Conflict*. Berlin: Walter de Gruyter, 1971.

Cross, F. M. *Canaanite Myth and Hebrew Epic*. Cambridge: Harvard University Press, 1973.

Dietrich, W. *Prophetie und Geschichte*. Göttingen: Vandenhoeck & Ruprecht, 1972.

Ellermeier, F. *Prophetie in Mari und Israel*. Herzberg: Erwin Jungfer, 1968.

Emmet, D. "Prophets and Their Societies," *JRAI* 86 (1956) 13–23.

Field, M. J. *Search for Security*. Evanston: Northwestern University Press, 1960.

Fohrer, G. *Elia*. 2d ed. Zurich: Zwingli-Verlag, 1968.

Friedland, W. H. "For a Sociological Concept of Charisma." *Social Forces* 43 (1964) 18–26.

Fry, P. *Spirits of Protest*. Cambridge: Cambridge University Press, 1976.

Guillaume, A. *Prophecy and Divination among the Hebrews and Other Semites*. London: Hodder and Stoughton, 1938.

Haldar, A. *Associations of Cult Prophets among the Ancient Semites*. Uppsala: Almqvist & Wiksell, 1945.

Hanson, P. D. *The Dawn of Apocalyptic*. Philadelphia: Fortress Press, 1975.

Hentschel, G. *Die Elija-erzählungen*. Leipzig: St. Benno-Verlag, 1977.

Herrmann, S. *Ursprung und Funktion der Prophetie im alten Israel*. Opladen: Westdeutscher Verlag, 1976.

Holladay, W. L. "A Fresh Look at 'Source B' and 'Source C' in Jeremiah." *VT* 25 (1975) 394–412.

Hölscher, G. *Die Profeten*. Leipzig: J. C. Hinrichs, 1914.

Hossfeld, F. L., and Meyer, I. *Prophet gegen Prophet*. Fribourg: Schweizerisches Katholisches Bibelwerk, 1973.

Huffmon, H. B. "The Origins of Prophecy." In *Magnalia Dei: The Mighty Acts of God*, edited by F. M. Cross et al., pp. 171–186. Garden City, N.Y.: Doubleday, 1976.

———. "Prophecy in the Ancient Near East." *IDBSup*, pp. 697–700.

———. "Prophecy in the Mari Letters." In *The Biblical Archaeologist Reader*. Vol. 3, edited by E. F. Campbell, Jr., and D. N. Freedman, pp. 199–224. Garden City, N.Y.: Doubleday, 1970.

Hyatt, J. P. "The Deuteronomic Edition of Jeremiah." In *Vanderbilt Studies in the Humanities*, 1. 71–95. Nashville: Vanderbilt University Press, 1951.

———. "Jeremiah and Deuteronomy." *JNES* 1 (1942) 156–173.

Jepsen, A. *Nabi: Soziologische Studien zur alttestamentlichen Literatur und Religionsgeschichte*. Munich: C. H. Beck, 1934.

Johnson, A. R. *The Cultic Prophet in Ancient Israel*. Cardiff: University of Wales, 1944; 2d ed., 1962.

Junker, H. *Prophet und Seher in Israel*. Trier: Paulinus-Verlag, 1927.

Kraus, H.-J. *Die prophetische Verkündigung des Rechts in Israel*. Zollikon: EVZ Verlag, 1957.

La Barre, W. "Materials for a History of Studies of Crisis Cults: A Bibliographic Essay." *Current Anthropology* 12 (1971) 3–44.

Leslau, W. "An Ethiopian Argot of People Possessed by a Spirit." *Africa* 19 (1949) 204–212.

Lewis, I. M. *Ecstatic Religion*. Baltimore: Penguin Books, 1971.

———. "Spirit Possession and Deprivation Cults." *Man* n.s. 1 (1966) 307–329.

Lindblom, J. *Prophecy in Ancient Israel*. Philadelphia: Fortress Press, 1962.

Macholz, G. C. "Jeremia in der Kontinuität der Prophetie." In *Probleme biblischer Theologie*, edited by H. W. Wolff, pp. 306–334. Munich: Chr. Kaiser, 1971.

Malamat, A. "Prophetic Revelations in New Documents from Mari and the Bible." VTSup 15 (1966) 207–227.

Marwick, M. G. *Sorcery in Its Social Setting*. Manchester: Manchester University Press, 1965.

Middleton, J. *Lugbara Religion*. London: Oxford University Press, 1960.

Middleton, J., and Winter, E. H. *Witchcraft and Sorcery in East Africa*. London: Routledge & Kegan Paul, 1963.

Moran, W. L. "New Evidence from Mari on the History of Prophecy." *Bib* 50 (1969) 15–56.

Muilenburg, J. "The 'Office' of the Prophet in Ancient Israel." In *The Bible in Modern Scholarship*, edited by J. P. Hyatt, pp. 74–97. New York: Abingdon Press, 1965.

Newman, M. "The Prophetic Call of Samuel." In *Israel's Prophetic Heritage*, edited by B. W. Anderson and W. Harrelson, pp. 86–97. New York: Harper & Row, 1962.

Nicholson, E. W. *Deuteronomy and Tradition*. Philadelphia: Fortress Press, 1967.

———. *Preaching to the Exiles*. New York: Schocken Books, 1970.

Noort, E. *Untersuchungen zum Gottesbescheid in Mari*. Kevelaer: Butzon & Bercker, 1977.

Obeyesekere, G. "The Idiom of Demonic Possession: A Case Study." *Social Science & Medicine* 4 (1970) 97–111.

Oppenheim, A. L. *Ancient Mesopotamia*. Chicago: University of Chicago Press, 1964.

Overholt, T. W. "The Ghost Dance of 1890 and the Nature of the Prophetic Process." *Ethnohistory* 21 (1974) 37–63.

———. "Jeremiah and the Nature of the Prophetic Process." In *Scripture in History and Theology: Essays in Honor of J. Coert Rylaarsdam*, pp. 129–150. Pittsburgh: Pickwick Press, 1977.

Parker, S. B. "Possession Trance and Prophecy in Pre-exilic Israel." *VT* 28 (1978) 271–285.

Perlitt, L. "Mose als Prophet." *EvT* 31 (1971) 588–608.

Petersen, D. L. *Late Israelite Prophecy*. Missoula: Scholars Press, 1977.

Plöger, O. *Die Prophetengeschichten der Samuel- und Königsbücher*. Greifswald: E. Panzig, 1937.

Prince, R., ed. *Trance and Possession States.* Montreal: R. M. Bucke Memorial Society, 1968.

Ramlot, L. "Prophétisme." *DBSup* 8 (1972) 811–1222.

Robinson, T. H. *Prophecy and the Prophets in Ancient Israel.* 2d ed. London: Duckworth, 1953.

Ross, J. F. "Prophecy in Hamath, Israel, and Mari." *HTR* 63 (1970) 1–28.

Rowley, H. H. "The Nature of Old Testament Prophecy in the Light of Recent Study." *HTR* 38 (1945) 1–38 (= H. H. Rowley. *The Servant of the Lord,* pp. 95–134. 2d ed. Oxford: Blackwell, 1965).

Schmitt, H.-C. *Elisa.* Gütersloh: Gerd Mohn, 1972.

———. "Prophetie und Tradition." *ZTK* 74 (1977) 255–272.

Schreiner, J. *Sion-Jerusalem, Jahwes Königssitz: Theologie der heiligen Stadt im Alten Testament.* Munich: Kösel, 1963.

Schüpphaus, J. *Richter- und Prophetengeschichten als Glieder der Geschichtsdarstellung der Richter- und Königszeit.* Bonn: Rheinischen Friedrich-Wilhelms-Universität, 1967.

Schweizer, H. *Elischa in den Kriegen.* Munich: Kösel Verlag, 1974.

Shirokogoroff, S. M. *Psychomental Complex of the Tungus.* London: Kegan Paul, Trench, Trubner, 1935.

Steck, O. H. *Israel und das gewaltsame Geschick der Propheten.* Neukirchen-Vluyn: Neukirchener Verlag, 1967.

———. "Theological Streams of Tradition." In *Tradition and Theology in the Old Testament,* edited by D. A. Knight, pp. 183–214. Philadelphia: Fortress Press, 1977.

———. *Überlieferung und Zeitgeschichte in den Elia-Erzählungen.* Neukirchen-Vluyn: Neukirchener Verlag, 1968.

Stuhlmueller, C. *Creative Redemption in Deutero-Isaiah.* Rome: Biblical Institute Press, 1970.

Thrupp, S. L., ed. *Millennial Dreams in Action.* The Hague: Mouton, 1962.

Tucker, G. M. "Prophetic Speech." *Int* 32 (1978) 31–45.

Van der Woude, A. S. "Deutero-Micha: Ein Prophet aus Nord-Israel?" *NedTTs* 25 (1971) 365–378.

Wagner, S. "Überlegungen zur Frage nach den Beziehungen des Propheten Amos zum Südreich." *TLZ* 96 (1971) 653–670.

Walker, S. S. *Ceremonial Spirit Possession in Africa and Afro-America.* Leiden: E. J. Brill, 1972.

Weinfeld, M. *Deuteronomy and the Deuteronomic School.* Oxford: At the Clarendon Press, 1972.

Westermann, C. *Basic Forms of Prophetic Speech.* Philadelphia: Westminster Press, 1967.

Widengren, G. *Literary and Psychological Aspects of the Hebrew Prophets.* Uppsala: Lundequist, 1948.

Willis, R. G. "Kaswa: Oral Tradition of a Fipa Prophet." *Africa* 40 (1970) 248–256.

Wilson, R. R. "Early Israelite Prophecy." *Int* 32 (1978) 3–16.

———. "Form-critical Investigation of the Prophetic Literature: The Present Situation." SBLSP 1973, 1. 100–121.

———. *Genealogy and History in the Biblical World.* New Haven: Yale University Press, 1977.

Wolff, H. W. *Amos the Prophet.* Philadelphia: Fortress Press, 1973.

———. *Hosea.* Philadelphia: Fortress Press, 1974.

———. *Joel and Amos.* Philadelphia: Fortress Press, 1977.

Worsley, P. *The Trumpet Shall Sound.* 2d ed. New York: Schocken Books, 1968.

Zaretsky, I. I. *Bibliography on Spirit Possession and Spirit Mediumship.* Evanston: Northwestern University, 1966.

Zimmerli, W. *Ezechiel.* Neukirchen-Vluyn: Neukirchener Verlag, 1969.

———. "Prophetic Proclamation and Reinterpretation." In *Tradition and Theology in the Old Testament,* edited by D. A. Knight, pp. 69–100. Philadelphia: Fortress Press, 1977.

Index

SUBJECTS

BIBLICAL REFERENCES